HISTORY OF THE
101ST AIRBORNE DIVISION

History of the
101st Airborne Division
Screaming Eagles

The First 50 Years

Edited by

Col. Robert E. Jones, USA (Ret)

Trade Paper
Press

Turner Publishing Company
200 4th Avenue north • Suite 950
Nashville, TN 37316

www.turnerpublishing.com

Copyright © 2005 by Turner Publishing Company

ISBN: 978-1-59652-746-1

Library of Congress Control Number: 2010926945

Printed in the United States of America.

11   10   9   8   7   6   5   4   3

Dedicated to the memory of
Major General William C. Lee, U.S. Army

General Lee, as a lieutenant colonel, was the insistent advocate who convinced the War Department that an airborne force was feasible and needed by the U.S. Army. He was and is still considered the father of the airborne.

His high standards for organization, training, equipment and people made the airborne divisions of World War II the place to be for all soldiers who sought to serve in units that were on the cutting edge of the profession of arms.

General Lee, as the first Commanding General of the 101st Airborne Division, provided the leadership and drive to make the Screaming Eagles the best trained, equipped and motivated soldiers who served in World War II. He gave them a motto - Rendezvous With Destiny - that has endured through World War II, the training years at Fort Campbell, Kentucky, Vietnam, and the war in the Persian Gulf

When a heart condition precluded command of the airborne assault of the 101st Airborne Division into Normandy, he presented Brigadier General Maxwell D. Taylor a superbly trained airborne division ready to embark on its first rendezvous with destiny.

Major General William C. Lee was truly the father of the airborne in the United States Army. His leadership began a fraternity of Screaming Eagles who for many years have trained hard to be ready, served in Vietnam where they never lost a battle and made military history during Desert Shield and Desert Storm in the Persian Gulf.

The legacy, created by General Lee, now binds more than 8,000 Screaming Eagle veterans and active duty soldiers in fraternal union as members of the 101st Airborne Division Association.

The 101st Airborne Division, which was activated on 16 August 1942 at Camp Claiborne, Louisiana, has no history, but it has a rendezvous with destiny.
—Major General William C. Lee, father of the airborne

I sent the 101st Airborne Division on so many important missions; never once did it's fighting men fail to add new luster to their reputation as one of the finest units in the Allied Forces.
—General Dwight D. Eisenhower

CONTENTS

PREFACE

There are many things about war that we are anxious to forget. We want to forget the necessary sordidness and cruelties of battle; to forget the mud and the muck and the mire; the painful days and the endless nights. We want to forget the sickening sensation of fear that comes at times to all soldiers.

War cuts down men in the prime of life. War is pain and rain and snow and cold. It is hunger and thirst and exhaustion, loneliness, separation from loved ones, and heartbreak. War should not be glorified. To attempt to do so would be the ultimate sacrilege.

But, this world is not always a flower garden - not now, never has been, nor ever will be. It is a battlefield between forces of freedom and those of slavery, between justice and injustice, and if you will, the forces of God and love against those of evil and hatred.

Sherman was not quite right when he said, "War is hell," for in hell there is no compassion, no love, no generosity, no empathy for the suffering. I believe most firmly that the American serviceman (and service woman) in combat exemplifies more than any segment of our society the virtues of love, of self sacrifice, of courage and of fortitude in the face of danger and death.

The men of the 101st Airborne Division did not philosophize deeply about the causes of war. But they did know that they were fighting for a way of life they loved, and that freedom is the inherent right of all. He fought without hatred, suffered without complaint, endured without despair.

When I first joined the Screaming Eagles I found a unit of immature boys, carefree and full of mischief. But they grew in a few short years into mature soldiers who supported each other and their units with great heroism. Their trials, sacrifices and suffering have given them a bond of fellowship that will never be broken, and a spiritual depth beyond description. I am proud to have served with them. Our beloved country is far richer for the quality of citizenship these veterans of the 101st Airborne Division continue to give to the United States of America.

—Major General Francis L. Sampson, Chaplain (USA, Ret.)

INTRODUCTION

This is a book about the people, places and events which combine to tell the story of a truly great and remarkable organization, the 101st Airborne Division. It is easy to make the case that this division was destined for greatness from the very beginning. Certainly its first commander, Major General William C. Lee, felt that very strongly, when, on 19 Aug 1942, just three days after his new division was activated, he issued his General Order #5. In it, disdaining Sam Goldwyn's famous advice: "Never prophesy-especially about the future," General Lee prophesied with all the-clairvoyance and wisdom of a biblical prophet. These were his words: "The 101st Airborne Division, which was activated on 16 Aug 1942 at Camp Claiborne, Louisiana, has no history, but it has a rendezvous with destiny."

One test of a good prophesy is the amount of amendment required to make it conform to what actually occurred. So tested, Bill Lee's prophesy deserves high marks, indeed. The only change one might make, would be to add that the rendezvous of the 101st with destiny would be a continuing event, going on and on. For example, "The 101st Airborne Division has an unending rendezvous with destiny."

Most assuredly, that has been the legacy of the 101st-always in the fore front; always where the stakes were highest and the going toughest, as in the night airborne assault into Normandy-into the teeth of Germany's "Festung Europa" (Fortress Europe), which General Eisenhower called his greatest gamble. So, too, in Holland, in the high stakes gamble of the 1st Allied Airborne Army to outflank all water obstacles short of Berlin itself, the Screaming Eagles played a key role and were highly successful in their part of a mission impossible without additional forces. Then, in their best remembered exploit, during the Battle of the Bulge, the 101st, with attached units, conducted the classic and justly famous defense of the key city of Bastogne.

After WWII, when the Army decided to keep only one airborne division, General Ridgway agonized in choosing between his old division, the 82nd Airborne Division and the 101st. Based on his analysis, and giving heavy weight to the greater number of operations of the 82nd, he recommended the 82nd be retained and the 101st deactivated. So there was a hiatus in the rendezvous until the 101st reactivation as a training division in 1948, 1950 and 1954! But the division's wartime commander, General Maxwell Taylor, then Army Chief of Staff, wanted to make the Army a more viable player in nuclear warfare, and, also, to see his old command again a part of the fighting Army. He accomplished both goals by converting the 101st to a "Pentomic" airborne division with an organic atomic capability in 1956.

The Pentomic 101st never had to fight an atomic war, but did play a key role in many of the civil rights disturbances of that era, before again being reorganized as a more conventional "Road" Airborne Division.

While the division was thus organized, its 1st Brigade deployed to Vietnam in July of 1965, one of the first brigade sized units to enter that war. After operating as a "fire brigade," all over South Vietnam, it was joined by the remainder of the division, which deployed to Vietnam in December 1967, in what was then the largest, longest airlift in military history. The Screaming Eagles were just in time to take part in throttling the enemy's highly publicized TET offensive which began the following month. Operations were many and highly successful as the Screaming Eagles adapted to this strange war which tried and divided our country-a war which asked our military to fight under unwinable ground rules, subjected to a new and totally different level of news media scrutiny, and with least inconvenience to the American people.

Then in 1968, in the midst of "Nevada Eagle," the largest single campaign ever fought by the 101st, on 1 Jul 1968, the division became the "101st Air Cavalry Division" and a year later the "101st Airborne Division (Airmobile). These were far more than mere name changes, they signified that in using the third dimension to leapfrog into an enemy's rear, henceforth the division would use helicopters, not parachutes. The division proved its mastery of this new airmobile warfare throughout the remainder of its service in Vietnam, in operations like Lam Son 719 and countless others.

The Screaming Eagles was the last Army Division to leave Vietnam, in late 1971 and early 1972 and received a well deserved welcome home at Ft. Campbell on 6 Apr 1972. Then in 1974, the 101st converted its one remaining brigade of parachutists to a third air assault brigade, and became truly helicopter oriented as the 101st Airborne Division (Air Assault). In this new format, the 101st is unique in being the only Air Assault Division in any army in the world.

In the 1980s, though based at Ft. Campbell, the division trained and served all over the map. It was during the rotation of a unit from service in the Sinai that a tragic plane crash at Gander, Newfoundland cost the lives of 248 Screaming Eagles.

In August 1990, the 101st deployed to Saudi Arabia to participate in operations "Desert Shield" and "Desert Storm" against the marauding Iraqi Army. Once more the division met its "rendezvous" in performing very difficult and critical operations with speed and precision, to include the longest air assault in history, 50 miles into Iraq.

With its brilliant and important contributions to yet another war ended, the 101st redeployed back to Ft. Campbell, where it is alive and well today, constantly honing itself for whatever new challenges fate may have in store. Wherever and how ever these new challenges may come, all of us, who have served as Screaming Eagles, are certain the division will once again proudly meet its "rendezvous with destiny."

This book makes it easy to understand why we feel the way we do about this extraordinary division and its unending "rendezvous with destiny."

—LTG Harry W.O. Kinnard (Ret)

HISTORY OF
101ST AIRBORNE DIVISION

CHAPTER ONE

World War II

FORMATIVE YEARS AND ACTIONS
John Hanlon

THE PROPER STARTING point for the history of the 101st Airborne Division, from its beginnings through its stormy and storied course in World War II, is with Bill Lee.

General William C. Lee, the acknowledged "father" of the U.S. Army's airborne force, was the first commanding general of the 101st Airborne. In one of his first General Orders, he told of the Division's place in time and its mission. Lee's words would be forever etched in the lore of the 101st Airborne Division.

"The 101st," he wrote in part, "has no history, but it has a rendezvous with destiny. Let me call your attention to the fact that our badge is the great American eagle. This is a fitting emblem for a division that will crush our enemies by falling upon them like a thunderbolt from the skies..."

As stirring and prophetic as these words were, there was a quiet talk given by General Lee to junior officers at one point early in the Division's training that remained equally moving to those who heard it.

The general, speaking softly, with the remnants of his North Carolina lineage in his voice, called briefly on his experiences in WWI. Then he was a 22-year old reserve officer leading a platoon in combat. Now, he was an impressive figure (a rugged man with a large head and square jaw), and he fixed us with these words on leadership.

"When you first lead your men," he said, "into the valley of the shadow of death" (a biblical phrase), they will look to you with pathetic eagerness for leadership, and you had better be ready."

Those meaningful words would never be forgotten by those who heard them.

General Lee was not the first man intrigued by "vertical envelopment," as the airborne operation came to be known. Ben Franklin foresaw "ten thousand men descending from the clouds" and "doing an infinite deal of mischief." No more apt description can be found for the parachute operations in Normandy, Holland and elsewhere.

Winston Churchill had seen the potential of the airborne in World War I. In the same war, Colonel Billy Mitchell had convinced General Pershing to make an air-landing unit of the 1st Division and use it to take the city of Metz. The war ended before the plan could be implemented. Russians and Germans employed parachutists to advantage in early World War II fighting.

In 1939 General George C. Marshall ordered the chief of infantry to make a study of the progress in air assault use by other countries. Lack of funds delayed the study until 1940, when Bill Lee, a major at the time, was named project officer to develop an airborne capacity for the U.S. Army.

Lee started from zero. He was instrumental in developing the very basic ingredient: a parachute for troop use. Then came tests of various items of equipment and training procedures. Eventually, these required "live" testing. To that end, on June 25, 1940, the order authorizing the Parachute Test Platoon arrived at Fort Benning, Georgia.

Volunteers for this unit came from the 29th Infantry Division, the demonstration troops for the Infantry School. The first order suggested that, because of the anticipated dangers, only unmarried men be accepted for the Test Platoon.

Under the overall direction of Major Lee, the Test Platoon consisted of 48 enlisted men, commanded by Lieutenant William T. Ryder. On the seventh week of an eight-week training course, the platoon was ready to begin jumping. The first jump was made by Lieutenant Ryder from a converted B-18 bomber. He jumped alone, then boarded the plane to witness the platoon in its first jump.

Ironically, the first soldier in the platoon scheduled to jump "froze" in the door and was sent back to a seat in the aircraft. The next man in line was Private William "Red" King, who did not hesitate, and thus became the first enlisted man to jump. It is a curiosity that the three pioneers: Lee, Ryder and King, of parachuting had the first name of William.

These jumps took place on August 16, 1940, and a few days later on August 29, the Test Platoon made the Army's first mass drop. Each man shouted the battle cry, "Geronimo," on leaving the door. This originated, reportedly, with Private Aubry Eberhardt. Later he said that he got the idea from a Western movie he and several other members of the Test Platoon had seen the night prior to the jump.

Although "Geronimo" may have been the cry of the earliest parachutists, later candidates were taught to call out "One thousand, two thousand, three thousand," marking the time in approximate seconds that the main parachute should have been, at the least, starting to open.

So impressive was the Test Platoon's development, that the War Department authorized in mid-September, the creation of the first tactical airborne unit, the 501st Parachute Infantry Battalion. Its commander was Major William M. Miley (yet another William). Among its officers were names that would be written large in 101st Airborne history: Sink, Michaelis, Ewell, Higgins, Strayer, Cole and Cassidy among them.

A control group was next, called the Provisional Parachute Group, Lieutenant Colonel Bill Lee commanding, with more names soon to be famous in parachutists' lore: Gavin, Yarborough, Ekman and Lindquist.

Its purpose was to furnish cadres for future parachute battalions and to continue the study of organizational matters, such as, integrating glider troops into the airborne. The 502nd Parachute Battalion was activated, followed in rapid order by the 503rd and 504th Parachute Infantry Battalions.

Out of the control group came the parachutists' distinctive gear—much of it the work of the young officer, William P. Yarborough, such as the winged badge, jump boots, the baggy and multi-pocketed battle dress. The wings, the cherished item awarded as the diploma from Jump School, said "for jumping from a plane in flight." Or, as the trainees put it, "jumping from a plane in fright."

The airborne battalions became regiments, leading to the formation of the Airborne Command with, now, Colonel Lee in charge. Part of this command was the 88th Infantry Airborne Battalion, the forerunner of the glider troops.

Lee was soon made a brigadier general and, in the spring of 1942, he was sent secretly to England with General Eisenhower, Arnold and Somervell. Lee's mission was to determine what role the airborne would play in the invasion of Europe and to determine what the British were doing by way of airborne troops.

On his return, General Lee recommended that airborne units be increased to a division size. The recommendation was accepted, and in the course of the war, five airborne divisions were activated and five more designated but never activated.

One of his suggestions was not immediately followed. Originally, the Army's plan was to include in the airborne division two glider regiments of two battalions each and one parachute regiment of three battalions. Lee had proposed a reverse ratio. In time, Lee's recommendation prevailed.

The Army activated its first two airborne divisions from the highly regarded 82nd Motorized Division, which had undergone its basic training under General Omar N. Bradley, as of August 15, 1942. One would be designated the 82nd Airborne Division, and the other the 101st Airborne Division.

Lee had been named for a second star on August 10; and on August 17, he arrived at Camp Claiborne, LA and took command of the 101st. Within a day, General Lee issued his General Order in which he wrote of the Division's "rendezvous with destiny."

The organizational task facing Major General Lee was formidable. He was charged with integrating the various units from the 82nd Motorized Infantry and moulding them into a fighting unit.

Some of the inherited combat and service units were old and established, others reactivated and renumbered. From this tangled web emerged the original troops assigned to the 101st Airborne as listed in its General Order #1.

HEADQUARTERS AND HEADQUARTERS COMPANY, 101ST AIRBORNE DIVISION

INCLUDED AMONG ITS units were two bands, one for Division Artillery, the other for the 502nd Parachute Infantry Regiment. The latter's commanding officer, then Lieutenant Colonel George Van Horn Moseley, ordered his adjutant, Captain Carlton P. Chandler, to form a band immediately. Chandler scrounged up instruments and musicians and, within two days, had the 502nd's band tootling lustily if not well.

327TH GLIDER INFANTRY REGIMENT

COMMANDED BY COLONEL George S. Wear. With just two battalions to a glider regiment, the excess men were used to fill out other glider units of the Division, including its 2nd Glider Regiment which became the 401st Glider Infantry Regiment.

401ST GLIDER INFANTRY REGIMENT

LIEUTENANT COLONEL JOSEPH H. Harper commanded this unit from the first day of its complicated organization. He was a former battalion commander of 326th Regiment, which remained with the 82nd. Essentially, the 1st Battalion of the cut down 327th and other of its units were transferred to the 401st.

502ND PARACHUTE INFANTRY REGIMENT

MOSELEY SUCCEEDED THE original commander, Lieutenant Colonel George C. Howell, who left to command the Parachute School. Moseley was a third generation West Pointer. "Old Moe," as he was known (out of his hearing) was a fairly short man. His jump boots seemed too high; and in his jump suit, he resembled a miniature Michelin man. He was demanding and severe. Only after he was gone, because of an injury on the D-day jump, was his tight discipline and insistence on perfection appreciated.

The regiment was often referred to in soldier talk as the "Five-Oh-Deuce," or simply "The Deuce," and for some inexplicable reason, "The Duck."

Once the glider/parachute ratio of regiments was reversed, among other Table of Organization changes, two other parachute regiments were attached to the Division before the Normandy invasion, and they fought with it throughout the war. On paper their attachment remained. Otherwise, they were considered by all to be integral parts of the Division. They were:

506TH PARACHUTE INFANTRY REGIMENT

COLONEL ROBERT F. Sink commanding. The regiment was called "colorful" and "rugged," reflecting its commander who always referred to the enemy as "hostiles." No one can recall ever seeing him with his overseas cap on straight. He commanded the regiment from the day it was organized through every one of its battles; he was revered by his men. A measure of his soldier's regard for Colonel Sink was shown in the regiment's sometime nickname, the "Five-Oh-Sink."

501ST PARACHUTE INFANTRY REGIMENT

COMMANDED BY COLONEL Howard R. Johnson. Unlike Moseley and Sink, Colonel Johnson did not attend West Point. Instead, he spent two years at the Naval Academy, then resigned to take his commission in the infantry. He was called "Skeets" by his intimates, but "Jumpy" by his men, for the vast number of jumps he made. A strong, vigorous, inspiring leader, he was killed in action while inspecting a front-line position in Holland.

Other original units assigned to the Division included:

377TH PARACHUTE FIELD ARTILLERY BATTALION

AT FIRST, THIS was a parachute battalion with few qualified jumpers. New men were sent to the Parachute School. Many of its parachute-trained replacements were schooled as infantrymen and required re-training as artillerymen. Lieutenant Colonel Ben Weisberg was its early commander.

Its main weapon, initially, was the 75mm pack howitzer (four howitzers in each of three batteries) which broke down into nine pieces intended to be carried by mules. As an airborne unit, the nine pieces were dropped by parachute bundles.

321ST GLIDER FIELD ARTILLERY BATTALION

LIEUTENANT COLONEL EDWARD L. Carmichael commanding. This unit had high scores in training, but its skills were gained using 155s and 105s. With airborne status, the battalion had to retrain with the pack 75mms.

907TH GLIDER FIELD ARTILLERY BATTALION

COMMANDED BY LIEUTENANT Colonel C.F. Nelson. Of World War I lineage, and was reactivated in March, 1942.

101ST AIRBORNE SIGNAL COMPANY

MADE UP LARGELY from a similar company in the 82nd Airborne.

326TH AIRBORNE
ENGINEER BATTALION
326TH AIRBORNE MEDICAL COMPANY
426TH AIRBORNE QUARTERMASTER COMPANY

THESE LAST FOUR units received about half their men from similar outfits in the 82nd Airborne Division.

Assisting General Lee in running the Division were Brigadier General Donald F. Pratt, formerly Assistant Division Commander of the 82nd; Brigadier General Anthony C. McAuliffe, commanding the division artillery, and Colonel Charles L. Keerans Jr., Chief of Staff. After the assignment of senior officers, others were parceled out by the toss of a coin. (Keerans, in a few months, would be assigned to the 82nd as Assistant Division Commander and was killed in that division's attack on Sicily.)

One of the first matters General Lee addressed was bringing the Division up to authorized strength, and, at the same time, weeding out older men and those not measuring up to the requirements of an airborne organization.

The call went out for volunteers from all arms and branches for airborne duty. Great numbers responded, and, in time, a definite airborne "type" emerged. President Bush would later refer to the airborne as the "special fraternity."

General Lee built on the fraternity's esprit by methods known to inspire young soldiers. Among them were the Division's distinctive shoulder patch and its nickname, "The Screaming Eagles." Early on, he obtained a live eagle as the Division's mascot. It was named "Young Abe," purportedly a descendant of the original "Old Abe," the mascot of the 8th Wisconsin Regiment of the 101st Infantry Division in the Civil War.

Old Abe was a hellion. He was acquired from a Chippewa Indian, who had captured it in the wilds of Wisconsin and sold him for a bushel of corn. He was then acquired by C Company of the 8th Wisconsin, an outfit known as the "Eau Claire Eagles."

Old Abe took his place between the regimental colors, screaming and swooping (on a tether) through 36 Civil War battles. He was so much a symbol and an inspiration to the regiment, it was said, that a Confederate general offered a reward for his capture, dead or alive.

Young Abe was also a product of the Wisconsin woods, but, alas, he was made of lesser stuff. He was presented by the state to Major Carmicheal and the men of the 321st Glider Field Artillery Battalion, many of whom were Wisconsin natives. They in turn gave Young Abe to the Division. The presentation ceremonies were deemed so significant that they were broadcast over the Mutual Broadcasting System. The acceptance speech for the eagle was made by General Lee himself.

Young Abe never soared in battle. Instead, he died infamously on July 6, 1943, eight months after his coast-to-coast induction into the Division. None of the 101st's troops were present to mourn him. They were away on maneuvers at the time in Tennessee.

Rigorous training went on for the Division for some 37 weeks, progressing from individual exercises to those for larger units. Soldiers were coming and going, as rejects or replacements, or off to Jump School. Complicating matters, shortages of equipment of every kind were the norm.

Typical was the experience of the 377th Parachute Field Artillery. For the longest time it was gunless. Finally, four pack howitzers were borrowed from the Airborne Command and rotated for training among other artillery units.

By March of 1943, the 377th Artillery Battalion began working with the 502nd, a pairing that was to continue throughout the war. By April it was making jumps of battery size. A month later, it made the first artillery-battalion jump in U.S. Army history.

This training was done at Fort Bragg. Most of the glider troops had their first ride in those "powerless boxes" at Laurinberg-Maxton Army Air Base in Maxton, North Carolina. Glidermen took a dim view of the fact that they were simply ordered to ride gliders, without receiving the hazardous duty pay of parachutists. They took pains to make this known in handcrafted posters carrying messages in large print.

"Join the Glider Troops," these proclaimed. Elsewhere on the posters, in and around drawings of smashed gliders, was this message: "No flight pay...No jump pay" "But never a dull moment." Extra pay was granted the glidermen in the Spring of 1944.

That summer gliders were used en masse in training for the first time. One person injured was General Lee, who suffered broken ribs when his glider made a rough landing. Glidermen did not appreciate his quoted remark afterward: "Next time I'll take a parachute."

Training continued, interspersed with demonstrations for dignitaries ranging from General George C. Marshall, chief of staff, to Anthony Eden, British foreign secretary, to movie star Dick Powell.

During this period, the Division's nickname progressed from "The Eagle Division," the winning name submitted by Private Jesse M. Willis, to "The Screaming Eagles." The last change just emerged. It was first applied to the 502nd's boxing team and appeared in the *Stars & Stripes*. Soon it was applied to the entire Division.

In early August 1943, a party of 76 officers and men were sent to England as an advance group, signalling that the Division would soon be moving overseas.

The Division started north by train on August 22, 1943, heading for its embarkation point, Camp Shanks on the Hudson River, some 30 miles above New York City. Twenty trainloads were required to move the troops and equipment.

Some elements of the Division sailed on the SS *Samaria*. The others, including the 502nd Parachute Infantry, the 377th Field Artillery, the 907th Artillery, engineer and ordnance companies and a detachment of unassigned members of the Women's Army Corps (WACs) sailed on an old British transport of the Peninsula and Orient Line called the SS *Strathnaver*.

The *Strathnaver's* voyage was a memorable saga, if somewhat inane and bizarre. The vessel was vastly overcrowded; set up to accommodate 4,300 troops, it sailed on September 5 with 5,800 officers, men and women aboard.

Troop accommodations below deck were abysmal. The British food and food distribution system were quite primitive, not to mention awful.

The WAC area was strictly out of bounds to other troops. This did not prevent a certain amount of distant fraternization, as well as a clinical demonstration of the boy-will-meet-girl syndrome.

When the WACs were given free time outdoors in the sparse confines of the foredeck and afterdecks, the men ogled the women from the decks above this recreation area. Many dropped notes on strings to the WACs, and many of these were returned. When the WACs were in their cabins, the men above lowered notes that were reeled in through the portholes.

No enemy action was encountered during the days at sea, but the *Strathnaver* was enemy enough. Six days out she developed engine trouble and was forced to leave the convoy and put into the small harbor at St. John's, Newfoundland.

The town itself was off limits to the *Strathnaver's* passengers, who were allowed off the ship only for hikes. Eventually, arrangements were made to rotate the men, about 1,400 at a time, to a local fort where showers and limited recreation (spelled "b-e-e-r") were available.

After 14 days in port and the repairs made, the ship headed out to sea. But passing through the harbor's narrow entryway, the *Strathnaver* struck a rock and took on 28 inches of water. Back she went to the dock for more repairs.

She was then relieved of her mission. On October 2, the SS *John Ericsson,* owned by the United States Line and crewed by Englishmen, arrived at St. John's to take her place.

The *Ericsson's* accommodations, compared to the *Strathnavers*, were luxurious. The food was American. The officers dined at table-clothed sittings, and their quarters served by a British batman. (The first morning out, a discreet knock on the door led to this man serving many a 101st officer his first cup of tea in his bunk.)

The *Ericsson* put to sea on October 4, bound for Halifax to join a convoy. Shortly before sailing from St. John's, Colonel Moseley of the 502nd discovered that his regiment had met the requirements for the North American Theater Ribbon, intended mainly for those who had served 30 days on such as the Murmansk run.

This blue service ribbon with red, white, and black vertical stripes, was somehow obtained in quantity and every member of the 502nd was ordered to wear it. The *Ericsson* finally docked at Liverpool on October 18, after a crossing in which the elapsed time from Camp Shanks to England encompassed 43 days.

There was one last incident concerning the ribbons. When the regiment disembarked, British longshoremen spotted the men's decorations. The English, always chary with ribbons, greeted the troops with the low whistle that constitutes booing in their country for troops newly arrived from America, already bemedaled, without hearing a shot fired in anger.

For the next nine months, the 101st lived in and around English villages with those wonderful names in Wiltshire and Berkshire counties: Greenham Commons, Chilton Foliat, Yattenden, Oglebourne, Yewden Manor and Denford House. The 326th Engineers had special quarters—in a 91 room, 232 year old manor house.

Training resumed and slowly the troops fostered friendly relations with the locals, drained their pubs, ate their baked goods and chased, and later, in some cases, married their daughters.

At the end of January, the Division's last unit, the attached 501st Regiment arrived in England. The majority of its troops had been assigned to the 501st at Camp Toccoa, following the departure of the 506th, and later took jump training a battalion at a time. The 501st was described as one of "the toughest and most spirited regiments" in the entire Army, commanded by a vigorous leader, Lieutenant Colonel Johnson.

Plans for the cross-channel invasion, in the works since 1942, progressed. Airborne units of the 82nd had been employed in earlier operations in North Africa, Sicily and Italy. Events had gone badly in terms of the drop; planes carrying parachutists had been mauled by trigger-happy men of the supporting naval and land forces, though once on the ground, badly scattered, the men fought superbly.

This, General Bradley would write later, "...seriously jeopardized the future of airborne operations; many of my infantry cohorts declared the paratrooper a dead dodo." After these fiascoes, Eisenhower, commander of the Mediterranean Theater, wrote General Marshall: "I do not believe in the airborne division." He suggested that airborne units the size of divisions be reduced to battalion size or smaller.

Bradley would remain a strong advocate of the airborne divisions, however, stating that he would not wish to make the Normandy Beach landings without their help, and Eisenhower would also change his tune.

In July of 1943, serious planning for the invasion, code-named "Overlord," was underway. General Lee went to London in August of that year, where he played a large role in the planning of the airborne phase. General Eisenhower was named to command the invasion.

On February 4, 1944, General Lee suffered a heart attack. A month later, he was told that his service with his Division must end. About a month after that, he began his journey home. It began on a train, on which the general sat propped up at a window with a pillow, waving goodbye. It was a sad occasion for this man, who by his foresight and effort could mark every step in the formation of the airborne forces, from the days of the Test Platoon, until almost two months before taking the 101st Division into combat.

After eight months of hospitalization and partial recuperation, General Lee was retired.

Brigadier General Maxwell D. Taylor came over from the 82nd Airborne and assumed command of the 101st Airborne on March 14, 1944. With the 101st, he was considered something of an outsider at first; he had made only one jump in training with the 82nd, three in all (two more in combat, Normandy and Holland) in his career. Lieutenant Eugene D. Brieure, assistant jumpmaster in Taylor's plane in the Normandy operation, is quoted in George Koskimaki's book, *D-day With The Screaming Eagles,* as saying this was General Taylor's fifth jump. A close associate once said of him, "He really didn't like to jump out of airplanes, but he liked to be around people who jumped out of airplanes."

He had an understanding of the early parachutists' mentality. A story is told of him on the occasion of his first jump, which was followed by a large-scale demonstration jump by the 504th Parachute Infantry Regiment. When it was done, the regimental commander said in Taylor's presence, "Well, that's it."

Taylor said angrily, "What do you mean, 'That's it.' They haven't done anything." Later, it was explained that Taylor meant that the troopers "hadn't made any tactical maneuvers on the ground, no military achievement, merely the jump itself." There was the definite feeling, he said, that the job ended with the jump. "They made the jump; they were all heroes, and they went home."

Emphasis on action after the jumps soon became a major part of training. All this about the general was beyond the knowledge of the 101st's soldiers. They took General Taylor at face value as a hard-charger, and it was not long before he gained their respect.

Meanwhile, planning for Overlord continued. General Bradley, as U.S. ground commander, fought for the use of two airborne divisions from the start.

Then the airborne part of the plan, which was thought to have full approval at the highest level, encountered an unforeseen snag. Ike's air marshall, Sir Trafford Leigh-Mallory, said he was against it. This happened at a meeting conducted by General Montgomery. The exchange between Bradley and Leigh-Mallory was heated.

Leigh-Mallory had expressed no concern about the airborne phase in the early planning. Now he shocked the high-level planners by saying of it: "I cannot approve of your plans. It is much too hazardous an undertaking— certainly far more than the gains are worth."

He turned to General Bradley and said, "I am sorry, General Bradley, but I cannot go along on it with you."

"Very well, sir," Bradley replied. "If you insist on cutting out the airborne attack, then I must ask that we eliminate the Utah assault. I am not going to land on that beach without making sure we've got the exits behind it."

"Then let me make it clear," Leigh-Mallory said across the table, "that if you insist on this airborne operation you'll do it in spite of my opposition."

Then he turned to Monty, the overall ground commander, and added, "If General Bradley insists upon going ahead, he will have to accept full responsibility. I don't believe it will work."

Montgomery quieted the two and said that he "would assume full responsibility for the landing."

Twice more, Leigh-Mallory went to the highest authority, General Eisenhower, asking that the airborne mission be cancelled. His second appeal, six days before the operation was scheduled, included the opinion that it would cost 50 percent casualties among the parachutists and 70 percent among the glider troops before they landed.

Eisenhower, after the second meeting, recalled that he withdrew alone to his quarters to ponder the matter, well aware that if Leigh-Mallory were right, he, Ike, could never forgive himself. He concluded that losses on the beach would be even higher without the airborne, and that success on that beach was a prerequisite to the success of the entire assault. He telephoned Leigh-Mallory and told him the operation would go as planned.

When the airborne phase resulted in 15 percent total casualties, Leigh-Mallory, in a letter to Eisenhower after D-day, said he was pleased to acknowledge his mistake about the mission.

There was a pointed and poignant sequel to this story. Four years later, on his retirement as the Army's Chief of Staff, a reporter asked Ike what he considered the high point of his 33 years in the military. He thought for a moment, then replied that he supposed "the natural thing would be to say that it was when the surrender agreement ending the war was signed."

But that occasion had been anticipated. Eisenhower went on to say, "I think the greatest moment was when I got word that the 82nd and 101st Airborne Divisions had landed and gone into action on the Cherbourg Peninsula."

Had it failed, he said, he would have gone to his grave haunted by the thought that he had killed 20,000 young Americans stupidly.

THE MISSION

THE MISSION GIVEN the 101st Airborne was essentially fourfold: (1) Secure the four causeways leading from Utah Beach; (2) Neutralize a battery of four 122mm howitzers virtually overlooking Utah; (3) Make contact with the 4th U.S. Division, leading the Utah landing and proceeding up the causeway; (4) These accomplished, march on and seize Carentan, the key to the roadnet leading up the Cotentin Peninsula to Cherbourg.

Three training exercises were held during the Spring, each duplicating as far as possible the 101st's mission in Normandy.

The first two, called Beaver and Tiger, simulated parachute drops and glider landings. The third, on May 9-12, closely resembled the actual operation-to-be on similar terrain, complete with a jump.

Beaver and Tiger were marked by much confusion, but they served a purpose in smoothing out procedures. Eagle was a dress rehearsal for the real thing. It, too, had its moments of confusion and turmoil, caused in part by high winds on the drop, presenting Taylor and staff with kinks that would have to be unknotted.

When specific missions were assigned to the regiments and battalions of the 101st, attacking and silencing the guns near St. Martin-de-Varreville (a Bradley priority) fell to Lieutenant Colonel Steve A. Chappuis' 2nd Battalion of the 502nd Parachute Infantry Regiment.

Aerial photos indicated that the guns were surrounded by a wall at least 12 feet high. Rehearsing the attack on these, it was determined that grappling hooks with ropes attached would help the parachutists scale the wall. A hurried call went out to find about a half-dozen of these hooks and eventually they arrived at the 2nd Battalion.

They were tried and tested on a model of the emplacement—not with great success, it must be said. Before the men boarded the planes for France, the grappling hooks were carefully packed in bundles and secured in the bomb bays of the aircraft carrying the men who were to use them.

When the parachutists jumped, the bundles were dropped, and were never seen again. If not at the bottom of a swamp or a swollen river, they might have been found in a field by a puzzled French farmer, who probably wondered why the Americans came to battle with so medieval a scaling device.

In late May, the 101st units scheduled to jump began moving to marshalling area at airfields in the Newbury-Exeter area, where planes of the 50th and 53rd Troop Carrier Wings of the IX Troop Carrier Command awaited them. Seaborne elements of the Division, namely, most of the glider units, moved to embarkation ports.

An exception to the glider units assigned to the Division's seaborne "tail" was a battery of the 81st AA/AT Battalion, commanded by Captain Thomas P. Moran, and B Battery, commanded by Captain Alphonse Gueymard. They were the only glider troops of the 101st who landed in Normandy by the means as a unit. They were part of Operations Chicago, as the lift was called, which arrived in Normandy about 3:35 AM, flying the same course as the parachutists' planes. A second, and later lift, called Keokuk, flew a direct course across the channel and over the Utah Beach to its landing area. One of the gliders in the first lift was assigned to Brigadier General Don F. Pratt, the Division's Assistant Commander.

A Battery's mission was to help clear the landing zone for Keokuk, then attach itself to the 506th Regiment for antitank support. It was particularly effective in supporting the attack on Carentan. B Battery had a similar mission, initially, then went over to division control. As the only glider troops of the 101st committed as such in Normandy, A and B Batteries were later awarded the Distinguished Unit Citation. At the airfields, the parachutists lazed about, eating well, studying sand table schemes of the various missions and going through the endless process of getting weapons, ammunition, gear and miscellaneous ready.

Among the last-named were two small items, air sickness pills and toy crickets. The pills had never been issued previously and were used before takeoff.

Their effect on many a parachutist was to cause sleepiness. More than one man recalled that shortly after dawn, when the first fire fight held up the column in which he was moving, he fell into a ditch by the side of the road and promptly fell asleep.

The crickets were an innovation of General Taylor's, and used only by the 101st, though some publications and movies later suggested that the 82nd Airborne used them as well.

General Taylor said that after the confusion following jumps by his former unit (the 82nd), he felt a need for some means of identification between troops in the dark. General Gavin of the 82nd disdained these "mechanical" devices. He said by the time of Normandy their use was superfluous, that signals by voice were sufficient.

In any case, the toy crickets, precisely the kind found in Cracker Jack boxes, were the most incongruous "weapon" in the 101st's armament. The idea was that one click was asking, "Who's there?" Two clicks in reply meant, "Friend." The sound of the cricket was heard often after the landing in the Normandy night; it played its role.

The crickets came to the 101st late in the game, and how so many of them were obtained was something of a mystery. Years later, after his retirement, General Taylor recalled that when the idea for the use of crickets was decided, he "put in a hurry call to London to a classmate of mine, Eddie Clark, on General Eisenhower's staff."

Brigadier General Edwin N. Clark was deputy chief of logistics at Supreme Headquarters, and he remembered General Taylor's call years later.

Where did he find so many crickets?

"I don't recall," said General Clark. "But I know we sent a wild holler to the United States. And for a friend like Max Taylor, we hollered a little harder."

The crickets arrived about four days before D-day. The matter of how to carry them was solved by an unidentified genius, who decided the best way was to drill a hole in the cricket's back, pass a length of string through it, place it around the neck, outside the jump jacket for easy access. Thus, the 101st troopers went into Normandy, crickets at the ready.

General Taylor visited almost every unit in its marshalling area. At each parachute unit, it was said, he urged the men to shout "Bill Lee" on jumping, in honor of the Division's first commander, according to Sergeant Thomas Buff of Division Headquarters. Buff said that he understood that many of the men in his outfit and others did so, but other units apparently did not get the general's message, or fell back on the call taught at jump school: "One Thousand...Two Thousand..."

General Eisenhower visited the 502nd Parachute Regiment's tent area on the eve of D-day. On his stop at the E Company Street, a picture was taken that became quite famous, including an appearance in 1992 on a U.S. postage stamp.

In the Photo, Ike is shown talking to Lieutenant Wallace C. Strobel, his face blackened and surrounded by members of the company similarly made up. Strobel, many years later, said the encounter was inadvertent. Word had spread through the company area that the general was accompanied by, among others, his comely driver, the English women Kay Summmersby. Strobel said he was running down the company street to see her when he ran into Ike.

There, in the picture, Ike is standing, hands in pockets, and appears to be talking seriously to Strobel (perhaps about the mission?) or whatever. Asked about the conversation, Strobel's memory of it was that Ike asked him a standard high-brass question.

"Where are you from, lieutenant?" Ike asked.

"Michigan, sir," Strobel replied.

"Michigan, eh?" said Ike, and then made a standard high-brass comment. "Good fishing in that country."

The men of E Company would be among those in the first flight of planes (their mission was the gun emplacement to be destroyed) in the main body of the great air armada that night. They were told that the distance of the flight from England to their drop zone was 136 miles and that the flying time to their jump was 58 minutes for the parachutists, 71 minutes for the glidermen coming later. The entire sky train took more than two hours to pass a given point.

Except for the awesomeness of the number of aircraft and the sea train below them, the flight was at first quiet and uneventful. Some men smoked, others fell under the spell of the pills and slept their way to France.

The orders to the C-47 pilots were to fly initially at 500 feet altitude in V's of three-plane V's. Crossing the coast of France, they were to climb to 1,500 feet and then slope down to 700 feet for the drop. The flying speed of 150 miles per hour was to be reduced to 110 miles per hour for the jump. The formations were to be tightly held, no evasive actions permitted.

Gliders were to come in two serials, one for each division, the first arriving just before dawn. The same evening, at 2100 hours, the second flight of gliders was to come in with 101st Headquarters personnel and signalmen, as well as jeeps for the regiments.

Just about 0100, the leading planes in the lift, all in good order, made a left turn at the Channel Islands and made for the Cherbourg Peninsula. Landfall was made in the vicinity of the small coastal resort towns of Carteret and Barneville. The drop zones were some 25 miles inland.

Jump masters could see the whitecaps on the shoreline below. The planes at that point rose to the appointed 1,500 feet. Within seconds they were engulfed by a deep and thick cloud bank. The result was near chaos. Planes lost their bearings and skittered and slithered out of formation. All was turmoil as planes went off course, every which way.

Tracers from ground fire began coming up, though the lead planes were not seriously troubled, apparently catching the Germans quite by surprise. Following elements received anti-aircraft fire in heavy doses, further flummoxing the flights.

The light signals at the plane doors were flashed on hectically, sending the parachutists out. In many a case, the red light to prepare for jumping was followed in seconds by the green light to go. In more than one case, jump masters saw the shadows of men from other planes already jumping and hastily gave the order to their own sticks.

In still other situations, pilots failed to give the signals, or flashed them after crossing the peninsula... Planeloads were dropped into the sea, where many perished. A few turned over the ocean and picked their way back over land, dropping their passengers safely. A few never did jump and returned to England.

Great balls of orange-colored flak reached up for the planes. Corporal John Marohen recalled that it seemed "thick enough to walk on." Planes were hit and crashed. Others burst into flames. Some parachutists managed to jump as these aircraft limped along or before they went in.

Pilots climbed or dropped steeply, attempting to avoid ground fire or other planes careening at crazy angles through the sky. Men waiting to jump were flung to the floor. Equipment bundles within the planes became jammed in the door and had to be manhandled out, causing delays to the men behind. Bundles in bomb racks, carrying ammunition, exploded when hit.

Men were hit and killed where they sat. Sergeant Robert Rader noticed that seconds after he heard the command to "Stand up and hook up," a shell pierced the seat on which he had been sitting. A man in line, waiting to jump, slumped to the floor. Others pushed him out when the signal came.

Planes flew dangerously low and fast. As a result, the opening shock for some was severe, ripping equipment from their bodies, tearing off leg bags carrying weapons and ammo. Release devices intended to drop those bags failed, causing men to plough violently to the ground. Broken legs and twisted ankles were prevalent.

It was chaotic. The 101st's pathfinders, led by Captain Frank Lillyman, jumped at 0015; he is generally credited with being the first man to land in the invasion. He noted wryly later that so many claimed to have jumped from the first plane it "must have had 1,000 people in it."

Some pathfinders landed in designated drop zones and were able to set up devices to lead the planes in. But most flights were so far off course that the pathfinder's help was ineffective.

Instead of a compact jump, the Division's drop encompassed a rectangle of some 25 by 15 miles. Scattered groups sought each other out, clicking their crickets, assembling and pushing out looking for a fight.

Landings themselves were equally harrowing in some cases. Men landed in flooded fields, in swamps shoulder deep, in rivers, even in the English Channel, where many perished. Some got hung up on trees, in mine fields and barbed wire near Utah Beach, in among the hedgerows, where Germans were ready and waiting. Still others landed all alone in fields where cows were grazing, contentedly.

General Taylor landed alone in a pasture and spent his first 20 minutes alone. Then he met a rifleman from the 501st at the corner of a hedgerow. Proper identification established by cricket, they approached each other and hugged, and, as the general said, "then we got busy."

It was some time before the general had a force to command. "If I had given an order," he said later, "there was nobody to hear it except cows."

In time, other officers turned up, including General McAuliffe and Lieutenant Colonel Julian J. Ewell, commander of the 3rd Battalion, 501st.

Major Larry Legere of the Division G-3 section made early enemy contact. Legere and Taylor's aide, Captain Tom White, were challenged by Germans while walking along a dark road. According to one version, the French-speaking Legere replied, "I come from visiting my sick cousin." In another, Legere said he was looking for his cows. ("Cherchez ma vache.")

Whatever, Legere tossed a live hand grenade into the midst of his German questioners and silenced them. Soon after, he and White met General Taylor.

Taylor ordered Colonel Ewell to lead a group of some 85 men they had gathered; they came from various units. Ewell's own battalion had been widely scattered in the drop and three planes carrying 35 of his men had perished when the aircraft were shot down.

Colonel Ewell was commanding a mixed batch. Legere led one squad that included artillerymen, a British correspondent and two generals. "Never were so few led by so many," General Taylor said.

Dr. Bill Best, a 30-year old battalion surgeon of the 101st Division, experienced a touching and busy few moments on D-day. Landing near St. Mere-Eglise, he and other medics and corpsmen set up shop to treat wounded in the home of a French family of one M. Jean Bartot. The situation was still unsettled. German 88s and mortars were firing outside the Bartot house.

On the evening of D-day, the man of the house came downstairs, waving his arms and babbling in French. A corpsman knew enough French to tell Dr. Best a little of the man's problem: his wife, upstairs, was about to have a baby.

Dr. Best said later that he had delivered many babies in civilian life, but this was the only time he had been called on to do so by kerosene lamp to the accompaniment of gunfire. He said he thought the latter might have hastened the mother's delivery. The woman had a son, Jean Yves-Bartot, and Dr. Best went back to the war.

There was no way of knowing it at the time, but the child became famous and is still celebrated as the first baby born in liberated France.

Colonel Ewell's grab-bag force moved on the village of Pouppeville, pronounced predictably as "Poopeville" by the troops. About opposite Causeway #1, the group encountered its first German opposition. Major Legere was seriously wounded in the stomach. An unidentified aidman of the 501st ran to help Legere where he fell and was himself killed by a bullet to the head.

Colonel Sink's 1st and 2nd Battalions of the 506th, charged with securing Causeways 1 and 2, had difficulty assembling. Only 10 of some 80 planes came close to the correct drop zone. The 2nd Battalion was dropped four miles from its assigned area. Some planes in the serial missed the drop zone by 20 miles.

The 502nd Regiment, charged with destroying the gun emplacement and securing Causeways 3 and 4, was put down largely some five miles south of its target area.

The Deuces' commander, Colonel Moseley, suffered a broken leg on the jump, but he enlisted Schuyler "Sky" Jackson to push him around in a wheelbarrow. When Generals Taylor and McAuliffe saw his plight, Moseley was ordered evacuated. His war was finished. The regimental executive officer, Lieutenant Colonel John H. "Iron Mike" Michaelis, took command of the regiment.

Colonel Chappuis, commander of the 2nd Battalion, suffered a twisted ankle on the jump, but he was able to function. He gathered about a dozen men and moved to the battalion objective; he was one of the few in the 2nd Battalion who was dropped close to the mark. He found it abandoned. The Air Force had done a thorough job of bombing it just prior to D-day. That eliminated the threat that had been a major concern of General Bradley, as well as nullifying the 2nd Battalion's prime mission and its use of the grappling irons.

Lieutenant Colonel Robert G. Cole, 3rd Battalion, 502, whose main mission was to secure Causeways 3 and 4, after helping out, if need be, with destroying the gun emplacement, wandered about after landing and found himself in the 82nd Airborne's area around St. Mere-Eglise.

Backing off, Colonel Cole and the few he had with him headed for the gun emplacement. Just before getting there, he learned that the German position was bombed out and deserted. He turned his attentions to the causeways.

G Company under Captain Robert L. Clements, was sent to the northernmost causeway, #4, and on the way cleaned out St. Martin de Varreville's barracks. Taking positions on Causeway 3 by mid-morning, they met German troops retreating along the thoroughfare and killed about 75 of them without sustaining any losses to themselves.

By 1300, Cole made contact with the 1st Battalion, 8th Infantry of the 4th Division. This was the first linkup of troops coming from the beach with the parachutists.

The 1st Battalion helped finish the mop-up of the barracks at the gun emplacement. The fighting to clear the five houses at St. Martin de Varriville was led by Staff Sergeant Harrison Sumers of B Company.

Sergeant Summers performed bravely and courageously, leading a mixed bag of 15 men, most notably Private John F. Camien Jr. Summers' actions gained him a Distinguished Service Cross and a battlefield commission. He and his gang killed 30 Germans in a clearing near one of the barracks. Another target was a mess hall, where they found and dispatched about 15 Germans still eating and not particularly moved by the by commotion outside.

The mess hall was part of a two-story building, the upper story of which was used for billets. Private William A. Burt, one of Summers' men, fired tracers into a haystack next to the mess hall. It caught fire and spread to a nearby ammunition shed. As the shed began to blow up, about 30 Germans fled the building and were shot down.

Staff Sergeant Roy Nickrent of Headquarters Company arrived with a bazooka and put seven rounds into the mess hall-barracks. When it began to blaze, about 100 more Germans abandoned the building. Many were casualties, when troops from the 4th Division came on the scene from the beach and another group, led by Colonel Michaelis, came from the west.

The four beach exits were secured, fully justifying General Bradley's insistence in using the airborne behind the beach.

Casualties among the landing force at Utah, led by the 8th and 22nd Infantry Regiments of the 4th Division were remarkably low. The spearheading troops suffered 12 killed in the invasion before noon of D-day. The entire Division sustained 197 casualties. Sixty of these were missing from an artillery battalion lost at sea. More than 20,000 troops crossed Utah Beach on D-day.

The task of the 501st was to capture the lock at La Barquette, north of Carentan, and to secure five crossings over the Douve River. The 506th was to take two wooden bridges further north on the Douve near Le Port.

The 501st was widely scattered on the drop. Some sticks landed south of Carentan. Lieutenant Colonel Robert D. Carrol, commander of the 1st Battalion, was killed, the battalion staff was unaccounted for, the battalion's executive officer, Major Phillip S. Gage Jr. was wounded and captured, and all three rifle company commanders were missing. The toll in leadership was devastating.

Colonel Johnson personally took charge of the battalion's mission at La Barquette. He had had the good fortune of landing on his assigned drop zone. He was luckier than some of his other parachutists. A bundle jammed in the door of his plane and delayed his jumping by 30 seconds, after which it was cleared. Other plane loads jumped without any such delay and came down in the marshes around Carentan. Most likely they were drowned.

At dawn, Colonel Johnson, with some 150 men he had gathered, made a dash for the lock at La Barquette and secured it without casualties.

Lieutenant Colonel Robert A. Ballard, commander of Johnson's 2nd Battalion, reported in by radio, that he had with him about 250 men. Johnson ordered Ballard to join him with his force in completing the second part of the 501st mission, securing other river crossings. However, enemy forces were between Ballard and Johnson. Ballard said he could not move and Johnson was receiving fire.

The colonel had a fitting, and lucky antidote to his problem. With him was a Lieutenant Farrell from the 1st Army who had been trained in directing naval fire. Colonel Johnson found the lieutenant in a ditch, his radio intact. Farrell was able to bring in fire from the cruiser USS *Quincy* offshore. A salvo of eight-inch shells soon quieted the German force separating the two units of the 501st. Soon the wooden bridges and the lock at La Barquette were under the tenuous controls of the paratroopers.

The 3rd Battalion of the 506th had a difficult time getting off the landing area losing 20 men in the ground fighting. Both Lieutenant Colonel Robert L. Wolverton, the commanding officer and his executive, Major George S. Grant, were killed. By D+3, only one of four company commanders was found. He was Captain Robert F. Harwick, who later took command of the battalion.

The battalion's mission was to take two crossings to the northeast of Carentan. But only the S-3, Captain Charles G. Shettle, two junior officers and 13 men were available. They elected to move on the two bridges, picking up men along the way. When they approached the bridges, the "battalion's" strength had grown to five officers and 29 men.

Private First Class Donald E. Zahn volunteered to cross one of the bridges and gained the east bank of the river under fire. He was later joined by Private First Class George Montilio. Zahn received the Distinguished Service Cross and a battlefield commission for his actions. Montilio also was awarded the Distinguished Service Cross and a promotion to sergeant; he was killed in Germany in April as the war wound down, one of the Division's last casualties in action.

At the end of D-day, along the Douve River, Captain Shettle's miniscule "battalion" held firm. So did Colonel Johnson's force at La Braquette. Something of a southern front was established for and by the 101st Airborne Division.

The 1st Battalion of the 502nd, Lieutenant Colonel Pat Cassidy commanding, was establishing the northern flank of the Division around

Foucarville (soldier's pronunciation censored), about two miles from Utah Beach.

Fighting around Foucarville began around 0200 when Captain Cleveland R. Fitzgerald, commanding C Company, and Lieutenant Harold Hoggard of A Company led 11 men into the village. Captain Fitzgerald was badly wounded in the chest when the group encountered the German command post in Foucarville. He lay where he was hit through the night. Eventually he was evacuated and survived to fight again at Bastogne. He was killed after the war was over when the jeep in which he was riding hit a tree.

At dawn, Hoggard's group was reinforced by Lieutenant Wallace A. Swanson and some 40 men, and they managed to secure the village with roadblocks on its outskirts. The Germans counterattacked, but the parachutists held their ground.

That night, A Company took the surrender of 82 Germans (and a French woman married to a German soldier). C Company routed Germans from its area, killing about 50 of them. At 0500 on June 7, Cassidy's battalion was relieved by the 502nd's 2nd Battalion.

Pat Cassidy was awarded the Distinguished Service Cross for his actions on D-day, and his battalion received high praise from S.L.A. Marshal, the military historian, who would write in his account of D-day, Night Drop:

"An examination of the record and accomplishments of Cassidy's battalion, weighed critically against all others in the American Army, warrants the estimate that on D-day, in point of fighting effectiveness and tactical scope, this was probably the outstanding battalion of the Normandy operation.

The 101st's buildup continued during the day, as men scattered in the drop joined various parties already formed into fighting groups.

Two glider lifts came in on D-day. The first was at 0400, essentially a night landing of the scope not attempted in training. It carried anti-aircraft and artillery guns and their personnel, and the 326th Airborne Medical Company. This seaborne group had been preceded by parachuting members of the company, who had set up aid stations near the landing fields. One such station was bombed by the Germans on D+3.

Three noncoms from the 101st Signal Company brought in a large radio and established what probably was the first contact from France to England. The signalmen's first glider had a hairy experience. It broke from its tow early in the flight and the glider landed four miles from its takeoff field in England. They hastened back to the field, loaded on another glider and took off with a subsequent serial. This time they landed under fire and hailed a jeep that took them to Division Headquarters. There they set up for business, serving the Division and other units in Normandy.

The 377th Glider Field Artillery Battalion, some of which had parachuted in, was reinforced by the seaborne element, but had few guns. The 321st Glider Field Artillery had much of its equipment on a ship that foundered (without loss of life), but had to wait a few days before it was ready for action.

The 327th Glider Infantry Regiment came by sea and was assembled and ready for action. Parts of the 326 Engineers were on the ship that sank, with the result that the men escaped harm but lost all their equipment.

Most gliders hit the right landing zone, but many of them crashed. One man killed in a landing was the Assistant Division Commander, General Pratt. He was riding in a glider called, *The Fighting Falcon,* flown by Lieutenant Colonel Mike Murphy, the senior glider pilot in the ETO.

General Pratt was delighted to be part of the air lift. Originally he had been assigned to lead the seaborne element of the 101st, the Division's so-called "tail." He preferred parachuting, but going by glider was his second choice.

Colonel Murphy's was the first glider to attempt a landing in France. His overloaded glider seemed headed for an easy flight in, heading for a field about 1,000 feet long. But he slid more than 800 feet on damp grass at high speed and smashed into a tree. Murphy survived with broken legs. General Pratt and the co-pilot lay dead in the crumbled wreckage. The jeep the glider was carrying had broken loose and crashed into the general. If that had not caused fatal injuries, it was assumed that his neck was snapped when the glider hit the tree.

The American glider pilots trained in British made Horsa gliders, capable of carrying large loads. Just before D-day, the pilots were informed that the first lift would be made in the smaller and more maneuverable Waco CG-4A gliders. They had been made in the United States, their manufacture parcelled out to companies that made furniture, pool tables, canoes and even coffins.

The men who flew these fragile birds were a colorful lot, something in the manner of World War I fighter pilots. They wore parachutes in training flights, but, as a point of honor, not in combat since their passengers had none.

The pilots usually stayed with the units they brought in to battle and were assigned to guarding prisoners. But many joined the fighting when matters got sticky and performed gallantly. Unlike British glider pilots, they received little or no tactical training.

They were called "the most uninhibited individualists in the Army. There seemed to be something about flying a glider...that freed many from the ordinary restrictions of Army life. Those who wanted to fought like lions. Those who wanted to go back to their bases, managed to get there before anyone else. They were usually right up front during critical moments when the need for men was greatest. But they successfully defied all attempts at organization."

Just before dark on D-day, the second glider lift came in using Horsas. They carried mostly command, communication and medical personnel. The size of these gliders and the small fields caused many to crash on landing, with the loss of about one-third of the riders. Much of the equipment carried was retrievable.

As darkness fell on D-day, the 101st Division could be fairly satisfied with its first day efforts. Its northern flank was relatively secure. On the southern front, most of its missions were at least under way, and the scatter-shot landings of its parachutists had thoroughly confounded the Germans. Reports of landings all over the landscape caused the enemy to overrate vastly their numbers, paralyzing and bewildering them.

For the Division generally, individual and small unit actions, the latter carried out by a mishmash of men from different units (even divisions), were still the order of fighting. Each played its part.

St. Come-du-Mont, north of Carentan, proved a stubborn proposition. It was strongly held by Germans who might use it as a corridor for a counterattack on Utah Beach from the south.

The first attack on the village, by the 1st Battalion of the 506th, petered out after some early success. The 1st Battalion of the 501st, fighting near Les Drouries, suffered casualties from friendly fire as it tried to take that town.

At La Barquette, the troopers were plagued by fire from German 88s. Colonel Johnson, fighting in the area, heard German voices shouting "Kamerad," signaling their intention of surrendering. Twice Colonel Johnson took a flag bearer (Private Leo F. Runge) and a German speaker (T/5 William F. Lenz) and marched toward the enemy lines to negotiate a surrender of the Germans, most of whom were in swampy areas.

The first time firing broke out from the German line, the Americans answered in kind. Another lull came in the shooting. Colonel Johnson made his second try. Two Germans approached and said most of the men wanted to give up, but that several soldiers had been shot by officers for simply talking about it.

German firing commenced again, gradually diminishing. Several Germans came out of the swamp, ready to give up. A shot from an American rang out, but this did not deter the Germans. In growing numbers they began surrendering, until more than 350 did so. About 150 had been killed or wounded and, during the night, still more came into the American lines.

Artillery support, usually problematical especially in the early fighting of an airborne force, was no less so in Normandy for the 101st. The 377th Field Artillery Battalion, jumping as usual with the 502nd, lost 11 of its

12 75mm guns. Most of its men were scattered and without their basic weapon, served nobly as infantrymen. Colonel Sink, at one point, provided a captured 105mm, but it blew up on the second round it fired, killing two and wounding four others.

Other captured guns were used until ammunition for them was exhausted. With the arrival of seaborne elements, the battalion consisted of 218 men and one 75mm that came in with the first jumpers and had fired 1,016 rounds.

On D+8, the 377th was split up among other of the division's artillery. A week later, it was reunited when it received 11 75mm's over the beach.

The 321st Glider Field Artillery Battalion had come across on two ships, one of which went down when it hit a mine. It was three days later that men and guns got ashore.

On D+2, 10 officers and 75 men from Division Artillery came over the beach and joined the group that earlier had parachuted in. Two Cub planes also came in on D+1.

The main artillery support afforded the Division during the first few days was provided by the 65th Field Artillery Battalion (Armored) which landed in the first three hours of D-day. It was equipped with self-propelled 105s. A similar unit, the 87th, also was assigned to the 101st for a time.

Three anti-aircraft batteries of the 81st Airborne Anti-Aircraft Battalion landed early on D-day and was soon manning anti-aircraft machine guns protecting the beach. The 101st Airborne Signal Company came across the beach on D+1. During the first week alone, the wire section of the company laid 600 miles of wire.

On D+2, Colonel Sink with a mixed bag of two battalions from his regiment, two more from the 327th Gliders, tanks and anti-tank guns and some artillery, attacked St. Come-du-Mont. Fighting was hard and confused, particularly for men of the parachute regiments who were already exhausted from previous fighting.

Six times the Germans counter-attacked during the day; at times the fighting raged with no more than a hedgerow separating the combatants. At mid-afternoon the main body of Germans retired. They blew up one of the highway bridges on the road to Carentan doing the job that the 101st had been trying to accomplish.

Captain Shettle's small force finally was resupplied. That evening (D+2), they were relieved by the 327th Glider Regiment. Shettle and company brought out 258 prisoners. Some 70 more Germans had been killed.

Now the 101st turned to its high-priority mission of taking Carentan. The main highway through the town ran from Cherbourg to Caen and St. Lo; its railway line went from Cherbourg to Paris.

The 101st's route of attack was to be down a causeway that ran through flooded fields and swamp. There were four bridges along the roadway, which rose six to nine feet above the flooded marshes.

The Screaming Eagles underestimated the German strength in the town. Indications and available intelligence were that it was held by less than one battalion, mostly German parachutists. The 502nd Parachute Infantry Regiment was chosen to attack the town, and the regiment's 3rd Battalion, Colonel Cole commanding, was assigned to lead off.

Although Carentan was the general objective, the 3rd Battalion's specific mission was to capture and hold Hill 30, about one-half mile southeast of the town in order to cut the German's route of withdrawal from Carentan.

The second of the four bridges was the first crisis point, covered as it was by German 88s. The real obstacle, though, was the fourth bridge, at the far end of the causeway. An iron gate there was jammed, opened just enough to allow one man to exit at a time. From a farmhouse forward and to the right of this bridge, the Germans brought fire to this obstacle. Ironically, at the height of the fighting, those durable Normandy cows strolled casually through the gate and up the causeway, taking no casualties.

By June 11, Colonel Cole had the bulk of his men across Bridge 4, but they were receiving heavy fire from the farmhouse. The marshes on either side held the men in their grip; Bridge 2 was shattered behind them, preventing a withdrawal. Maneuver room was limited.

Colonel Cole made his decision. He would lead a bayonet charge across the field to the German-held farmhouse. He gave the men the order, "Fix bayonets," the first time this chilling order was sounded in Normandy, and instructed that they would charge at the sound of his whistle. He also called for an arc of smoke around the farmhouse.

But in the noise of battle, few heard the orders, or it was not understood. In late afternoon, Cole blew his whistle and took off across the open field. About 20 men, their bayonets fixed, followed him. Major Stopka, Cole's executive officer, with about 50 men, saw the colonel run ahead and shouted to his own group, "Let's go! Follow the colonel."

Most of the men in charge were from G Company. Cole stopped about halfway across the field, winded, and knelt on one knee and looked back. Most of the men had stopped.

Cole ran among them, urging them individually or in small groups, "Get up and go on!" He pointed his Colt .45 at the farmhouse and began firing. "__damn," a soldier heard him shout, "I don't know what I'm shooting at, but I gotta keep on."

Major Stopka, running up the road, overtook Cole. The latter and his radio operator hurdled a low hedgerow. Cole landed up to his neck in water. Eventually, they reached the farmhouse and flushed Germans out of it and the surrounding buildings.

An officer of the 2nd Battalion, which was in reserve, met Colonel Cole on the road near the farmhouse shortly after the bayonet charge. He was helmetless, flushed and his adrenalin was pounding, but the charge had nullified the German position, even though more fighting was to come.

For his actions that morning, Colonel Cole was the Division's first Congressional Medal of Honor awardee, and the Army's first in Normandy. He was killed in Holland by a sniper's bullet while setting out panels to mark his position for American planes, before he learned of his award.

Major Stopka received the Distinguished Service Cross for his actions. He was presented the medal at Bastogne. A few days later, he was killed by a direct hit of an artillery round.

The bayonet charge had marked the fate of many Germans, but the bitter battle continued. The jammed gate at Bridge 4 was torn away and Bridge 2 was made crossable, thanks to the engineers. But the wounded were many and ammunition was low.

Captain Lillyman secured a half-ton truck and made several dashes along the causeway and across Bridge 4, bringing supplies in and the wounded out. Near Bridge 2, three battalion surgeons: Captain Frank Choy, Captain Adolph Blatt, and Captain Charles "Mike" Althoff, tended the injured.

Cole's Battalion, what was left of it, was near exhaustion, and Cassidy's 1st Battalion was committed to join it, but not relieve it. The objective was still Hill 30, and the advance on it continued. The parachutists did so under heavy shelling; A and B companies took the worst of it. Later Cole's battalion was relieved by the 502nd's 2nd Battalion.

The hard fighting was unrelenting. The Germans counterattacked, and some of the soldiers thought the order once had been given to withdraw. It had not, and turning the troopers back to action took some doing.

At noon the next day, June 11, regiment sent word to cease firing; the Germans, it was said, sought a truce. Nothing came of it. The battle raged throughout the afternoon, close-joined. Another German counterattack got closer to success, and only American artillery turned the day. It was slow in coming, but when it arrived, it was so close that many parachutists suffered from friendly fire. It lasted only about five minutes, but it turned the Germans back. Then their firing diminished and by morning most of them had given up the battle.

Meanwhile, the 327th Glider Regiment was fighting toward Carentan from the east. The regiment was the closest unit to Omaha Beach, where stiff resistance met the landing force. On the afternoon of June 10, the 327th made the first linkup with troops of the 29th Division from Omaha Beach.

Carentan was clear by 1000, after the 327th's strong push from the northeast. Near the town's railroad station, Colonel Harper of the 327th met with Lieutenant Colonel Bob Strayer of the 506th and Colonel Allen of the 327th's 3rd Battalion. The three officers went to a nearby wine shop and got a bottle to celebrate the joining of the two beachheads. Still the fighting was not over.

The end of the Normandy operation was nearing for the 101st Airborne Division. Its last task was to hold a defensive line at the approximate base of the Cotentin Peninsula, about halfway between Carentan and Cherbourg. It was a relatively quiet sector, covered largely by patrols.

In the Division's first combat experience, none were more involved than those who administered to the souls and bodies of the fighting soldiers, the unarmed chaplains, the aid men and the doctors.

One of the chaplains was Father Francis L. Sampson, who as a 30-year old Catholic priest, volunteered for airborne training unaware that jumping from an airplane in flight would be required of him. He jumped in Normandy and Holland with the 501st Parachute Regiment and was taken prisoner while in search of casualties at Bastogne. Later, he rose to the rank of major-general and was, after service in Korea, named chief of chaplains in the Army.

Father Sampson's D-day experiences were typical of other clergymen. He landed in the middle of a stream with water up to his neck. Struggled to free himself from his parachute, he lost his Mass kit in the water. Further, his canopy was still open and wind "sailed" him downstream about 100 yards into shallow water. Once free, he returned to the stream's edge near where he had landed and began diving for his Mass kit. He found it after five or six dives.

One of the regiment's doctors, Major Francis Carrel, had insisted that clergymen be knowledgeable in giving first aid, and this activity occupied Father Sampson throughout D-day.

A colorful personality was the 502nd's Protestant chaplain, Raymond S. Hall. He was one of the first to join the airborne, which helped gain him the nickname of "Jumping Jesus;" in hearing range, he was usually referred to as "Chappie."

On D-day, he ran to a crashed glider and found both the pilot and co-pilot had suffered broken legs. When snipers opened up on him, Chappie Hall hid under the jeep in the glider and gave both men hypo shots.

He often said that he was so busy attending his flock in the marshalling area before Normandy that he was not issued a cricket or given the password. In France, he was almost shot because of his inability to identify himself quickly.

Hall's Catholic counterpart in the 502nd was Father John Andrejewski. One of the sublime moments of D-day in France was hearing Andrejewski, of Polish background, conversing with a French priest in the one language common to them - Latin.

Captain Stanley E. Morgan, a 506th surgeon, was captured shortly after landing near St. Come-du-Mont. He gave care for three days to a large number of German and American casualties. He was assisted by Sgt. Mainard D. Clifton, also a German doctor and aid man.

Private First Class John H. Wilson of the 502nd landed in a flooded area behind Utah Beach, and he treated wounded in an aid station he had established without a doctor. T/5 Ray Barton, a 501st medic, landed in a canal and attached himself to a group of men from the 82nd Airborne and, alone, treated their wounded for several days.

Private Albert Hutto of the 501st and others maintained an aid station on their own for three days. Several other noncombatants joined them, including Chaplain Kenneth Engle, Private First Class Robin Plager, and Sergeant Lee Edwards.

At one point, Hutto and Edwards went out and brought in a wounded German. He was a 19 year old boy, wounded seriously in the abdomen. He died the next day.

T/5 Wayne Walton, 501st, attended American and German wounded on a clump of high ground in a marsh. A German patrol overran them and later they were liberated by Americans. An officer with the latter group instructed Walton to remain with the wounded and that help would be sent. It arrived three days later.

So it went for these brave and dedicated men.

On July 10, the Division was relieved and moved by truck to a bivouac area just back of Utah Beach. From July 11-13, the troops were moved by landing craft back to England. All its missions had been accomplished, with a toll of 4,670 casualties. As General Lee had forecast two years previously, the first step in the 101st Airborne Division's rendezvous with destiny had been taken and fulfilled.

The 101st were the first combat troops in the invasion to return to England as a unit. The Screaming Eagles were roundly greeted on the return to their old billets. Back pay was forthcoming, furloughs granted. Most headed for London and the riotous life. A London joke had it that the MPs were going to receive a Presidential Citation for service above and beyond the call during the time the now cocky 101st troopers were in town.

After their celebratory holiday, the Division underwent refitting and re-equipping. Training started once more in the English summer. Also, they were presented with a succession of false starts that had them making other combat jumps on the continent.

During the summer of 1944, the first Allied Airborne Army was formed, consisting of the three American airborne divisions (the 17th Airborne had arrived in England), plus British and Polish airborne units. Some 16 airborne missions were considered for this command through the summer. Some reached the stage of moving the troopers to marshalling area and almost enplaning. Each time the rapid advance of Allied ground troops caused them to be cancelled.

Then there was one that became a reality. It was called "Market-Garden."

HOLLAND

MARKET-GARDEN WAS to be a concentrated thrust on a single axis, south to north, of Eindhoven, Zon, St. Oedenrode, Vechel, Uden, Grave and Nijmegen, taking the large Nijmegen Bridge across the Waal River; then on through the British sector and the bridge at Arnhem, the one that would become famed as "the bridge too far."

The operation would begin with an enormous airborne phase, the "Market" of it, taking and securing this Dutch corridor of about 100 miles in length.

Then, in the "Garden" of it, British armor would dash from the Belgium-Holland border below Eindhoven along this corridor, turn the German flank at Arnhem and forge an opening into Germany's industrial heart, the Ruhr Valley.

German troops in the area were thought to be of poor quality and poorly organized. Further, the shock of an airborne attack would easily neutralize them. These would prove to be misconceptions about the capability of the German troops involved.

The Allied plan was entirely the concept of General Montgomery, and after some initial reluctance, approved by General Eisenhower. Ike had also been pressured by his superiors, General Marshall and General Arnold, to "make use of the valuable (and expensive) airborne forces."

General Bradley was vehemently opposed, because it would supplant his preference for continuing the American advances on a broad front. Bradley would write later that "in permitting Monty to launch Market-Garden, Eisenhower committed his gravest tactical error of the war." Bradley added that "it was dangerously foolhardy, the wrong plan at the wrong time in the wrong place." Ike, for his part, insisted to the end of his life that Market-Garden "was a risk that had to be run."

Initially, the British plan called for the 101st Division to be used in units of battalion size or less. They would lay a "carpet" along the corridor over which the British XXX Corps would advance, led by the Guards Armored Division. The area assigned to the 101st along the roadway in this plan would cover some 30 miles.

Major General Maxwell Taylor (he had gained his second star during the first week of Normandy) protested vigorously at this proposed use of his force. Finally, an alternate plan was drawn up that would permit the Division to make a more compact drop and attack in larger numbers.

Specifically, the revised plan called for the Division to seize rail and highway bridges near the town of Vechel, take an important highway bridge over the Dommel River at St. Oedenrode, a canal crossing at Zon and another crossing of the Dommel at Eindhoven. Further, the 101st was to secure the corridor northward some 30 miles from Eindhoven.

As Taylor insisted, his paratroops were to drop as regimental units close to their objectives, in keeping with the now accepted concept of airborne tactics. The 502nd and the 506th Parachute Infantry Regiments would land on the same field north of Zon. The same area would be used by glider elements in the first lift, following within an hour after the parachute drops.

The 502nd was charged with securing the landing zone, capturing the bridge at St. Oedenrode and attacking the village of Best to the West to afford flank protection and to secure the lower section of the axis of the British advance.

The 506th was to seize the main bridge of the Wilhelmina Canal at Zon, then move south and take Eindhoven and its bridges over the Dommel. Quick action was important on this last mission, because the British predicted that the first advance of the Guards Armored would put them at Eindhoven in two or three hours. In fact, they reached there 36 hours after the start of Market-Garden.

The 501st was to land north of the other parachute regiments and take four bridges at Vechel over the Aa River and the Zuid Willems Vaart Canal.

During the planning, General Brereton made the bold decision to make all the parachute drops and glider landings in daylight. It was a decision, it was hoped, that would eliminate many of the failings of the Normandy operation.

The terrain of Holland was described as "basically just a big, glorified jump field." D-day, September 17, was a clear and cloudless Sunday. The planes flew over the channel without opposition, made a left turn at Bourg-Leopold, 14 miles south of the Belgian border and flew straight for the front lines. Flak was thick at the latter point; many of the German anti-aircraft were set up on barges in the various waterways. Five minutes from the drop zones, the fire was still heavy.

This time, the formations held firm, though some planes were hit and burning. The jump was the most orderly and successful ever for the 101st, resembling an Infantry School demonstration at Fort Benning. In a 30-minute period, starting at 1300, some 6,700 parachutists landed on or near their intended places, with less than two percent casualties and five percent loss of equipment. The pilots did their job splendidly.

Gliders were not as successful. Of the 70 that left England in the first life, only 53 made it to Holland. A few landed within enemy lines. Subsequent glider lifts changed course and came in behind German lines, with fewer losses. Still, some of the gliders underwent hair raising experiences.

General McAuliffe demonstrated the qualities of a leader. In Normandy he had parachuted in without formal jump training "in order to organize his artillery expeditiously," as the citation read for his award of a Silver Star on that occasion.

In Holland, he chose to come in by glider to show his support for these troops. He rode the first craft on D+1, a lift that included the 2nd and 3rd Battalions of the 327th Glider Infantry Regiment and others.

Most gliders flew without co-pilots in order to increase the number of 101st men brought in. Corporal Mike Field, a medic with the 327th, rode the co-pilots seat of his glider. What he knew about landing a glider was explained to him by the pilot on the flight to Holland.

Staff Sergeant Grayson Davis' tow plane was hit by flak, and he and the pilot had to knock out their glider's windshield and cut the tow line with a knife. Their landing was made safely.

One tow plane was totally lost in clouds soon after takeoff. The plane and glider flew for two hours above the clouds, then came through a break, but still not knowing where they were. When the glider was released, it landed just below London.

Others had it better. A medical officer, Captain Willis McKee, and the command pilot flying his glider, picked in advance, from an aerial photo, their landing spot near a gate on their field. The glider on landing, stopped with its nose 20 feet from the gate. And the first lift, landing about an hour after the parachute drops, despite some difficulties, managed to bring 250 officers and men to battle and 32 much-needed jeeps with them.

Parachute units were assembled and operational within an hour. Many Dutchmen came onto the fields at the height of the drop. One American officer recalled a Dutch boy about 12 years old, pushing his bicycle, approaching him and saying, "I am Dutch. I can help you." Asked the location of German troops in the area, the boy repeated the only English he knew: "I am Dutch. I can help you."

Colonel Sink started groups of men of the 506th toward Zon and its bridges as soon as they arrived at the regimental assembly point. German 88s slowed the drive on the bridge, and when the 1st Battalion, led by Major Jim LaPrade, was about 150 yards from its objective, previously set explosives sent the bridge up with a roar. Some men of the battalion swam to the opposite shore of the Wilhelmina Canal, others crossed in a rowboat and took positions.

A night attack on Zon was ruled out. The British tankers had been held up by the enemy. By nightfall, they were only half way to Eindhoven. The taking of the city could wait until D+1.

The 1st Battalion, 501st, landing separately north of the others, was one of the few units that did not benefit from the troop carriers' preciseness. It landed compactly but about three miles above its scheduled drop zone. It formed quickly and had little opposition in taking a railway bridge and two other smaller ones, as well as the town of Vechel itself. Its stiffest "opposition," in fact, came from the burghers of Vechel, plying them with food and drink.

The 502nd was guarding the landing zone. H Company was ordered to take the village of Best, one mile southwest of the corridor. Colonel Pat Cassidy's 1st Battalion moved to secure the road at St. Oedenrode.

Best was a village off to the west of the main avenue of advance, but General Taylor felt it would (as it did) afford an alternate route if Zon was impassable.

Originally, it was considered a mission for a platoon, then a company (H Company) reinforced. Later it became a job for a battalion. Then it required two battalions and finally half the division and a squadron of British tanks before it was suppressed. Best was defended by 1,000 Germans.

Captain Bob Jones, H Company commander, was sent with his unit through woods to seize the main bridge over the Wilhelmina Canal at Best. They came out of the woods, below the objective, on the highway to Best. There, they encountered a convoy of German trucks carrying men to reinforce their position. Jones was ordered to pull back to a defensive position.

Then he sent his 2nd Platoon, under Lieutenant Edward L. Wierzbowski, and a squad of engineers to seize the canal bridge.

Shortly after nightfall, rain began falling. The men reached the canal but were still some distance from the bridge. With Private Joe E. Mann as lead scout, they moved toward the bridge only to find it was strongly defended. They withdrew under fire.

By then, Colonel Michaelis, the 502nd's commander, realized that the mission required more fire power than Jones' outfit could produce. So he sent another reinforced company into the engagement.

Best still considered a secondary mission was growing more difficult. The 2nd Battalion, 502nd, was ordered to join Colonel Cole's 3rd Battalion in the fight. The 2nd Battalion with a classic attack employing three companies in line, struck across a wheat field. They took considerable losses from machine gun fire. Colonel Chappuis withdrew his men.

Cole's 3rd Battalion was still engaged. He called for air support. P-47s came in too close and began strafing Cole's men, whereupon he went out and placed orange panels and orange smoke to define his lines to the aircraft. Shading his eyes to the sun, he looked up. A sniper's bullet cracked from a house about 100 yards away. The bullet struck the colonel in the temple and he died immediately, never knowing that the Medal of Honor had been awarded him for leading the bayonet charge at Carentan.

Cole's radio operator, T/5 Robert Doran, was killed within minutes of Bob Cole, when he left his foxhole to improve his radio reception.

T/5 John Fitzgerald, who had been instructed previously by the colonel to look for a jeep load of ammunition, returned in time to see Colonel Cole's body on the ground.

Fitzgerald knelt beside him. He turned to the battalion surgeon and asked, "Why don't you do something for him?"

The surgeon replied, "I'm sorry, John. There's nothing I can do for him now."

Back in the Best area, enemy soldiers moved up close to Lt. Wierzbowski's position, close enough to attack with potato mashers. One landed on the machine gun of Engineer T/5 Vincent Laino. Groping about, he located one of the German grenades sputtering at his feet. He picked it up and hurled it back at the Germans, thereby saving his own life and that of three of his comrades. He was awarded a Silver Star for this act.

Joe Mann, the scout, had been wounded in both arms and hands the previous day. His arms had been bandaged and bound tightly in slings, but Mann was still fighting. On D+2, Germans again threw grenades at Lt. Wierzbowski's group. A potato masher came flying toward Mann, who was sitting in a large trench with six other men. The grenade landed behind Mann.

He shouted a warning to the others, but he was unable to pick up the explosive. Instead, he lay back on it, and seconds later, took the full force of the explosion. Some of the men in the trench suffered shrapnel wounds, but they lived. Mann was able to say only, "My back's gone," and he died within minutes.

He was awarded the Congressional Medal of Honor. It was tragically ironic that the Division's only two recipients of the Medal of Honor died with a day of each other on the same general battlefield.

Not long after Mann died, Wierzbowski and his men were overwhelmed by a superior German force and had to surrender. During the 2nd Battalion's successful attack on Best the next day, the group was freed, and in turn, took prisoners of the Germans who had been guarding them.

British tanks had reached Zon during the night, and their engineers had thrown a Bailey Bridge across the Wilhelmina Canal in darkness. One tank squadron, consisting of six Churchills and one Challenger, was assigned to the Division. With the help of these, Best finally fell, along with a large bag of prisoners.

To the north, counterattacks hit the 501st around Vechel and the neighboring town of Eerde. The 501st's Colonel Johnson moved his 1st Battalion into Vechel, to back up his various counter moves. The Division itself was bolstered by the glider lift of D+1, the one led by General McAuliffe, bringing in two battalions of the 327th Regiment. One of those in that lift was Walter Cronkite, a young correspondent for the United Press.

Cronkite had initially started parachute training at the Division's school in England, intending to jump into Holland. Then orders came down stating that none of the newsmen would be permitted to jump, and Cronkite, much to his displeasure, was assigned to go in by glider.

Cronkite later told of his glider landing, a typical controlled crash. His helmet and shoes were blown off and his trousers were filled with dust. He surmised, as any parachutist could have told him, that jumping with a parachute was much "safer" than glider riding.

On the morning of D+1, Colonel Sink sent his three battalions of the 506th in column to take Eindhoven. When his 3rd Battalion in the lead was held up, he sent his 2nd Battalion in a sweeping movement to the left.

This unit and the 3rd Battalion converged in Eindhoven, and after close street fighting, finally gained control of the city—the first such in Holland to be liberated.

At 1230, two British armored recon cars arrived, marking the Division's first actual link-up with the British. At 1830 the first tanks of the Guards Armored Division clanked into Eindhoven and their advance units approached Zon 30 minutes later.

There, the 326th Airborne Engineers were working to clear the debris of the blown bridge, and British engineers worked all night installing a Bailey Bridge. At 0645 on D+2, the first squadron of British armor moved across the bridge and onto the "carpet" laid by the 101st Division. From there, the tankers proceeded through Zon, St. Oedenrode and Vechel, on into the area of the 82nd Division.

Thus, Montgombery's plan was working, but under the strain of two major shortcomings. The British tanks were 36 hours behind schedule, and the the British parachutists north at Arnhem were locked in desperate fighting for their lives. Heavy weather would delay subsequent parachute and glider reinforcements and high-level communications were not established. The seeds of the plan's destruction were sewn.

More glider units were to go in on D+2, bringing the 3rd Battalion of the 327th and much needed artillery pieces. Bad weather thwarted the lift, causing many of the artillery outfits to turn back. Of 385 gliders leaving England, twice as many as originally planned, only 209 of these made it to Holland.

Losses were heavy: 26 gliders were never accounted for; 16 were known to have landed in German territory; of 136 jeeps leaving England, only 79 made it; of 86 artillery pieces, just 40 reached Holland. Most devastating was the fate of the 907th Glider Field Artillery. All planes towing its dozen 105mm Howitzers and crews turned back.

Meanwhile, the Germans directed counterattacks against Best, St. Oedenrode and Zon. At Zon, the location of Division Headquarters, glider pilots were needed to man its defensive perimeter. For a time, the pilots were the command post's sole line of defense.

The counterattack on St. Oedenrode produced one of the great characters on the Allied side of the operation. He was Sergeant James W. McCrory, called "Paddy," a tanker with the Irish Guards. His tank was almost put out of commission by enemy fire and just limping along. Paddy and tank came to a halt at the command post of the 1st Battalion, 502nd.

This was on D+2, when the battalion was moving toward the village of Schijndel under fire. Colonel Cassidy sent a message asking Paddy if his tank was able to help. McCrory's reply was, "Hell, yes."

American parachutists volunteered to replace McCrory's injured crew. They were Sergeant Roy Nickrent and Private John J. O'Brien. Paddy and his tank, the latter still "wounded," caught up with the lead company already under severe fire. He dispatched three German 20mm guns. Next he finished off a heavy weapon, then a truck loaded with ammunition.

John O'Brien stood in the tank's turret and sprayed the ground ahead with a Sten gun until a German bullet killed him.

The German opposition ceased. Cassidy felt he did not want to become engaged in a longer and larger fight and called his units back. Fifty-three prisoners had been taken and more than 30 Germans killed.

Paddy McCrory, on being thanked for his help, replied, "When in doubt, lash out."

Soon thereafter, the Division was put to holding off hostile thrusts at the corridor. This involved, General Taylor said, "a matter of nice judgement" in deciding how to discourage attacking any cuts in the corridor without becoming involved in a serious engagement. "Almost like Indian fighting," the general said.

There were several "nice decisions" to be made at Eindhoven, at the villages of Eerde and Heeswijik and Dinther, minor players until now.

At Dinther, A and B Companies of the 506th pushed the Germans back against C Company and trapped them. In the doing, they bagged 418 prisoners, with 40 German dead and 40 more wounded. These "Indian" attacks on the corridor continued until D+10.

On D+5, the 502nd Regiment lost key members of its command echelon injured by an artillery shell that burst in a tree above them. The shell hit as the group was conferring at a forward command post; the regiment was attacking toward Schijndel at the time. Fourteen men were casualties.

Among them was Colonel Michaelis, the commanding officer, who sustained fragment wounds of the arms, legs and stomach; he had previously suffered wounds in Normandy. He returned for Bastogne, but reaction to his wounds forced him out of action.

His orderly, Private First Class Garland E. Mills, was killed by the burst. Michaelis' S-2, S-3 and assistant S-3 (respectively Captain George Buker, Captain R.B. Clements and Captain Henry "Hank" Plitt) were wounded.

Visiting the command post at the time were General Taylor's G-2, Lieutenant Colonel Paul Danahy, and his G-3, Lieutenant Colonel Harold Hannah, were also downed by the blast. From the 377th, Major Elkins suffered a wound, as did one of his observers. Colonel Chappuis, the 502nd's senior officer remaining, was called back from the Schijndel attack to take command of the regiment.

Later that afternoon, D+5, a report by radio to the 501st said that the Germans had cut the corridor between Oden and Vechel to the northeast. The subsequent fighting, mainly by the 501st, to restore the cut was called one of the hardest battles fought by the Division in Holland.

The 501st 2nd Battalion was the first to confront the attackers. It was later joined by the 2nd Battalion of the 506th, which had been hurried to the area by truck. The 327th offered strong support.

Three times the Germans directed furious charges and each time the units of the 101st held. Once more, the corridor was re-opened.

The 502nd kept the roadway clear around St. Oedenrode. The 327th defended it around Vechel and the 501st kept it operational in the vicinity of Earde. Small, sharp attacks continued on the highway, but all were repulsed.

On September 24, D+7, the 501st was consolidated around Eerde facing a familiar antagonist from Normandy, the German 6th Parachute Regiment. The battleground was a collection of sand dunes ranging in height from 15 to 40 feet. Early in the day, some 250 Germans backed by five tanks, attacked.

Colonel Johnson sent the 501st's 3rd Battalion and nine British tanks to fend off the attackers. Heavy, close-in fighting resulted.

Lieutenant Henry Mosier, leader of the 1st Platoon of A Company, led a daring attack through mortar and machine-gun fire into the German position in the dunes, clubbing the enemy in foxholes and shooting others at close range. Lieutenant Murphy, the platoon's second in command, said of Mosier's action, "It was courage such as I had never imagined possible, almost foolish courage..." The dunes were cleared.

By D+10, the 101st Division's initial mission had been accomplished, though there were subsequent assignments, with more hard fighting to come.

Market Garden, however, was faltering and soon was a failure. Arnhem had not been taken. The German flank could not be turned. The British at the northern extreme of the corridor had been plagued by the bad weather, which botched reinforcing air lifts. Communications were faulty. There had been miscalculations of German strength in the area. All doomed the British phase of the operation to failure and to heavy casualties.

There were a few pluses. Significant advances were made over some major geographical obstacles. Large parts of Holland were relieved of the crushing German occupation. The number of Germans killed or wounded was sizable, if inestimable. The number of 101st Division men killed, according to a recent Dutch source, has been put at 854. American figures list an additional 2,151 wounded or injured and 398 missing or captured.

An historian of the American airborne forces would later write: "The gallantry of the officers and men of the 82nd and 101st Divisions in all their actions in Holland showed an excellence which has not been in any operation in the European Theater."

The rest of the Division's fighting in Holland was, in a sense, anticlimactic. It consisted of holding defensive positions, assigned by the British, on the "Island."

This was the name given a long, narrow stretch of terrain, some 10 miles of miserable land, to the north and west of Nijmegen. The assignment there went on and on, until the Division was finally relieved after 71 days on the front lines of Holland, a record for such continuous service.

The Division, on loan to the British 2nd Army, began its move to this new position on October 2, 1944. The 506th took over from the British near Opheusden, out near the narrow end of this pie-shaped sector that was between the Lower Rhine and the Waal rivers. With it was the 321st Artillery, B Company of the 326th Engineers and all batteries except C Battery of the 81st Airborne Artillery. Preliminarily, in support of the 82nd Airborne near Nijmegen, the 321st fired the Division's first round to fall on German soil.

The next day the 506th took over front-line positions near Ophuesden, and in the same week, other units of the Division joined the 506th on the Island.

It was a difficult and dreary position, low and flat. Large dikes held back the water of the two rivers. The area between was farm land. The weather was as miserable as were the British rations, except for the supply of rum that came with them.

The Germans occupied high ground on the north side of the Rhine, making movement in the low lands hazardous. British artillery, augmented by guns of the 101st, engaged in almost constant exchanges. Men were forced to occupy their foxholes, often in heavy rain that rose the water levels in these shelters almost three feet. The British rations included tea instead of coffee. But plenty of wine did help ease the pain of the position.

Nijmegen was the location of the hospital of the 326th Airborne Medical Company, with an advanced field hospital out on the Island. Indicative of the severity of the artillery exchanges and of German mines in the area was the number of casualties; 2,765 were treated.

Fighting of major proportions occurred around Opheusden. A German force of more than 300 with artillery and mortar support unleashed an attack that went on from October 6 to October 14. The first day the Germans sent in three attacks, mostly at the 506th. At the end of the day, the 506th had lost 91 men and 11 officers.

The next day they attacked again with fresh troops. The 327th was committed to the action, as was a battalion of the 502nd and attached British troops of the Duke of Cornwall's Light Infantry.

That night the 1st Battalion, 506th, and the British troops were withdrawn to a new position, which meant that some 120 seriously wounded might have to be left behind. During the day Captain Joseph Warren, the battalion surgeon, had set up an aid station in a windmill. Major Louis R. Kent, the regimental surgeon, sent up a small convoy of six jeeps and an ambulance. These removed about 20 of those on litters. Six German prisoners carried three litters. The rest were taken out by unwounded men, two to a casualty, using a seat carry with M-1 rifles.

On October 6, after the 501 had gained control in its attack, Colonel Johnson, the dynamic leader of the regiment, was killed. At the time, he was inspecting a front line position with other officers of the 2nd Battalion.

A heavy caliber German shell roared in near the group. Characteristically, Johnson strode on. The others ducked for cover. The shell landed almost at his feet, causing severe wounds to the colonel's neck, arms and spine. On the way to the hospital at Nijmegen, he died.

Colonel Johnson's last words to Lieutenant Colonel Julian Ewell were, "Take care of my boys." Ewell, the 3rd Battalion commander, took over the regiment.

General Taylor was later wounded while inspecting front line positions. A fragment from a self-propelled gun nicked him in the lower back, putting him out of full action for about two weeks. Still later, on a similar inspection tour of the 1st Battalion, 502nd, at Bastogne, he sustained a similar wound in the same general place. This one did not put him out of action.

Now the 327th Glider Infantry took over responsibility for the Opheusden area. From October 7 through the 14, the Germans launched a series of attacks, almost non-stop, against the 327th. The regiment fought brilliantly, under heavy artillery and ground fire and prevented any penetrations.

The 506th's 2nd Battalion, with the help of the Dutch Underground, assisted 138 British soldiers and four American pilots, in a daring night crossing by pontoon boats of the Rhine. This was one of the last groups from the battered British force at Arnhem to make its escape. Patrolling became the order of the day (or night) around the heavily mined area at Opheusden.

Lieutenant Fred J. Rau and a sergeant of the 327th's reconnaissance patrol were killed. A patrol from the 502nd lost seven men and an officer. The Division recon patrol leader lost a foot. Lieutenant Hugo Sims Jr., the 501st's regimental S-2, led a unit in search of prisoners on a 24-hour patrol deep into German lines that gained fame as the "the incredible patrol."

In mid-November, the 101st Division sent advance parties to a World War I airfield in France called Camp Mourmelon, an ancient pile on which Caeser had camped, and most recently, Germans had used as a tank depot.

Later in the month the Division began moving there. As they proceeded along the once embattled corridor, the Dutch stood on the edges shouting, "September 17, September 17," signifying that day they would long remember as the day their liberation began. The Dutch have, to this day, continued to lavish their kindness on men of the 101st Airborne Division who have returned for sentimental visits.

BASTOGNE AND BEYOND

The market town of Bastogne, Belgium, population about 4,000 in 1944, stands on a plateau in the Ardennes region. It is at the center of five major highways and three secondary roads and a railway, with few other distinguished or attractive features.

Historically, it has been fought over several times in other wars because of its strategic location. Marshal Ferdinand Foch in World War I avoided it, describing it as "an almost impenetrable massif." In 1944, Allied strategy plotted attacks to the north and south of it, rather than attacking through it.

Germans struck through the Ardennes into France in 1914 and again in 1940, in their assaults on Holland and Belgium—attacks facilitated by the drier conditions of late spring and summer.

General von Runstedt led these latter strikes. Von Runstedt made his headquarters in Bastogne during part of these campaigns, and Hitler himself was familiar with the town. He arrived there by car with a large entourage to confer with von Runstedt on May 17, 1940.

On that day he was to boast of the drive that took him to the French coast, "All the world harkens." Almost five years later, the world would witness at Bastogne the beginning of his last hurrah.

In the early days of December 1944, life for the 101st Division troopers at Camp Mourmelon was easy. Passes to nearby Rheims were plentiful. The 502nd Regiment fielded a football team. Champagne was in ample supply if you brought your own empties Only the bottles were hard to come by in the champagne district of France. USO troops were frequent visitors to the camp.

One of these featured baseball's Mel Ott and Frankie Frisch, both managers of major league baseball teams at the time. After doing their turn one evening, they adjourned to a small private bar arrangement in the officers' barracks that Lieutenant Earl Henricks of the 502nd had set up in a vacant room.

At first, Ott and Frisch were properly circumspect. As the night wore on and the champagne flowed in excess, Ott took over as bartender and Frisch began telling his supply of baseball yarns. Before they were done, the two began buying and selling each other's ball players, paying for them with wads of worthless German marks they had acquired along the way.

The next day was December 17, 1944, a Sunday, another dull and greasy day, of which nothing is more dull and greasy than a December Sunday in France.

The 502nd's football team was off somewhere to the south playing an Air Force team. Many men and officers were away on passes and leaves in Rheims and a few in Paris. A call came, an officer on duty at a battalion command post remembered, to go to a meeting at regimental headquarters.

The old man did not have much to tell, except that the Germans had attacked some 200 miles to the north of us and that the 101st had been alerted to move there. He said we would go by trailer trucks and the first units would leave as soon as the vehicles arrived, without those off recreating.

Not everyone had finished the refitting, but they were ordered to move out "as is." The 463rd Parachute Field Artillery Battalion, a battle-hardened outfit of Italy and Southern France, at Mourmelon awaiting assignment to the 17th Airborne Division, headed out under unusual circumstances.

As the 101st made ready to leave, the 463rd's commander, Lieutenant Colonel John Cooper, offered the services of the unit to General McAuliffe. The latter said the 463rd was outside his command, but he suggested that Cooper talk with Colonel Harper of the 327th Glider Infantry. Harper readily accepted Cooper's offer and the 463rd went off to war "attached" to the 101st. Technically it was AWOL. It would perform with distinction at Bastogne.

Few were exactly sure where the 101st was headed; a town called Werbomont was one of those mentioned. The 82nd Airborne, farther along in its refitting would precede the 101st.

The troops piled into the open cattle trucks for the journey in frigid cold. Once during the night, the column stopped so the British drivers could have a "brew-up." At one point, a lieutenant came along with a map and told an officer sitting in a jeep that their destination had been changed.

"Where is it now?" he asked the lieutenant.

"Someplace called Bastogne," the latter said.

The officer in the jeep said, "Oh." He sat there and waited for the convoy to move. "Bastogne" meant nothing to him; he had never heard the word before. Soon the trucks pulled out for this meaningless town. It would not be long before it would be the most memorable place he would ever know.

The Americans, under the German thrust, were losing ground in their thinly held defensive line. They were under the command of Major General Troy H. Middleton, in charge of the VIII Corps, with headquarters in Bastogne.

General Middleton was an experienced soldier. He was twice promoted on the same battlefield in WWI, and became one of the youngest regimental commanders in the Army. He was called back to the service in 1942 and named commander of the 45th National Guard Division, which was called by a historian "probably one of the best-trained divisions in the American Army."

Now, his VIII Corps had mostly new and untried divisions brought to this "quiet" sector for indoctrination. Such was the 106th Division, part of the 9th Armored Division and a cavalry outfit. There for a "rest" were the experienced, but battered, 4th and 28th divisions.

The weather was bone-freezing cold and, typically, dank. About dawn on December 16, a furious artillery barrage was directed at the VIII Corps front, some 80 miles long. Massive infantry units and 10 armored divisions followed the German barrage. The Battle of the Bulge was in the making.

The Germans hit hard at the north flank of the VIII Corps, aiming to take St. Vith, another town with a vital road net about 25 miles northeast of Bastogne. They drove through the 28th Division, advancing eight miles in some places, which put them close to Bastogne.

The 101st was short of senior officers. General Taylor was in the United States to discuss changes in the size of Airborne units. The Assistant Division Commander, General Gerald Higgins was in England with some other staff officers to lecture on the Holland operation. The senior officer remaining with the Division was Brigadier General Anthony "Tony" McAuliffe, who took command of the 101st.

Most of the troops were unaware of these absences, and who was commanding the Division was an immaterial matter to them. Their main thought at the time was simply, "Here we go again."

In a fast developing situation, the 82nd Division moved northward to

Werbomont, and the 101st moved eastward into Bastogne. Some accounts tell of this happening inadvertently; but as that officer in his jeep down the road was informed a few hours previously, Bastogne was long the Division's destination.

In retrospect, the defense of Bastogne by the 101st Division and supporting units, evolved into four major battles, roughly at the four points of the compass. In the sometimes vague and fluid fighting, it was not that pat, of course, and one battle overlapped the other with some mingling of units.

The four were, first, the initial contact with the Germans east of Bastogne, around Longvilly and the "satellite" villages of Neff, Bizory, and Wardin. Involved were the armor of Team Cherry and Team O'Hara and Colonel Julian Ewell's 501st Parachute Regiment.

Shunted off there, the Germans began sliding counter clockwise around Bastogne's perimeter and renewing their assaults. Thus, to the northeast, came Noville and Foy, involving largely the 506th Regiment under Colonel Sink, and parts of the 501st.

Next was the fighting around Champs, Longchamps and Hemroulle to the northwest and west of the circle, with the 502nd deeply involved, particularly in the German attack on Christmas Eve.

Finally, the 327th Glider Infantry held the front from the 502nd's left, around Mavie to the south, swinging a considerable distance back to the 506th. There was something for everybody in the 101st.

The lead unit in the 101st's column of trucks was Lieutenant Colonel Julian Ewell's 501st Regiment. An element of good fortune would soon stem from this placement. In early November, Ewell had taken a busmen's holiday from Holland and by chance spent two days looking around the Bastogne area.

Now, on this cold December night, the 501st was the first to arrive at its bivouac just outside Bastogne. The regiment closed by midnight on December 18 and Ewell made his way to the Division Command Post.

General McAuliffe, told that the Division was to defend Bastogne, knew little of the enemy situation, to say nothing of his own, except that American tank units were supposedly almost surrounded on the road to Noville to the northeast.

The general ordered Ewell to move to a position beyond Longvilly and "to clear up the situation."

At 0600, December 19, the 501st moved out, led by the 101st Reconnaissance Troop, then Major Ray Bottomly's 1st Battalion, followed by Battery B of the 81st Airborne Artillery Battalion of seven 57mm anti-aircraft guns. The rest of the battalion stayed in the bivouac until the parachutists found the enemy.

Lieutenant Colonel Ewell's familiarity with the area saved the column

from an early mistake. He realized the troops had made a wrong turn outside Bastogne and was headed for the village of Marvie, below Longvilly.
He turned them around and put them on the right road.

About this time, two more battle-tested units were ordered to Bastogne:
Combat Command B, 10th Armored Division, located in France; and the
705th Tank Destroyer Battalion, then about 60 miles north of Bastogne.
Each would play an important role in the defense of Bastogne.

The VIII Corps Headquarters received orders to withdraw from Bastogne, and in the process of pulling out, added to the traffic and the confusion on the main roads.

Ewell's troops engaged the enemy in other villages in the area, Bizory
and Neff, on what would become the perimeter of Bastogne. In the end,
he had three battalions abreast along with Team Cherry of Combat Command B and help from artillery. Team O'Hara of Combat Command B was
holding on the right flank.

Ewell felt he had the situation under control, although I Company had
lost 45 men and four officers at Warden, to the right, and had withdrawn
to a better position. Ewell had asked for and received a battalion of the
327th Glider Infantry to help in the protection of his right flank and to
form a reserve.

Ewell's 3rd Battalion, under Lieutenant Colonel George M. Griswold,
was ordered to the village of Mont, about one mile south of Neff. The battalion was stymied by the road clogged with traffic and sought a route other
than one direct to Mont.

The delay had a redeeming feature. Some of the men of the 101st in
their hasty departure from Mourmelon, like many other soldiers of the
101st, were forced to leave without helmets, rifles and ammunition. Now
they were able to borrow or beg these items from Combat Command B, still
in town, and thus, approached battle with more equipment.

Norville, to the north, was another hot spot. Strays from the 28th Division filled the roads. In a foggy dawn of the 19th, outposts at Houffalize and
Bourcy were beaten back on Noville. At mid-morning when the fog lifted,
the Americans found the countryside filled with German armor. With the
609th Tank Destroyer Battalion, the Americans had a duck shoot, knocking
out 10 of 14 German tanks in the area.

The situation was still tense. A small armored force commanded by
Major William Desobry of the 10th Armored, tried to place a small minefield
along the road, but was thwarted by stragglers on the roadway. Team Desorby managed to knock out 11 tanks. With enemy on three sides, Desorby
called Colonel Roberts, his CO, and asked to withdraw to high ground near
the village of Foy.

Roberts did not give an immediate answer. Instead he left his command post in a hotel at Bastogne to visit General McAuliffe nearby. On the way, he met the assistant Division Commander, General Higgins. As they talked, the 1st Battalion of the 506th Parachute Infantry Regiment came passing by. Colonel Sink was with the battalion's leader, Lieutenant Colonel Jim LaPrade.

Convinced by Roberts that the Noville situation left his unit "out on a limb" and required reinforcements, General Higgins on the spot sent LaPrade's battalion to Noville. The remainder of the regiment went into Division Reserve along the Noville road.

A subsequent attack on Noville flagged under severe German artillery, and American casualties were many. By dark, the troopers were digging in around Noville. Lieutenant Colonel LaPrade set up his command post near the town. He reinforced the building by pulling an armoire (clothes closet) in front of the window facing the street.

A tank retriever parked outside the house took a hit from a German 88mm shell. Fragments pierced the armoire and flew about the room. LaPrade was hit and killed instantly and Desobry was seriously wounded. Major Robert Harwick, who had raced back from leave and joined the battalion that afternoon, took command in LaPrade's place. Major Charles Hustead took over the armor.

The two battalions of the 506th in reserve, were moved into line with the 705th Tank Destroyer unit attached. The 506th was in contact with the 501st on their right and the 502nd on their left.

That night to the west of Bastogne, Germans came down the road from Houffalize with a force of armor and half tracks and overran the Division's Field Hospital, the 326th Clearing Station. Firing lasted a brisk 15 minutes on the clearly marked and defenseless hospital unit. A few men and officers escaped back to Bastogne and told of the devastating attack.

Most were captured, 11 medical officers and 119 men of the medical company, three officers and two men of the Division surgeon's group and four officers and three enlisted men of the 3rd Auxiliary Surgical Group. They were marched to the German rear under harrowing conditions. Valuable supplies were also taken by the Germans.

The losses were costly, one the Division would feel acutely later. The 501st Aid Station in Bastogne became the main collecting point. One part of this installation would be hit by an incendiary bomb, and many of the wounded in it would burn to death.

Supplies of all kinds were running low. A cache of German flour was found and for a time pancakes were the standard meal for the wounded and others. Resupply missions flown by the C-47s later augmented this diet. On the sixth day, two volunteer surgical teams were airlifted by glider into Bastogne. The pilot, Lieutenant Charlton "Corky" Corwin, suffering a large hangover from a Christmas party at his base in France, put the surgeons down safely, but right in front of a gun muzzle sticking out of the woods. It was a German gun, but fortunately, manned by American parachutists.

It was at this aid station that one of the most famous of the many stories of wry remarks to come out of Bastogne emerged. This one was a product of, perhaps, the too-vivid imagination of Jimmy Cannon, a New York sportswriter serving as a war correspondent.

Cannon wrote that a 101st Division "doughboy" (WWI term never applied to a WWII soldier) was evacuated to the aid station at Bastogne. The man said he never saw so many wounded and asked a medic why they were not sending them on for further treatment.

"Haven't you heard?" the medic replied.

"I haven't heard a damn thing," the man said.

"They've got us surrounded, the poor bastards."

Perhaps the medic did say it, but more likely we prefer to think he said it. In any case, it goes along with "The battered bastards of Bastogne" as one of the most-told tales of the battle.

With the written authority of General Middleton, Colonel Roberts was given permission to impress any and all stragglers into a fighting force: Team SNAFU was the result.

Colonel Roberts set his net. Military Police were posted on the roads leading south from Bastogne with instructions to turn stragglers back to the Combat Command B area in the town. There, hot food and billets awaited. Men from the 9th Armored and the 28th Division were snagged in the net. Within a week, Team SNAFU numbering some 600 men were set to defending Bastogne or providing replacements for regular units.

Outfits that still had a degree of organization were made part of the Bastogne force. Roberts commandeered a field artillery battalion and put it in with the other guns centered in Bastogne. The 969th Field Artillery Battalion (a much appreciated Negro outfit) was inducted in the force. Roberts also found in Bastogne eight new and undelivered tanks with crews. They were signed on and put to work.

South of Bastogne, a group of Armored Engineers and an anti-aircraft Artillery Battalion were, for a time, the only units between the Germans and the town. General McAuliffe sent two battalions of the 327th Glider to beef up the line southward, around the Arlon-Bastogne highway. Some of Team SNAFU went with the 327th. A German attack in the area was held off with the help of the artillery in Bastogne.

Heavy snow fell on the night of December 21. Several outfits appealed to the few Belgians left in the area to provide sheets and table clothes for camouflage.

Not all stragglers continued drifting westward away from the battlefield.

The 109th Field Artillery Battalion of the 28th Infantry, still relatively intact, attached itself to the 907th Glider Field Artillery Battalion. A platoon from the armored infantry of the 9th Armored joined the 2nd Battalion, 501st and fought with it for several days. Seven tanks from the 9th Armored also joined the battalion and held positions on the flank at Bizory.

On the same day, Bastogne was totally encircled by the Germans and the siege, so called, set in.

On the morning of the 22nd, General McAuliffe received the message that the 4th Armored was on the way to break through the siege. It would be an arduous journey for the tankers.

Just before noon of the 22nd, near the highway to Arlon, men of a platoon of F Company of the 327th Glider were amazed to see four Germans, one of whom carried a large white flag, appear in a clearing near the hamlet of Remoifosse. The German party included a major and a Captain Henke. The captain spoke English.

Out to meet them went two sergeants, Oswald Y. Butler and Carl E. Dickinson, and a medic, Private First Class Ernest D. Permetz, who spoke German. Henke spoke first and quite formally.

"We are parliamentaries," he said.

The major spoke sharply to him and Henke then said, "We want to talk to your commanding officer."

They were blindfolded and taken to F Company's command post, where Captain James F. Adams was handed a written message from the Germans. One copy was in English, the other in German. Word went up the chain of command to Division Headquarters that the enemy was attempting to arrange a surrender of the Americans.

Major Alvin Jones at regiment, acting in place of Colonel Joe Harper absent at the time, hurried the Germans to Division. There, Jones met with General McAuliffe and Lieutenant Colonel Ned Moore, acting chief of staff.

Moore read the message. In exaggerated phrasing, it told of how the Germans had Bastogne encircled. "All that was left for the Americans," it said, "was the honorable surrender of the encircled town."

The last two paragraphs of the note read: If this proposal should be rejected, one German artillery corps and six heavy A.A. Battalions are ready to annihilate the U.S. troops in or near Bastogne.

All the serious civilian losses caused by this artillery fire would not correspond with the well known American humanity.

The signature at the bottom was simply, "The German commander," afterward identified as Lieutenant General Heinrich von Luftwitz, commander of the 47th Panzer Corps.

"What's it say, Ned?" McAuliffe asked Moore.

"They want you to surrender," Moore answered.

"Aw, Nuts," said McAuliffe.

McAuliffe was fully aware that the German reference to "the encircled town" was not a true bill of the battle situation. He felt he was giving the Germans a beating.

He sat down, pen in hand, and thought about his answer. Puzzled, he said to no one in particular, "Well, I don't know what to tell them." He asked his staff gathered around him what they thought.

Colonel Kinnard, his G-3, spoke first.

"The first remark of yours would be hard to beat," Kinnard said.

McAuliffe had to ask, "What was that?"

"You said, 'Nuts,'" Kinnard replied.

The staff agreed. Without further hesitancy, McAuliffe wrote his answer. It read: "To the German commander: Nuts."

General McAuliffe asked Colonel Harper, who had joined the group at the command post, to see that the answer was delivered. "I'll deliver it myself." he said. "It will be a lot of fun."

Colonel Harper proceeded to Smith's platoon, where the Germans waited. He said to them, "I have the American commander's reply." The captain asked whether it was written or verbal. Harper said, "It is written," and handed it to him.

The message was translated. The major asked, "Is the reply negative or affirmative. If it is the latter, I will negotiate further."

Colonel Harper was impatient with the German's patronizing manner. "The reply is decidedly not affirmative." He then added, "If you continue this foolish attack, your losses will be tremendous."

The German nodded. Harper put the two German officers in a jeep and took them back to the road, where the German enlisted men were waiting.

Speaking through the translator, Harper said, "If you don't understand what 'Nuts' means in plain English, it is the same as 'Go to hell. And I will tell you something else," Harper said. "If you continue to attack, we will kill every German who tries to break into this city."

The German saluted stiffly. The captain said, "We will kill many Americans. This is war."

"On your way, Bud," said Colonel Harper. "And good luck to you." The colonel immediately regretted his last five words.

The German general, von Luttwitz, made the surrender offer to the Americans without consulting his superior, who was said to be furious when he heard of it. Among other reasons, the Germans did not have the artillery to carry out their threat, but the Luftwaffe did bomb Bastogne that night and for four nights following.

These raids were brief and noisy, but not particularly damaging. They caused a commotion and some damage in Bastogne, but those in position on the perimeter were scarcely troubled. When word of McAuliffe's reply spread among the troops, they had a chuckle at his use of this pure Americanism.

After the Battle of the Bulge was closed, General McAuliffe, already a hero at home and now more so, was called to Paris for a press conference about his answer. On his return to Bastogne, he told some of his staff, chortling with pleasure, of the meeting with the correspondents.

"I fortified myself before I spoke to them," he said, "and I might be a bum tomorrow, but I gave them a helluva story today."

The 4th Armored was well on its course to Bastogne. McAuliffe sent them a message on December 24, saying, "Sorry I did not get to shake hands today." A staff officer sent another message reading, "There is only one more shooting day before Christmas."

By the 24th, Hitler was said to be indignant that the German drive could be hindered by such a relatively small American force. The previous night, he insisted that the burr of Bastogne be removed.

By December 22, the 101st had units defending the entire perimeter of Bastogne, some 16 miles around in total. Still strange incidents of battle occurred. There was the so-called Ghost Patrol, not further identified, which more than one American reportedly saw wandering about behind American lines unhindered.

In Champs, northwest of Bastogne, a high-ranking German officer and an assistant came boiling into the center of this tiny village in an American jeep. They were easily captured. The senior officer indignantly insisted that he could not be captured because his map (and he produced it) showed clearly that Champs was in German hands.

Four huge German attacks to the south around Marvie were repelled, others turned back in the vicinity of Senonchamps, where the Germans attacked in captured Sherman tanks. They did cut the road.

The attacks gained nothing. But the Division G-2 wrote laconically in his periodic report that the cutting of the roadway "had no effect on our present situation, except to make travel hazardous."

And Lieutenant Colonel Kinnard, G-3, was asked by radio telephone from VIII Corps to describe the Bastogne situation after the town was surrounded. Not wishing to be specific if any Germans were eavesdropping, he replied, "You know what a doughnut looks like? Well, we're the hole in the doughnut."

At Marvie, after the heavy fighting there, the 327th Glider Infantry was ordered to defend the perimeter from that village on the southeast, all along the line northward to the 502nd in Hemroulle, on the other end of a half-moon that encompassed almost half the Division's sector, about two and one half miles in all.

"Look at it!" Bud Harper said to General Higgins of his sector. "This is half the Division's perimeter."

"It's all yours, Bud" Higgins said quietly. "Do what you can with it. There isn't any other solution."

About this time, a crisis was building in the matter of diminishing supplies. The Germans were building in strength in front of the 101st Division, unhampered because of the shortage of artillery shells. The 463rd Field Artillery, in support of the 327th Glider, had only 200 shells remaining. By the time the first resupply mission came in, the battalion was down to nine rounds of high explosive shells and no rations. Other battalions were suffering similarly. McAullife was faced with the prospect of rationing guns to 10 rounds per day. Small arms ammunition was also critically short.

On the 22nd, word came that an airlift of C-47s would be on the way. But winter storms would ground the planes. The next day, 257 planes dropped 1,466 bundles of much needed supplies in a drop zone near the 327th's position.

In about three hours the bundles were recovered, and in some cases, artillery shells in the drop were being fired on the enemy before the area was entirely cleared of bundles.

The next day about 100 tons of material were dropped from a lift of 160 planes, not all of which made it safely through the flight. These supplies helped immeasurably, but gasoline and K-rations were not included in sufficient amounts.

By now, the disparate groups assisting the 101st Airborne were melding into smooth, working teams, the artillery, firing in a 360° radius, the tank destroyers, even Team SNAFU.

An Air Force captain, Jim Parker, of the 9th Air Force made his way into Bastogne on December 19, and once he was able to get his radio working, did a remarkable job of designating targets for fighter planes. In many cases, planes flew 250 sorties a day, replying to calls for air support in 20 minutes or less, once the weather cleared.

Now, the Germans ordered by Hitler to eliminate Bastogne, shifted their attacks to the northwest sector of the Division's line, defended essentially by the 502nd and the 327th.

A German column came down the road from St. Hubert. Men of the 3rd Battalion of the 327th, under the mistaken impression that this was the route the American 4th Armored would be using, let it proceed until it was too late to offer any great resistance. One company attempted to execute a planned withdrawal and suffered casualties. A Company of Colonel Allen's 1st Battalion, instead of going through with its withdrawal, was ordered to return to the line.

"This is our last withdrawal," Allen told the men. "Live or die, this is it." They held their ground.

It was Christmas Eve. From Division came an overlay to the troops on the line showing German positions in red, surrounding Bastogne. In the center, in green ink, was the message: "Merry Christmas."

From the German side, artillery shells carried leaflets with the message that the Americans could find succor by surrendering to enemy forces "only 300 yards away." The few Americans who saw the leaflets ignored them.

Bastogne itself suffered heavy bombing. One shell landed near the field hospital of the 20th Armored Infantry Battalion. It buried 20 American wounded and killed a Belgian woman serving as a nurse.

Another shell landed near Combat Command B's headquarters, causing much damage and knocking over a small Christmas tree in the command center. When the tree was set up again, a sergeant pinned a Purple Heart on it.

A Belgian nun died, when by a freak accident, a bomb landed outside the town's hospital. A steel fragment entered a ventilator, followed the path of the piping and came out in the basement at the instant the nun was passing by. The fragment struck her in the temple, killing her immediately.

Early on the morning of Christmas Day, the Germans launched a last-gasp attack at the seam between the 327th Glider and the 502nd Parachute Infantry. At the same time, they hit A Company of the 502nd, commanded by Wally Swanson, in the village of Champs. A large German force, supported by 11 tanks (some said it was as many as 18), dented the 327th's line.

Meanwhile, the rest of the 502nd's 1st Battalion, in reserve in the hamlet of Hemroulle, a mile or so back of Champs, was ordered to the latter village to reinforce A Company.

As the parachutists of the 1st Battalion moved along the road to Champs, with dawn nearing, across an open field to the column's left came part of the German force that had hit the 327th. The Germans in white camouflage cover, came with seven tanks, perhaps more, and more than 100 infantrymen, some riding, some walking. This was the curtain raiser of the last ditch German attack.

Fred MacKenzie, a Buffalo newspaperman and the only reporter with the 101st Division throughout the battle, would write that "it was the most desperate hours of the siege." To the right of the 502nd marching column, some 750 yards away, was the 502nd's command post. Beyond that, it was a clear run to the center of Bastogne and the Division command post.

The company commanders of B and C companies on the road, gave in effect, an order to face left and engage the enemy. At regimental headquarters, every available man was rallied to its defense, including many of its wounded in a stable. Major Douglas T. Davidson, the regimental surgeon, had called on wounded who could manage it, scratched up rifles and led this force to join the defenders.

The fighting along the Champs Road was brief but vicious. The Americans forced the Germans back across the field. They destroyed six tanks and captured a seventh after it made a run for Champs.

Another tank attempted to run up the road. But a soldier from C Company, manning a bazooka in a foxhole at a crossroad, held his position and waited, and waited, until the tank was almost upon him. He fired. The bazooka shell disabled the tank's right track. When the crew attempted to bail out, rifle fire converged on them and all were killed. In all some 37 Germans were killed and 35 prisoners taken, with not a single friendly casualty in this brief encounter.

Captain Jim Hatch, the regimental S-3, had gone for a look at A Company's situation. When he heard shooting outside A Company's command post, he drew his pistol and opened the door to see what was happening. There, 15 feet away, staring him in the face was a German tank's 75mm gun. Hatch quickly slammed the door and said to no one in particular, "This is no place for my pistol."

Meanwhile, the 327th was undergoing a heavy attack. Some German armor supported by infantrymen had reached almost to the regiment's command post. Colonel Harper, it was reported, avoided capture by escaping through a rear window of the house in which his headquarters was located.

By mid-morning the 327th re-established its position, with the considerable help of the 463rd Artillery. That outfit accounted for eight of 11 tanks in one spearhead moving on Hemroulle.

Captain Fitzgerald, executive of 1st Battalion, 502nd, in rummaging through the battalion's headquarters in a house in Hemroulle, had uncovered a cured Belgian ham, a local delicacy, in a chest. He brought up the rear of the battalion's advance to Champs on Christmas morning, carrying the ham in his knapsack. He was determined, he said later, to have it for Christmas dinner.

When the matters at Champs had quieted, he took over a sizeable house in the village, heated the ham and, with supplemental items from K-rations, served a relatively scrumptious dinner to the staff.

Almost at the instant the group sat down at the table, an artillery shell rattled off the roof of the house. Fitz did not move.

"I'm going to eat this dinner," he said, "even if it kills me," which seemed a possibility as the shelling continued for a few minutes more.

This meal, incidentally, demonstrated one of the few advantages afforded front-line troops. The regimental commander, Colonel Chappuis and his exec, Lieutenant Colonel Cassidy, dined Christmas Day, it was said, on a can of sardines and a box of crackers.

The Screaming Eagles' Christmas present came December 26, the day the 4th Armored Division broke through the circle around Bastogne.

At 1650, a light team of tanks and infantry, led by Captain William A. Dwight, was ordered to attack through the village of Assenois and to keep going until it reached the Bastogne lines. Armored Artillery was to fire in support.

Some of this fire fell on friendly troops as Assenois, and Dwight's force was slowed by enemy mines. But three tanks under 1st Lieutenant Charles P. Boggess kept pushing and entered the lines of the 326th Airborne Engineer Battalion.

A message to Lieutenant Colonel Creighton W. Abrams suggested that the remainder of the 37th Tank Battalion be brought forward. The encirclement was over, but much more fighting was to come before the breakthrough was firm and the siege lifted.

The cost to the 4th Armored had been brutal during its advance on Bastogne. It lost 1,000 men. Its tank strength was reduced to the number in a single battalion.

With the tankers came General Taylor, at the end of a hurried trip from the United States. With him were his jeep driver, Staff Sergeant Charlie Kartus and his aide, Tom White. He had flown to France on Christmas Eve on a C-54 carrying freight. He asked permission to parachute into Bastogne, but General Bedell Smith, Ike's chief of staff, refused him permission.

Meeting the 4th Armored on its advance, a member of the Division warned him not to try to get into Bastogne. "The corridor is so narrow," the man said, "you can spit across it."

Cornelius Ryan, then a correspondent for the London Daily Telegraph, remembered the general saying to a number of his associates, "I've got to get in tonight. I've got room for one correspondent."

Ryan answered, "No volunteers today, General."

Half an hour later, Taylor walked down the stairs of McAuliffe's cellar command post.

"Well, boys," he said, after a boisterous welcome, "you're heroes."

"Who, us?" McAuliffe replied.

"Everybody's been worried about you," Taylor said. "What is the condition of the Division?"

"No damned reason to be worried about us," said McAuliffe. "We're ready to attack."

Much more fighting remained for the 101st, but the German drive had been blunted. Bastogne might have been bypassed, but the Germans could not leave the 101st in their rear like a festering abscess in their drive to the

Meuse River. Therein, rested Bastogne's continued importance.

And when the encirclement was broken, the Germans had given up their main objective to concentrate on Bastogne. By the first of the year, eight additional German divisions had been thrown into the battle. German attacks at various points (17 of them) continued.

G-2 reported a buildup of German troops in the northern sector. To the south, the corridor was gradually widened. The 4th Armored joined the 101st on its semicircle defensive line, and the 501st and the 506th staged limited attacks to secure high ground to the northwest.

The weather at the time was deplorable. Temperatures hovered near zero at night. Snow was waist deep. Roads were icy and virtually impassable for armor. And Germans were present in large numbers. They still held the diminishing hope of restoring the vise around Bastogne.

A few days after New Years, the 501st was involved in a hectic attack towards Foy. The regiment pierced German lines and was counterattacked. German tanks with artillery came across open ground, then side slipped left and unleashed on the 501st a mortar barrage at the rate of a round a second, described afterward as "the most terrific barrage the regiment was to experience in the war."

Fighting for the 2nd Battalion, 501st, was close-in and hectic. Thanks to individual heroics, they held the ground, but casualties in the area around the Bois Jacques approached 200, most from artillery bursts in the tall trees.

The 502nd also stood off attacks by some 30-40 tanks and a battalion of infantry. To the command post of D Company, near Longchamps, Sergeant Lawrence Silva reported in from his outpost: "I can see 14 tanks... no there's 18, no, 20!"

Silva then said, "I can't tell you anything more."

"Why not?

"There's a tank right over my foxhole," Silva said.

The tank tried to crush him, but the frozen ground did not give. So the tank parked over the foxhole, its motor racing. Carbine monoxide flooded the hole. In a few minutes, Silva was dead.

Private First Class Bruno Mecca had the same experience, but escaped suffocation. He said later, "I'll fight any son of a bitch, but I can't fight those tanks with a carbine."

Medic Warren Cobbet, attached to D Company, refused the shelter of a foxhole during the fighting. Instead, he roamed the battlefield, treating or bringing in wounded. He was, those who watched him said, the hero of the day.

For F Company, 502nd, the fighting around Longchamps was called the most difficult since Normandy. It lost 47 men, including the company commander and two other officers; D Company lost 48, with 17 killed and 13 others missing. After a three-hour struggle, Division asked Colonel Chappuis his situation. He said it was under control.

Chappuis' men were helped by the 326th Engineers, who moved in with mines and bazookas. In a notable action, Battery C of the 81st AA Battalion knocked out 10 Mark IV tanks. Tank Sergeant Joe O'Toole; section chief, Sergeant Ed Forand; assistant gunner and Private First Class Acardio Navarre fought until their ammunition was spent. Each was awarded the Silver Star.

While this fighting was going on, General Taylor formed Task Force Higgins to strengthen the front held by the 502nd and the 327th. It had a lot of punch, consisting of the 502nd, the 327th, Team Cherry from the tankers, two companies of the 705th TD Battalion and A Company of the 326th Engineer Battalion. General Higgins would be on the scene to direct operations in the event Division lost communications with that front.

On January 4, the Germans launched another attack on that sector, but the Americans were ready. The attack was of regimental strength, driving hard against the 1st Battalion of the 327th with 11 tanks in support.

The Germans moved to within 100 yards of the battalion's command post at Champs in fighting as fierce as any the 327th faced. The 1st Battalion of the 502nd helped stabilize the situation from its position in reserve. By the morning of the 6th, the front was considered secure enough to dissolve Task Force Higgins.

After these two days of hard struggles, the Division G-2 report noted that the Screaming Eagles had "maintained defensive positions and contact with flanking units." Eight words, in short, summing up two days of dire fighting.

The next few days were relatively quiet. There was one disastrous blow. A truck carrying 200 land mines was hit by an enemy shell near the 501st command post and blew up. No one could be certain of the exact cause. Because the truck disintegrated and nothing remained of its crew.

On January 7, 1945, General McAuliffe was given command of a division of his own, the 103rd Infantry Division. At a farewell dinner, senior staff officers of the 101st presented him with a set of canvas leggings, symbolic of his coming change from jump boots to the gear of "ordinary" infantrymen.

Sometime previously, General McAuliffe took pains to refute a sore point in an unusual way for one of his rank. Some publications had termed the break-through into Bastogne by the 4th Armored as a "rescue."

An indignant McAuliffe, to the troops of the 101st's great delight, wrote a letter to the Stars & Stripes' letters column, called its "B Bag."

"I know of no man inside Bastogne," the general wrote, "who ever doubted the 101st Airborne Division's ability to hold the town."

He followed this with another letter to the newspaper, saying this time:

"We resent any implication that we were rescued or needed rescuing."

The 17th Airborne, which had gone into action on January 3, came abreast of the 101st on its left flank. On January 8, the 101st was ordered to attack and capture Noville. On the same day, Hitler finally permitted withdrawal of his forces east of Bastogne.

Three days later, the 101st was part of an attack toward Houffalize, aimed at joining the Americans on the northern shoulder of the Bulge. German troops west of the juncture would be trapped.

One of the most telling losses of the day was Colonel Ewell, who had succeeded to command of the 501st after Colonel Johnson was killed.

Ewell was one of the most brilliant and gallant of the regiment's officers. He suffered a wound to the foot which ended his battle career.

The advance on Houffalize was relatively easy at the start, but grew increasingly difficult. On the 13th, German resistance was formidable as they fought to keep open their escape route. The 506th, with Team Cherry, took the brunt of the battle.

The 502nd was assigned to protect the left flank of the 506th in the latter's advance through Fazone Woods. Resistance grew markedly as the parachutists advanced into the woods.

Small arms fire and tree bursts of artillery slowed the movement. Also for the first time, the Americans encountered tactical wire, indicating a well-prepared defensive position.

Lieutenant Colonel Stopka, Colonel Cole's successor, was killed during the advance by a friendly airplane's bomb. A few days previously, Stopka had been presented the Distinguished Service Cross for his part in the bayonet charge at Carentan. The bomb hit Stopka directly and only scraps of his leather jacket were found.

At 0945, advancing units from the north and south made contact at Houffalize, signalling that the main battle of the Ardennes was almost over.

On January 13, the 101st advanced on Noville, its sought-after objective since almost the start of the Bulge. The 502nd, leading the advance, suffered heavily: 84 casualties, including 17 killed. A German force slipped behind the 327th when the gap with the 502nd widened. The 502nd took fire from three directions. Staff Sergeant William N. Tucker of the regiment's medical detachment was one of the day's heroes. He carried out five wounded men under enemy fire and directed the evacuation of 25 more. The break between regiments eventually was closed.

On the last day of fighting, the 502nd, with part of Combat Command

B of the 10th Armored, took Bourcy and 84 prisoners. That night, the 10th Armored, which had performed so gallantly throughout the Bulge, was relieved from attachment to the 101st to fight elsewhere. It left with exchanges of mutual admiration.

Bastogne was over for the 101st. Late on the afternoon of the 18th, the 501st, in reserve, began entrucking for its relief. Other units followed to billets in Luxembourg to the south.

On the morning of the 18th, as part of an awards ceremony in the battered square of Bastogne (later renamed Place McAuliffe) the town's mayor presented General Taylor with the community's flag in appreciation for what the Division had done in its defense.

General Middleton of VIII Corps spoke highly of the 101st, saying that the men of the Division "were the best bunch of fighting men in the United States' or any army in the world."

Later, Middleton wrote Taylor personally to tell him: "I have been permitted to serve with or have personal contact with some 30 divisions of the U.S. Army. I am pleased to say that I place your Division at the top of the list."

At the same ceremony, General Taylor asked General Middleton for "a receipt" for turning Bastogne back to him. With that, Taylor gave Middleton a hand-printed document for his signature. It read:

"Received from the 101st Division for the town of Bastogne... Condition used, but serviceable, Kraut disinfected."

Middleton signed, with obvious pleasure.

In Luxembourg, the Division was quartered in various villages, warm, safe and secure. Soon the 101st was on the way to its next mission, assigned to General Alexander M. Patch's 7th Army in the Alsace region of France, 160 miles south. The trip was again made in trucks and the weather was cold and snowy.

The Division was assigned to one corps and then another, ending up in the VI Corps area near Hochfelden, on the Moder River.

The Division learned that the VI Corps was worried about a German breakthrough. Major Leo H. Schweiter, acting 101st G-2, reassured them, saying, "What the hell are you so worried about. The 101st alone can lick five German division simultaneously; we just did."

As a further example of the Division's self-assuredness, a liaison officer told them of Lieutenant Tom Downey of the 502nd who called himself the "Rock of Bastogne" and who had a sign that read, "Holds Anything."

The Division was there for about a month, mid-January to mid-February, and life was good. There was little action, lots of movies, showers and good food. And winter gear finally arrived.

There was one sizable operation. It was a raid, or more exactly, a reconnaissance force, to assist in removing a German "bulge" on the American side of a stretch of the Moder.

The raid was meticulously planned, involving A and B Companies of the 501st, C Company of the 327th and B Company of the 326th Engineers. The operation went almost like clockwork, but not without American casualties, and with a number of German prisoners taken.

Two members of the 327th, Privates Philip Nichols and Joe Seny, made several trips into the woods, where the raid occurred, to bring out wounded, and Seny took time to destroy a German pillbox with a bazooka, killing eight Germans.

After a month, the Division returned to Camp Mourmelon. For most of the outfits, the trip was made in the infamous World War I boxcars, called the 40&8's, lined with straw.

At Mourmelon, medical units had taken over the Division's barracks, and most of the 101st lived in tents. After a rest period, the Division began preparing for the parade at which the Division would receive the Distinguished Unit Citation, or, as it is now known, the Presidential Citation.

The 101st was the first division in history to receive the award as an entire division. On March 16, 1945, after much spit and polishing, the Division received the presentation, then passed in review before a group of high-ranking officers, the highest among them General Eisenhower, who made the award.

A full (and unpopular) training schedule resumed. Missions were scheduled, only to be cancelled. The Germans, pushed back behind the Rhine River and prepared to hold it, were attacked by a huge airborne operation. The mission was the job of the 17th Airborne.

The Division, less the 501st Parachute Infantry (which stayed behind if needed to jump and secure prisoner of war camps), was ordered to the Ruhr with its position on the Rhine itself in the vicinity of Dusseldorf.

The troops were in modern and mostly undamaged houses. There were movies and USO shows, and the products of local breweries flowed freely. Sports teams were formed. Passes were available to the Riviera, England, Paris and Brussels.

Most of the fighting, if any, was done by patrols, and casualties were mostly freakish. The Germans often threw over artillery shells, largely from a railway gun. One of these landed in the vicinity of the 327th's 3rd Battalion command post, wounding four and killing two members of the anti-tank platoon. A fragment penetrated the command post of the battalion and cost Lieutenant Colonel Ray C. Allen a leg. He had been with the battalion since its first action in Normandy and was the battalion's last casualty of the war.

Another late casualty was Major William Leach, who had been S-2 of the 506th, later on the Division staff. He elected to accompany a regimental patrol across the Rhine. Germans opened fire and hit the boat he was in. His body was discovered downstream two days later.

Operating the military government of the area was an assigned task for the regiments. Of prime importance was administering the camps of thousands of displaced persons who had been brought unwillingly to Germany to work.

In mid-April, the Division was alerted to move to South Germany. This was the area where, it was thought, the German army would make its last stand in the so-called National Redoubt. A vast number of Germans would, the American senior commanders believed, assemble in the mountains with tanks, planes and other armament, numbering as many as 100 divisions. These would be manned by German fanatics. As it developed, few such dedicated Germans remained.

Again the troops moved by truck and 40&8s. The first stop was at Merchingen, in the foothills of the Alps. On the afternoon of April 25, as the last 101st Division unit closed in to Merchingen, Russian and American troops met on the Elbe River in central Germany.

In south Germany, a great tidal wave of French and Americans chased the Germans, then in full retreat. Thousands of Germans filled the roads, shorn of leaders, disorganized, incapable of offering resistance. There was always the threat, however, of a bullet from the German mob.

The chase went from Merchingen into Bavaria in late April. Along the way, the 506th relieved a regiment from General McAuliffe's 103rd Division. Near Memingen, came the first look at a concentration camp in all its horror.

Then came the Screaming Eagles' last mission: capture Berchtesgaden, the place of Hitler's mountain home and the symbolic "capitol" of South Germany. On May 4 at 0600, Colonel Sink's 506th Parachute Infantry, with two artillery battalions attached, moved out by truck along the autobahn on the mission. At the town of Inzell, they ran into a column of stalled tanks from the French 2nd Armored Division under the famed General Jacques Phillipe LeClerc.

A bridge was out, causing the French delay. Far up the hillside, Germans were firing on Sink's troops attempting to throw up a Bailey Bridge. Men from the 506th descended the bank of the creek, crossed it and climbed the opposite side to reach and neutralize the enemy.

Other barriers were encountered, including the commander of the American 3rd Division, who did not look favorably on allowing the 506th to bypass his outfit. Everyone, it seemed, was thirsting to be first into Berchtesgaden. Sink's solution to the roadblock: Backtrack and proceed along another route.

The 506th reached Berchtesgaden on the morning of May 5, 1945. Two men of the regiment suffered the fate that every soldier dreaded: that of being among the last killed at the end of the war. They were Sergeant Nick Kosovosky of Headquarters Company and Private Claude E. Rankin.

On May 7 the first reports of an Armistice were heard on the radio, and the official announcements came the next day. Some cheered the event, but for the most part there was nothing in particular by way of marking the day. Silently, most thanked God, or Allah, or whoever, that there would be no more shooting.

Next morning the order came to hold fast in present position, with no firing on Germans unless fired upon first.

The 502nd took up comfortable quarters in the village of Kempton, a pleasant village outside Berchtesgaden. Their main mission was to receive the flow of prisoners into the village. In a week's time, the Division took in 14,935 Germans, captives from every kind of unit.

Also uncovered were a number of ranking Hitler officials who had taken refuge (but not to fight) in the mountains. The bag included a field marshall, Albert Kesselring, living on his nine car train on a siding below Berchtesgaden.

Others were Dr. Robert Ley, leader of the Nazi Labor Front; and Julius Streicher, the infamous "Jew baiter," so-called. These two had lost whatever bearing and dignity they possessed.

Streicher posed as a simple painter and denied he was Streicher to Major Plitt of the 502nd. Only when Plitt, taking a guess, said to him, "Well you look like Streicher," did he admit he was. There was poetic irony in Plitt's taking this man. Plitt himself was Jewish.

The Eagle's Nest became a premiere attraction to all who visited Berchtesgaden, though it was bereft of furniture and burned out by RAF raids.

The 327th Glider found Herman Goering's stolen art collection and other valuables sealed in a tunnel near Berchtesgaden. Also found was Goering's luxurious private train and Hitler's Mercedes-Benz; the latter was turned over to General Taylor, which he used in place of a jeep. A large number of horses used by the German army was discovered. The 501st organized these into what it called "the parachute cavalry."

General Taylor came into possession of a large set of silver goblets belonging to Goering. These bore his family crest. The general had these engraved with the names of the Division's campaigns and presented one to each of his battalion commanders, bearing the individual's name.

Berchtesgaden was a luxurious resort and life there was pleasant for everyone. Hotels were utilized as troop billets, their kitchens staffed by Germans or displaced persons. German wines were in copious supply, as were German vehicles and weapons. This combination was the cause of many mishaps.

The pleasant summer wore on. In mid-June, word came through that the Division would move to the Pacific. Earlier, back at Mourmelon, Taylor had announced at a Division formation that he "was doing all in my power to have the Division sent to Japan." Generals, of course, have ambitions not in keeping with the average combat soldier. They booed, softly at first, from the rear ranks, then louder and louder, until most joined in the chorus. General Taylor was quite furious at this reception of his announcement. Later, the plan to move to Japan was rescinded. Then it was announced that the Division was to proceed to the United States as part of the general reserve. This, too, did not materialize.

In July came the Army's system of releasing men from the service by means of a point system. Men with 85 points or more, based on service, decorations etc., would be released; soon, some 2,500 veterans left the Division.

In a sense, this departure of the Division's "old soldiers" was sad. Trucks to carry them away would appear in the picturesque villages of Bavaria where the journey homeward for the high point men would begin.

The men leaving piled in with their gear. Those staying would gather in small groups around the trucks to say farewell. Those leaving made little attempt to hide their delight, and the banter was noisy. It was also tinged with small touches of regret.

For never again would these men experience the bond that is forged between men who have seen battle together. The intense camaraderie that needs no telling and lasts a lifetime, their days with the Screaming Eagles were over. For most, they would not know its like again.

In time, the Division, what was left of it, would move to Austria, then to the French city of Auxerre. Only a few of the Division's old regulars, mostly officers, would make the last moves. Changes were many, particularly among senior officers, moving along in their careers.

The Division learned that it was to be designated a Regular Army Airborne Division and the 82nd Airborne was to be inactivated. This decision was later reversed and the 101st Airborne Division was the one destined to be inactivated there in France. By then, on November 30, 1945, only five of the division's original officers were left.

The 101st Airborne's rendezvous with destiny was fulfilled and finished.

CHAPTER TWO

The Training Years

INTRODUCTION
John L. Burford

1956

IN THE EARLY 1950S, two major events forced the U.S. Army to rethink the mission and shape of the Army Division. The first of these events was the birth of the Atom bomb in 1945 and its transformation in 1951 to a battlefield weapon of massive destructive force that was easily deployed. The Atomic age caught the Army with an unwieldy division structure that didn't allow the units the dispersion required to reduce their exposure to a nuclear attack. In the Second World War, a division needed its units to be close together for supply, communications, and combat strength. Now this structure needed to change because the Army could ill afford to present the enemy with the fat target of a regular Army division.

The second major event was the war in Korea. The U.S. Army was caught flat-footed by the outbreak of hostilities on the Korean Peninsula, and had no way to react early in the conflict. Early intervention in the war by a combat ready American force could have had a dampening effect on the war and may have stopped or at least shortened it. The Army found it didn't have the needed transport to move a combat unit quickly or a ready and trained unit to move.

In 1954 the Military Chiefs of Staff started to formulate the plans for a new type of Army Division that would be both new in structure and mission. The Reorganized Army Division (ROAD) was to be known as the Pentomic Division. This name was taken from the idea that the Division would have five battle groups instead of the three regiments under the old triangular division system, i.e. the Pentagon, and it would fight on the atomic battlefield. This Division would be smaller than its World War II counterpart but would be equipped with more firepower, and the unit would have nuclear weapons attached to it as well as the means to deliver them via the new Honest John Rocket. The basic building block of this Division was the Battle Group which would have a Headquarters and Headquarters Company, a

Mortar Battery of 4.2 inch mortars, five rifle companies with 240 men in four rifle platoons, and a heavy weapons platoon with three 81mm mortars and jeep mounted 106mm recoilless rifles. There would be an anti–tank section in the Headquarters Company that was equipped with the new M-56 Scorpion 90mm self-propelled anti-tank gun (SPAT). The division artillery would have five artillery batteries with 105mm howitzers that would be attached to the various battle groups on an as needed basis.

The new mission given to this Pentomic Division was to move anywhere in the world and quickly get on the ground ready to fight. The unit would maintain the highest training standards and provide the Army with a test bed for the Pentomic Army concept. It was evident from the start that this new unit would have to be an airborne division able to fulfill its many mission roles and light enough to move everything by air. Early in the planning stage, requirements were sent out to the defense industry to develop air mobile equipment and the air lift to carry it. The unit was to have another new feature added to its growing list of firsts. This feature was an expanded division aviation section with extra helicopters.

In late 1955 the Army and Navy Journal reported that the Army had briefed House Appropriations Committee members during a secret session on plans for a radically new type of division organization which would be activated in 1956. The Army had hinted in some recent public statements that the new divisions' design was calculated to meet the requirements of the atomic battlefield. Waiting in the wings was the 101st Infantry Training Division, which had been the 101st Airborne Division during World War II. The Army planners decided that this unit would be the vehicle for the activation of the new Pentomic Division.

On March 24, 1956, Army Secretary Wilber H. Brucker announced the formal reactivation of the 101st Airborne Division would take place September 21, 1956, at Fort Campbell, Kentucky. The Division would be organized as a brand new type of paratroop division with its own atomic weapons, and this division would be ready to deploy to overseas trouble spots by February 1957.

With this simple announcement the great eagle was poised to scream again. The new Pentomic 101st Airborne Division was started on another rendezvous with destiny. This time the whole world would watch as the Screaming Eagle Division unfolded her mighty wings and prepared to take to the sky as the most powerful division in the American Army.

This was a division capable of landing every man and every weapon by parachute, and while she was smaller, about 11,500 men, she was more powerful than any of her sister airborne divisions. This division could be fully deployed using one half of the number of aircraft needed to move a standard airborne division. The 101st Airborne was the first Army division to be issued the Honest John Artillery Rocket. This weapon system had always been held at the Corp and Armies level up to this time due to its nuclear warhead. It was understood that the Division would get a new weapon system in the near future that would be an atomic cannon of a smaller caliber than the 280mm weapon that was in service.

Major General Thomas L. Sherburne Jr. was appointed to be the 101st Airborne Division Commander. He had served with the Division during World War II as the Division Artillery Commander. The general did all he could to pull together members of the Division from the Second World War to man this new Division. The Department of the Army published a letter which encouraged commanders to approve request for transfer to the 101st Airborne Division from enlisted men of their command who were wartime members of the Division, if they were entitled to such a transfer.

Major General Thomas L. Sherburne officially arrived at Fort Campbell on the 23rd of May and was welcomed home by the Assistant Division Commander Brigadier General Charles H. Chase, an honor guard from the 187th Airborne Regimental Combat Team, and an honor guard from the 674th Airborne Field Artillery Battalion. The general announced that the 101st Airborne Division would be formally reactivated on September 21, 1956. The next day to make his homecoming official, the general made his first parachute jump in three years.

The 187th Airborne Regimental Combat Team was the first unit to be assigned to the new 101st Airborne at Fort Campbell, Kentucky. The new 187th Airborne Combat Group was made part of the 101st Airborne Division (Advance) on the 19th of June. During the change-over ceremonies, Colonel Melvin Zais, a member of the original 501st Parachute Battalion, had his men remove the Rakkasan patch from their left shoulder to reveal the 101st Screaming Eagle patch that had been hidden under the old unit patch. When the patch removal was completed the men of the 187th passed in review showing the proud new shoulder patch to the world.

The 508th Airborne Regimental Combat Team was transferred from its overseas duty station in Japan to become part of the 101st Airborne Division. The unit was scheduled to start arriving in late July, and its men would be used to furnish the cadre to form the other four combat groups.

Operation Stateside, the 10,000 mile journey of the 508th Regimental Combat Team (Red Devils) from Japan to Fort Campbell, Kentucky, was completed on July 29, 1956. The men of the 508th joined with the men of the 187th to prepare for the coming reactivation in September. General Sherburne welcomed the Red Devils to Fort Campbell in a train side ceremony. In his speech the General said, "Your homecoming is a big day for the 101st Airborne Division. Here is the job you and I have been chosen to do: Organize and train a completely new kind of airborne outfit. Give it the newest and finest equipment the military mind can devise. Give it more firepower than any unit its size ever had, including atomic weapons. Give it plenty of light aircraft and helicopters, new communications equipment including battlefield television. Give it the kind of organization that will permit it to operate rapidly over great distances. In brief, build a division of the future, and if you build it right, the Army may use it as the model for widespread reorganization. That's why the eyes of the Army, the country, and the world are on Fort Campbell right now - and will be for a long time to come. No question about it - today you join the Army's elite."

Colonel William A. Kuhn had been appointed to command the 327th Airborne Infantry Combat Group. He was serving as the chief, Plans and Operations Division, Troop Test Jump Light. The Jump Light Test was a series of test maneuvers to determine the adequacy of the new concepts of doctrine and organization of the airborne division as developed under project ROTAD (Reorganization of the Airborne Division). This series of tests evaluated the various components of the new division rather than the division as a whole.

The 101st Airborne Division Museum was started at Fort Campbell in August 1956. Lieutenant Yvonne G. Trout was made the museum curator, and she was instrumental in getting a number of artifacts and relics for the museum which add to the chronological picture of the Division during World War II.

The 508th Airborne Infantry School Command was tasked to start the Basic Jump School at Fort Campbell. The mission of the school was to graduate qualified parachutists to fill the airborne slots in the new Division, and to train all non-airborne qualified replacements assigned to the Division in the future. The school was also used to teach an advance airborne school that trained jump masters and pathfinders for the Division.

All activity of the cadre of the 101st Airborne Division (Advance) was directed toward the task of getting the unit ready for the official reactivation of the Division. The tempo of activity around Fort Campbell rose to a fever pitch. New units were being formed, new men trained, and new tactics were being developed. The target date of September 21, 1956 was closing in fast, and all had to be ready.

In dramatic ceremonies at Fort Campbell, Kentucky, the reactivation of the 101st Airborne Division gave a preview of American's newest threat to potential aggressors, a completely reorganized airborne division. The Screaming Eagle had once again bared its talons as one of the world's most formidable fighting forces.

Secretary of the Army, Wilber M. Brucker, and General Maxwell D. Taylor, former wartime commander of the 101st and now Chief of Staff of the United States Army, headed up the list of dignitaries who attended the colorful reactivation ceremonies. Other noteworthy dignitaries were Continental Army Commander, General Willard M. Wyman; Commander of the Tactical Air Command, General O.P. Weyland; 3rd Army Commander, Lieutenant General Thomas F. Hickey, and XVIII Airborne Corp Commander, Major General Paul D. Adams. Distinguished members of the wartime Division included General Anthony C. McAuliffe (DIVARTY), Major General Gerald M. Higgins (Div. HQ) and Major General Robert F. Sink (506th Parachute Infantry Regiment).

Thousands of spectators gathered at Fort Campbell's Yamoto drop zone for the airborne demonstration that kicked off the reactivation day program. Drops featured men making their first jumps, combat veterans of the wartime Division, men with the most combat jumps, men with the most total jumps, and a mass jump of 120 combat veterans. Other events included air dropping artillery and landing more by helicopter, laying communications wire by airplane, live fire demonstrations including the Honest John Rocket, and a visit to the jump school to watch parachute training.

The Division Commander and his Assistant Division Commanders arrived at the reviewing field via helicopter, a move that truly foretold the future of the 101st Airborne Division. One of the more moving moments of the reactivation was when the entire Division knelt in prayer on the parade field prior to the order to pass in review.

While the 101st was really new, the Division went to great lengths to retain the proud tradition of the old Division. The old battle flags, draped in their museum cases since 1945, had been unfurled and once more they appeared with the units bearing the numerals of their World War II predecessors. The Screaming Eagle patch, borrowed by the wartime division from the Civil War Iron Brigade of Michigan, was back on every left shoulder. The Division mascot was a live American Bald Eagle, and the amplified scream of an Eagle marked the noon hour every day of the week.

Many of the officers who served with the Division in the Second World War had commands in the new Division. Colonel Harry W.O. Kinnard who commanded the 1st Battalion 501st Parachute Infantry Regiment (PIR) in World War II, now commanded the 501st Airborne Combat Group. Many of the enlisted men who crossed Germany with the Division in the Second World War came back to the ranks of the new Division.

General Sherburne visualized the Division as having two types of mission capabilities. Since the Division was completely air-transportable, it was to be a "Fire Brigade" that would move instantly to deter or stop a small brush fire war. Its role in a major war was to plunge deep into hostile territory to wreak irreparable damage to the enemy force. The Division was capable of being air-lifted out of action, quickly being refitted and going back into action someplace else.

The balance of 1956 was spent in intense field training with the Troop Test Jump Light maneuvers that were to climax with the Skyraid maneuvers in early 1957. The February 1957, date for the Division to be ready to deploy and fight overseas was coming up fast.

1957

1957 DAWNED WET and cold at Fort Campbell, Kentucky, as the winter rains soaked the men of the 101st Airborne Division while they slogged their way through the last of the Troop Test Jump Light exercises. Exercise Sky Raid was the climax of four months of field testing that started at the squad level and tested every level of the Division structure. This was the big one, as military leaders from all over the world came to Fort Campbell to watch the four day division size maneuver. The weather came into the act, and the major parachute jump of the exercise was cancelled. General Sherburne had the units make a simulated jump by tailgating from two-and-a-half ton trucks at the drop zone, and the Division went on to play out the attack that was called for in the original plans. The war games had simulated Honest John Rocket firings, mock atomic weapons hits, displacement and counter-attack by helicopter-born troops. Every action was played out to the fullest extent, and movement of replacements, casualties, resupply and diversified support problems were thrown at the commanders all four days.

In other operations conducted as part of the Jump Light Test, Colonel Melvin Zais's 187th Airborne Combat Group left Fort Campbell for Operation Market II. 1,800 men with five 105mm howitzers, 185 jeeps, 44 three-quarter ton trucks, and 187 tons of equipment were flown out of Sewart Air Force Base to Fort Bragg, North Carolina in 49 lifts by 20 giant C-124 "Globemaster" aircraft of the 18th Air Force. The 187th, fully reinforced as for a combat mission, again demonstrated its complete air transportability. On the 11th of January, 1,240 paratroopers hit the silk and 300 tons of equipment and supplies were dropped from 66 C-119 "Flying Boxcars." Shortly after the paratroopers secured Normandy drop zone, 91 C-123 "Providers" made an air assault landing to disgorge additional men and equipment. This was the largest tactical air drop since World War II, and it set the pace for four days of realistic combat maneuvers. The men of the 101st were fighting an aggressor force from the 82nd Airborne Division. On the third day of the operation, another 16 C-123s made combat assault landings to bring 160 tons of supplies to the fighting men in an airhead behind enemy lines.

Some men of the 81st Rocket Battalion (formerly the 81st AA Battalion) drew better duty in January and took two of the Honest John Rockets to Washington, DC. The men and the missiles were on display for President Dwight D. Eisenhower at the Inaugural Parade in Washington.

The 101st Airborne Division set the stage for sweeping changes in the Army organization and doctrine with the completion of one of the most important field tests in Army history. Since its reactivation in September 1956, the Division was rushed through a series of tactical tests to meet an urgent deadline. Lieutenant General Thomas F. Hickey, the 3rd Army Commander, had to have the completed report on the successes and shortcomings of the streamlined 101st Airborne Division on the desk of the Continental Army Commander no later than the 22nd of March 1957. There was much speculation that, based on the results of the Jump Light Test, the Army wouldn't wait for the final evaluation before it started to reorganize the 82nd Airborne Division into the Pentomic concept.

The final Jump Light report was rushed through top-level Pentagon analysis and examined the difference in structure between the standard airborne division, like the 11th, 82nd, and the new Pentomic 101st. The report studied the ramifications of the decision to slash the strength of an airborne division from 17,000 men to 11,500 men. The Army's drive for mobility had seen the 101st Airborne eliminate 138 medium tanks, two light tanks, 19 tank recovery vehicles, nine armored personnel carriers, 24 twin 40mm guns, 48 quad 50 caliber machine guns, 346 50 caliber machine guns, 18 155mm howitzers, 29 105mm howitzers, and 547 two and a half ton trucks. General Sherburne noted that the Division would need a lot of support, but the light weight would allow the Division to move into a situation fast, get the job done, and move out. The 101st Airborne was designed for the assault mission. The Division was to be kept slim and quick.

Jump Light also studied the effects of the elimination of a level of command by the creation of the five combat groups of integrated arms in place of the three infantry regiments with their nine infantry battalions. Another command that came under close scrutiny was the Combat Support Group commanded by Colonel Alan Strock. The support command was responsible for all logistics support for the Division and eliminated many logistic responsibilities at the company and regimental level.

Despite its reduced manpower, the 101st packed increased rifle power. The Pentomic Division had 300 rifle squads with 3,300 riflemen, compared to the 243 rifle squads with 2,187 riflemen in the other airborne divisions. Each combat group had five rifle companies compared to the three rifle companies in the old style battalion. The increased use of organic aircraft in the 101st was a feature that would be expanded as the Division got ready to go into a combat ready status. The Division started with 53 organic aircraft, and the number was doubled in the Spring of 1957.

There was an unusually high experience level throughout the Division with almost all of the officers having seen combat in two wars, and the same held true for hundreds of enlisted men. The Division Jump School graduated 4,500 new jumpers for the Division, while the units conducted the five month testing phase.

Another more familiar mobility test was given to a unit of the Division when Company B of the 501st Airborne Combat Group left Fort Campbell for a 94 mile foot march. The company left on the 21st of February and moved in combat formation over back roads and trails to Sewart Air Force Base, south of Nashville, Tennessee. Moving with the company was the heavy weapons platoon with their mortars and the new jeep mounted 106 recoiless rifle. The resupply of ration, water and essential equipment was made by helicopter. The company arrived at Sewart Air Force on the 26th and returned to Fort Campbell the airborne way by making a parachute jump at Fort Campbell the next day.

During training at Fort Campbell, the men of the 187th made use of a new tactic with a helicopter raid on a mock atomic missile launcher site. The 500 troopers loaded into 37 helicopters and flew to the attack site in 20 minutes. The lift crossed over a river and numerous land barriers that would have required days of marching and fighting had the attack been made on foot. When the mission was completed, the men loaded up and were returned to their base to prepare for a new mission. In a second action, the 187th made a counter attack by helicopter to demonstrate the air mobility of the new light weight division.

The 101st Airborne was the first to receive three new items of equipment in 1957. The Army Mule, a small light weight four-wheel drive vehicle came into inventory in May 1957. The low, flatbed vehicle weighed 900 pounds and could carry a 1,000 pound payload. Each rifle platoon had a mule assigned to it to carry the extra platoon equipment like water, rations, and ammunition. The Division got a new radio unit mounted on the 3/4-ton truck. The AN/GRC-46 unit was air-transportable and had a range of 50 miles. Two jeep mounted 106mm recoilless rifles were issued to each rifle company's heavy weapons platoon, and the vehicles could be either parachuted in or lifted by the H-34 helicopter.

The 101st Airborne was the first division to redesignate most of its major commands under the Army-wide "Combat Arms Regimental System." Under this new system a total of 164 of the Army's most distinguished regiments became institutionalized with all active Army units being designated as elements of one of these parent units. There were nine Airborne regiments included in the 164 parent units. Those units were the 187th, 325th, 327th, 501st, 502nd, 503rd, 504th, 505th, and the 506th and every airborne infantry unit was assigned to one of them. The five major commands of the 101st Airborne Division were the 2nd Airborne Battle Group 187th Infantry, 1st Airborne Battle Group 327th Infantry, 1st Airborne Battle Group 501st Infantry, 1st Airborne Battle Group 502 Infantry, and 1st Airborne Battle

Group 506th Infantry. As a general rule, the first battle group of a regiment is assigned to the division that it fought with in combat. The 1st Airborne Battle Group 187th was assigned to the 11th Airborne Division and the 2nd Airborne Battle Group 502nd was assigned to the 82nd Airborne Division. All airborne, cavalry, infantry, armor, field artillery, anti-aircraft artillery and special forces units were redesignated under the new system.

The first year of training and building the 101st Airborne Division wasn't without tragedy. On June 13, 1957, 14 members of Company A, 1st Airborne Battle Group, 327th Infantry were killed and nine more men were injured when their truck overturned at Fort Campbell. Quick action by men of the 326th Engineers and a H-34 Cargo Helicopter saved some of the injured from being killed. In peace and in war, death and injury are always at a soldier's side.

September saw the 101st pass the one year mark, and the new Division was lean and mean. New units had been added to the five major combat commands. The Division has Support Command, Troop A 17th Cavalry for reconnaissance, and an aviation company for its expanded organic aviation assets. The administrative weight was reduced to add foxhole strength; every weapon was air-transportable and capable of being parachuted into action; and every man was a qualified parachutist. The Division was a strategically ready Army force that could be picked up, in part or in whole, and be delivered in a matter of hours to any destination in the world where a show of force or application of force would be in the national interest.

September 1957 saw the first use of the 101st Airborne in a civil rights incident when the 1st Airborne Battle Group 327th Infantry was ordered to Little Rock, Arkansas. September 24th President Dwight D. Eisenhower ordered units of the 101st to move to Little Rock to join with the federalized National Guard units to prevent civil disturbances as Governor Orval Faubus defied the federal court decision on integration of the schools. The center of the action was Central High School in Little Rock and 1,000 101st Airborne troops and the federalized National Guard remained on guard at the school for 34 days. While on duty at the school, the troops had to respond to bomb scares, mob attacks, and charges by the governor that the men had invaded the girl's dressing room. The worst incident came when an ex-marine tried to take a weapon from one of the paratroopers. The ex-marine got a cut on his hand from the bayonet on the rifle and a few lumps on the head from other paratroopers coming to the aid of their fellow trooper. The men of the Division did a difficult and unpleasant task with a discipline dignity that was the earmark of the modern airborne soldier.

General Sherburne received a telegram from Secretary of the Army Wilber Brucker, which congratulated him on the excellence of the airborne movement to Little Rock and the high degree of combat readiness and mobility achieved by the Division. The men of the 1st Airborne Battle Group 327th were returned to Fort Campbell before the end of October.

General Taylor's report to the Armed Services Committee for the fiscal year 1958 stated that the Army's FY 1958 budget would field an Army of one million men that would be in 17 reorganized divisions, nine separate battle groups, several atomic support commands and additional anti-aircraft units. The purpose of the reorganization was to improve the ability to fight effectively on the atomic battlefield without the loss of capability to conduct so-called conventional warfare. The 101st Airborne Division had proved the concept and the Pentomic Army was born.

1958

THE ARMY ANNOUNCED the formation of the Strategic Army Corps in early 1958, and the 101st Airborne Division was selected as the first ready division of that force. STRAC, as the force was called, was designed to meet the initial requirements of a limited war or to provide initial reinforcements to overseas units in a general war. STRAC's mission was to be operationally ready on a moment's notice. STRAC could place fully armed and equipped elements into action on a few hours notice, and have the rest of its elements ready for phased deployment as the air and sea lift became available.

STRAC consisted of four Pentomic Divisions and a headquarters unit. The divisions were the 101st Airborne Division at Fort Campbell, Kentucky; 82nd Airborne Division at Fort Bragg, North Carolina; 4th Infantry Division at Fort Lewis, Washington; and the 1st Infantry Division at Fort Riley, Kansas. The headquarters element was the 18th Airborne Corps stationed at Fort Bragg, North Carolina. The 101st was the high priority unit in STRAC and always got the most modern equipment first. STRAC was the U.S. Army's first Rapid Deployment Force (RDF) and was assigned to the commanding general's U.S. Continental Army Command. In the case of war, the STRAC elements deployed overseas would have come under the command of the combat theater commander. STRAC's motto was, "Skilled, Tough, Ready Around the Clock," and at Fort Campbell that motto was the law of the land.

In an emergency, elements of STRAC would have deployed to meet the contingency requirements. New units would have been assigned to STRAC and reserve units would have been called up to reconstitute the Strategic Army Force. Using this system, adequate readiness was maintained for both a general war and units were available for limited war duty.

The 101st Airborne was tested many times to prove the Division could meet the movement schedule. One morning the Division was alerted at 0400 hours, and 36 hours later the entire Division - men, weapons, ammunition, vehicles, and supplies were marshalled at Campbell Army Airfield in chalk order ready to load on aircraft for a trip to any part of the world where they would be required to land and fight.

The 101st Airborne was the only one of the four STRAC divisions that was really maintained at full war strength and was ready to go on call. Although the Division was at full strength, there was a great deal of skepticism about the readiness or even the existence of adequate airlift power to move the entire Division overseas on short notice. In the words of General Sink, Commander of the 18th Airborne Corps, the 101st Airborne was reduced to hitchhiking with its sister services if it had to go to war in an emergency. The mobility of the 101st Airborne required airlift to get it to the war zone and modern sea lift to sustain it in combat.

The Army decided that it too should be included in the next round of development for modernization of the military airlift fleet. The Army even went so far as to propose the construction of an additional 100 C-133 transport aircraft for its use only. The concern among the joint services about the lack of airlift would lead to the development of the C-141 jet transport in the early 60s.

March 1958 saw a new Division Commander arrive at Fort Campbell, Kentucky. Major General William C. Westmoreland, who had just turned 44, was given the command of a lifetime. General Westmoreland was one of the youngest and most distinguished major generals in the U.S. Army. He had served with the 9th Infantry Division during the Second World War and the 187th Airborne Regimental Combat Team in Korea.

General Sherburne said that he couldn't have wished for a better successor than General Westmoreland. The Division was in good shape in training, condition, equipment, and strength and ready to continue on towards its "Rendezvous with Destiny." General Sherburne built a new division capable of meeting the demands of a new era in land warfare; yet he was able to retain the high morale, discipline, and standards that had characterized the World War II 101st Airborne Division.

On April 23, 1958, tragedy again struck the 101st Airborne Division during a training exercise. Five paratroopers were killed and 158 paratroopers were injured when the 1st Airborne Battle Group, 502nd Infantry jumped unsuspectingly into a sudden and violent wind gust on the drop zone.

The disaster struck so suddenly that General Westmoreland, who jumped with the battle group on the other drop zone used for the exercise, didn't find out until later in the day. All of the prescribed safety precautions were being taken at the time of the drop. The wind speed readings from the drop zone were 10 knots, and wind under 12 knots is considered safe for a jump. The 15th Field Hospital, which was expecting to handle simulated casualties as its part in the Eagle Wing exercise, soon found itself very busy with real casualties as 102 of the injured paratroopers were brought in for treatment.

Exercise Eagle Wing was canceled on the 28th of April when the final mass jump by the Division was stopped due to poor weather conditions at Fort Campbell. General Sink, Commander of the 18th Airborne Corps and deputy exercise director, announced the cancellation after a jump by General Westmoreland showed that there were marginal wind conditions on the drop zone. Westmoreland himself would have been dragged had there not been extra men on the drop zone to catch his chute.

Never before in peacetime had the Army required its first line troops be so well trained. In truth, the men of the 101st Airborne were not intended to be peacetime soldiers. They were combat troops at all times, and it showed in the realistic training they went through every single day. When those five men gave their lives, they gave it for their country as surely as if they had died with their brothers of the Eagle in Normandy, Holland, or Bastogne. As a result of the accident, the Army developed the Capewell Canopy Quick Release for the T-10 parachute. Therefore, out of death during training, new lessons were learned that would save many lives in later years.

The Division continued to train and sharpen the skills that would prepare it for combat. The assignment to STRAC meant the Division had to be ready to move its alert force on one hour's notice. There was a tremendous amount of work required to get all of the loading tables made up for the Division's equipment. When a unit went on alert, every vehicle was loaded with its combat equipment, including live ammunition. Every piece of equipment had to be loaded the same way every time a unit went on alert. Mock-ups of all of the Air Force's major transports were built near the jump school area so the Division's vehicle drivers could practice loading their vehicles night or day under any weather conditions.

May 1958, saw the first real test of the STRAC concept, the Tactical Air Command and the 101st Airborne Division. President Eisenhower ordered U.S. paratroopers into a standby position in the Caribbean in the wake of mob violence against Vice President Nixon in Caracus, Venezuela. TAC responded to a "no notice" call from the Pentagon and rushed 40 C-130s from Sewart Air Force Base near Nashville, Tennessee, to Fort Campbell, Kentucky. The aircraft picked up 577 battle ready paratroopers of the 1st Airborne Battle Group 506th Infantry and flew them non-stop 1,600 miles to San Juan, Puerto Rico. The aircraft also carried 44 jeeps, 10,000 pounds of ammunition, a helicopter, three 106mm recoiless rifles, four mortars, and extra gasoline for the vehicles. The violence died down, Mr. Nixon left Caracas, and the men of the 506th came home to Fort Campbell.

The summer of 1958 was used to get the troops of the Division ready for the first Strategic Army Corps Maneuvers ever held. Exercise White Cloud was conducted at both Fort Campbell, Kentucky, and Fort Bragg,

North Carolina, under the direct supervision of Major General Robert F. Sink, the commander of the 18th Airborne Corps. The maneuvers ended on November 5 after 19 long days of concentrated training in all phases of airborne operations under conditions of atomic, radiological, and electronic warfare.

The 101st Airborne Division was the key striking force of the Strategic Army Corps and was used as the maneuvering force during the exercise. A Battle Group of the 101st was detached and used as aggressor forces during the Fort Campbell phase, and a battle group of the 82nd was used as the aggressor force when the Division went to Fort Bragg.

The 101st Airborne had completed two years of testing and training as the Army's pioneer Pentomic Division when it completed exercise Eagle Wing in April and May of 1958. Now it was employed in its first STRAC maneuver, and all of the missions assigned to the Division were typical STRAC missions.

The U.S. Air Force provided 12 C-124 aircraft from the Military Air Transport Service (MATS), 45 C-123 aircraft from the 9th Tactical Air Command (TAC) and 50 C-119 aircraft from the Air Force Reserve. During the course of the operation, the Division was committed to a ground action, refitted for an airborne assault, moved by both tactical and strategic aircraft to five dispersal airfields, conducted a mass airborne assault, and fought in a second ground action.

In the final phase of the operation, 4,000 paratroopers were withdrawn from a ground action in Tennessee, moved by C-124 to South Carolina where they boarded C-130 aircraft, and made a mass drop at Fort Bragg, North Carolina. The following evening Company E of the 327th Airborne Battle Group made a helicopter assault on an aggressor missile launcher site at Camp Mackall. The company used 15 H-34 and H-21 helicopters in the raid. The men landed, attacked, and were lifted out in less than one hour. The next day more elements of the 327th were lifted by helicopter to an airfield where they boarded 26 C-123 aircraft, put on their parachutes after take off, and made an airborne assault on aggressor forces at Camp Mackall.

The last action of the maneuver had the 506th Airborne Battle Group do a force march of 13 miles through thick woods and swamp to assault an aggressor force that was equipped with tanks. General Sink commented that STRAC, with the 101st Airborne Division as its spearhead, was in better shape than ever before to protect the nation's interest in a limited war.

The 101st maintained its instant capability to move anywhere, anytime, and fight during the exercise. There was a company ready with all of its combat gear and ammunition loaded on alert during the entire exercise. STRAC never let its guard down, even when training.

General Westmoreland was proud of his Division, but he saw some shortcomings in the small unit leadership of the Division. The General had always been a firm believer in the importance of small unit tactics. He believed the squad leaders in the Division were the most important men in the unit, but many lacked the polish and confidence men gained from combat or Ranger School. The U.S. Army Ranger School at Fort Benning, Georgia, was eight weeks long and limited as to the number of men it could take from the 101st. The General wanted to train at least three men in every squad in the Division in Ranger skills.

Lieutenant Donald Bernstein brought the idea of a mini-Ranger School run by Ranger qualified instructors to the Division G-3. General Westmoreland liked the idea and selected Major Lewis L. Millett to form the school at Fort Campbell. Late in November of 1958 the Recondo School was born. The name was thought up by General Westmoreland, who used the word "reconnaissance" that was needed on the atomic battlefield and the skills of the "doughboy" to develop the name Recondo. The design of the Recondo patch was a joint effort of General Westmoreland, Major Millett, and Chief Warrant Officer John McClosky. They picked an arrowhead, the symbol of woodlore, and had it point towards the ground to symbolize jumping from the air. The patch was black and white to symbolize operations night or day, and the 101st was across the face of the arrowhead to symbolize the proud Division they would lead into combat.

1959

THE NEW YEAR brought with it a new training cycle for the men of the 101st Airborne Division. The rigorous training cycle started at the squad level in January with the Infantry Squad Army Training Test (ATT). Each infantry squad in the Division would spend almost every week in the field during the month of January and February. The training was designed to sharpen the skills of the basic building block of the Division, the infantry rifle squad. During the last weeks of February, special umpires would grade each of the Division's 300 rifle squads in a series of concurrently run exercises that included a night and day live fire exercise. The best squad in the 101st Airborne Division for 1959 was the 3rd Squad 2nd Platoon of Company A 1st Airborne Battle Group 501st Infantry.

The next step in the training cycle was the platoon level ATT. The training schedule got tight as the four infantry platoons and the heavy weapons platoon in each of the Division's 25 rifle companies took to the field for the numerous training exercises that would climax with the platoon level competition.

There were ATTs for all of the various units that made up the Division: Artillery, Aviation, Engineers, Medical and Support Command. Fort Campbell rattled around the clock with live artillery and small arms fire.

There were night firing exercises, live missile firing exercises, and tear gas training. This Division was a combat ready division waiting for a war, and it showed in the realistic and constant training.

More new equipment poured into the Division, and the Army even issued the new man-portable foxhole digger to the Division. Another new piece of training equipment was tested by the men of the Division. The new sub-caliber pneumatic mortar trainer was first used by the men of Company D 1st Airborne Battle Group 327th Infantry. This new trainer would allow the mortar men of the Division to spend more practice time with their weapon at a low cost and not take up live fire range time. Brigadier General C.H. Chase was the trigger man for the first firing of the Little John Rocket that was given to the Division to replace the larger Honest John Rocket. The new rocket made the Division truly air-transportable, and now all of the equipment was air-droppable.

An older piece of equipment was still with the Division in 1959. Master Sergeant William King, the first enlisted paratrooper to jump with the parachute test platoon July 1940, was a member of the 521st Parachute Supply Company and still was jumping with the 101st Airborne at the ripe old age of 41.

Alabama Governor John Patterson came to Fort Campbell on April 11 to take part in the Civic Day program. After watching a mass parachute drop by a division unit, the veteran of both the Second World War and the Korean War, commented that the strength and character of the nation was reflected in units like the 101st Airborne Division.

In late May the troopers of the 1st Airborne Battle Group 501st Infantry went west in Operation Utah Eagle I. The men traded the blue grass of Kentucky for the rocks and sand of the Nevada desert and got a few bruises in the deal. The exercise was part of the ongoing training that made the mainstay division of the Strategic Army Corps ready to move anywhere, anytime, and fight.

July 1959, Private Michael McKean of the Command and Control Battalion's Administrative Company became the 10,000 man to graduate from the 101st Airborne's Jump School since the Division was reactivated in 1956. Later in the month, the actor, Gregory Peck, stopped by Fort Campbell to meet with Captain Joe Clemens. Mr. Peck was on a national promotion tour for the movie Pork Chop Hill. Captain Clemens was the central figure in the story about the battle on the hill. While at the fort Mr. Peck watched a jump by men of the 506th Infantry.

Major General Westmoreland became a member of the Century Club when he made his 101st parachute jump. To add to the moment, the general was the first 101st Airborne trooper to jump from the Air Force's new C-130 B aircraft built by the Lockheed Aircraft Company in Georgia.

The Division sent 43 men to Holland for the 1959 Liberation Day ceremonies. The men went to the Eindhoven ceremonies and the dedication of the Veghel Memorial to the men of the 101st who died there in 1944.

During Exercise White Cloud II, conducted at Fort Campbell, the 101st Airborne unveiled another piece of new equipment. The M-56 Scorpion was a 90 millimeter self-propelled antitank gun that was air-droppable. The SPAT, as it was affectionately called by the men of the Division, was a welcome addition to the Division's anti-tank fire power. Too many times the paratroopers of the Division had been chased across the fields and over the hills by aggressor forces with tanks. Now they could get in a few licks of their own.

Major General Westmoreland was on hand for ceremonies at Fort Campbell, Kentucky, to welcome two Golden Eagles from their home in Alaska, to their new home in Kentucky where they would serve as mascots for the Division. The two Eagles were a gift from the men of Company D 40th Armor 1st Battle Group 23rd Infantry stationed at Fort Richardson, Alaska.

In its role as the spear point of STRAC the 101st Airborne established the Division Ready Force concept to make sure the 101st could be anyplace, anytime, and fight. STRAC's world-wide mission counted on the 101st Airborne to be able to start moving a battle group that was ready and equipped to fight, within one hour of the alert signal. Unlike their World War II counterparts, who had the luxury of knowing weeks or even months in advance that they were going to war, the young men of the 101st lived with the knowledge that in any given hour the balloon could go up. The Division would have the DRF equipped to deploy to the world trouble spot of the time. During the winter the men of the DRF could be in summer camouflage and have their summer combat gear in their packs if the current world trouble spot was in a tropical area. This was a period of general world instability and the men were constantly being briefed on the changing political winds that could affect their lives. Europe, Southeast Asia, Africa, South America, or the Middle East were all potential combat situations for the men of the 101st Airborne Division in the age of the brush fire war.

Age was another factor that had a profound affect on the men of the Division. The average age of a combat infantryman in the Second World War was 26 years old. The average age of the combat infantryman in the 101st Airborne was 19 years old. There were many men in the Division who were jump qualified and assigned to combat units before they were 17 and a half years old. During the Second World War, the men of the 101st had a common bond or goal of winning "the big war," and this bond drew out the deep reserve of resolve men need to fight and be willing to die in a war. The Cold War didn't have the same clear cut goals, and the men of the Division drew on their youth to provide the resolve they would need to move out and fight in a brush war that wouldn't have a lot of patriotic fever behind it.

The battle groups rotated the ready force duty, with a battle group being the Division Ready Force (DRF) for two weeks at a time. One of the five infantry companies would be the 1st Ready Company for a week while the other companies would be the 2nd, 3rd, 4th, and 5th Ready companies. After seven days the 5th Ready Company would become the 1st Ready Company and the order would reverse. The 1st Ready Company's task was to be able to move to the airfield in one hour after the alert was called. The company would have all of its combat gear, ammunition, vehicles, and personnel loaded and ready to go. The Air Force would have aircraft ready at the airfield to move the company anywhere in the world to establish an airhead for the Division. The rest of the battle group would move a company at a time on a very tight schedule until the entire battle group was on its way to the conflict within 36 hours. The other division battle groups would start loading and moving in such a manner that would allow the entire Division to be in combat anywhere in the world in less than 30 days.

The first ready company would be locked in the barracks during the week, and all of the companies men, married or not, would be included. There were guards on the doors and there would be barbed wire surrounding the company area. All of the company vehicles fully loaded with fuel, rations, water, and ammunition would be parked under armed guard in the alert area. There were briefings every day on the world situation and map and mission studies for all of the men. Every man had his alert package updated before the alert started, and all wills, next of kin notification form, shot records, and pay records were updated. The men's civilian clothing and personal belongings were packed in a foot locker to be shipped home in the event the Division should go to war. This box was the "C" box. The uniform items not needed for combat would be packed in a duffel bag called the "B" bag that was marked to follow the Division at a later date. The extra clothing items needed for combat were packed in a duffel bag called the "A" bag that was carried by the men as they left for the airfield, and their combat gear was in their pack and on their pistol belt.

General Westmoreland would test his DRF at any time night or day. Sometimes the alert call would come and the 1st Ready Company would move to Campbell Army Airfield and have a shake down inspection to make sure every man had the right equipment and that it was serviceable. There were times when the alert force would board C-124 aircraft and fly off to a distant airfield, land, unload, eat a meal of C-rations, reload and fly home. Every time the alert company was called out, it was under the clock and the company had best be well under the hour. The men of the company never knew if it was practice or the real thing, and there were times when the world situation was hot and nerves were on edge.

Life in the 101st Airborne Division was never dull, and the troopers of the Division gave 100% all the time. The salute salutation "All the way, Sir" was the only one used in the 101st Airborne Division and it was backed by the true spirit of the statement. The men and officers of the 101st were "All the way" in every way.

1960

WITH THE NEW year came more new equipment for the 101st Airborne Division. January 1960, the first eight HU 1 A model Iroquois turbine powered helicopters were delivered to the men at Fort Campbell. The helicopter could carry four men and a crew of two, and had the added feature of an easy to remove rotor blade that made the chopper air transportable in the Air Force C-130 aircraft.

During Operation Straight From The Heart, the men of the Division donated 1,125 pints of blood. The blood drive was the single largest drive in the history of the Red Cross. General Westmoreland was the first donor and, later in the day, sent his congratulations to the men of the 101st who opened their hearts and their arms for the Red Cross.

The 101st Airborne Division NCO School and the Recondo School both started a new tank killer course as part of their training program. The men were trained to blind the tank with smoke and come up behind the tank with field expedient napalm bombs to hit the engine compartment. An old tanker commented that he knew paratroopers had to be brave to jump out of airplanes but attacking a tank with small arms fire and homemade fire bombs was well beyond the call of duty.

The troopers of the Division continued to train more and more with the helicopter. The 1st Airborne Battle Group 187th Infantry's Mortar Battery spent a week in a training exercise with H-24 helicopters to gain proficiency in the rapid movement of their equipment by helicopter. The training consisted of a series of movements which had the men sling loading and unloading their jeeps and 3/4 ton trucks from the H-34. Rapid movement by helicopter had become the Divisions ace in the hole. The light and mobile paratrooper could now move faster and further and still pack a punch.

The 501st Airborne Infantry Regiment was designated the Honorary Regiment of Veghel and a special standard was presented to the unit. General Westmoreland requested, in accordance with Army regulations, that the 501st be authorized to bear the standard at all ceremonial occasions.

The 101st Airborne was picked to be the first unit in the Army to receive the new M-14 rifle. The 7.62 NATO weapon would replace the M-1 Garand, Browning Automatic Rifle, M-1 and M-2 Carbine and the M-3 submachine gun. The original delivery schedule called for delivery of the weapon in

1960, but it was delayed until 1961.

May 1960, two Battle Groups of the 101st took part in Operation Puerto Pine. This was a combined operation with both regular Army troops and reserve troops working side by side. General Robert Sink, commander of the Strategic Army Corps, was the director of the operation. The exercise was a mass movement of 21,000 troops to Puerto Rico by air. The troops were to prepare for combat in Puerto Rico and then be returned to their home base. Part of the test was to see if the Air Force could move a number of troops a long distance. There was a growing concern in many areas that the Air Force couldn't move one division with equipment to any part of the world. During this period the majority of the Air Force money was going to buy bombers and fighters, while the strategic air lift was left to suffer.

During hearings before a house subcommittee, it was disclosed that the Air Force had only 29 of the new C-133 Turbo-prop aircraft in inventory, with 21 more on order. The only other aircraft that could move the 101st Airborne Division long distance were the 291 C-124 piston engine aircraft, and they were becoming obsolete. L. Mendel Rivers noted in an address that the Air Force had only 50 million dollars allocated in 1961 for development of a new transport that wouldn't be ready for five years, and he was right. The Lockheed C-141 jet transport wouldn't touch down at Fort Campbell, Kentucky, until 1965. It was noted in the *Washington Post* that the troops moving to Puerto Rico couldn't carry any ammunition due to the lack of available airplanes.

The troops of the Puerto Pine Task Force hardly had time to clean their gear before a division exercise, called Quick Strike, took the Division back to the field for 11 days of airborne assaults, river crossings, and simulated atomic warfare. The exercise was staged across the mighty Cumberland River and involved a number of major river crossings. The training was set to simulate European warfare conditions. The exercise had the Army Engineers build a 300 ton float bridge across the Cumberland River as well as operate a ferry to move the Division's SPAT guns across the river to enable the paratroopers to hold the bridge head and cover the construction. The 101st Airborne Division once more proved it was the tip of the STRAC spear and ready to move and fight under any conditions.

The Division had the honor of naming four of its new drop zones at Fort Campbell after great World War II 101st Airborne battles. The four drop zones were named Carentan, Zon, Veghel, and Bastogne. The other drop zones on the post had been named by the 11th Airborne Division and reflected the many battles they had fought in the Pacific Theater and the battles of the 187th Regimental Combat Team in Korea.

The Puerto Pine exercise had brought out the strategic air lift shortages of the U.S. Air Force, but it didn't shine the spot light on one of the Air

Force's strong points. The American paratrooper in 1960 had the largest number of tactical jump aicraft available to him in the history of airborne forces. A few C-46 and C-47 were still in the Air Force inventory but weren't used for troop drops, but there were plenty of other aircraft designed with the airborne forces in mind.

The C-119 Flying Boxcar was a paratrooper's dream due to the fact it was the easiest aircraft in the world to jump out of. The twin engined aircraft had its jump doors located in the clam shell doors at the rear of the fuselage and the prop blast was very light. The wide body of the airplane gave it a feeling of spaciousness.

The C-123 was designed as a cargo glider but was redesigned in to an assault transport. The twin-engined aircraft was cramped inside when it was full of paratroopers and the jump door was just behind the wheel well. The exit from a C-123 was hard to make and many a jumpmaster heard the sound of a trooper bumping the side of the plane due to a weak exit. There wasn't any feeling in the world that would compare to the feeling of making an assault landing or take-off in a C-123. Minutes after the airplane hit the ground, in a barely controlled crash, the men's stomachs would catch up with them.

The C-124 was the largest airplane in the Air Force troop carrier force during this period. The four engine airplane was called "Old Shaky" and it lived up to its name. The aircraft had a double deck that folded down when there was a need to carry extra troops. The worst position in the jump stick in the C-124 was the last half of the stick if they used the upper deck. The men on the upper deck would have to climb down a miserable little ladder from the top deck while the men on the lower deck jumped. Then they would have to hook up on the run as they tried to catch up with the first half of the jump stick and make their exit. The prop blast on the C-124 was very strong and it gave the T-10 parachute an unaccustomed opening shock. The brakes on the C-124 made a sound that every trooper on Fort Campbell knew by heart. The brakes made a squeal unlike any other sound, and many nights the troops would know something was afoot with the alert Battle Group by the sound of the brakes on "Old Shaky" as they taxied to the apron after landing to pick up the alert force.

The C-130 was a great aircraft that was built with the paratrooper in mind. The side jump doors had a step and a prop blast deflector that made the airplane easy to exit from. The turbo prop engines gave the aircraft a strong prop blast but the jump set-up helped cut that down. Heavy drop of vehicles and equipment was easy with the built in floor roller system and wide opening rear tail gate. The plane could hold 64 fully equipped paratroopers, yet all of the men had enough room to stand up and hook up without being crushed by the other men.

The Division was also using the U-1A Otter, a single engine utility aircraft, to drop pathfinders and small reconnaissance units. The helicopter was being used as a drop aircraft and many of the Division's men jumped from the H-21 and H-34 helicopter. The helicopter always gave the first-time jumper a start because there wasn't any prop blast, and the straight down drop from the chopper was a strange sensation. Most of the men in the Division made 12 to 14 jumps per year with all of the various training exercises always going on.

The morning of August 20, four air trains of C-119 aircraft converged over seven drop zones on Fort Bragg and nearby Camp Mackall. At 0930 hours the sky over Fort Bragg literally darkened as 10,000 parachutes opened in the largest one day airborne effort since the Second World War. Operation Bright Star was under way. Besides the troops there were four million pounds of equipment, vehicles, and weapons dropped. This count included 350 vehicles and 25 of the Division's 105mm howitzers. The drop wasn't without its cost. Sp/4 Weinrich of the 1st Airborne Battle Group 506th Infantry was killed when his parachute malfunctioned during the drop.

The exercise was a joint operations exercise involving both reserve and active duty military personnel, and another test of STRAC and its ability to fight a brush fire war. The ground phase of the action only lasted three days, and the men of the Division outfought the aggressor force, which was equipped with tanks. The ground action was only a small part of the exercise. The real test was moving the troops and equipment to the staging areas, the drop, and returning the 101st Airborne to Fort Campbell, Kentucky.

The Division rounded out 1960 with another blood drive called Operation Straight from the Heart and donated a whopping 1,124 pints of blood to the Red Cross. Private First Class Patrick made the 100,000 jump for Jump School when he made his fifth qualifying jump. The 101st Command General Ben Harrell made his 65th jump and got his Master Jump Wings.

1961

IN JANUARY, THE 101st Airborne Division sent five enlisted men to Washington, DC to take part in the oath of office ceremony for the new President of the United States, the Honorable John F. Kennedy. The men were part of a 101 man cordon that was surrounding the President while he took the oath.

The first new Army Jeep in 20 years, the M-151 built by Ford Motor Company, was issued to the 101st in February. The first 500 jeeps were off loaded at the post motor pool and issued to the Division units after they received their new-in-service maintenance. The M-151 was a new vehicle from the ground up. The body and frame was built as one unit and the vehicle had four-wheel independent suspension. The M-151 had a four-speed transmission and a top speed of 66 miles per hour. There was a serious flaw in the design of the vehicle, that would take the life of many troopers before the proper driving techniques were developed. As with many new weapons, the problems that arise in the use of the equipment didn't show up during the field test. The M-151 didn't have the same driving characteristics as the M-38 jeep that it replaced. The M-151 had a nasty habit of rolling over if the driver made a high speed turn. The first men to make this fatal discovery were the drivers from the recon section of the 17th Cavalry, 101st Airborne. Many of the recon platoon's vehicles had machine guns mounted on them, and the recon mission called for the unit to move forward quickly to find the enemy or use their speed and fire power to screen the division's flanks. The drivers of the gun jeeps were known for their wild driving and daring antics and were used to the more stable M-38 jeep. After the first few accidents, the Division placed restrictions on the recon drivers and set up a Driver Training School for all of the Division's M-151 drivers. Within a few weeks, the accident rate started to drop and the M-151 took its place in the Division.

In March, the men of the Division set up lines of tables and vats of solvent, as they got ready to clean their trusty M-1s, BARs, M-1 and M-1 Carbines, M-3 SMGs and the M-1919A3 light machine gun for the last time. The M-14 rifle and the M-60 light machine gun were ready to issue, and the 101st Airborne was the first in line for the new weapons. Both of the weapons used the NATO 7.62 round (U.S. 308 Caliber) and the ammunition was common with our European allies. The shift to a common ammunition for use by NATO troops would assure the 101st would have a ready supply of rifle and machine gun ammunition if they deployed to meet a threat in Europe.

All of the M14s came with a select fire option that would allow the rifleman to choose either semiautomatic or fullautomatic fire, but the Army decided to remove the selector from all of the weapons, except for the rifles carried by the two automatic riflemen in each infantry squad. The basic M-14 rifle was lighter than the M-1, but the 20 round magazine used in the weapon made the fully loaded M-14 a bit heavier. The M-14 had an advanced gas piston system and was a very accurate weapon. The Division's automatic riflemen were glad to trade the 19.5 pound Browning Automatic Rifle for the lighter M-14, even though the automatic rifleman's weapon had a detachable bipod that added about two pounds to the overall weight of the weapon. Although the BAR-men were happy about the weight reduction of the weapon, they still complained about missing the carrying handle that was standard on the BAR, and the fact that they couldn't use the sling during assault fire.

The men of the 101st Airborne were quick to find the only flaw in the weapon. The barrel of the M-14 was long and unsupported by a full length stock, and the rifle had a four inch flash suppressor. After some of the division's first parachute jumps with the new M-14s, many rifles were sent to ordnance with bent barrels. There never was a good solution to the barrel problem, when it came to making a parachute jump with the weapon. In training, the men would break the weapon into the three main groups and put it in the Grizwald weapon container. This solution was far from ideal and a lot of time was lost on the drop zone, as the men scrambled to assemble their weapons after the landing. There were a few times when a trooper in a hurry wouldn't get the trigger group locked into position and ended up losing part of his weapon as he ran from the drop zone. Sometimes the men would pack the assembled weapon in the Grizwald container with the barrel pointed up, so if they made a hard landing the stock would take most of the impact and the barrel wouldn't hit the ground first. There were times when a man would pack the weapon muzzle up and make a hard landing during the jump. When that happened, the force on the stock could drive the barrel out the end of the container and injure the jumper.

The M-60 light machine gun was another good weapon, but it wasn't as well built as the old M-1919A3 machine gun. The Division's machine gun crews did enjoy the light weight and the speed and ease with which they could change the barrel; but the gun was made with stamped out parts and it wasn't as sturdy as the old machine gun that it was replacing. The gun crews of the Division had a hard time learning to check the feed paw before they closed the feed tray cover. This simple check could prevent the breaking of the feed paw, which would put the gun out of action. Many an excited gunner slammed the cover with the feed paw in the wrong position and suffered the embarrassment of a weapon malfunction at a critical time.

More new equipment in the form of the TPS-21 Ground Surveillance Radar was issued to the Division in April. This set was one of the Army's most advanced electronic devices. The radar was unaffected by inclement weather, and had a range of one mile. In the hands of a good operator, the radar could pin point the location of either troops or vehicles to within 19 meters.

Another first for the Division Jump School came when the huge C-124 Globemaster aircraft was used as a training aircraft for a class making their qualifying jumps. The C-124 was one of the hardest aircraft in the Air Force inventory to make a parachute jump from, and the prop blast had to be a real experience for the trainees.

Some really good news came to the Division, and the Army as a whole, when the "Castro" style block hat, that had been worn with the utility uniform since 1957, was traded in for the new baseball style headgear. The old style block hat was hard to keep neat looking and got crushed at the blink of an eye.

Major General C.W.G. Rich took command of the Division in July, just prior to the 101st Airborne's participation in the largest free area Army maneuver held since the Second World War. Exercise Swift Strike I covered a maneuver area that extended from Fort Jackson, South Carolina, north to Fort Bragg, North Carolina. The west boundary was U.S. Highway 1, and the east boundary was U.S. 301. The exercise pitted the 101st Airborne Division against the 82nd Airborne Division, so there was more to the exercise than just war games. Both divisions had proud traditions and a heated rivalry that only could be had in the Airborne Forces. The 101st had the upper hand at that time by virtue of its position as the first ready Division of STRAC, and the fact that the men of the 101st were armed with the M-14 rifle, while the men of the 82nd still carried the old M-1 rifle. There was no doubt that the men of the 101st looked down on their lesser airborne brothers in the 82nd Airborne as being somewhat like stepchildren. The 101st always got the new equipment first.

The 101st marshalled at Shaw Air Force Base and North Field in South Carolina to prepare for the jump to start the exercise. The drop zones were located between Sumter and Florence, South Carolina, and in most cases they were watermelon fields. The men of the Division were a little slow at running off the drop zones after the jump, and many a trooper had his parachute over one shoulder, his rifle in one hand, and a watermelon under his other arm. The civilian population of the rural area was out in force to watch the jumps, and during the entire maneuver they would line the roads to watch the men march by. The local people went out of their way to make the Division troops feel welcome; and many times farm trucks going down the road would toss off fresh apples and peaches to the troops during a tactical road march along the highways. It wasn't unusual for a rifle squad, stationed near a farm house, to find themselves invited to a country breakfast by the family that lived there.

During the exercise, the 1st Airborne Battle Group, 506th Infantry made two parachute jumps to complete the encirclement of the 82nd Airborne and finish the mock battle. The Division engineers outdid themselves when they completed a float bridge across the Big Pee Dee River in record time. There were a number of minor incidents, like the time a platoon from the 506th got trapped by a unit from the 82nd near a small church on a hilltop. Blanks were fired, hand grenades and artillery simulators were thrown, and the battle raged around the church until the wedding party inside the church came out, dressed in their best, to see what had happened. The umpire stopped the battle and both of the platoon leaders came up to apologize to the newlyweds. After a round of congratulations from members of both of the division's forces, the troops quietly left, and the wedding party went back into the church.

The 101st Airborne was trucked back to Fort Bragg to wait for their airlift back to Fort Campbell, while the 82nd Airborne got to walk back to Fort Bragg to set a world road march distance record. The morning that the 82nd Airborne got back to Fort Bragg, a few units of the 101st Airborne were still marshalled on Range Road, and the catcalls flew as the bone weary men of the 82nd Airborne walked by the tents of the still sleeping 101st Airborne men.

In response to the Berlin crisis, the Pentagon ordered a crack Battle Group of the 101st Airborne deployed to Europe to take part in a NATO war game as a test of the combat readiness of the U.S. Army. The 1st Airborne Battle Group, 327th Infantry was selected as the unit to go, and the first elements of the battle group air lifted out of Fort Campbell on the 9th of September. The 1,884 men of the 327th flew to Turkey to participate in the Southern Europe part of the war game called Operation Checkmate II. The troops landed at the American airbase in Adana and were marshalled there to prepare for the jump. The morning of September 15 the first wave of the 327th boarded C-130 aircraft and flew northwest to jump 16 miles from the Bulgarian border. The civilians living in the area had waited two days at the drop zone to watch the jump, and they got the full show. The first wave made a smooth jump and cleared the drop zone quickly to allow the heavy drop to come in. After the heavy drop, the men of the first wave moved to the high ground to secure the drop zone for the afternoon drop.

The afternoon jump got off to a bad start when the lead C-130 mistook the VIP tents at the far end of the drop zone for the release point. The troops on the hills around the drop zone watched in fascination as the C-130s flew over the drop zone and started to release the jumpers after they had flown beyond the drop zone. To compound the error, the heavy drop made the same mistake and released the heavy equipment over the VIP tent. The troops of the first wave roared with glee, as the brass ran out of the VIP tent and scattered to escape the falling heavy drop. It looked like ants boiling out of a disturbed mound as the little black dots ran from the tents. No one was hurt, but the second wave spent a few hours gathering up stragglers and scattered equipment.

Once the battle group got gathered back together, the unit started a 16 mile road march to the Bulgarian border. The supply trains for the battle group stayed at the drop zone because they had a basic load of live ammunition for the unit, and while the deployment of the battle group was to show the Russians the military might they would face in a Berlin showdown, it was decided that the ammunition being moved forward would be too provocative. The battle group set up a defensive perimeter for two days and then road marched back to a small town near the drop zone, boarded trains, and moved back to the Istanbul International Airport to set up a marshalling area. All of the troops were required to bring two sets of Class A uniforms on the trip, and the men were allowed to go to Istanbul every day until the aircraft arrived to take them back to Fort Campbell. The Turkish people greeted the men of the 101st Airborne with open arms, and the city belonged to the paratroopers. The men shopped in the ancient bazaars of Istanbul and took wild cab rides across the city until they were either broke or on a manifest to fly out.

After the 327th Infantry returned to Fort Campbell, Kentucky, a new mission came down to the Division. The 101st Airborne was tasked to send three battle groups to winter maneuvers with the NATO forces in Germany. This troop movement was the very first time the Army had tried to move a large reinforcement group to Europe; and it was designed as a show of force to the Soviet Union, and to demonstrate the ability of the Army to respond to any Warsaw Pack aggression.

The three battle groups picked for the mission were the 187th, 501st, and 502nd. The entire post got into the act and went so far as to put out German road signs to help the division's drivers learn the NATO rules of the road. Extra men were borrowed from the 327th and the 506th Infantry to round out the combat strength of the units. The battle groups were ready to move out in early October. The heavy equipment had been loaded on rail cars for movement to ports of embarkation, and the troops were ready to move out. With only two days left until the airlift started, the men were in high spirits and looking forward to a chance to visit Germany. At 2200 hours, the night of October 6, the Division was given a war alert. All of the clubs on the post were closed, and all personnel living off the post were ordered to report to their units. The entire Fort was a churning flurry of action, and the troops were told the movement to Europe had been cancelled.

The next morning the men were ordered to change from winter camouflage to summer camouflage, and to change out the heavy winter uniforms in the A-bags to the lighter summer uniforms. Later in the day, the first briefings were given to the troops. The Geneva Accord had broken down in Laos, and the United States was preparing to send in troops. The 1st Airborne Battle Group, 503rd Infantry and the Marine force on Okinawa had been alerted, and the Marines had put out to sea. The men of the 101st were told that the three battle groups from the Division would leave on the morning of the 8th of October for Laos. At 0500 hours on the morning of the 8th, the word was passed down that the Division was to stand down. A new agreement was reached in Geneva, and Laos was declared neutral. All troop movement stopped, but the Division was on the alert for another week after the accord went into effect. The NATO war games were cancelled, and the Division's equipment trickled back in from the ports. The men of the Division were both relieved and disappointed; they were trained to a razor's edge and ready to fight.

In 1961 President John F. Kennedy emphasized the need for a military power that would be swift, effective, flexible and selective. This force would give the nation flexibility to answer threats on a scale less than all out nuclear war. That Spring the Secretary of Defense directed the Joint Chiefs of Staff to develop a plan for such a force. In the summer, they presented a plan that recommended that the combat ready forces of the Continental Army Command and the Tactical Air Command be tied together, for operational purposes, under a new unified command. In September the President approved the plan, and the United States Strike Command was born. The Headquarters was established at MacDill Air Force Base in Tampa, Florida. The Army's part of the command were eight combat ready divisions stationed in the Continental United States. There were two airborne, three infantry, one mechanized infantry, and two armored divisions assigned to the force, and the 101st was the only Division that was fully combat ready at that time. On December 28, 1961, the United States Strike Command reported ready for duty, and STRAC faded into history.

1962

CLASS #96 WAS the final class of the 101st Airborne Division's Basic Airborne School. After the class graduation, the school cadre was transferred to Fort Benning, Georgia, to staff the Jump School there. Both the 82nd and the 101st would get all of their future paratroopers from the consolidated Basic Airborne School at Fort Benning.

The Division got ready for one of its busiest years in the field, as the new Strike Command got ready to test its might. The first exercise was a two week deployment of Division units for exercise Red Hill. This was a joint exercise that had units of the 101st Airborne being air lifted by Military Air Transport Service (MATS) aircraft from Fort Campbell, Kentucky, to various air bases in the United States. The troops would unload from the MATS aircraft, draw parachutes, load up on Tactical Air Command (TAC) C-130 aircraft, fly back to Fort Campbell, and parachute in for a combat assault. Red Hill was designed to develop the joint operational tactics between Strike Command's Army and Air Force units in the event of a general war or a show of force.

The next exercise saw the 1st Airborne Battle Group 506th Infantry off to the Philippine Islands for exercise Great Shelf in February. Great Shelf was the first exercise for the 101st that used a small aggressor force dressed like the civilian population that lived in the maneuver area. After the flap over Laos in late 1961, the Army had decided to start practicing for the upcoming war that was building on the horizon, and Great Shelf was a taste of things to come.

The men of the 506th Infantry flew to Okinawa on Military Air Transport Command (MATS) C-118 and C-121 aircraft. MATS used a mixture of Air Force and Navy transport aircraft. All of the men of the 506th voted for the Navy transports as having the best food on the trip. The Battle Group marshalled for five days on Okinawa, then boarded MATS C-121 aircraft for the trip to the Philippines. The men were disappointed when the Battle Group didn't get to make a parachute jump in the exercise. The 506th Infantry was being brought in as reinforcements for the 1st Airborne Battle Group, 503rd Infantry, that was stationed on Okinawa, and a battle group from the 25th Infantry Division that was stationed in Hawaii. The 503rd got the honors of making the combat assault to start the maneuvers in the Philippines. Years later, it would be the 1st Brigade, 173rd Airborne Infantry, stationed on Okinawa, that would be the first Army combat unit sent to Vietnam. A brigade of the 25th Infantry Division, stationed in Hawaii, would be the second Army combat unit, and the 1st Brigade, 101st Airborne Division would be the third Army combat unit in the country.

The men off loaded at Clark Air Force Base and spent the next six days being heli-lifted all over the Clark Air Force Base reservation. There were two helicopter assaults made by the battle group; and in one movement A&E Company moved 10 miles on foot, over mountains and through jungle, to close a trap on the aggressor force. The aggressor forces kept constant pressure on the 506th Infantry with numerous small harassing attacks, with their forces dressing in native garb. The civilian population got into the act with the local population setting up drink stands to sell iced sodas, boys on water buffaloes with coconuts, and both sides in the mock war using civilians for information gathering. There were many lessons learned by the men of the battle group during Operation Great Shelf. The amount of water needed to keep the unit moving in the tropical heat was astronomical, and the supply section had its hands full keeping the battle group in food and water. The pilots of the 101st Aviation Battalion braved treacherous winds in the mountain passes to bring up needed water and food. The Air Force made an aerial resupply drop to the battle group, but there was always a shortage of both food and water.

Sunburn was the single largest casualty producer in the unit. The men came from Fort Campbell, Kentucky, in February, and the tropical sun took its toll on the men. The heavy cotton fatigue uniform was uncomfortable, and the men took their shirts off at every chance. The battle group drivers, who had been left on Guam Island with the ammunition vehicles, got sunburned the worst. The 506th Infantry as a whole had at least 35% sunburn casualties.

As a climax to the exercise, the men gathered at the Crow Valley Gunnery Range near Clark Air Force Base for a combined Army, Air Force, and Negrito fire power demonstration. The demonstration opened with a high speed pass by two RC-101 Voodoo reconnaissance aircraft that used their special camera to take a picture of the battle group. The RC-101s flew to Clark and landed. The pictures they took were developed and flown back to Crow Valley before the fire power demonstration was finished. The Air Force used F-100s to make the bomb runs, and all of the troopers were awestruck at the raw power of the 500 pound bombs and the napalm bombs. The Army did a demonstration of the 4.2 inch mortar and a rapid fire mission with the 90mm M-56 SPAT gun, but the best "fire power" was demonstrated by a hand full of Negrito warriors who used bows and blow guns with extreme accuracy.

The battle group marshalled at Clark Air Force Base four days before loading up on MATS C-118 and C-121 aircraft for the long flight home. The last of the unit closed into Fort Campbell on the 2nd of March, and Operation Great Shelf was over. The men of the 506th spent a week cleaning equipment before they joined the rest of the Division in the annual cycle of Army Training Tests and special exercises.

An exercise that saw the Division set another first was held at Fort Campbell by the Military Air Transport Service. For the first time in MATS 14 year history, the MATS pilots flew formation airdrops using 18 of their giant C-124 Globemaster aircraft. Normally, MATS would move the troops to a marshalling area near the combat zone, and the Tactical Air Command would furnish the aircraft to take the troops into the combat zone for the jump. The Division furnished 2,100 paratroopers for the two day exercise, and the MATS pilots got their fill of formation flying at 1,250 feet over the small drop zones at Fort Campbell.

The Division joined the 82nd Airborne for exercise Swift Strike II in July. This was the first major exercise conducted by the U.S. Strike Command, and it pitted the 82nd and 101st Airborne divisions against an armored division and a mechanized infantry division. The maneuver was held in North and South Carolina, and it was a large free area war game. Both of the airborne divisions found that they had their hands full with the tanks and infantry's Armored Personnel Carriers (APC). The farmers in the maneuver area had to put up with some damage to their crop lands even though there were rules about the employment of armored forces over crop areas. The Headquarters for U.S. Strike Command published 65,000 special handbooks for the troops that spelled out the rules of conduct while in the maneuver area, and the war game was quite an experience for the folks of the Piedmont area. They had never seen four divisions of Army troops, plus all of the attached Air Force fighters, battle it out over their farm land. There was a mass parachute drop to start the battle, and then there were seven days of air strikes, tank battles with the tank guns firing blanks, artillery firing simulators and night flare missions, and the constant rattle of small arms fire as the two forces clashed and fought a seesaw battle over the Great Pee Dee River. In the end the U.S. Forces prevailed, but there wasn't a paratrooper there who didn't have a new respect for the legs of the armor and mechanized infantry units.

The Division was the host to the Burgomaster of Eindhoven in August, and the Honorable H.B.J. Witte spent two days visiting all of the units making up the Division. General Rich rolled out the red carpet, and Mr. Witte met with many of the Division's veterans who had made the combat jump into Holland and still served with the 101st Airborne. The units of the Division awarded Mr. Witte with honorary Jump Wings and Rigger Wings as well as honorary membership in all of the Division units.

The 101st Airborne Division Aviation Battalion gave the 101st Airborne another first when it became the first aviation unit in the Army to be issued the new AO-1 Mohawk reconnaissance aircraft. The Mohawk was a twin turbo jet prop engine aircraft that was able to take off from a 400 foot strip and land in only 250 feet. The aircraft was capable of speeds up to 310 MPH. The AO-1 would give the Division all-weather eyes and a new ground search radar called Side Looking Airborne Radar, or SLAR for short. This radar would greatly enhance the way enemy forces could be found, and it would play a large surveillance role in the upcoming Vietnam War.

September 30, 1962 saw the 101st Airborne being alerted for another civil disturbance mission in the United States. The Oxford Military Operation would require the Division to move three battle groups to Memphis, Tennessee, and Jackson, Mississippi, for emergency use in the integration flap when James Meredeth entered the University of Mississippi at Oxford. All of the battle groups were on alert to backup the National Guard in case of riots at the University. The Army used the parts of the 18th Airborne Corps, the 82nd Airborne, the 101st Airborne, and other resources of the 3rd U.S. Army stationed at Fort McPherson, Georgia. The 101st Airborne had units assigned to the Oxford Task Force until July 1963.

The Cuban Missile Crisis in October, 1962, brought the Division to a full war alert on October 22, 1962. In a few hectic days, over 350,000 troops were amassed in Florida for the full scale invasion of Cuba. The combat invasion troops were the 82nd Airborne to make the invasion jump, the 101st Airborne to be the second wave, and the Atlantic Amphibious Force to hit the beaches. The troops were marshalled at Homestead Air Force Base in Florida; once again, the young paratroopers of the airborne divisions packed their combat packs and loaded the magazines for their M-14s with ammunition. Briefings were held, maps were studied, and prayers were said by the men of the invasion force. October 30 was set as the D-Day for the invasion, and the Airborne forces were the only Army troops who were instantly ready to go to war. The one Marine division of the Atlantic Amphibious Force and the two airborne divisions would have faced the Cuban Armed forces and three Soviet divisions. At the time of the planning for the invasion, no one knew the Soviets had a full strength motorized division, an armored division, and an elite guards division on the island. The world breathed a collective sigh of relief as the two super-powers stopped short of war and solved the crisis through diplomatic means.

The rest of the year the 101st spent on an upgraded state of alert while it balanced the two tasks of supporting the Oxford Operation and being the U.S. Strike Commands first ready alert force. The 82nd Airborne had been designated the home guard division with its area of responsibility being the Western Hemisphere, and the 101st was the fire brigade unit to be used in any area outside of the Western Hemisphere.

1963

THE 101ST AIRBORNE Division was the first Army division to be assigned U.S. Air Force fighter pilots under a new Army-Air Force exchange program. The two pilots were assigned to the Division G-3 Air Operations Section to serve as forward air controllers and help train the Division in close air support tactics. Both of the pilots served an 18 month tour with the Division. Being parachute qualified, they were allowed to make parachute jumps with the Division while performing their duties. The men were experienced fighter pilots with over 100 hours of flight time in jet fighters.

The 506th Airborne Battle Group won the coveted Parachute Rifle Award for the best rifle team again. The award was a modified M-1 Rifle, originally designed for jungle warfare by paratroopers, and it was presented to the 101st Airborne in 1957 to be used as a trophy by Major Thomas Roswell, a World War II veteran of the 101st. The 506th won the trophy in 1958, 1959, 1962, and 1963.

Major General C.W.G. Rich left the Division for a new assignment as Commandant of the Infantry School at Fort Benning, Georgia. Brigadier General Harry W.O. Kinnard also left the Division for a new assignment at Fort Benning. He would be working with the Howze Board on the new role of the helicopter in warfare. General Kinnard would soon start to form the 11th Air Assault Division and test the new tactics that would evolve into the 1st Air Calvary Division.

The 101st headed for the Carolinas to participate in Swift Strike III, the largest joint training held by the Army to date. The 80,000 plus men formed two major task forces and battled across the Piedmont area of the Carolinas for 26 days. The citizens in the maneuver area were getting used to seeing the men of the 101st, since this was the third year in a row that the Division had jumped onto their farms.

The Division continued to sharpen its combat skills as Company D 502nd Airborne Battle Group won the Howze Trophy for the highest live firing score with the 106mm recoilless rifle, and Troop B 17th Cavalry Recon Platoon won the highest live firing score with the M-60 machine gun.

The Division's Advance Airborne School conducted a jump master training course for a group of West Virginia National Guard Special Forces men, and had a number of foreign exchange officers visit the Division, and many of the guest soldiers attended the 101st Airborne Division Recondo School.

Some of the men of Company E 187th Airborne Battle Group and the 101st Aviation Battalion became television stars during the filming of "Mock Village" for the U.S. Army Big Picture series. The men were showing off some of the new helicopter and airborne tactics developed by the Division.

Lieutenant General William C. Westmoreland, who commanded the 101st from 1958 to 1960, stopped to visit the Division in his new capacity as the Commander of the XVIII Airborne Corps. General Westmoreland visited with the various battle groups and stopped in to see how the training was going at the Recondo School he started back in 1958.

All of the units in the Division started to see a number of the officers and senior enlisted men get overseas orders to some duty station called Vietnam. The 101st was still assigned to Strike Command and the Division's focus was on Europe, so little thought was given to that distant second unknown country. Many of the men in the 101st Aviation were wearing combat patches, Air Medals and Purple Hearts. The storm clouds of war were gathering on the horizon, and 101st was being slowly bloodied.

Miss Annie Mabry Barr, affectionately known to the Division as "Stockade Annie," was honored in special ceremonies at the Division Headquarters by Division Commander, Major General Harry Critz. Stockade Annie was a living legend at Fort Campbell for her devotion to the men in the Army Stockade. Miss Barr was the only person who was issued a 24 hour, seven day a week pass to the Fort Campbell Stockade by every Commanding General of the Post. Any time a man in the stockade needed to talk to her, she would come. She not only visited the stockade, but she spent time at the Fort Campbell Army Hospital as well. She would spend hours talking to the young men who needed her, and her Bible was always at hand. There was never a shortage of love for the men of the 101st Airborne where Stockade Annie was concerned. Miss Annie was born near Fort Campbell in 1877 and passed away in 1969.

1964

THE BIG NEWS for the Division in 1964 was a new Table of Organization and Equipment (TO&E). The Army had decided the Battle Group concept was not suited for limited brush fire wars. The structure of the battle group was more suited to fight a NATO ground war in Europe on the nuclear battle-field, and the Brass knew the next war for the U.S. Army wasn't going to be fought in Europe.

Under TO&E 57E, the 101st Airborne Division was changed from the Pentomic Division structure with five battle groups assigned to the Division to the brigade structure with three tactical brigades assigned to the 101st. This structure was designed for increased flexibility, greater battlefield mobility, and stepped-up firepower. The Division also had the Division Artillery, Support Command, 101st Aviation, 2nd Squadron 17th Cavalry, 501st Signal Battalion, and 326th Engineer Battalion.

Each brigade was built around three battalions, and each battalion had a Headquarters Company of 252 men and three infantry companies with 180 men in each company. In the 101st Airborne, the 1st Brigade was made up of the 1st and 2nd Battalion 327th Airborne Infantry and the 2nd Battalion 502nd Airborne Infantry. The 2nd Brigade was the 1st and 2nd Battalion 501st Airborne Infantry and the 1st Battalion 502nd Airborne Infantry. The 3rd Brigade was the 1st and 2nd Battalion 506th Airborne Infantry and the 3rd Battalion 187th Airborne Infantry. The Division Artillery was built around the 319th, 320th, and 321st Airborne Artillery Battalions, and Support Command consisted of the 326th Medical Battalion, 801st Ordnance Battalion, and the 426th Supply and Transportation Battalion.

This gave the Army a new flexibility to tailor any division or brigade as needed to fit the combat situation. A division could have a fourth brigade attached as needed or an extra Artillery Battalion. The independent battle groups, like the 1st Airborne Battle Group 503rd Infantry stationed on Okinawa, were converted to brigades to allow them to have a better command and control structure. The 503rd became the 173rd Airborne Brigade while the Alaska Command got the 171st and 172nd Brigades which were mechanized infantry units. The war in Vietnam would see the full justification of the brigade concept.

The change-over left the Division with a surplus of men in occupations that had been deleted by the restructuring of the Division. These men were retrained in new Military Occupation Specialties (MOS) in a special school set up by the Division. The goal of the Division Commander was to not lose a single man in the transition and keep every man on jump status that wanted to stay with the Division.

General Westmoreland, the commander of the XVIII Airborne Corps, visited Fort Campbell to present the original guidon of the 3rd Battalion 187th Airborne Infantry, that he commanded in the Korean War, to the newly activated 3rd Battalion 187th Airborne Infantry. Meeting with the General were five NCOs that were combat veterans of the 3rd Battalion 187th during the Korean War.

The Division picked up the pace in sending and receiving men for Vietnam. In one month the commanding officers of the Division Artillery and the 1st Airborne Battle Group of the 502nd Infantry would get orders for Vietnam. Major General Beverley E. Powell, the new Commanding General of the 101st Airborne, would spend time presenting Bronze Star Medals to SFC Bjornstal and Captain Barge for action in Vietnam and the seventh Oak Leaf Cluster to the Air Medal for 75 combat missions in Vietnam to SP/6 Davis. The war was heating up.

Exercise Delaware and exercise Deep Furrow, a joint Airborne Armor linkup exercise was held in April to get the Division ready for Operation Desert Strike that was held in May at the Army Training Center Fort Irwin, California. The Screaming Eagles hit the desert and linked up with their armor support for one of the toughest maneuvers in the Division's history. The heat and the terrain combined to punish the men of the Division even more than the Carolina Swift Strike series had, and realistic combat was the order of the day. The desert training was needed since the 101st Airborne Division had been given an additional mission in the defense of the Middle East.

During the summer the Division provided training for the men of the United States Military School. The cadets from West Point were put through their paces by the men of the 101st Airborne. On the lighter side, the Division was the host to a Boy Scout Jamboree, and the boys had one of the best times they could ever expect as the men of the 101st rolled out the red carpet for the Scouts. The boys were shown Recondo School in session and taken to the firing ranges to see all types of weapons in a live fire demonstration.

Late September, the Division received the new M-16 rifle, the first Army Division to receive the weapon. Once again a major weapon system was fielded with a serious flaw in the design. The design of the M-16 was a radical departure from prior U.S. Army rifle designs by the way the bolt of the rifle was completely enclosed by the upper receiver of the weapon. The problem occurred when the bolt of the rifle wouldn't seat the bullet completely in the chamber of the weapon. The bolt didn't rotate and lock, and the weapon couldn't be fired. With the M-1 or M-14, the soldier could push forward on the operating rod handle of the weapon and force the bolt to close. The M-16 didn't have an operating rod handle, so the men had no way of pushing the bolt closed in case of a weapon malfunction. The manufacturer of the M-16, Colt Firearms Company, recalled the weapons and added the forward bolt assist assembly to solve the problem.

The Division was once more issued the M-16 in mid-October and a new range schedule was set up to get the men of the Division out to the weapons zero ranges to battle sight their weapons. After the men had finished on the weapons zero range, they moved to the train fire range to qualify with the M-16 rifle.

On the 11th of November, the 1st Battalion 506th Airborne Infantry was put on special alert for a possible combat mission. A decision was made that, due to a lack of a satisfactory supply of 5.56mm ammunition available to support a battalion in combat and the fact that the men of the battalion were not used to the M-16, the men of the 506th would turn in their M-16 rifles and draw M-14s for this mission. Tension ran high as the riflemen of the battalion were rushed to the weapons zero range to battle sight their M-14s.

The plan for the mission was laid out at a meeting held for the unit's squad leaders and up. There was a hostage rescue mission required deep in the Belgian Congo. Over 1,600 foreigners including 29 Americans, 500 Belgians, 400 other Europeans and 400 Indians were being held in Stanleyville. On September 5 they all became hostages and would suffer through an ordeal that would include rape, beatings, and humiliation. The first stage of the operation would have an Airborne force parachute onto the Stanleyville airport runway to secure the airfield and remove the steel drums and automobile bodies from the runway so the rest of the battalion could land and move quickly into town to free the hostages before the rebel forces could kill them. Speed was the key to the operation, and one platoon of the first company that parachuted in would run to town and secure the road for the follow-up force. The follow-up air landed force would use jeeps that were brought in by C-130 aircraft to speed into the town square where the majority of the hostages had been gathered together.

The American Government wanted a joint Belgian-American military rescue mission, but there was a problem. The Belgian Military didn't have any aircraft capable of moving an airborne force that far, and the Belgian 1st Parachutist Battalion of the Paracommandos Regiment didn't have any experience in jumping from the American C-130E that could get them there. For three days the governments of both countries debated the solution to the sticky political problem, and for three days the men of the 506th prepared for the mission. The men practiced house to house combat and riot control, packed their bags and got mentally ready for a short war.

A political solution was reached with the U.S. Air Force furnishing the airplanes and the Belgians furnishing the paratroopers. The Belgian Airborne was flown to Ascension Island in the Atlantic where they spent a few days practicing jumping from the C-130E, and then they flew into Africa. At 0600 hours November 24, 1964, the "Red Berets" of the 1st Parachutist Battalion jumped into history and made a spectacular hostage rescue, according to plan, while the men of the 506th cooled their heels at Fort Campbell, Kentucky.

1965

THE M-16 RIFLE was adopted as a fully deployable weapon for the 101st Airborne early in January 1965. There were adequate supplies of the 5.56mm ammunition stockpiled to support the Division in any combat situation, and all of the men in the Division were train fire qualified with the weapon. The overall reaction of the division's riflemen to the M-16 was great. The weapon was light, easy to carry, accurate, and simple to take apart and clean. A soldier could carry three times the amount of ammunition for the M-16 that he could carry for the M-14. The major drawback to the weapon was the need to train the men in fire discipline. The temptation was there to flip the selector to full automatic and let it rip, but the men had to be taught to fire semi-automatic fire with aimed shots.

The Division sent a contingent of men to Washington, DC, for Lyndon B. Johnson's Inaugural Parade, while the rest of the men in the Division got ready to start the yearly cycle of Army Training Tests. This year the men of the units would work a little harder to sharpen their combat skills. The ominous clouds of war were gathering over Southeast Asia, and it didn't take a rocket scientist to figure out that the 101st Airborne Division's young Screaming Eagles would soon bloody their talons.

In March the Division had two major field exercises, back to back, as the training for air mobile operations was increased. The Division also made a major training move with a division wide push to get as many qualified as possible for the Expert Infantry Badge (EIB). The test for the badge was a grueling three day test that was scored by senior NCOs and officers. There was a special physical training (PT) test and weapons qualifications as well as practical tests in map reading, weapons knowledge, compass courses, first aid, and radio procedure. The training that was given in conjunction with the testing was important to every man whether or not he passed the test, and this training would be called on in a few short months.

May 14, 1965, brought a new TO&E for the Division. TO&E 57 F was the final fine tuning for the brigade and battalion concept, and there was a slight increase in the rifle firepower for the infantry company. The Heavy Weapons Platoon was left alone, but the Weapons Squad in each infantry platoon was issued the 90mm recoilless rifle to replace the old 3.5 inch rocket launcher. The 90mm was a much heavier weapon to carry but it gave the Airborne infantryman a much greater anti-tank punch. The 3.5 rocket launcher had been in service since 1953, and the new armor on the Warsaw pact tanks was more than it could handle.

The Division was alerted for movement to the Dominican Republic when the island was racked with revolution. The 82nd and the 101st were alerted, along with a Marine Task Force, to go to the troubled area and restore order.

Since the 82nd was assigned to the Western Hemisphere, it was deployed to the Dominican Republic first. The 82nd and the Marines were able to quiet the trouble in a few days and the 101st was released from the alert. The Army had other plans for the 101st Airborne Division.

On the 3rd of May the first Army combat unit sent into the war zone, the 173rd Airborne Brigade, landed in Vietnam. The movement of the 173rd Airborne sent a chill throughout the Division. The Airborne community was small and many of the men of the 101st had good friends in combat. The men of the 101st Airborne knew that they would soon follow their sister Airborne Brigade to war.

Movement Order #5-116 dated May 27, 1945, put the 1st Brigade of the 101st Airborne Division on call to CINCSTRIKE for a permanent change of station (PCS). The marching orders were in and the 1st Brigade was picked to go. Colonel James S. Timothy was the 1st Brigade Commander. Colonel Timothy was promoted to Brigadier General later. Fort Campbell, Kentucky, became a beehive of activity as men were shifted from the 2nd and 3rd Brigade to round out the 1st Brigade. There wasn't any time for special training for the men of the brigade, and no one really knew what to expect. The brigade had 40 days to pick up, packup, and catch the train for Oakland, California. No time was wasted as paperwork was updated, shots were given, and the men prepared to go to war. The 1st Brigade was ordered to move by train to the Oakland Army Terminal in Oakland, California, where it would be shipped to Vietnam via Army transport ship. As the train neared the Oakland Army Terminal, anti-war demonstrators picketed and laid on the railroad track to block the train. The 173rd deploying from Okinawa and the 3rd Brigade of the 25th Infantry Division deploying from Hawaii got much better send-offs.

The combat strength of the 101st was cut by a third, and a new series of levies was coming around. The Army ordered the 11th Air Assault Division to change its name to the 1st Air Cavalry Division, and prepare to move to Vietnam in September 1965. The men of the 11th Air Assault Division were disappointed by the order to change the division's name, but the Army thought the name, 11th Air Assault, sounded too aggressive. The 1st Air Cavalry had an Airborne Brigade attached to it, and the 101st Airborne Division was a natural place to get more paratroopers to round out that Division before it entered the war zone.

To meet the upcoming manpower requirement of the growing war in Southeast Asia, Fort Campbell was given the additional task of becoming an Advance Infantry Training Center where the Army would give selected soldiers their second eight-weeks of Advance Individual Training (AIT) in a military occupation specialty of 111.00 Light Weapons Infantryman or 112.00 Heavy Weapons Infantryman MOS. Many of the men who went to

AIT at Fort Campbell would volunteer for Airborne training at Fort Benning and return to serve with the 101st Airborne Division.

The levies to fill out the 1st Air Calvary Division dug deep into the Division's supply of trained and seasoned manpower. New replacements were brought in as fast as could be, and the training cycles were stepped up. There was another drain on the Division as the call kept coming in for airborne qualified replacements to go to Vietnam to replace casualties from the three airborne brigades in combat. There was a lot of strain put on the Jump School at Fort Benning, Georgia. The school had to train enough paratroopers to bring the two brigades of the 101st back up to strength, keep the 82nd Airborne Division full, send replacements to the three airborne brigades in Vietnam, supply airborne troops for the airborne units in the Canal Zone, Germany, and the Special Forces units world-wide. There were never enough men to go around and all of the units suffered from a shortage of enlisted men and NCOs.

The Division absorbed the lessons learned from Vietnam as fast as they were sent back, and the training for the Division took on a new slant. All career NCOs and any enlisted man with two or more years left in the Army knew they would be going to Vietnam in the next 18 months.

1966

IN JANUARY, BRIGADIER General Willard Pearson departed Fort Campbell, Kentucky, to assume command of the 101st Airborne Division's 1st Brigade in Vietnam. There was a flow of men from the Division going to Vietnam as replacements, and in July the first group of Vietnam combat veterans started to arrive at the Fort Campbell replacement detachment for assignment to the 2nd and 3rd Brigade. Every unit had young enlisted men with the 101st Airborne Division combat patch on their right shoulder and a Combat Infantryman Badge (CIB) on their chest. These men had spent a year fighting the war in Vietnam, and it was very difficult for them to adjust to a peacetime Army unit.

The 101st Airborne was still committed to Strike Command for use in Europe, in case of war with the Warsaw Pact, and the Division had to train for that action. The career officers and NCOs took the training in stride, but most of the young enlisted men who were just marking time to finish their enlistment didn't care for the day-to-day routine of garrison life or field training exercise with blanks and umpires.

In 1966 no one in the Army or the Government had any idea of the ticking time bomb inside all of these men. The signs of Post Traumatic Stress Disorder were there and they showed up a number of times during training, but they were misread. There was a marked increase in disciplinary actions taken against Vietnam combat veterans for such offenses as disobeying orders, absent without leave, fighting, and petty crime. The divorce rate went through the roof at all military posts as the men took out their anguish on their family and loved ones. The use of narcotics was growing at a rapid pace as the men tried to recapture the adrenaline rush and high of combat. There was a saying among Vietnam Veterans, "When you were there you wanted to be home, and when you got home you wanted to be back there." The single biggest loss for the returning men was the personal relationship that was formed with a few close friends under combat conditions, and a nagging worry about friends left behind in Vietnam. Some of the men blamed themselves for the death of a buddy in combat after they left Vietnam. Many a young man would breakdown and cry after hearing that a friend in his unit got killed and say, "It wouldn't have happened if I had been there."

Fort Campbell took on the additional task of training basic trainees in late 1966. The Fort was pushed to the limits for barracks space and most of the old World War II barracks on the post were refurbished and put into service.

1967

In January, Brigadier General S.H. Matheson, the Assistant Division Commander of the 101st Airborne, was transferred to Vietnam to take command of the Division's 1st Brigade, and the 2nd and 3rd Brigades participated in Operation Eagle Prey. Operating against the men of the 101st was a Special Forces Operation group of guerrilla raiders who would give the men of the Division the type of opposition they would run into when they got to Vietnam. Even the weather got into the act when it rained during the entire operation. The use of psychological warfare teams and 60 civilian prisoners played by wives and children of military families from Fort Campbell gave added realism to the operation.

There was a special awards ceremony held for 2nd Lieutenant Herbert D. Williams, the aero rifle platoon leader in Troop A 2nd Squadron 17th Cavalry. Lieutenant Williams was presented the Robert P. Patterson award for being named top Infantry Officers Candidate School Graduate for 1966. The final selection was made by the committee that administered the Patterson Memorial award, and the high honor included a cash award and an engraved service pistol.

In March, Major General Sternberg presented the Presidential Unit Citation Streamer for valor in combat action in Vietnam to Company A 101st Aviation Battalion. The citation, approved by the President of the United States, was for extraordinary heroism in action June 1-13, 1965, near Dong Xoai, South Vietnam. The company flew 2,700 sorties under heavy enemy fire to airlift 3,500 troops in the battle area. The 101st Airborne Division had received this award for its defense of Bastogne in World War II, and Company A 101st Aviation Battalion was the first Division unit to get the award for action in Vietnam.

The U.S. Strike Command's exercise One Shot 3-67 saw a battalion of 101st paratroopers jumping into Fort Bragg, North Carolina, to free hostages being held by an aggressor force. The men jumped on Salerno Drop Zone and made a 25 mile forced march to assault the air strip at Camp Mackall.

July was a changeover month for the Division as Major General Stenberg got orders to Headquarters U.S. Army Pacific, in Hawaii. General Stenberg was replaced by Major General O.M. Barsanti. The Division also had a changeover in the top NCO slot as Sergeant Major and Congressional Medal of Honor winner, Paul D. Huff, left the Division for a tour of duty in Vietnam.

The Division launched Operation Goblin Hunt I in July. This exercise was a major anti-guerrilla operation designed to sharpen the talons of the 101st Airborne's 2nd and 3rd Brigade and get them ready for their upcoming deployment to Vietnam.

The race riots that broke out in Detroit in late July saw the Division once again called out to help restore civil order in an American city. Four infantry battalions from the 101st were sent to Detroit to join units from the 82nd Airborne Division to stop the riots. The men of the 501st, 502nd, and 187th arrived at the Detroit Airport and moved to take up positions on the east side of the city at dawn. The troops had been issued 60 rounds of ammunition and instructed to cordon off trouble spots, run frequent patrols, and be firm in the handling of the civilian population. Many of the troopers were Vietnam Combat Veterans and they had come to do a job. When the troops took some sniper fire, they stood their ground and returned effective fire. It didn't take long for the word to get out that the paratroopers meant business, and the rioters started to cool down quickly.

September 7, 1967, the 2nd and 3rd Brigades of the 101st Airborne were alerted for movement to the Republic of South Vietnam, and the Division had a major replacement problem on its hands. There were a large number of men in the Division that weren't eligible for reassignment to Vietnam due to the rotation policy in force during the war. The 101st was going to lose almost all of the combat seasoned veterans presently assigned to the Division. There were 1,000 officers, NCOs, and enlisted men who volunteered to go back to Vietnam with the Division, but there were still a lot of holes left in the fabric of the Division. There was a quick shuffling of eligible men from the 82nd Airborne to replace the ineligible men sent from the 101st to the 82nd. In a three week period the Division was brought up to combat strength and by late September the Division was trying to sort itself out. To add to the confusion there was a 3rd Battalion of the 506th Infantry being formed that was departing for Vietnam in October to reinforce the Division's 1st Brigade. September 28, 1967, Letter Orders #9-105 was published for a permanent change of station on call to CINCSTRIKE for the 101st Airborne Division.

In October the training started in earnest as the men of the Division worked to build a fighting team. There was new equipment to issue, new tactics to learn, and newly promoted NCOs to train. When General Westmoreland requested that the Division deploy to Vietnam at an earlier date than was originally planned, all of the training programs were accelerated and the 101st Airborne Division was ready as requested.

The Division completed another first when it became the only unit in Army history to deploy from the United States directly to the combat zone by air. The 101st was flown from Fort Campbell, Kentucky, to Bien Hoa Air Base, South Vietnam, on the Air Forces new C-141 Starlifter Aircraft built by Lockheed Aircraft at its Georgia facility. On December 13, 1967, Major General O.M. Barsanti reported to General Westmoreland, "Sir, the 101st Airborne Division reports for combat duty in Vietnam."

CHAPTER THREE

Vietnam
Gary Linderer

BACKGROUND

IN THE LATE 50s and early 60s, most Americans knew or cared little about the southeast Asian nations of North and South Vietnam. And those who did, had little more than a passing knowledge of the two, small third world countries that formed the east coast of what was known worldwide as Indochina. Ancient history buffs may have been aware of the rich cultural background of the lost empires of the Chams and the Annamese. Students of modern history were undoubtedly familiar with the French conquest of Indochina in the late 1800s, and their subsequent colonization of Vietnam.

The French subjugated the Vietnamese people and milked the region's rich resources for over sixty years, taking everything that they could mine, harvest or levy, and giving back little of any real value. Little that is, except a puppet government rife with the seeds of graft and corruption that would manifest itself at its very worst during the coming American debacle in Vietnam.

Ruthlessly putting down several attempted rebellions, France ruled Vietnam, Cambodia, and Laos with an iron fist until her defeat early in World War II at the hands of the Axis powers. But there was no relief for the subjugated peoples of Indochina: French rule had dissolved only to be replaced by an even tougher taskmaster—Imperial Japan.

The Vietnamese people saw this change in colonial administration as a golden opportunity to win back their freedom and independence. They fought back doggedly, determined to help the Allies overthrow the Japanese occupation forces. Realizing that their liberation from Imperial Japan could mean an independent Vietnam, the Nationalist movement under Ho Chi Minh sought help from the United States to guarantee their sovereignty after the victory over Japan. The U.S. government, however, chose to support the newly empowered French government in its effort to re-establish its hegemony over its "lost" colonies. Spurned by the U.S., Ho Chi Minh, already a devout communist, turned to the Soviet Union and Communist China for help. The Viet Minh communists, fresh from fighting the Japanese, immediately redirected their efforts against the newly arrived French occupation forces, and the bitter conflict was on.

The war ebbed and flowed for ten long years, until the devastating defeat of the elite French forces at Dien Bien Phu caused the government of France to sue for peace and withdraw its territorial claims to Vietnam.

The Geneva Conference on July 21, 1954, divided the country into a communist North Vietnam and a democratic South Vietnam. It also established a demilitarized zone along the 17th parallel to separate the two fledgling nations. The partition of Vietnam saw a mass exodus of Catholics and non-communists from North Vietnam into South Vietnam. Supporters of Ho Chi Minh migrated north, but thousands of Viet Minh communist troops remained in the south to continue the battle for a unified Vietnam.

Recognizing its age of empire was at an end, the French government granted independence to Laos and Cambodia as well as Vietnam. Although French influence would still be felt in the area, colonial France was no more.

Coming on the heels of the U.N. compromise with the Red Chinese and the North Koreans, and the recent signs of burgeoning communist aggression worldwide, the U.S. government was stunned by the defeat of its western ally, France, in Indochina, and especially by the subsequent loss of the northern half of Vietnam to the communists. When it soon became evident that pro-communist insurgents in the south were still unwilling to accept the U.N. mandated status quo, the United States was forced to take on an expanding military role in the area to fill the void left by the departing French. The paranoia of the "Domino Theory" was in full force. Senator Joe McCarthy and his ilk had Americans seeing "commies" everywhere. The Red hordes of heathen communism had to be stopped somewhere—why not in Vietnam?

When the first U.S. civilian/military contingent arrived in Vietnam in 1957, their mission was neither clear nor concise. They were tasked with providing economic and military aid to the fledgling South Vietnamese government, and equipping, instructing and advising a badly trained, poorly motivated, and ineptly led South Vietnamese army that was having a difficult time effectively dealing with a relatively small force of local communist insurgents who were remnants of the old Viet Minh infrastructure. The Americans were ordered to avoid active participation in actual combat of any kind at all costs. Escalation was not yet a point of necessity.

By 1962, American advisors under the command of U.S. Military Assistance Advisory Group (MAAG) began to play an increasingly important role in South Vietnamese military operations against the Viet Cong, the successors to the Viet Minh. Although the American government downplayed the role of U.S. military personnel in the growing conflict, the sometime hostile minions of the international press corps were telling an alarmingly different story. It was the harbinger of things to come. Vietnam was destined to become the most publicized and widely covered war in the history of mankind.

By 1964, the United States had nearly 5,000 officers and enlisted personnel serving in Vietnam. Because of the failure of their South Vietnamese counterparts to carry the war to the insurgents, the U.S. military's role as advisors and instructors had changed to the point where they were often forced to accept responsibility for direct leadership in combat operations without the official authority to do so. Their jobs became increasingly more dangerous as the Viet Cong became even bolder in their hit-and-run ambushes and terrorist attacks on U.S. military personnel. The war was expanding at a faster pace than the South Vietnamese government could keep up with.

In 1964, a large number of ARVN (Army of the Republic of Vietnam) military disasters made it readily apparent that the role of the U.S. Military Assistance Command—Vietnam (MACV), the successor of MAAG, would have to change, or be forced to become a spectator to the demise of the South Vietnamese Army. As MACV's role expanded and it became more and more active in taking the war to the Viet Cong, the U.S. found it necessary to likewise expand its commitment to the South Vietnamese government. Without realizing where it was leading, MACV discovered that it was soon fully involved in a first class shooting war without a defined objective. The Vietnam conflict was heating up and the United States military machine was inadvertently becoming its fuel.

Presidents Eisenhower and Kennedy did their very best to keep the U.S. involvement in Vietnam at low key, but with the assassination of South Vietnamese President Ngo Dinh Diem and his brother, Ngo Dinh Nhu, on November 1, 1964, during a U.S.-condoned military coup that overthrew the South Vietnamese government and replaced it with one more in tune with current American policy, the United States was fully committed.

U.S. President John Fitzgerald Kennedy's assassination in November of 1963 placed Vice President Lyndon B. Johnson in the presidency, and soon America found itself in an upward spiraling vortex that would over the next ten years suck the might of the U.S. war machine into its deadly grasp. It would divide our country, polarize our two-party political system into a tradition of grid-lock and inane bi-partisanship, and create a generation of military veterans destined to carry the guilt and shame of a war they did not lose. The final, irrefutable result of ten long years of war was the blackening of America's image worldwide, and the tarnishing of the honor and prestige of our military.

On the second and fourth of August, 1964, the United States announced unwarranted attacks by North Vietnamese gunboats on two U.S. destroyers patrolling outside of the internationally recognized territorial limits of North Vietnam. Outraged by these "unprovoked" attacks on U.S. forces in neutral waters, President Johnson immediately ordered U.S. air attacks against targets on the North Vietnamese mainland. This was the first overt American military action in the growing conflict. The Gulf of Tonkin Incident—as it soon came to be known—as did Pearl Harbor at the onset of World War II, served to steel the will of U.S. society and to justify our president's decision to commit military forces to protect our threatened national interests.

By the fall of 1964, the conflict had escalated to the point that the Pentagon decided to send the 5th Special Forces Group to South Vietnam to expand our role in the theater of operations. The unit arrived in Nha Trang with many of its members already veterans of a previous tour in-country. During the succeeding months, the soldiers of the Fifth Special Forces Group would develop the Civilian Irregular Defense Group (CIDG) program; set up small, fortified outposts in the heart of the central highlands of South Vietnam and along her borders with Laos and Cambodia. They would also run top-secret, specialized raids and reconnaissance operations into NVA/ VC strongholds and sanctuaries on both sides of the border. But the best efforts of America's finest and most professional soldiers was not enough to stem the rising tide of communist aggression in South Vietnam.

In the face of heavy ARVN losses (nearly a battalion a week in early 1965), and a deteriorating military situation throughout South Vietnam, the U.S. government began to feed logistics, aviation, and security units into the meat grinder of Southeast Asia, escalating the war far beyond the advisory stage. In response, the enemy became even bolder, attacking Camp Holloway and the U.S. Army helicopter base at Pleiku, and two weeks later the U.S. military advisory barracks at Qui Nhon. President Johnson reacted by launching Operation Rolling Thunder—United States and Vietnamese airstrikes against targets in North Vietnam.

Now, fully aware of the vulnerability of U.S. military bases in South Vietnam, President Johnson sent the 9th Marine Expeditionary Brigade— two full battalions of Marines (over 3,500 troops)—to Vietnam from Okinawa on March 8, 1965, to guard the U.S. air base at DaNang. When the Viet Cong responded by bombing the American embassy in Saigon, the Marines were put on full combat alert.

The first U.S. Army troops to arrive in Vietnam under the 1965 troop build-up was the 716th Military Police Battalion, arriving in Saigon on March 19th. As vast quantities of supplies and materials poured into South Vietnam, storage depots and fuel dumps became susceptible to sabotage and Viet Cong attack. The 173rd Airborne Brigade from Okinawa arrived at Bien

Hoa on May 5th, and set up to secure the burgeoning U.S. military complex being constructed around the Bien Hoa air base. Two months later, the 2nd Brigade of the 1st Infantry Division landed at Vung Tau.

The increased American presence in South Vietnam only served to demonstrate the further need for more American forces to secure and protect the growing number of U.S. facilities being created to support the growing number of American units—it generated a self-perpetuating escalation.

FIRST BRIGADE ODYSSEY

ON JULY 28, 1965, President Johnson announced U.S. forces in South Vietnam would be increased to 125,000 men. The next day, July 29th, the 1st Brigade of the 101st Airborne Division, sailing aboard the U.S.S. *Leroy Eltinge*—a converted World War II "liberty ship"—landed at Cam Ranh Bay in the Republic of South Vietnam. They had departed Ft. Campbell, Kentucky, full of "piss and vinegar and loaded for bear." As with the generation of Screaming Eagles before them, they were anxiously in search of their "rendezvous with destiny."

The 101st Airborne Division was alerted to prepare a brigade for assignment to Vietnam in May 1965. When Major General Beverly E. Powell, the division commanding general, had selected the 1st Brigade to fill the role, he knew he was sending one of the top infantry brigades in the United States Army. Physically stronger than the 173rd Airborne Brigade, with three intrinsic infantry battalions—the 1/327th, 2/327th, and 2/502nd—instead of two, the 1st Brigade, commanded by Colonel James S. Timothy, comprised the finest officers and enlisted men of the elite 101st Airborne Division based at Ft. Campbell, Kentucky.

Although trained to operate in all types of environments, the 1st Brigade had specialized in desert operations, and there was some initial grumbling within the 2nd and 3rd brigades which had trained specifically for mountain and jungle fighting. There was also a flurry of last minute 1049s (Personal Action Forms) from paratroopers in the 2nd and 3rd Brigades attempting to transfer to the 1st Brigade, and even though there was little time to muddle through excess paperwork, some of the best soldiers in the other two brigades found their transfers quickly approved. The 1st Brigade was insured that it would arrive in Vietnam fully manned with the finest the 101st Airborne Division could provide.

Thanks to the remarkable ability of the Brigade operations officer—the legendary David Hackworth—the 1st Brigade was already in a fine state of combat readiness. This was most fortunate, because there was very little time for extensive pre-deployment training. Equipment had to be issued, inventoried, serviced, and prepared for shipment half way around the world. Individual and crew served weapons had to be zeroed, unit tactics had to be rehearsed, and military skills had to be honed to some semblance of combat readiness. Transferees had to be quickly integrated into their new units. Administrative records and shot cards had to be updated. Men had to go on final leave. Brigade personnel with families had to see to the care and disposition of their dependents. And finally, wills had to be written or amended.

Ft. Campbell, Kentucky, was a very busy place during the torpid months of June and July 1965, but the Screaming Eagles of the 101st Airborne Division's 1st Brigade went about their tasks with the usual pride, spirit and enthusiasm that had always characterized United States Army paratroopers. For the first time in twenty years, Screaming Eagles were going into harm's way. It had been too long. For most of the young paratroopers, it would be their first taste of war, but to their good fortune, a large number of the Brigade's officers and NCOs were combat veterans of World War II and Korea. Many had already completed one or two tours in Vietnam as advisors, or with Special Forces. All in all, the 1st Brigade of the 101st Airborne Division was one of the finest military units in the United States Army. America was sending the "cream of the crop" to Vietnam to get the job done. At that time, no one suspected that the addition of the Screaming Eagle Brigade to US forces already in Vietnam would not be nearly enough. Halfway around the world a determined and resolute enemy waited.

Besides the three maneuver battalions, the Brigade was composed of the Brigade Headquarters and Headquarters Company, Troop A 2/17th Cavalry, 2/320th Field Artillery, the Brigade Support Battalion (Quartermaster, Medical, Maintenance, and Administration companies), Company A 326th Engineer Battalion, a platoon of the 101st Military Police Company, a platoon of Company B 501st Signal Battalion, a Long Range Reconnaissance Patrol Platoon (LRRP), a Radio Research Unit, and a Military Intelligence Detachment. On July 6, 1965, the paratroopers of the 1st Brigade arrived at Travis Air Force Base aboard chartered civilian airliners. They were bused to Oakland Army Terminal, where they were greeted by an Army band and a contingent of Red Cross "Doughnut Dollies", and then introduced to the USNS *General Le Roy Eltinge*, a five hundred ten foot long rust bucket of a World War II troopship that had somehow or another gotten a reprieve from its role as a U.S. Navy target ship.

The *Le Roy Eltinge* came as a shock to the hard-core 1st Brigade paratroopers. Appearing too small for its own smokestacks, the rusting antique liberty ship seemed even smaller as the Screaming Eagles began filing aboard. Much to their dismay, they soon discovered the ventilation system below decks was wholly inadequate to sustain life as they knew it, and the toilet facilities, better known as "heads" by the ships crew, were primitive at best and were to be avoided at all costs. The sleeping accommodations were the ultimate in "stacked decks," allowing the cramped soldiers less than twenty-four inches of head space between bunks. Claustrophobia would be the order of the day for those who would survive the rampant seasickness. It wouldn't be long before men ready to die for each other in combat were ready to kill each other for elbow room.

Once at sea, the already atrocious conditions steadily worsened. The *Le Roy Eltinge* proved to be about as seaworthy as she was beautiful. The continual pitching and rolling, combined with the poor ventilation and the overcrowded conditions, had most of the rugged, hard-bitten paratroopers lining the rails marking their backtrail with the partly digested remains of their previous meal. Miraculously, the rusted railings managed to hold under the combined weight of hundreds of "pea-green" troopers, each trying to avoid the side spray from flanking friendly fire. Fortunately, the questionable quality of the shipboard food prevented this from being a great personal loss for the individual soldiers, although it was undoubtedly an environmental hazard to deep-sea ocean life.

On July 29th, the *Le Roy Eltinge* waddled slowly through turbulent seas off the coast of South Vietnam, buoyed by little more than the stagnant air in its crowded holds, and limped gratefully into the quieter waters of Cam Ranh Bay. The "surviving" troopers of the 1st Brigade gathered along the rail for a final time, anxious to see land again, in spite of the unknown perils it held. Ambassador Maxwell D. Taylor and General William Westmoreland, both past commanders of the 101st Airborne Division, were on hand at dockside to great the Screaming Eagles as they disembarked the *Le Roy Eltinge*.

Battalion by battalion, company by company, platoon by platoon, the men of the 1st Brigade moved off the ship and formed up on Vietnamese soil for the first time. Colonel James S. Timothy, the brigade commander, moved proudly forward to accept the official greetings of the Vietnamese government and the division's two famous former commanders. The 1st Brigade of the 101st Airborne Division had arrived.

At the time, Cam Ranh Bay was little more than a collection of small fishing villages occupying the sandy coastal area around the large bay that faced the South China Sea. MACV had developed plans to turn the bay and its surrounding shoreline into a first-class deep-water harbor, an air base, and the largest military logistics depot anywhere in the world. The 1st Brigade was tasked to establish perimeter security for the large-scale construction activities that would soon turn this isolated pocket of South Vietnamese coastline into one of the busiest seaport facilities anywhere.

It took a while for the troopers to become accustomed to the oppressive heat and humity, but gradually the brigade began to settle down to the

Winston Churchill inspects members of the 327th Glider Infantry Regiment.

The tri-colored flag of France floats in the breeze over a street in Carentan, France as members of the 501st Parachute Infantry Regiment move into the town on 14 Jun 44.

Major General Maxwel D. Taylor, CO of the 101st Airborne Division waves good-bye from a C-147 aircraft prior to Normandy jump.

Catholic Chaplain, Captain Francis L. Sampson of the 501st PIR sits astride a captured German motorcycle given him by one of the partroopers. Father Sampson used this method of transportation to visit men in the scattered battle areas of Holland.

Paratroopers of a 75mm howitzer section, Battery C, 377th Field Artillery, 101st Airborne, put on their parachutes before loading into C-47 cargo plane, Newburg, Berks, England, 3 Oct 44.

Bastogne, Belgium - 101st Ariborne Division, December 1944. From left: LTC Paul Danahy-G2, BG Anthony McAuliffe-Acting CG, and LTC Harry W.O. Kinnard-G3.

LtGen George S. Patton (right) confers with BG Anthony C. McAuliffe and LTC Steve Chappuis shortly after awarding them the Distinguished Service Cross for their actions to the defense of Bastogne, Belgium.

During an impressive ceremony in France, the 101st Airborne Division receives the first Presidential Citation ever to be awarded to an entire division in the history of the United States Army, 15 Mar 45.

Paratroopers of a 75mm howitzer section, Battery C, 377th Field Artillery, 101st Airborne, put on their parachutes before loading into C-47 cargo plane, Newburg, Berks, England, 3 Oct 44.

Troopers prepare to jump.

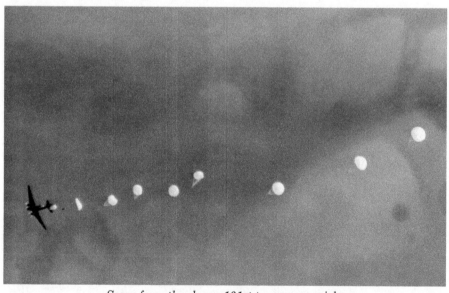

Scene from the sky as 101st troopers go airborne.

A paratrooper of the 377th Parachute Field Artillery Battalion comes in for a landing somewhere in Holland on 23 Sept. 44.

For men of the 101st, fighting and training in close quarters creates a lasting bond of friendship.

Members of the 907th Glider Field Artillery Battalion loading a 75mm pack howitzer into a glider in preparation for the invasion of Holland on 16 Sep 44.

Lt. Alex Bobuck looks over part of his platoon of the 506th just before boarding the plane for the Normandy Invasion.

General Colin Powell watches the 1-187th during their live fire exercise. Major General Peay also observes.

"The Chief of Chiefs," Muscalero Apache Chief, Silas Naiche, one of the many Indians who served with the Screaming Eagles, was asked to have his picture made with the eagle mascot of the 101st Airborne Division in 1956. A few weeks before the reactivation of the Divison, the eagle was strangled in his cage in front of Division Headquarters. Another eagle was found as a replacement but the culprits were never found.

Trooper standing beside "The Assassins" 1st Bn., 327th Inf., 101st Airborne "Screaming Eagles" marker.

A Screaming Eagle from the 2nd Brigade, 101st Airborne Division (Airmobile) is silhouetted against the setting sun at his squad prepares to move out to their night ambush position on the coastal plain near Camp Evans in northern I Corps.

Camp Eagle Vietnam (101st IP) – Marching medical man, Capt. Charles Herron, battalion surgeon for the 2nd Bn., 32nd Airborne Infantry, carries a heavy load as he leaves on a mission with paratroopers of the 101st Airborne Division.

SP4 Leland W. Brooks, A/2-502 IN, gives a wounded buddy water from his canteen as they wait for a medical helicopter.

Screaming Eagle point man on search and destroy mission.

MG Melvin Zais (center), CG, 101st Air Cav Div., discusses the operation with MG C.B. Drake (left), DCG, PROVCORPS V, USMC and BG John S. Lekson 8/7-10/68.

Pfc. Richard A. Gosnell, Stockton, CA, is about to throw a grenade into a VC tunnel discovered by paratroopers of the 101st Airborne. Covering security is provided by Pfc. Clarence H. Ward, Baltimore, MD.

UH-60 Black Hawk is the Army's first true squad carrying assault helicopter.

An Apache gunship feared by enemies of the 101st.

Vietnam, a trooper of the 101st poses in front of his company sign.

Desert Storm, Screaming Eagles get ready to move.

1-187th Infantry Tactical Operations Center during live fire training in the Gulf.

Interrogation of an Iraqi prisoner of war at the 101st Abn. Div. (AASLT) POW collection point in Saudi Arabi, February 1991. (Courtesy of Dobraomir Neikor)

routine, hum-drum task of providing area security. The paratroopers' initial excitement over impending combat operations soon gave way to the tedious boredom of idleness and inactivity. The United States Army's finest infantry brigade was discovering the lesson of that age old axiom of combat: "90% of war is the waiting."

The 1st Brigade spent nearly a month guarding the massive construction effort at Cam Ranh Bay, running patrols outside the perimeter, and participating in five major but unproductive operations within the province. On one operation near Nha Trang, 1st Brigade troopers killed a dozen black pajama clad "VC," only to discover a short time later their first enemy KIAs were actually a patrol from a friendly local PF (Popular Forces) unit that had not been given the word American soldiers were operating in the neighborhood.

In spite of their best efforts in the field, 1st Brigade units failed to find the enemy during their first month in-country. The VC, unprepared to meet arriving United States soldiers and Marines face-to-face, were satisfied to sit back and watch while they learned more and more about these American units.

Hoping to win the war before major U.S. forces arrived on the scene, Ho Chi Minh sent his NVA units into South Vietnam in strength during the late summer of 1965. Their objective was to defeat the ARVN units stationed along Route 19, effectively cutting the country in two. MACV got wind of the plan and ordered the 1st Cavalry Division, still at sea, to move ashore and establish a base at An Khe astride Route 19.

But during the final week of August, it appeared that An Khe might fall before the 1st Cavalry Division could arrive. MACV moved quickly and ordered the 1st Brigade of the 101st to move to An Khe and secure the base area until the twenty-thousand-man-strong air mobile division with its 400+ helicopters could disembark and move inland. The Brigade was tasked with opening up the stretch of Route 19 running between An Khe and Qui Nhon on the coast, in what would begin Operation HIGHLAND. The plan for this operation was to have the 1st and 2nd battalions of the 327th Infantry secure the An Khe area; the 2nd Battalion of the 502nd Infantry was to guard the An Khe Pass; while a composite force, called Task Force Hansen, consisting of A Troop 2/17th Cavalry and the reconnaissance platoons from each of the three maneuver battalions, was to patrol Route 19 and provide convoy duty from Qui Nhon to An Khe. This clearing and security operation would last nearly a month and would conclude without enemy contact. The VC were still avoiding the troopers of the 1st Brigade, but the honeymoon would soon be over.

Shortly after arriving in An Khe, a patrol from A Troop 2/17th Cav, the Brigade's reconnaissance unit, recorded the Screaming Eagle's first legitimate enemy kill. The recon troopers, patrolling along Route 19, came under fire from a single VC sniper hidden in a tree. Spotting the source of the sniper fire, they immediately brought the courageous but foolish enemy soldier under the combined firepower of the entire patrol, quickly ending the VC's budding career as a killer of American paratroopers. Tying the dead VC across the hood of a jeep, the patrol returned in triumph to An Khe, anxious to show off their grisly trophy to the rest of the Brigade.

The dead enemy soldier would be the first of many to fall to the 1st Brigade paratroopers of the 101st Airborne Division. Over the next two years, their role as MACV's "Fire Brigade" would send them up and down the South Vietnamese countryside, putting out hot spots wherever and whenever they occurred.

While the Brigade was holding the fort for the arrival of the cavalry, it received reliable intelligence that a main force VC unit—the 95th Battalion of the 2nd NVA Regiment—was in the Song Con River valley just north of the An Khe Pass. Besides the obvious threat to Route 19 and arriving 1st Cavalry Division convoys, Colonel Timothy wanted badly to tangle with a main-force VC unit in order to test the Brigade's combat readiness. On September 18, 1965, the Brigade kicked-off Operation GIBRALTAR.

The ground phase of Operation GIBRALTAR would consist of a mechanized column which would drive north along the Song Con River. An airmobile force consisting of the 2/502 under the command of Lieutenant Colonel Wilfrid K.G. Smith would air-assault into the jungle foothills near An Ninh and push the suspected VC battalion into the advancing mechanized task force. But during the initial stage of the combat assault, Charlie Company and a portion of Bravo Company of the 2/502nd became heavily engaged on the landing zone. Colonel Smith soon found himself trapped on the LZ with only 224 paratroopers from his battalion. The remainder of the battalion assault was aborted as the dug-in VC battalion inflicted heavy casualties on paratroopers and helicopter crews alike. Captain Robert E. Rawls, commanding officer of Charlie Company, requested immediate help before he was killed trying to organize the remnants of his company and Bravo Company into a defensive perimeter.

The mechanized column was experiencing its own problems, having a major difficulty moving forward through the boggy terrain. It soon became obvious that the column would not be able to reach the beleaguered infantry companies in time to do them any good.

Fighting off the encircling VC with helicopter gunships and air strikes, the Strike Force troopers dug in, attempting to hold on until a relief force could reach them. Several heroic attempts were made to medevac wounded paratroopers, but it soon became obvious that no one was going to be evacuated until the entrenched VC were either driven off or destroyed in place.

The remainder of Company B and Company A attempted another air assault to the south of the trapped paratroopers. But they were forced to give up after they were able to get only thirty-six men on the ground alive. Unable to reach the remnants of Bravo and Charlie companies, the undermanned relief element was forced to form its own perimeter, and hold on until rescued themselves. All in all, the failed attempt to reinforce the trapped infantry companies had resulted in the loss of all twenty-six of the battalion's supporting helicopters. During the night flare ships kept both U.S. defensive perimeters lit up like day. The VC initiated several probes but failed to make a serious assault on the trapped paratroopers.

The next morning, a combined relief force composed of the remainder of the 2/502nd, elements of the 2/327th, and the 23rd ARVN Ranger Battalion, reached the battleground with little opposition. The VC had quietly pulled out during the early hours of the morning, leaving behind 226 of their dead. Only twenty-one enemy weapons were recovered, but twelve prisoners were captured during subsequent sweeps of the battle area. Fortunately, American casualties were not as bad as originally believed, with thirteen KIA and forty WIA. Not only was this action the first major enemy contact for the Brigade, but it was also the first actual conquest of a VC main-force unit by any U.S. Army element in South Vietnam.

The VC had proven that it could stand up to the best America had to offer. No longer could the United States government get by with calling Vietnam a "police action." Operation GIBRALTAR and other early Army operations demonstrated the United States was now involved in a full-fledged war. After Operation GIBRALTAR, the Brigade quickly resumed routine patrolling through its area of operations. On September 21st, the 1/327th moved to the An Khe Pass to relieve the 2/502nd's lead elements from the 1st Cavalry Division began arriving at An Khe. The "cavalry had arrived" in the heart of "Indian country" without suffering a single casualty, courtesy of the soldiers of the 1st Brigade, 101st Airborne Division.

Having successfully screened the arrival and deployment of the 1st Cavalry Division, the 1st Brigade was immediately given a similar mission to secure a base of operations at An Nhon for the first South Korean division to arrive in South Vietnam—the Republic of Korea Capital (Tiger) Division. Unlike the mountainous terrain around An Khe, the area in the immediate vicinity of An Nhon consisted of expansive flatlands of rice paddies, interspersed with a large number of small villages nestled amid a few low hills. After establishing a base camp perimeter near An Nhon, the three battalions began extensive patrolling through the immediate area. The brigade conducted a series of ten battalion-sized operations, between October and early November, the largest of which was called Operation SAYONARA. The individual operations made sporadic contact with small enemy groups and resulted in the detainment of large numbers of suspected VC. Major Viet Cong units avoided detection, however, unwilling to risk destruction at the hands of the Screaming Eagles carrying out operations in the midst of torrential monsoon rains.

The most significant event of the entire operation was the chance discovery of over 200 tons of cached rice. Dubbed Operation RICE BIN, the effort to remove the huge cache proved to be a difficult task. For five days, under adverse weather conditions, helicopters, APCs, and even VC prisoners were utilized to remove the huge supply of captured rice. To its credit, the brigade succeeded in relocating all but eight tons of rice, which was left behind for the local villagers.

On November 15th the last elements of the brigade turned over defensive responsibility for the area to the ROK Capital Division, and moved south to join the rest of the 1st Brigade, busily engaged in constructing a permanent base camp at Phan Rang.

Phan Rang, a coastal area twenty-five miles south of Cam Ranh Bay, proved to be an in-country R&R area for the weary troopers of the 1st Brigade. Secure from any known VC activity, Phan Rang allowed the Brigade its first break from continuous field operations since its arrival in Vietnam. Although local patrols were still conducted as a precautionary measure and a training aid, the entire Brigade enjoyed the short standdown from combat operations. The rugged paratroopers were even able to make a few parachute jumps in order to keep their "jump pay" requirements current.

But the party ended two weeks later, when the 1/327th and the 2/502nd received orders to move to Bien Hoa near Saigon to counter increased enemy activity in that area. A joint operation involving the 1st Brigade, the 1st Infantry Division, the 173rd Airborne Brigade, and Australian and ARVN troops was already getting underway. It would be given the name Operation CHECKERBOARD.

The two battalions of the 1st Brigade assumed defensive responsibility for the Bien Hoa air base on November 30th. Screaming Eagles patrolled outside the perimeter of Bien Hoa until December 8th, with only light enemy contact to show for their efforts. On December 9th, the two maneuver battalions departed for Lai Khe by motor convoy, where they were attached to the 1st Infantry Division as part of Operation CHECKERBOARD. The 1/327th quickly ran into VC command detonated mines a few miles from Ben Cat, losing three vehicles, and suffering five men killed and ten more wounded. When they finally pulled into Lai Khe, they hurriedly prepared defensive positions and prepared themselves for offensive deployment.

In the opening phase of Operation CHECKERBOARD, the 1/327th air-assaulted into an unsecured LZ to set up as a blocking force, while the 2/502nd and a maneuver battalion from the 3rd Brigade of the 1st Infantry

Division combined to conduct a sweep toward them.

The 1/327th assaulted into a hot LZ, but the enemy broke contact immediately as the paratroopers expanded their perimeter. Phase One produced no significant results, and the operation moved into Phase Two.

In Phase Two of the operation, the 2/502nd secured the original LZ used by the 1/327th. Paratroopers from the 1/327th then moved out in a search and destroy mission to the north. They quickly discovered a cache of 15,000 pounds of rice; a large logistical complex containing food, clothing, and ammunition; and a small fuel cache containing cans of gasoline. Held up in their search by numerous booby-traps and the time it took to destroy the caches, the battalion was forced to spend the night of December 13th set up in the open in a hasty defensive perimeter. Later in the night, ambush patrols "outside the wire" radioed that two VC companies were moving toward the battalion perimeter. "Time-on-target" artillery was called in, resulting in numerous screams from the target area. A sweep at first light discovered a number of heavy blood trails leading away from the scene of carnage. The 1/327th then rejoined the 2/502nd and established a joint perimeter from which platoon and company-sized patrols were dispatched to look for any remaining VC units still in the vicinity.

In this third and final phase of Operation CHECKERBOARD, 101st patrols uncovered a carefully concealed hospital complex and several Viet Cong base camps in various stages of construction. Although there were several encounters with small VC patrols, large main-force units avoided engaging the Screaming Eagles. Operation CHECKERBOARD terminated on December 16th, and the two 1st Brigade battalions returned to the brigade base camp at Phan Rang. The entire brigade spent the remainder of December, 1965, conducting security patrols in the Phan Rang area. The 2/327nd conducted a parachute proficiency jump on December 31st. The paratroopers of the 1st Brigade looked forward to 1966 as being the year that would see the destruction of the Viet Cong. If they had only known it was but the beginning of eight more years of an expanding war!

THE BEGINNING OF 1966 saw the 1st Brigade engaged in security and screening operations to protect the Vietnamese rice harvest in the coastal areas of the central South Vietnamese provinces. In conjunction with the recently arrived Korean 2nd Marine Brigade and the 47th ARVN Regiment, two battalions from the 1st Brigade, the 2/327th and 2/502nd, moved north from Phan Rang by Air Force C-123s and C-130s and a Navy LST to set up base camps near Tuy Hoa. The 1/327th remained behind to secure the brigade base area at Phan Rang. The Tuy Hoa operation, called Operation VAN BUREN, was officially kicked off on January 15, 1966. Both 101st battalions had established base areas two days after their arrival, and began running patrols around Tuy Hoa on January 18. On January 21, Company B 2/502nd landed at Hoi Tin and helped to evacuate the Mang Lang orphanage to Tuy Hoa. The soldiers of Bravo Company sponsored the Catholic orphanage during their stay in the area, providing for the welfare of the displaced orphans as they adapted to their new home.

On January 28, 1966, the brigade commander, Colonel James S. Timothy, was replaced by Brigadier General Willard Pearson, who had been serving as the assistant division commander for the 101st Airborne Division back at Fort Campbell, Kentucky. Under the leadership of its new commander, the Brigade immediately intensified its offensive operations. Operation VAN BUREN produced significant contacts with main-force VC units.

On February 6, the 2/502nd made heavy contact with a VC battalion. Two days later, Lieutenant Colonel "Hank" Emerson's "Strike Force" troopers again initiated contact with a large NVA unit, and with the aid of a task force from its recently arrived sister battalion, the 1/327th, commanded by Lieutenant Colonel Joe Rogers, succeeded in inflicting heavy casualties on the enemy, killing over 100 NVA—66 confirmed by actual body count. It was during this action the Brigade's first Congressional Medal of Honor was earned by 1st Lieutenant James A. Gardner, commanding officer of the 1/327th's reconnaissance platoon, better known as "Tiger Force."

Charlie Company 2/502nd had been pinned down in the ruins of a bombed-out village called My Canh 2 by a large NVA force of unknown size. Task Force Hackworth, commanded by the legendary Major David Hackworth, the 1/327th's Operations officer, consisting of the 1/ 327th's Bravo Company and Tiger Force elements, combat assaulted into the area to come to the relief of the trapped "Strike Force" company. With Bravo Company moving into an ambush position, Major Hackworth ordered Lieutenant Gardner's Tiger Force to roll up the enemy's flank and push it into the arms of Bravo's waiting troopers. Advancing on line across an open rice paddy, Gardner's paratroopers closed on the enemy positions dug into a dense hedgerow. The entrenched enemy soldiers from the NVA 95th Regiment allowed the Americans to close within twenty meters before they opened fire, killing and wounding a majority of the Tiger Force troopers. Those who survived the initial onslaught immediately charged the hedgerow where bloody hand-to-hand fighting ensued. The Tigers succeeded in taking the tree line but were held up again in the enemy trench line by four well-placed NVA machine guns. Gardner saw that his attacking Tiger Force troopers had stalled and were in danger of being destroyed. Taking as many grenades as he could carry, he courageously charged the machine gun positions. He succeeded in knocking out the first one with a grenade and moved on to the next. He tossed a grenade into the bunker, only to have it thrown back out at him. It exploded, wounding Gardner. Refusing to give up, the young officer pitched another grenade into the bunker, successfully destroying it. Bleeding badly, the young officer moved on, wiping out an NVA anti-aircraft emplacement, before falling mortally wounded when the NVA in the final bunker fired a burst of machine gun fire into his chest. It was reported that when he was hit, he turned and said, "It's the best I can do!" For his actions that day, 1st Lieutenant James A. Gardner was posthumously awarded the Congressional Medal of Honor. It was the first such award for a member of the division since World War II. But it would not be the last.

The battle would go down as a U.S. victory, but the price had been very heavy. The task force alone had suffered 26 KIA and 28 WIA. The NVA had prepared their defenses well, and had gone toe-to-toe with the attacking American forces. The battle would be a harbinger of things to come.

Three more weeks in the Tuy Hoa area uncovered numerous supply caches and precipitated sporadic contact with the suddenly elusive NVA/VC forces. Operation VAN BUREN finally came to an end on February 20. Thanks to the protective paratrooper barrier thrown around Tuy Hoa, its residents had been able to harvest over 30,000 tons of rice, much of which would have ended up in the hands of the enemy. VC cooking pots would be empty for months to come because of the aggressive actions of the 1st Brigade. Operation VAN BUREN had resulted in heavy losses for the enemy, with 679 confirmed KIA and 49 captured during the U.S. deployment in the vicinity of Tuy Hoa. Over 4,700 area residents had been removed from the influence and control of the VC by their relocation to safe areas. In addition, nearly 200 hundred Viet Cong guerrillas defected to American forces during Operation VAN BUREN.

WITH THE RICE harvest successfully "in the bag," the entire 1st Brigade was ordered to remain in the Tuy Hoa area to continue offensive operations to the north and west of the city. Their mission was to locate the 95th NVA Regiment and destroy it. It was given the official name, Operation HARRISON, and would begin on February 21. This time the Brigade's three maneuver battalions would employ checkerboard patrolling operations, pioneered by the 2/502nd's commander, Lieutenant Colonel Hank Emerson, better known as the "Gunfighter." This involved dividing a company operational area into grids and then sending out a large number of platoon-sized or smaller patrols. If nothing was discovered within a particular patrol grid, the patrol would move diagonally into the next grid, skipping the grids on its four borders. This enabled the battalions to cover five times the ground it normally covered. The concept operated under the premise that thoroughly searching a single grid would reveal any sign of enemy activity in adjoining grids. Emerson also emphasized night movement and ambushes, and ground entry into suspected hostile areas without extensive artillery preparation or helicopter activity. Emerson's theory was the traditional American methodology, preceding an operation, achieved little more than warning the enemy in the vicinity that U.S. military forces were on the way. Operation HARRISON also incorporated the first extensive use of long range patrols and night airmobile assaults.

Prior to the operation, the brigade had established a Long Range Reconnaissance Patrol detachment for the purpose of conducting tactical long range reconnaissance ahead of brigade maneuver elements. An absence of accurate and reliable intelligence concerning enemy activity in their AOs indicated a distinct need for such a reconnaissance capacity. Volunteers for the new "provisional" long range reconnaissance unit poured in from all over the brigade. The detachment was soon staffed by a well-qualified veteran force of recon men whose professionalism and ability would set the standard for future LRP (Long Range Patrol) and Ranger operations within the division.

The first significant contact of Operation HARRISON was made on the morning of March 4, by elements of the 1/327th. Acting on a tip from an elderly Vietnamese man that he had just seen "men from the North" wearing khaki and carrying "long stovepipes" moving toward the village of Thanh Phu. Companies A and B, just returning to camp from another operation, were quickly air-assaulted into the area from two different directions. Bravo Company immediately made contact outside of the village of My Phu, catching an NVA company on the move. Alpha Company also made contact as it moved up to encircle the enemy. The ensuing battle lasted the rest of the day. Tiger Force was brought in as a blocking force after dark to help close off the NVA escape routes.

When the smoke cleared early the next morning, 118 enemy bodies littered the battlefield. But again, as at My Canh, the cost of success had been very high—twenty-one U.S. paratroopers had paid the ultimate price for the victory.

A week later, the 2/502nd achieved a "first" when it conducted the first battalion-sized night airmobile operation. The 2/327th also had some successes when it attacked and destroyed a Viet Cong redoubt and seized a small weapons cache. When Operation HARRISON was officially terminated on March 25, the Brigade had done well, decimating two entire NVA battalions and throwing the local VC forces off balance.

Operation FILLMORE followed immediately behind Operation HARRISON. Running from March 25th to April 7th, the operation involved both the 1/327th and the 2/502nd. The 2/327th remained in the Tuy Hoa area until July 21, while the first two battalions were airlifted to Phan Thiet in mid-April. Operation FILLMORE was characterized by company-sized immediate reaction forces responding to intelligence gathered by numerous small reconnaissance elements. These tactics proved very effective and kept maximum pressure on NVA/VC units in and around the Tuy Hoa area.

The "Nomads" of the 1st Brigade remained for several months in Phan Thiet to counter what intelligence reports indicated was a large Viet Cong stronghold located somewhere along the boundary between II Corps and III Corps. Named Operation AUSTIN II, the two battalions of the Brigade were to work in conjunction with ARVN forces, Civilian Irregular Defense Groups, Popular Forces, Regional Forces, and National Police Units from Binh Thuan Province. The Brigade sent out a number of long range patrols into suspected VC sanctuaries, trying to locate the elusive enemy. Companies from the 1/327th and the 2/502nd acted as reaction forces for the long range patrols and Vietnamese units conducting operations nearby. Operation AUSTIN II came to an end on April 21st, netting only 21 enemy dead and the destruction of over a hundred VC emplacements. However, it succeeded in proving an American military force was capable of successfully coordinating joint operations with the South Vietnamese, something no other U.S. unit had been able to do.

On May 1st, the 1/327th and the 2/502nd, kicked off Operation AUSTIN IV in the Nhon Co area of Quang Duc Province near the Cambodian border north of Saigon. The two battalions were tasked with the mission of locating and breaking up NVA troop concentrations along the border and astride the II Corps-III Corps boundary. The two battalions conducted intensive patrols along the Cambodian border for eight days without making contact with the enemy. Then they received intelligence reports there was heavy enemy activity in the vicinity of Bu Gia Map in nearby Phuoc Long Province. Brigade dispatched Recondo Force, the recon company from the 2/502nd, into the area ahead of the rest of the battalion and the 1/327th, along with a task force from the 173rd Airborne Brigade located at Song Be. During normal checkerboard patrolling, an element from the 2/502nd captured an NVA prisoner, who under interrogation pointed out the location of an NVA battalion-sized ambush site. Recondo Force executed a flanking movement that sprung the ambush prematurely, resulting in an hour long firefight that left 35 enemy dead on the battlefield. With the element of surprise lost to them, the NVA broke contact and scattered in an effort to escape the battle. One of the NVA companies chanced into an artillery barrage along their escape route and was decimated. A second NVA prisoner later verified this. A B-52 arc-light on the following day caught more of the fleeing enemy soldiers and added to the impressive score of enemy dead being run up by the U.S. paratroopers. While the 2/502nd chased the surviving NVA across the border into Cambodia, the 1/327th swept to the south and east, uncovering a Viet Cong provincial headquarters and a recently abandoned

POW camp. Both enemy camps were subsequently searched and destroyed. Operation AUSTIN IV terminated on May 18th.

FROM MID-MAY to early June, the maneuver battalions of the 1st Brigade were dispersed in three separate locations. The 2/327th remained in Tuy Hoa, providing area security while standing down from major operations. The 1/327th and the 2/502nd were airlifted to Cheo Reo, the capital of Phu Bon Province, just south of Pleiku. Their mission was to serve as a reserve for I Field Force, operating in II Corps Tactical Zone. On May 28th, the 2/502nd moved from Cheo Reo to Pleiku and established a base camp near the II Corps USMACV compound. All three battalions conducted routine patrols during this period of relative inactivity, but the bulk of their effort was centered around rebuilding their strength, training, and resupplying. Brigadier General Pearson ordered an intense critique of prior unit actions from battalion down to squad level for the purpose of recording "lessons learned" so they could subsequently be imparted to new 1st Brigade replacements as they arrived in country. In the future, each new replacement would receive an intense eighty-hour bloc of instruction during a six day (and night) "P" (for proficiency) Training course designed to acclimate him to Vietnam and to enhance his ability to survive the initial phase of his tour. Taught at Phan Rang, the course was designed to improve a soldier's physical conditioning, familiarize him with the weapons and tactics (and those of the enemy) that he would be using in combat, while stressing the importance of intelligence collection and the maintenance of friendly relations with the Vietnamese populace. In addition, combat-seasoned officers and NCOs were selected to instruct squad leaders from each rifle company, cavalry troop, and engineer company at the Phan Rang base camp for six days of intensive leadership training in a Squad Leaders' Combat Reaction Course. In the eleven months the Brigade had served in Vietnam, it had paid an extremely heavy price in American lives to learn some valuable lessons. General Pearson wanted to insure these lessons would not be lost on the uninitiated. In the future, countless lives would be saved from lives that had been lost in the past.

REFRESHED BY ITS period of rest and recuperation, and sharpened by the additional training, the Brigade was ready when it was airlifted to Dak To in Kontum Province, in the heart of the Central Highlands to relieve an ARVN Regional Forces garrison besieged by a large NVA force at the Toumorong outpost twenty kilometers northeast of Dak To. The timely arrival of the 1/327th, along with the 42nd ARVN Regiment and the 21st ARVN Ranger Battalion in early June soon turned into more than MACV had bargained for. When the 2/502nd was airlifted to join the relief force on

June 7th, it ran head on into the 24th NVA Regiment, which was building up for a major drive from Dak Tan Kan Valley through Dak To to Kontum. The action began when a fire base west of Toumorong manned by Battery B 2/320th Field Artillery, and Company A 2/502nd, with elements of the 326th Engineer Battalion, were attacked by an estimated battalion of the 24th NVA Regiment. The initial assault, begun shortly after midnight, was savaged. One of the 105mm gun positions was twice lost and recaptured by Battery B artillerymen who killed 13 of the attacking NVA inside the artillery position. At dawn an additional 73 enemy bodies were found outside the American defensive perimeter. The action saw U.S. paratroopers fix bayonets to retake the captured artillery tube, and NVA soldiers attacking behind a 122mm rocket barrage with bugles and whistles blowing. For his heroic actions in defending his artillery pieces, the battery commander, Captain Don Whalen was awarded the DSC. The battle for Toumorong was over but the campaign at Dak To was just beginning. When the relief force from the 1/327th finally climbed the heights to the beleaguered CIDG camp, they pressed on beyond it, only to run headlong into the "meat" of the 24th NVA Regiment. Surprisingly, the enemy was no longer on the run. The mountains around Dak To belonged to them, and they had decided to stay and fight for it. From captured NVA prisoners, Brigade S-2 soon learned the 24th NVA Regiment had moved into the area in November of 1965. They had spent the next seven months digging in and preparing strong, mutually supportive fighting positions.

When the 1/327th and the 2/502nd discovered they were up against a hard-core NVA regiment that wasn't giving any indication it intended to cut and run for the border, General Pearson immediately contacted MACV and requested additional troops. All he got was a company from Tuy Hoa and a tongue-in-cheek promise if they ran into more than they could handle, the 1st Cav would "probably" come in to give them a helping hand. The 1/327th found "more than they could handle" just a short walk outside the wire at Toumorong. They didn't even have to look for it, because "it" was looking for them. Advancing in a three-pronged echelon, three companies abreast, each prong ran head on into heavily entrenched enemy forces blocking access to the high ground above the valley. Within minutes all three companies were embroiled in contact and up to their necks in alligators. The NVA had prepared their trap well. In six long days of jab and parry, attack and withdraw, the warriors of the 1/327th made little impression on the entrenched NVA. On the sixth day, now physically exhausted and suffering from a major loss of motivation, the Screaming Eagle battalion paused to catch its breath. It was at that moment two fresh NVA companies attacked the battalion's isolated Tiger Force recon platoon. The Tiger Force troopers fought off the NVA companies but were very nearly overrun in the process. The other three companies of the 1/327th pulled back into separate defensive perimeters and fought ferociously to avoid encirclement. Tiger Force, trapped in the middle of an NVA base camp, had already taken heavy casualties, and its new commander was showing signs of coming unglued under the intense strain of close combat. Charlie Company, commanded by Captain Wayne Dill, moved out of its perimeter to reinforce Tiger Force and immediately found itself in the midst of a wild battle for its own survival. The NVA seemed to be everywhere.

General Pearson went for the "brass ring" and decided to insert the 2/502nd behind the NVA front lines and deep into the heart of their fortifications. Under cover of monsoon mists, the companies of the O' Deuce combat assaulted into a scattered number of small LZs and quickly consolidated their positions before the surprised NVA had a chance to turn and destroy them piecemeal. As the O' Deuce moved out in a checkerboard configuration designed to force the NVA elements facing the 1/327th into separate pockets, no one realized they were charging up the back of an enraged dragon.

Major David Hackworth put Charlie Company 2/502nd, under his operational control, and moved them into a blocking position to cut off what he believed would be a retreating 24th NVA Regiment, while Alpha and Bravo companies maneuvered to relieve the 1/327th. But the 24th NVA Regiment was not cooperating with Hackworth's well-designed plan, and worst of all, they were definitely not retreating.

With Tiger Force and C Company 1/327th pinned down and in danger of being chopped to pieces, Captain Ben Willis, Alpha Company 1/327th's commanding officer, attempted to go to the rescue of Tiger Force and Charlie Company 1/327th, and by nightfall had linked up with the survivors of the two trapped units. Their forces now consolidated, the three 1/327th elements managed to survive the night.

On the morning of June 9th, having evacuated their most critically wounded, Alpha and Charlie companies 1/327th, along with the remnants of Tiger Force began to withdraw back toward Toumorong. Before they could reach the security of the camp, Lieutenant Colonel Hank Emerson, the commander of the O' Deuce, radioed Hackworth his Charlie element was pinned down and in imminent danger of being overrun. Alpha Company 1/327th was the only unit in position to effect a rescue. Captain Ben Willis, without complaint, turned his worn out soldiers around and moved out to rescue their trapped brothers. Charlie Company 2/502nd had gotten itself encircled moving into position to cut off the escaping 24th NVA Regiment. Surrounded, taking heavy losses, and believing he was being overrun, with the NVA troops hugging his perimeter, Captain William S. Carpenter, Jr., Charlie Company's commander, took the only course of action available to him—he called in napalm on his own positions. The air strike, coming within thirty meters of his perimeter, enabled Carpenter to pull back another 125 meters as a second strike was called. Charlie Company survived the night in a driving rainstorm. Low on ammo, hiding from NVA probes trying to locate and kill the wounded, individual Charlie Company survivors fought off several attempts to penetrate its new positions. During the night, Alpha Company 1/327th finally reached them and effected a link-up. Many of the Charlie Company survivors credit their lives to the inspiration and confidence provided by their legendary First Sergeant Walter "Ski" Sabalauski, who seemed to be everywhere during the night. The 55-year old NCO's courage and leadership kept many of the Strike Force soldiers from giving up during the long and terrible night. Captain William S. Carpenter and Sabalauski were awarded the Distinguished Service Cross for their heroism. With both the 1/327th and the 2/502nd now out of the fire and back into the frying pan, Task Force Schroeder, a relief force consisting of volunteers from the 2/502nd Battalion rear at Phan Rang and commanded by the 2/502nd executive officer, Lieutenant Colonel Don Schroeder, arrived on the scene. All eighty-four of the volunteers were O' Deuce paratroopers who had survived their tour and were waiting to go home. Combat-assaulting onto the high ground above the encircled companies, they drove off the NVA entrenched on the ridge crest and established a small landing zone, holding it until the besieged survivors of Alpha and Charlie companies struggled uphill and were extracted. Nine of the volunteers were wounded, but through their courageous efforts their comrades were saved from annihilation.

Now that the positions of the NVA regiment along the ridges lining the Dak Tan Kan Valley had been pretty well fixed by the points of contact over the past three days, the two Screaming Eagle battalions moved back in and executed a double-envelopment to prevent the NVA from using its escape routes. Then the battalions moved back, away from the NVA positions utilizing dummy radio traffic to fix the enemy in place. On the 13th of June, I Field Force brought in an arc-light in an effort to bring the curtain down on the six-day show. Thirty minutes later 1/327th and the 2/502nd went in right behind the bombers and discovered nearly two hundred enemy bodies among the wreckage of a systematic gridwork of well-prepared bunkers, some over fifty feet deep. The battalions remained in the area for a few days, chasing down survivors of the 24th NVA Regiment as they fled back across the border into Laos, until Operation HAWTHORNE was officially terminated on June 20th.

Operation HAWTHORNE had succeeded in blunting the NVA's well-organized plan to move against Kontum. It was one of the most successful military operations of the war to date. An entire major enemy unit had been rendered combat ineffective. The 24th NVA Regiment had suffered over 1200 KIA in its encounter with the 1st Brigade, compared to U.S. losses of

48 dead and 239 wounded.

The I Field Force commander, General Stanley Larsen, on a trip to the U.S. following the action at Toumorong, publicly announced that the 1st Brigade of the 101st Airborne Division was "the best fighting unit in Vietnam." For its efforts during Operation HAWTHORNE, the 1st Brigade was awarded the Presidential Unit Citation for extraordinary heroism.

After Operation HAWTHORNE, the 1/327th and the 2/502nd withdrew to Dak To for a brief rest and recuperation. Three days later, Operation BEAUREGARD commenced as the two battalions moved back into the area recently occupied by the 24th NVA Regiment. Their mission was to locate and destroy any elements of the NVA regiment that were still in the vicinity of Toumorong.

The battalions rotated companies into the area of operations over five-day periods. Most of the companies infiltrated into the operational areas at night, carrying five days' rations. This was done so that the NVA would not be able to locate the Screaming Eagles by watching where their helicopters went in. The "Above the Rest" and "Strike Force" soldiers discovered a few small rice caches, but enemy contact was almost non-existent. The destruction of the 24th NVA Regiment was complete. The stunned survivors had withdrawn to their sanctuaries in Laos. On July 6th, a possible contact with a small enemy unit eighteen miles north of Dak To was developed by a Brigade long range reconnaissance patrol. Two companies air-assaulted into the area to sweep toward a third company acting as a blocking force. The enemy avoided contact but succeeded in leading one of the companies into an unmarked Special Forces mine field. When the dust had settled, five O' Deuce soldiers were dead. All the 1st Brigade elements returned to their base camp by July 15th, and Operation BEAUREGARD was concluded. The two battalions were then air-lifted back to Tuy Hoa to rejoin the 2/327th.

WHILE THE 1/327TH and the 2/502nd were busy destroying NVA units throughout II Corps and III Corps, the 2/327th was still back at Tuy Hoa carrying out the mission requirement of Operation FILLMORE—to protect the rice bowl of Phu Yen Province. On June 19th the 1st Cavalry Division kicked off Operation NATHAN HALE. The 2/327th, commanded by Lieutenant Colonel Joseph Wasco Jr. (less Company B which was still participating in Operation HAWTHORNE with the rest of the Brigade) was placed under the operational control of the 1st Cavalry Division, and assigned the task of locating a suspected enemy force of unknown size operating in the area west of Tuy An.

Company C, 2/327th, air-assaulted into position in the heart of the Trung Luong Valley and immediately began a search of the area. It wasn't long before it was in heavy contact with the enemy. The battle lasted all day, with the NVA hugging close to the Charlie Company positions making air strikes and artillery support risky. By dark the company withdrew to a nearby sugarloaf hill and established a defensive perimeter. The NVA followed after them and continued attacking the American positions throughout the night and into the next day.

Alpha Company, 1/327th, commanded by Captain Charles T. Furgeson, combat assaulted into an area near Don Tre to relieve some battered CIDG companies. Within an hour of landing they were engaged by sniper fire from an unknown enemy force. Two of Alpha's platoons swept the village where the fire was coming from and took into custody 17 Viet Cong suspects. The next morning, Alpha Company was ordered to move out to reinforce Charlie Company which was still in contact. One of its platoons walked head on into an NVA ambush at the edge of a hamlet. The battle lasted all day, through the night, and into the morning of the 21st, with Alpha Company attempting to assault the village three times. The final U.S. assault was in conjunction with the arrival of Charlie Company 1/8th from a 1st Cavalry battalion that had been air-lifted into the battle. After the battle, U.S. forces discovered the entire area was honeycombed with a myriad gridwork of NVA tunnels.

Alpha Company, 2/327th, commanded by Captain Joseph Mack, was fed into the fray early in the afternoon of June 20th, combat assaulting into LZ Axe on a nearby mountain top called Hill 258. The NVA were waiting for them. They allowed the paratroopers to land, firing on them sweeping the LZ with small arms and automatic weapons fire. Heavy fighting raged all day, with a lack of water causing more of a problem than the enemy fire. By the end of the day, the enemy forces began to disengage, but Alpha Company had taken heavy casualties and was still on the LZ.

Just before dark on the 20th, Bravo Company, 1/8th from the 1st Air Cav, commanded by Captain Gerald E. Plummer, combat assaulted unopposed into LZ Axe. They spent the entire night in a defensive position on the mountain, then moved out at first light on the 21st to relieve Charlie Company, 2/327th, still holding out on the sugarloaf in the Trung Luong Valley. The two units joined before dark and remained in a defensive position on the sugarloaf overnight. Mortared and probed by grenades throughout the night, the two companies were ready when the NVA attacked at first light. The battle lasted until approximately 1000 hours when the NVA withdrew.

Charlie Company, 1/8th Cav landed on Hill 258 to replace the battle ravaged Alpha Company, 2/327th, which was withdrawn from the operation at 1430 hours on June 21st. Only 47 of the 144 soldiers who had begun the assault with Alpha Company were still on the ground. The majority of the 97 casualties were heat related, but they were casualties just the same.

Charlie Company 1/8th then moved off the hill to assault down into the Trung Luong Valley.

On the third day, additional reinforcements arrived in the form of Bravo Company, 2/327, just back from Operation HAWTHORNE, and the majority of the troops assigned to battalion headquarters company. In addition, two entire battalions from the 1st Cavalry Division had to be fed into the meat grinder before the remnants of the 18B NVA Regiment decided to call it a day and go home. The additional reinforcements enabled the Screaming Eagle battalion to finally break out of its defensive perimeter and go back on the offensive. The battle officially ended on the morning of June 22nd, when the surviving NVA withdrew. When Operation NATHAN HALE officially concluded on July 1st, the Screaming Eagle battalion had been credited with 237 enemy killed and 14 captured.

Mid-July found the Brigade back at Tuy Hoa, united again for the first time since April. With adequate time to rebuild and re-equip its shattered battalions, the Screaming Eagles prepared for Operation JOHN PAUL JONES. Their mission would be to secure Vung Ro Bay and the highway north out of Tuy Hoa, and, as in Operation FILLMORE, to protect the important rice harvest in Phu Yen Province.

Operation JOHN PAUL JONES successfully concluded on September 5th, and was succeeded by Operation SEWARD, again seeing the Brigade tasked with the mission of guaranteeing a successful rice harvest in the area. Operation SEWARD ended on October 24th. The only event during the operation occurred on the night of September 17th, when the command post of Company B 2/327th was overwhelmed by a surprise attack from a reinforced Viet Cong company. When the smoke cleared, the company commander, the executive officer, and the company FO were among the American dead. But during the two operations, Brigade companies utilizing saturation patrolling, extensive night ambushes, and occasional sweeps through the neighboring mountains, accounted for over 200 enemy dead.

In late October, the 1st Brigade turned over responsibility for the security of the area around Tuy Hoa to elements of the Republic of Korea 9th (White Horse) Division and the U.S. 4th Infantry (Ivy) Division, which had just arrived in Vietnam.

The Brigade moved to a secured area on the coast south of Tuy Hoa, and spent several days resting and recuperating from their nomadic role as the MACV "Fire Brigade." During this lull in the action, the Brigade was notified to ready itself for Operation GERONIMO I. Intelligence reports indicated the 95th NVA Regiment was operating in the mountains in western Phu Yen Province, and their presence was a threat to the rice bowl area around Tuy Hoa. Once again, the battalions of the 1st Brigade were given the task of finding, fixing, and finishing the enemy.

On October 31st, the 1/327th infiltrated into an area south of the Son Be River. Setting up company-sized bases, the battalion stayed in the area for a week sending out numerous small reconnaissance patrols to develop contact with the enemy.

On November 6th, all three battalions of the 1st Brigade air-assaulted into the Dong Tre area. Advancing in three different directions, all three battalions made significant contacts within the first two days of the operation.

On November 8th, companies from the 1/327th engaged approximately 100 NVA in what proved to be a vicious fight. Two days later, on November 10th, the 2/502nd, now under command of Lieutenant Colonel Frank L. Dietrich, surrounded the 5th Battalion of the 95th NVA Regiment. Over a two day period, paratroopers from the O' Duece kept intense pressure on the entrapped NVA battalion, as PSYOPS units continually called for the enemy to surrender. Many of the NVA, realizing the situation was hopeless, surrendered to the paratroopers. When the battle ended the next day, enemy losses stood at 13 KIA, with another 35 captured. Large amounts of weapons and equipment were discovered inside the overrun NVA positions. The total NVA losses during Operation GERONIMO would exceed 150 KIA.

Operation GERONIMO continued with its search and destroy operations amid torrential monsoon rains until December 4th, when the Brigade was pulled back to Tuy Hoa for a much needed rest.

With many 1st Brigade troopers recovering from foot problems brought on by continuous patrolling in the rain-soaked coastal plains, no one was happy when orders came down three days later to prepare to move out by airlift for Operation PICKETT in the mountains west of Kontum in the heart of the Central Highlands. On December 9th and 10th, all three battalions deployed into landing zones in and around the Plei Trap and Dak Akoi valleys, twenty-four miles west of Kontum. It was the first time in the Vietnam War an entire brigade had been moved from one place to another in less than 48 hours.

The battalions moved out on search and destroy operations and immediately encountered well-used enemy trail networks, base camps, and numerous weapons and food caches. However, enemy contact was light. The NVA had made the decision to pull out rather than tangle with the infamous Screaming Eagles.

On December 26th, the 2/327th was pulled out of the field to begin a one-week period of training at a base near Kontum, which included a parachute jump. The battalion traded places with the 1/327th on January 2nd, which in turn, swapped roles with the 2/502nd on January 9th. Throughout Operation PICKETT, the NVA units in the area west of Kontum avoided contact, except for a few squad-sized actions.

With allied forces gaining offensive momentum, Headquarters, I Field Force ordered the 1st Brigade of the 101st Airborne Division to move 400 miles south to its base camp at Phan Rang and to prepare for Operation FARRAGUT, with the mission of going after enemy secret base camps in Binh Thuan, Ninh Thuan, and Lam Dong provinces. The Brigade left Kontum on January 21st by air and by land. The motorized convoy completed the trip to Phan Rang without incident in six days. It was the longest overland military convoy made over Highway 1 to that date. For most of the Brigade's soldiers, it was the first time they had been at their base camp.

However, they weren't there for long. The Screaming Eagles stayed in Phan Rang just long enough to see off their old brigade commander, Brigadier General Willard Pearson, and welcome aboard their new commanding general, Brigadier General S. H. Matheson. Like Pearson, Matheson's last duty station was Assistant Division Commander of the 101st Airborne Division at Ft. Campbell.

General Matheson had little time to get comfortable in his new role, for as quickly as the change of command ceremony came to an end, the hard-charging brigade initiated Operation FARRAGUT.

Hard on the heels of a B-52 strike, elements of the 2/502nd conducted a feint against a suspected NVA base camp approximately twenty klicks north of Phan Rang.

While the enemy was recovering from the massive arc-light, and his attention was focused on the sweeping elements of the O' Duece, the 2/327th combat assaulted into a second suspected enemy base camp nearby. Without giving the enemy a chance to recover from this new turn of events, the 2/502nd wheeled and moved overland toward the second area also. Both battalions conducted coordinated search and destroy operations in their Area of Operations over the period of January 28-29, but with minimal enemy contact. Caught unprepared by the swiftness of the Brigade's assault, the enemy had gone to ground. The Brigade succeeded in opening the road from Phan Rang to Song Mao, which had been in enemy hands for over a year. On the night of January 30th, the 2/502nd was extracted by helicopter to regroup in preparation for employment with the 1/327th in Operation GATLING. The 2/327th remained in the AO (Area of Operations) and continued its search and destroy efforts as part of Operation FARRAGUT until February 16th. Operation FARRAGUT resulted in only 115 enemy killed, but the South Vietnamese government's Chieu Hoi—"Open Arms"—program had picked up momentum with 475 enemy soldiers giving up freely to allied forces.

Operation GATLING was carried out in Lam Dong, Binh Tuy and Bin Tuan provinces during the month of February. Like Operation FARRAGUT, Operation GATLING was planned in response to intelligence reports indicating a suspected secret meeting place for a high level enemy command conference in Lam Dong Province. Precautions were taken to insure surprise, but an arc-light on February 1st on the suspected location, followed by a combat assault by the 2/502nd and the 1/327th discovered no sign of the enemy. The two battalions spent two weeks running search and destroy operations in the area without contact.

On February 17th, the two battalions rejoined the 2/327th in conducting search and destroy patrols in the Le Hong Phong Forest and Di Linh areas until February 28th. The enemy had remained unwilling to come out and play. In spite of the limited contact during the two operations, the Brigade was credited with destroying a VC province headquarters and a district headquarters, and disrupted VC tax collection and recruiting efforts in the province. The operations also revealed a scarcity of water which made it unlikely the AO could support enemy or friendly forces during the dry season without organized and reliable resupply. In addition, the Brigade discovered with irrefutable proof that NVA troops were being integrated into VC units to maintain the strength and the will to fight of those units.

Headquarters, I Field Force ordered the Brigade to move to Khan Duong, along the coast north of Phan Rang, and to prepare for Operation SUMMERALL in Khanh Hoa, Phu Yen, and Darlac provinces. Operation SUMMERALL began on March 29th with half the Brigade and three-quarters of its vehicles moving into the area of operation by road convoy. Two convoys, one starting out from Tuy Hoa with 166 vehicles and another originating at Phan Rang with 248 vehicles, reached Khanh Duong on Highway 21 without hitting a single ambush, mine or sniper. The balance of the Brigade's personnel were airlifted from Phan Rang by C-130.

On March 30th, the 2/327th kicked off Operation SUMMERALL with an air assault northeast of Khanh Duong. Intended as a diversion, it masked the Brigade's real intention to converge on the Buon Mi Ga area. Three days later, the 1/327th and the 2/502nd began operations around Buon Mi Ga.

Operation SUMMERALL proved to be much like Operation FARRAGUT—a lot of time beating the bush with little or no contact to reward for the effort. One half of the Brigade's enemy body count of 29 were killed by the provisional LRRP (Long Range Reconnaissance Patrol) detachment, commanded by 1st Lieutenant Dan McIsaac. Nine VC were killed in one operation when a six-man team split into two-man sections to capture a single VC the team had observed. Following his trail, a two-man element, Sergeant Jim Cody and Sp4 Virgil Palk, walked into what proved to be a company-sized VC base camp. Believing it was only a small camp, the two recon men fired on a group of astonished Viet Cong. In the confusion of everyone trying to distance themselves from the source of the gunfire, the two Lurps escaped. The next day, leading an infantry platoon back into the camp, the Lurps captured a VC suspect who told them the camp was a Viet Cong provincial headquarters, and had been occupied by over 100 Viet Cong guerrillas when the two Americans had "attacked." Nine Viet Cong had been killed. Operation SUMMERALL was concluded on April 29th without a single major contact.

The Brigade stood at Khanh Duong until May 1st, when it began movement to Duc Pho in Quang Ngai province far up the coast in I Corps. The Brigade was placed under the operational control of Task Force OREGON.

Task Force OREGON had been created in response to the general military situation existing in South Vietnam in the early part of 1967. While the Brigade had been busily engaged in operations along the coast in II Corps, the major MACV effort had been directed at relieving pressure against Saigon in III Corps. Operations CEDAR FALLS and JUNCTION CITY had proven very successful and had given MACV the offensive momentum in III Corps it had been seeking. To make up for its losses in III Corps, the enemy began to exert increasing pressure on U.S. and ARVN forces in I Corps. Unable to spare a division from operations currently going on in II and III Corps, MACV created Task Force OREGON in an attempt to consolidate its momentum without losing its gains around Saigon. Creating a provisional HQ out of I Field Force assets, borrowing support units from various U.S. Army commands, and consolidating three separate and independent brigades—the 196th Light Infantry Brigade, the 3rd Brigade of the 25th Infantry (Tropical Lightning) Division, and the 1st Brigade of the 101st Airborne Division—under a single command, MACV succeeded in forming Task Force OREGON.

The arrival of Task Force OREGON in southern I Corps in May 1967, gave the hard-pressed Marines working the AO a little breathing room, and allowed them to move units that had been tied up in Quang Ngai Province north to reinforce the DMZ. This also allowed the 1st Cavalry Division to extend its operations north along the coastal plain, opening up Highway 1 all the way to DaNang.

Phase One of Operation MALHEUR—or MALHEUR I—began on May 11th, with air assaults by the 1/327th and the 2/502nd into the mountains west of Duc Pho. Their mission was to locate and destroy VC/NVA forces, and neutralize their base camps. Their sister battalion, the 2/327th, combat assaulted into the same area the next day to establish a blocking position to cut off escaping enemy units. During the early phase of this Operation, the 1st Brigade was awarded its second Congressional Medal of Honor. Each of the three battalions had made contact with enemy units soon after inserting in their AOs. The 2/502nd was busy recovering casualties from one of these contacts. Sp4 Dale E. Wayrynen, a member of Bravo Company, 2/502nd, was assisting in the evacuation of his company's wounded when his platoon blundered into a fortified enemy bunker. The point man, directly in the initial line of fire from the enemy emplacement, was hit and went down. Without regard for his own welfare, Specialist Wayrynen immediately rushed forward and dragged the wounded man to the safety of his platoon. Suddenly, an enemy hand grenade landed among the clustered paratroopers. Wayrynen shouted a warning to his fellow soldiers and fell across the grenade, smothering the blast with his body. His action saved the lives of his platoon leader and fellow squad members.

As the well-equipped enemy soldiers of the 2nd VC Regiment attempted to break contact, they collided repeatedly with elements of the three battalions. By June 7th, the Brigade had killed 399 of the enemy and captured 157 weapons, 78 tons of rice and more than 40 tons of salt.

Intelligence reports arrived indicating survivors of the VC regiment were fleeing to the northwest in an attempt to evade the Brigade. On June 8th and 9th, the 2/327th and the 2/502nd were redeployed to cut off the fleeing VC. The two battalions combat assaulted into the area west of the Song Be valley and began conducting intense offensive operations in an attempt to locate the 2nd VC Regiment. They didn't have far to look. Each battalion found itself heavily engaged in numerous contacts within hours of inserting into the mountains overlooking the Song Be valley. But within a few days the enemy once again broke contact. Intelligence reported they had had enough and were withdrawing from the area.

The province chief requested the Brigade's assistance in evacuating the civilian population from the rich rice growing areas of the Song Be and Song Tra Can valleys. The VC had been extracting a heavy burden in taxes and food from the local population for years.

This phase of the operation known as MALHEUR II lasted from June 15-22. During its sweep up the Song Tra Can valley, paratroopers from the 1/327th made contact with the 1st VC Regiment at the mouth of the valley. However, the enemy unit decided not to follow the course of action taken by its sister regiment, and left the valley for safer points north. At the same time, the 2/327th launched an assault up the Song Be valley in search of remnants of the 2nd VC Regiment which were reported still in the area. The 2/502nd moved in to assist the 2/327th. On June 29th, the 1/327th gave up trying to locate the "ghosts" of the 1st VC Regiment and moved into the Song Be valley to assist its two sister battalions.

On July 3rd, the 1/327th was pulled from the field by the Task Force commander to conduct Operation LAKE. Operation LAKE would keep the "Above the Rest" troopers occupied with providing security for engineer units working on the portion of Highway 1 from Dien Troung to Sa Huynh. On July 14th, its mission completed, the 1/327th rejoined its sister battalions still searching for the survivors of the 2nd VC Regiment.

Operation MALHEUR II concluded on August 2nd. Over the three month period of combined operations, the Brigade had varying success at making and maintaining contact with the enemy. VC losses were over 800. The 1st Brigade paratroopers had collected over 300 weapons, 133 tons of salt, and 260 tons of rice. Friendly casualties were 81 dead and 594 wounded. In addition, the Screaming Eagles had successfully relocated 6,256 villagers and 1,341 head of cattle to the relative safety of government controlled areas at Nghia Hanh.

WITH HARDLY ENOUGH time to catch their breath, the 1st Brigade paratroopers were thrown into Operation HOOD RIVER. Quang Ngai Province was proving a hotbed of enemy activity, so MACV decided to maintain constant pressure on the enemy units operating in the province by keeping Task Force OREGON in their faces. HOOD RIVER was a four-pronged allied attack converging on a newly discovered enemy base area Intelligence believed was the location of the missing 1st VC Regiment and the 2nd NVA Division.

On the 2nd of August, two battalions of the poorly performing 2nd ARVN Division conducted an overland assault from Quang Ngai, while two battalions of ARVN rangers air-assaulted onto the high ground above the suspected enemy base area. Two ROK (Republic of Korea) battalions moved in on the area from the northwest. American forces consisting of the 2/327th and the 2/502nd inserted on the high ground just to the west of the enemy positions, while the 1/327th moved in to conduct sweeping search and destroy operations six miles to the south of the suspected NVA/VC base area, focusing their attention on likely avenues of escape from the massive Allied entrapment.

The terrain in the area consisted of steep, heavily foliated mountains. Temperatures at that time of the year consistently reached in excess of 100 degrees F, resulting in excessive heat casualties.

The operation lasted only eleven days and resulted in several sharp, small-unit clashes, but, once again, the major enemy units in the area proved to be elusive. Accurate sniper fire and entrenched NVA/VC squads effectively delayed the advancing allied elements while the bulk of the enemy forces escaped with most of their weapons and equipment intact. The search and destroy sweep by the 1/327th netted 63 enemy KIA with 42 weapons, 23 tons of rice, and three tons of salt. The 1st Brigade suffered two killed and 20 wounded, nearly all from the 2/327th. The nature of this operation typified the combat experiences of most American units in the Vietnam war to date. Operating almost entirely on agent reports and civilian intelligence, the Brigade discovered that only about half of this intell was reliable. This resulted in a lot of "ghost chasing" as 1st Brigade elements tried to close with and destroy the enemy. Although intelligence reports indicated the presence of a main-force VC regiment and a full-strength NVA division, prisoners taken during the operation proved to be no more than local guerrillas. There had been no indication the two main-force units described in the intell reports were ever in the area.

THE 1ST BRIGADE'S odyssey continued on August 13th, as its paratroopers deployed southwest of Chu Lai in Operation BENTON. The Brigade was assigned the task of locating and destroying NVA forces in the area, believed to be the 21st NVA Regiment and the elusive 2nd NVA Division. Intell also showed the probable presence of the 70th Battalion of the 1st VC Regiment.

On the morning of August 13th, the 2/327th air-assaulted into LZs in the mountainous jungle southwest of Chu Lai, closely followed that afternoon by the 2/502nd. The 1/327th, designated as the Brigade immediate reaction force, waited at Chu Lai.

Neither battalion encountered hostile fire on their LZs, but each made contact with enemy forces as soon as they moved away from their landing zones. Shortly after the 2/327th inserted, its tactical command post area was set ablaze by a "friendly" smoke grenade. By mid-afternoon, the grass fire had roared out of control and consumed the artillery battery firing in support of the battalion. Simultaneously, Bravo Company 2/502nd was forced to retreat to its original landing zone after its patrols ran into intense enemy resistance. That night, Bravo Company's third platoon perimeter was attacked by an estimated enemy company. Nearby, the 2/327th was also receiving night attacks by unknown enemy forces. This time the NVA was not proving as elusive as they had in previous operations.

There was little action on the second day of the operation, but on August 15th, Alpha Company 1/327th, air-assaulted into the area and found itself up to its elbows in NVA. The remainder of the Brigade's reaction force was committed. All three maneuver battalions continued to make sporadic contact with enemy forces during the remainder of Operation BENTON. However, the magnitude of the individual contacts began to decrease as NVA/VC forces pulled out of the area. When Operation BENTON officially ended on August 29th, it was apparent that such operations were discovering a familiar pattern was being established by the NVA/VC: heavy contact with enemy forces soon after insertion which usually retarded U.S. offensive operations, followed by days of diminishing contact with small local force units sacrificing themselves in delaying actions as the main-force NVA/VC units split into small groups and moved out of the area of operations. This was making it exceedingly difficult for the large American maneuver units to close with and destroy the enemy. In spite of the frustration caused by these new enemy tactics, Screaming Eagle paratroopers still accounted for 303 enemy killed, with 131 weapons, 31 tons of rice, and four tons of tea captured. A side-benefit of the Brigade's presence in heavily-populated Quang Nghia Province during Operation BENTON was the Viet Cong infrastructure was prevented from effecting the Vietnamese national elections.

The Brigade extracted from the mountains southwest of Chu Lai by helicopter and was then transported by C-130s to Duc Pho for a much needed standdown. But, as usual for the "Nomads of Vietnam," plans were already in the works to see that their well-deserved vacation was short-lived.

OPERATION COOK WAS launched on September 4th by the 1/327th. Basically a holding operation to prevent the enemy from interfering with the upcoming national elections, 'Above the Rest" troopers ran patrols in the northern reaches of the Song Be River valley, killing six enemy soldiers and capturing two weapons.

While Operation COOK was keeping the enemy off balance, Operation STRIKE FORCE, utilizing elements from the 2/502nd, conducted raids on two enemy prisoner-of-war camps. Both camps had been vacated about two weeks prior to the raid, but the O' Duece still succeeded in liberating sixteen South Vietnamese, and destroying the camps.

STILL OPCON TO Task Force OREGON (now designated the Americal Division), the Brigade returned to Chu Lai to kick off Operation WHEELER, which was to prove the Brigade's most significant action of 1967. Underway on September 11th, the Brigade finally encountered elements of the elusive 2nd NVA Division west of Tam Ky.

The 2nd NVA Division had an estimated strength of nearly 5,000 men. It was made up of the 3rd and 21st NVA Regiments, the 1st VC Regiment, and various support units, including engineer, artillery, anti-aircraft, and signal battalions. There were also independent VC forces in the area: the 70th VC Battalion, attached to the Quang Nam Province headquarters; and the 72nd Local Force Battalion, and seven local force companies. To make these enemy forces even more formidable, they had the support of most of the local population, since most of the province's districts had been under communist control for the past twenty-odd years.

The 1/327th air-assaulted into multiple landing zones among the lower mountains on the southern portion of the area of operations on the morning of September 11th. The next morning, the 2/327th and the 2/502nd combat assaulted into the northern and western portions of the area. The Brigade's three maneuver battalions assumed a semi-guerrilla profile by breaking into small saturation patrols, setting multiple squad-sized ambushes, implementing stay-behinds, conducting raids, maintaining a large and flexible area of operations, and limiting resupply missions. Designed to throw the enemy off-balance and promote favorable contact, the brigade's tactics seemed to misfire when the first week of Operation WHEELER produced only light contact, accounting for 76 enemy killed in seven days.

However, intelligence reports began coming indicating large enemy forces, including the 2nd NVA Division's headquarters, were located farther back in the mountains, ten miles west of the Brigade's current area of operations. The initial phase of the operation had surprised the enemy, and had forced him into consolidating with local VC forces in the area. On September 27th, Brigade units quickly redeployed to exploit this new situation. Over the next four days, numerous significant contacts developed as the enemy reacted to the Brigade's presence.

Enemy activity was also noted in the original area of operations, and the 23rd Infantry Division (Americal) placed the Brigade's reaction force, the 1/14th Infantry Battalion, and an additional battalion under the Brigade's operational control for use in that area.

On October 8th, Alpha Company 2/327th, slammed head-on into two NVA companies and lost 17 men KIA in a vicious firefight with savage hand-to-hand combat. This was the largest single encounter loss suffered by the Brigade since it arrived in Vietnam. The subsequent awarding of seven Silver Stars and a Distinguished Service Cross indicated the severity of the fighting.

Rainy, overcast weather set in, helping the enemy avoid further contact in the western portion of the area of operations. Taking advantage of the inability of the Brigade's companies to maneuver in the slippery, muddy mountains west of Tam Ky, the NVA/VC units tried to move eastward back into their original deployment areas. Brigade elements followed as soon as the weather permitted.

On October 14th, thirty-three days into the operation, contact was again established with large enemy units. On October 15th, Staff Sergeant Webster Anderson became the third member of the 1st Brigade to be awarded the Congressional Medal of Honor. His unit, Battery A, 2/320th Artillery, was in a defensive perimeter at its fire support base near Tam Ky when it was hit by a large NVA ground assault at 0300 hours. The intensity of the attack surprised and stunned the unprepared defenders. Realizing the fire base was in imminent danger of being overrun, Staff Sergeant Anderson mounted the exposed parapet of his howitzer position and directed his gun crew in placing accurate and devastating point-blank fire on the assaulting NVA. Two enemy hand grenades destroyed Anderson's legs, but the crippling wounds did not stop him from carrying out his duty. In intense pain, he remained in his exposed position to continue directing his gun crew. When another enemy grenade landed between him and a wounded companion, Anderson grabbed it and at tempted to throw it away, only to have it explode in his hand. Only partially conscious, he continued to in-spire his men until the NVA attack had been thrown back. Only then did he allow himself to be evacuated.

On October 22nd, and again on October 27th, the Brigade made signifi-cant contacts with battalion-sized enemy forces. But it was now apparent that the enemy had had enough. Between October 28th and November 4th, a lack of further contact with the NVA alerted the American forces that the enemy units were attempting to flee the area. The 1st Brigade soldiers moved quickly and intensified their efforts to find the 2nd NVA Division.

New intelligence reports came in placing the NVA division's headquar-ters just to the north of the Brigade's area of operation, prompting a new plan of action. Brigade soldiers hurriedly went into blocking positions east and southwest of the suspected enemy headquarters, while a U.S. Marine battalion was inserted as a blocking force to the northwest. Elements of the 1st Cavalry Division then moved into blocking positions to the northeast, from which they began to attack from that direction. There were numerous small unit contacts over the next seven days, and one more major battle on November 11th when Charlie Company, 2/327th, caught an escaping NVA company and bloodied them in a prolonged firefight.

When Operation WHEELER came to a successful close, 1st Brigade Intelligence estimated that approximately a full one-third of the 2nd NVA Division—nearly 1,100 enemy soldiers—had been killed during the opera-tion. The Brigade had also located and destroyed a battalion base camp, captured numerous small arms and crew served weapons, and "liberated" a 200 pound stash of high-grade marijuana valued at $100,000.

The Brigade's three maneuver battalions were relieved in place by ele-ments of the 196th Light Infantry Brigade, transported to the airfield at Tam Ky, and then redeployed to the Brigade's permanent base camp at Phan Rang in time for a well-deserved four-day Thanksgiving Day standdown.

OPERATION KLAMATH FALLS, the Brigade's final offensive activity of 1967, began early in December. The operation was initiated in response to intel-ligence reports indicating a VC regional headquarters, reinforced by the 482nd VC Battalion and local VC forces, was operating in Tam Dong and Bien Thuan provinces south of Phan Rang. The Brigade's three maneuver battalions along with its newly arrived sister battalion, 3/506th, deployed on December 2nd, and found numerous indications of the enemy's presence, however, the VC units proved evasive and avoided heavy contact. A bi-lateral truce between the warring parties enabled the "Always First" Brigade to celebrate Christmas in the field without interruption. After a full month in pursuit of the elusive enemy, Operation KLAMATH FALLS was terminated on January 7th, 1968. Enemy losses were only 156 killed in action.

DURING OPERATION KLAMATH FALLS, the 2nd and 3rd brigades of the 101st Airborne Division, plus divisional support units, arrived in Vietnam from Ft. Campbell, Kentucky, in Operation EAGLE THRUST. It was the longest and largest military airlift ever attempted. In an elaborate ceremony at the 101st's new division rear, Division Commanding General O. M. Barsanti reported to General William Westmoreland the 101st Airborne Division to be "ready for combat in Vietnam." The 1st Brigade's lonely odyssey had come to an close. It was now once again an intregal part of the 101st Airborne Division's "Rendezvous with Destiny."

PREPARATIONS AT FORT CAMPBELL

WHILE THE "ALWAYS First" Brigade was establishing its own reputation as the finest brigade in the American army, the 2nd and 3rd Brigades were fighting a losing battle in their efforts to fill their ranks and prepare for possible deployment to Vietnam in 1968. The Division was suffering severe manpower shortages. Levies from the Republic of Vietnam caused a continuous drain on the 101st as the 173rd Airborne Brigade and the Division's own 1st Brigade attempted to maintain a fresh source of airborne qualified replacements to overcome losses due to rotation and battlefield casualties. In August 1967, the 101st Airborne Division received its official notification for deployment to Vietnam. Over the ensuing months, the division collected airborne qualified personnel from wherever they could be begged, borrowed, stolen, or scrounged. Many were replacements from the 82nd Airborne Division and XVIII Airborne Corps at Ft. Bragg. As the Division's ranks began to swell, training cycles were established to prepare the new Screaming Eagles for the upcoming deployment. Personnel were shipped all over the country to attend specialty schools to fill critical MOS slots, while individual units at Ft. Campbell concentrated on combat qualifying their soldiers regardless of MOS. Cooks, bandsmen, clerks, mechanics, supply personnel, medics, signalmen, artillerymen, infantry were all honed to a fine steel edge. Volumes of logistical planning and administrative paperwork were created in the mad rush to make the Division combat ready. Transportation to move 10,000 plus paratroopers more than 10,000 miles along with their vehicles and equipment had to be laid on and coordinated. Major General O.M. Barsanti, the Screaming Eagle Commander, had his hands full. The question was, "Could he and his staff handle the job in such a short period of time?" Just when things began to come together, General Westmoreland requested the Division report at an earlier date than planned. This called for an immediate acceleration of the training program, along with a revamping of the entire shipping manifest. But when the time arrived for the Division to deploy, the Screaming Eagles were ready. The Division had trained together in defensive/offensive tactics;

squad/platoon/company maneuvers; ambush, weapons familiarization and qualification; night movement; and anything else necessary to insure the completion of their mission. Although most of the Division's troopers were green and untried in the arena of armed combat, all were airborne volunteers and anxious to be underway. A large number of the 101st's officers and NCOs were veterans of World War II and Korea, with an additional salting of nearly 1,000 seasoned, second tour Vietnam veterans to insure that the Division's transition from garrison duty to combat duty would go as smoothly as possible.

RENDEZVOUS WITH DESTINY

ON OCTOBER 2, 1967, the Currahees of the 3/506th arrived at Cam Ranh Bay in the vanguard of its 101st Airborne Division parent unit. Before the rest of the division arrived two months later, the 3/506th was redeployed as a mobile task force for the entire II Corps Tactical Zone. The "Stand Alone" battalion began its own "odyssey" which was to last until the 3/506th Mobile Task Force rejoined the rest of the Division at Camp Eagle in I Corps Tactical Zone on August 26, 1970. When the battalion landed at Cam Rahn Bay, it was given a week to acclimatize before being committed to its first operation. Moving a short distance south, the Currahees moved into the coastal mountains below Phan Rang in what was to become Operation ROSE. However, VC units avoided contact with the newly arrived paratroopers and the operation proved to be little more than a "walk in the woods."

Next came Operation KLAMATH FALLS, and the 3/506th was joined by its sister-battalions from the 1st Brigade of the 101st Airborne Division. Concentrated sweeps throughout the area turned up plenty of indications that the enemy was in the area, but the VC avoided any major contact. Again, the 3/506th paratroopers failed to close with the enemy, but the operation proved invaluable as a confidence builder. With a couple of shakedown missions under their belts, the Currahees were gaining the experience that would be necessary to get them through the bloody days of Tet '68. On January 17, 1968 the battalion was detached from the 101st Airborne Division and sent south to Phan Thiet with the new title of Task Force 3/506th. A battalion base camp was soon established at LZ Betty in AO Byrd, and the battalion's maneuver companies moved out to secure LZs Bartlett and Judy in the mountains below Phan Thiet. The mission of Task Force 3/506th was to locate and destroy MR-6, the VC/NVA base area located somewhere in Binh Thuan Province.

ON DECEMBER 13, 1967, Operation EAGLE THRUST succeeded in relocating 10,356 soldiers and all their equipment, vehicles and aircraft half way around the world, closing out the Division from Ft. Campbell, Kentucky, in 41 days. Never before had an entire division been deployed so far, so quickly. General Barsanti and his staff arrived at the Bien Hoa air base and reported immediately to General Westmoreland, "The 101st Airborne Division reports for combat in Vietnam." With these prophetic words, the Screaming Eagles began their three-fold mission: to win the people, to win the battle, and to win the war in Vietnam.

Division headquarters for the newly arrived 101st Airborne Division was established at Bien Hoa, just north of Saigon. With the 1st Brigade already established at Phan Rang, the 2nd Brigade was ordered to move west by convoy to establish its area of operations around Cu Chi, in support of the U.S. 25th Infantry Division. The 3rd Brigade redeployed to the countryside outside of Phuoc Vinh, northwest of Bien Hoa about 60 miles from Saigon. While the 1st Brigade was resting and recuperating from extended combat operations, the 2nd and 3rd Brigades began a thirty-day in-country training program. "Tropical Lightning" soldiers of the 25th Infantry Division, shared their experience with the newly arrived Screaming Eagles by running the 2nd Brigade troopers through daily instructions on booby traps, explosives, reconnaissance, and ambush techniques.

While the Division's new arrivals were becoming acclimatized to Vietnam, the enemy was quietly moving its forces into position around key military installations, and district and province capitals throughout the country. The cities of Saigon and Hue had been singled out for "special" treatment in what was to become the biggest, most widespread enemy offensive of the Vietnam War—Tet 1968.

TET OFFENSIVE: 1968

THE ENEMY'S 1968 Tet Offensive caught the South Vietnamese military and its foreign allies completely by surprise. Although MACV had been expecting an offensive, it had not really accepted the possibility the NVA/VC forces were capable of mounting an offensive of such unparalleled magnitude. All of the obvious warning signs had been there, but the U.S. and ARVN intelligence agencies had ignored them and "played down" the danger of a country-wide offensive. Year-end intelligence reports in 1967 indicated the existence of a major NVA effort building along the DMZ followed by heavy NVA movement into the area around Khe Sanh, effectively surrounding the U.S. 26th Marines garrisoned there. With both the 1st and 3rd Marine divisions already involved in heavy combat, the situation in I Corps Tactical Zone was shaping up as a potential disaster of major magnitude. With only the newly formed Americal Division situated to back up the Marines in I Corps, MACV had little choice but to pull the divisional headquarters and the 1st Brigade of the crack 1st Cavalry Division out of Binh Dinh Province and move it north to the Hue/Phu Bai area. The 1st Cav's 3rd

Brigade, already OPCON to the Americal Division, rejoined the divisional headquarters and its sister-brigade on January 21st, 1968. The Cav's 2nd Brigade was unable to rejoin the division until March, so the 2nd Brigade of the 101st Airborne Division, under the command of Colonel John H. Cushman, comprising the 1/501st, 2/501st, 1/502nd (less Company C which had remained behind at Bien Hoa as a base security force) infantry battalions and miscellaneous support units, was pulled out of Cu Chi and rushed north to join the 1st Cav as its third maneuver brigade. At full strength once again, the 1st Cavalry Division would quickly leap-frog even further to the north, headlong into the NVA build up in Quang Tri Province. In the next two months they would destroy the enemy at Quang Tri, play a major role in defeating the NVA forces holding the city of Hue, and succeed in rescuing the trapped U.S. Marines at Khe Sanh.

On the night of January 30th, 1968, all of South Vietnam was busy celebrating Tet, the Vietnamese lunar New Year. Most South Vietnamese military and police units had furloughed most of their personnel and were staffed by skeleton crews. All over Vietnam American forces were standing down in observance of the bi-lateral Tet cease-fire agreement. Some American units had put out ambushes and had inserted long range reconnaissance patrols to screen the approaches to critical military installations, but all in all, the allied military establishment was unprepared for the storm about to descend upon them.

In Saigon, the city was alive with celebration and excitement. Fireworks and lively music created a festive atmosphere as its citizens ushered in the Year of the Monkey. There was plenty of reason for optimism. The American military buildup had succeeded in bringing the Communist forces under a semblance of containment. Pacification seemed to be working, with more and more villages and hamlets coming under government control all the time. Saigon seemed sheltered from the impact of the war raging the countryside . The government promised that 1968 would bring better things for the people of South Vietnam.

But shortly before midnight, throughout the city of Saigon, heavily armed Viet Cong guerrillas jostled through the throngs of jubilant celebrants and disappeared into the shadows of Saigon's back alleys. No one seemed to take notice—or even care—that something unusual was underway. In the early hours of the morning the Viet Cong struck. Achieving complete and total surprise, VC sapper and assault squads attacked key ARVN and U.S. military and government installations throughout Saigon and the surrounding countryside. Among their initial targets were the Presidential Palace, the ARVN Joint General Staff compound, the U.S. Embassy, the South Korean Embassy, the Philippine Chancery, Saigon's National Broadcasting Station and the Vietnamese Naval Headquarters. In addition, well-coordinated attacks were also directed at buildings housing American officers, district police stations and various ARVN military installations. By dawn, with several precincts in Cholon firmly under VC control, and numerous government and military buildings in the hands of the enemy, it became obvious that the VC were intent on more than mere hit and run terrorist attacks.

Word reached MACV Headquarters that two squads of VC sappers had attempted to seize the United States Embassy. Killing several guards, the VC had succeeded in breaching the outer wall to the embassy compound and taking over the lower floors of some of the surrounding buildings, but they were being held at bay by American government officials and the Marine guard detachment holed-up in the upper floors of the chancery. Company C 1/502nd, the base security company at the 101st Airborne Division headquarters at Bien Hoa, was quickly ordered to go to the relief of the embassy. Captain Jack Speedy, Charlie Company's commanding officer, selected the third platoon for the mission. The 35-man reaction force boarded Huey helicopters and headed for the section of Saigon where the American and French embassies were located. At 0500 on the morning of January 31, 1968, the rescue force, led by Major Hillel Schwartz, the assistant Division Intelligence officer, flying in the C&C bird, attempted to land on the roof of the embassy, but was driven away when a heavy volume of small arms fire erupted from the courtyard around the chancery building, striking the lead helicopter and wounding one of the door gunners. Major Schwartz and the Screaming Eagle reaction force succeeded in a second attempt to insert onto the roof of the embassy at 0800 hours. Breaking into the building, the paratroopers quickly assaulted through the embassy, searching every nook and cranny, room by room, for VC commandos until they were finally able to establish a defensive perimeter in the courtyard surrounding the embassy building. The Screaming Eagle "First Strike" troopers killed nine of the nineteen Viet Cong sappers found dead on the embassy grounds. While the VC were heavily engaged in Saigon, a massive enemy ground assault attempted to overrun the huge military complex and the air base at Bien Hoa. The 2/506th was rushed by helicopter from the 3rd Brigade AO near Phuoc Vinh and combat assaulted into an open area behind the division headquarters. The battalion found itself embroiled in heavy combat within thirty minutes of its arrival. Seven hours of intense fighting saw the battalion kill over 100 VC just outside the main gate of the division compound. Continued contact the next day accounted for another 58 enemy killed. During the first two days of intense fighting and subsequent mopping up operations, the Division accounted for a total of 851 enemy killed. The defense of the Bien Hoa area was given the designation of Operation UNIONTOWN.

WHEN THE NATION-WIDE Tet offensive erupted on the night of January 30th, NVA/VC forces surfaced in Binh Thuan Province intent on winning a decisive victory and humiliating the American and ARVN forces operating in their district. But the 3/506th Currahees had responded quickly to blunt enemy attacks wherever they occurred. The paratroopers pursued the demoralized enemy over the next several months, destroying the VC infrastructure throughout the province and breaking up large concentrations of main force Viet Cong units, by keeping them off balance and reeling from one military operation after another. In three operations—ROCKNE GOLD, BANJO ROYCE, and HARMON GREEN—the Battalion fought from the Southern Free Strike Zone to the Le Hong Phong Forest and inflicted severe losses on the enemy in southeastern II Corps Tactical Zone with over 500 killed and another 18 captured. The 3rd Battalion Currahees also uncovered nearly a hundred tons of food and weapons. For its efforts and achievements, the Battalion received the Presidential Unit Citation.

FARTHER NORTH IN I Corps, newly arrived 2nd Brigade troopers teamed with the 1st Air Cavalry Division and the tough ARVN 1st Infantry Division in Operation JEB STUART. Landing and setting up on the Phu Bai airfield, the 2nd Brigade consolidated its forces and moved north to LZ Sally. At the outbreak of the Tet Offensive, 2nd Brigade troopers moved north again, and OPCON to the 1st Air Cav Division, shared the burden of the heavy fighting in the battle for Quang Tri, accounting for 94 enemy dead. With Quang Tri City finally cleared of NVA, the 1st Air Cavalry Division and the 101st's 2nd Brigade turned and moved south to set up blocking forces in the countryside around Hue, while U.S. Marines and ARVN forces fought to retake the city from the NVA. During the following weeks, the tally of NVA soldiers killed and captured climbed as 2nd Brigade soldiers cleaned out pockets of enemy resistance between Hue and Quang Tri, and intercepted NVA units attempting to reinforce the former Imperial City. In one incident, the 1/501st, conducting road clearing operations along Highway 1 south of Quang Tri, received a timely warning from local South Vietnamese villagers that enemy soldiers were hiding along the highway ahead of them. Utilizing helicopter gunships and artillery, the Screaming Eagles broke up a battalion-sized NVA ambush, killing 72 enemy soldiers. During the heavy fighting around Hue, two 2nd Brigade soldiers distinguished themselves in combat and were awarded the Congressional Medal of Honor.

On February 21, 1968, Staff Sergeant Clifford C. Sims, a squad leader with Delta Company 2/501st, was assaulting a heavily fortified enemy position hidden within a densely wooded tree line, when the company came under heavy fire from entrenched NVA defensive positions. Reaching the tree line, Sergeant Sims led his squad in a furious attack against the enemy forces that had pinned down the 1st Platoon and was threatening to overrun it. His leadership enabled the 1st Platoon to regain the initiative. Sergeant Sims was then ordered to move his squad to a position where it could provide covering fire for the company command group and then link up with the 3rd Platoon, which was also under heavy enemy pressure. After moving a short distance, Sergeant Sims spotted a nearby brick structure containing a stockpile of ammunition. Seeing it was on fire and realizing the danger to his nearby squad, he took immediate action to get them out of danger. But before they could clear the area, the structure exploded, slightly wounding two members of his squad. His actions prevented more serious casualties. Continuing to advance into the woods amidst heavy enemy fire, Sergeant Sims led his squad toward an enemy bunker. Suddenly, the paratroopers heard the sound of a hidden booby trap being triggered. Sergeant Sims shouted a warning to his squad and threw himself on the concealed booby trap, absorbing the full impact of the explosion with his body, and killing him instantly. His actions prevented further casualties among the men of his squad. On the same day that Sergeant Sims was killed, Staff Sergeant Joe R. Hooper, also a squad leader with Delta Company 2/501st, was assaulting a well-armed and heavily defended enemy position and was engaged by heavy B-40 rocket fire and automatic weapons. Ignoring the danger, Sergeant Hooper assaulted the enemy position and destroyed several bunkers with grenades and rifle fire. He returned to his squad and treated several wounded soldiers, helping them to safety. During the evacuation, Sergeant Hooper was seriously wounded, but refused evacuation and returned to his squad, still pinned down by enemy fire. Hooper once again assaulted the enemy positions, destroying three enemy bunkers and killing two enemy soldiers. Pushing on, he destroyed four structures housing enemy soldiers and killed an NVA officer. Wounded again by grenade fragments, Sergeant Hooper ignored the pain and went after more grenades. Returning to the battle, he charged a line of enemy bunkers, destroying them as he ran past, and killed another enemy soldier and three more NVA officers in close combat. Out of grenades, he returned to his squad to reorganize them, choosing not to be evacuated until the next morning. He was awarded the Congressional Medal of Honor for his actions.

WITH THE TET Offensive all but contained near Saigon, the 1st Brigade—now under the command of Colonel John W. Collins—was airlifted from its base camp at Phan Rang to central I Corps, along with Division headquarters. In two weeks, the 1st Brigade troopers would clear the route following Highway 547 to the A Shau Valley, cutting enemy supply and escape routes, interrupting troop movements, and uncovering numerous caches containing arms, ammunition, food and medical supplies intended for NVA units still holding out in Hue.

Operation JEB STUART ended with the destruction of the 812th NVA Regiment and the 324th NVA Division. Paratroopers from the 101st Airborne Division and sky-soldiers from the 1st Air Cavalry Division had killed over 1000 NVA and VC in bitter fighting along Highway One—the "Street without Joy"—and in the rolling countryside and sandy coastal plains around the former Imperial City.

WHILE THE 2ND Brigade was engaged in supporting the 1st Air Cav Division, and the 1st Brigade was working the area west of Hue, units of the 3rd Brigade were parceled around III Corps to search for enemy units in the hills around Song Be, and to probe deeply into the southern part of War Zone D and the Filhol rubber plantation. They would gain much needed combat experience ferreting out the remnants of the VC units withdrawing to their sanctuaries to lick their wounds. Song Be, especially would be the scene of heavy fighting for the 3rd Brigade troopers.

A NEW HOME IN I CORPS

INITIALLY SLATED TO provide a much needed shot in the arm for III Corps Tactical Zone, the 101st Airborne Division—less its 3rd Brigade which continued running operations in III Corps—had been redirected to I Corps to become part of General Westmoreland's northern buildup, freeing up the 1st Air Cavalry Division to come to the relief of the Marines surrounded and trapped at Khe Sanh. Protected by a "heavy" 12-man team from F Company, 58th Infantry (Long Range Patrol), Brigadier General Frank B. Clay, the Assistant Division Commander, searched I Corps from DaNang to Hue to Quang Tri, for a suitable location to serve as a forward operational base for the Division. It wasn't long before a site was selected among the low, rolling hills about 8 kilometers southwest of Hue. The site was secured by the two Lurp teams until the rest of F Company, 58th Infantry (Long Range Patrol) arrived to "hold the fort" until combat engineers from the 326th Engineer Battalion arrived a week later to begin constructing what was soon to become Camp Eagle. The newly arrived 3rd Brigade of the 82nd Airborne Division deployed to I Corps on February 14, 1968, and was put under the operational control of the 101st Airborne Division in place of its own 3rd Brigade still conducting operations in III Corps. The three paratrooper brigades and their support elements quickly launched Operation CARENTAN I, a campaign designed to keep the NVA/VC forces north of the Division's new forward base camp, off balance, and on the defensive. The initial series of combat assaults along the Perfume River included "All Americans" from the 82nd, helicopters, and mechanized infantry from B

Troop 2/17th Cav, Lurps from F Company 58th Infantry (LRP), and paratroopers from the three 2nd Brigade battalions rejoining the Division after participating in Operation JEB STUART. Two days into the operation, Alpha Company 1/501st discovered two large weapon caches, while paratroopers from Charlie Company 2/501st ran into an enemy company and killed 25 NVA soldiers in a fierce firefight. By the close of the first week, Charlie Company 2/501st killed another 41 NVA who decided to stand and slug it out in a two-day battle two kilometers north of Hue. While 2nd Brigade's companies were busy punishing the NVA among the rolling hills north of the Perfume River, Screaming Eagles from the 1st Brigade also decided to share in some of the action. Paratroopers from the 2/327th, patrolling Highway 547 out toward Fire Base Bastogne, killed 25 NVA who tried to trade fire with the Americans from reinforced bunkers located along the highway. Continued sweeps along both sides of Route 547 flushed snipers and stay behind parties, but failed to turn up large enemy units.

On March 21st, troopers from the 2/501st repulsed an all out NVA attack on their night defense perimeter. Bringing to bear direct artillery fire, the Screaming Eagles dealt the charging NVA a mortal blow. The Americans found 22 enemy dead and numerous blood trails outside their perimeter during a sweep the next morning.

The next day, Huey gunships from the 101st Aviation Battalion caught an NVA company "half-stepping" in the open five miles west of Hue and left 34 of them lying in the sun, while a light fire team operating nearby destroyed three sampans, killing nine more VC.

Subsequent company-sized sweeps by the 1/501st trapped elements of the Viet Cong 810th Battalion inside the deserted village of Thuan Hoa along the banks of the Perfume River. Establishing a hasty multi-company cordon around the village, and keeping night-long illumination overhead, Lieutenant Colonel Procup's troopers sealed the fate of the VC defenders holed up amid the abandoned buildings of Thua Hoa. Navy patrol boats joined the cordon to prevent the enemy from escaping by water. The Screaming Eagles turned back several attempts by VC elements to escape the trap, killing over 20 enemy soldiers by actual body count, but the net had been drawn too tight. When the sun came up the next morning, loud speakers were used to broadcast last minute surrender appeals to the trapped VC, then Delta Company 1/501st moved into the village. Meeting no enemy resistance, they found the bodies of more than 30 uniformed VC soldiers. But the 101st Airborne Division had learned a lot about conducting cordon operations. In spite of their valiant efforts to totally surround the village, a large number of enemy soldiers still succeeded in escaping during the night. In future operations, flare ships would be standing by early, with a replacement ship requested well ahead of time. As insurance, a helicopter flare ship or artillery flares should be utilized to fill in the gaps. In other words, entrapped NVA/VC should be given no opportunity to sneak out of the trap under cover of darkness. A net can only be as strong as its weakest point. The 2nd Brigade, under the direction of Colonel Cushman, would set the standard for cordon operations in the future. It would become their trademark.

A classic cordon operation in Phuoc Dien village along the south bank of the Perfume River by the 1/502nd accounted for another 70 dead NVA and 13 NVA taken prisoner. Delta Company 2/501st discovered an additional bonus when they uncovered a mass grave containing 31 NVA killed in earlier fighting.

When Operation CARENTAN I came to a close on March 31, 1968, the Screaming Eagles and their brother "All Americans" had killed 861 enemy soldiers, captured 186 individual and crew-served weapons, 1,027 rocket, mortar and artillery rounds, 41,000 small arms rounds and 45 hand grenades. American paratroopers also prevented 17 tons of rice and grain from providing much needed sustenance to NVA soldiers operating in the area.

Immediately on the heels of CARENTAN I came Operation CARENTAN II, conducted in the same area, northwest from the coastal plains, south of Hue, and west toward the A Shau Valley. Another successful cordon operation by 2nd Brigade paratroopers from the 2/501st set the pace for CARENTAN II. Elements of the 2/17th Cav, assisted by the 2/501st, had been sweeping the area known as "The Street without Joy," destroying numerous bunker complexes and other NVA fortifications, but not finding any enemy soldiers. An enemy agent reported the presence of two enemy companies entrenched in strong defensive positions in the village of Phuoc Dien. Late in the afternoon on April 10th, Lieutenant Colonel Richard J. Tallman, commander of the 2/501st, sent in his A and D companies to see if the agent had been telling the truth. Within minutes both companies were pinned down and in heavy contact. It soon became obvious the two U.S. companies would be unable to take the village without suffering heavy casualties, nor would they be able to cordon off the village without additional reinforcements.

General Barsanti ordered the paratroopers to "stay with the enemy" and agreed to send them whatever they needed—which in this case was extra helicopters. Lieutenant Colonel Tallman immediately moved his Bravo Company into the fray, and by last light had succeeded in completing his cordon. Individual American positions were established no more than ten meters apart all the way around the village. When it was completed there were no holes in the cordon. Orders came down from Colonel Tallman that the Screaming Eagles would remain on 100% alert during the night.

Continual illumination was maintained over the village by flare ships and artillery.

Between 2000 hours that night and 0730 hours the next morning, the trapped NVA made at least twelve separate attempts to break through the cordon. The next morning three dozen NVA soldiers were found dead within hand grenade distance of the cordon positions. Two dazed NVA were captured and taken prisoner. At 0800, companies B and D assaulted the village in a coordinated attack that met only moderate resistance. When the smoke had cleared and the dust had settled, the 2/501st troopers had killed a total of 70 NVA from the 6th Battalion, 812th NVA Regiment and had captured another thirteen.

After the battle of Phuoc Dien, the 2nd Brigade's command post moved back to LZ Sally, leaving behind its three battalions and the 2 /17th Cav to continue searching for the enemy. In late April came the opportunity for the "classic" cordon operation.

Companies of the 1/501st and local South Vietnamese forces, along with the Black Panther (Hac Bao) Company from the 1st ARVN Division, were scouring the countryside looking for large enemy units reportedly hiding among the villages in the Brigade's area of operations. Although most of the villages had been abandoned during the height of the recent Tet offensive, NVA units were still digging in and using them, moving from village to village, never spending more than two days in the same place.

Around noon on April 28th, the Hac Bao executed a recon in force into the village of Phuoc Yen. They were greeted by a heavy volume of small arms and RPG fire, which drove them out of the village. The Black Panther commander estimated they had stepped into an NVA battalion.

Company A 1/501st and Company B of the 2/501st were quickly moved into blocking positions on the west, south and southeast sides of the village, as the Black Panther Company set up on the north side. Three platoons of PFs (Popular Forces), sent in by Huong Tra district chief, Major Nguyen Huu De, established blocking positions along the river line east of the village. By 1800 the cordon was 80% complete and the village was clear of all friendlies. Company A 1/502nd was moved into a nearby landing zone and set up positions along the northeast edge of the cordon. Attempting to bypass the small neighboring village of Le Van Thuong, Alpha Company troopers drew fire from hidden enemy positions within the village. They backed off and soon realized they would have to include the village of Le Van Thuong within the cordon, or risk leaving a hole in the net for the enemy to escape through. Major De ordered a platoon-sized hamlet militia unit from a small village across the river to form blocking positions across the Song Bo River from the village of Le Van Thuong, while Company A 1/502nd infiltrated a platoon along a hedgerow all the way down to the river. The trap was sprung. There was no way out.

When the lights were turned on after dark, the NVA forces inside Phuoc Yen and Le Van Thuong knew they were trapped. There was scattered firing throughout the night, but the enemy avoided any major break-out attempts, that is until 0500 when heavy firing erupted along A Company 1/502nd's left flank, right where its platoon had closed the last gate on the cordon around the two villages. Three different times, the enemy attempted to break through and escape the encirclement at the point were the Alpha Company troopers had thrown up defensive positions along the river. Each time the attacks were thrown back. When daylight finally arrived, the enemy forces were still in the bag.

Company A went on the offensive around 0900, attempting to gain a foothold in the village of Le Van Thuong. But heavy enemy resistance from entrenched, well-camouflaged defensive positions inside the village stopped them dead in their tracks. The commanding officer of Company A pulled his troopers back and adjusted artillery fire from batteries of the 21st Artillery onto the hardened enemy bunkers.

Later in the day, the ARVN 1st Infantry Division Black Panther Company advanced to the edge of the village of Phuoc Yen where they, too, ran into stiff enemy resistance and were forced to pull back. That evening, another company from the 2/501st was brought in to strengthen the cordon. The operation's commander realized the enemy in their desperation would have to attempt a breakout. As during the first night of the cordon, the battleground was illuminated at all times. This time the enemy continually probed all sides of the perimeter attempting to find a weak spot. There were none.

On April 30th, the third day of the operation, the Screaming Eagle companies took turns probing the trapped enemy positions, themselves looking for the one weak link in the chain that would crack the defensive "nut" of Phuoc Yen. Turned back at every point, they withdrew and brought in artillery and tactical air strikes on the village.

At the end of the day, the Black Panthers were pulled out of the cordon and airlifted back to another operational commitment outside of Hue. The now exhausted U.S. paratroopers adjusted their lines to tighten up the slack left in the cordon by the departing ARVNs. Both friend and foe were reaching the end of their reserves. One side or the other would have to give. At Phuoc Yen, it would be the NVA.

The U.S. paratroopers held the cordon for the third night, and in the early morning hours of May 1st, the NVA took advantage of a short break in the illumination, and made a final desperate attempt to once again break out of the cordon on the left flank of Alpha Company 1/502nd. Three Americans died during the ferocious attack, but the cordon held.

When the sun rose over the battlefield, enemy defenses began to collapse. A Division PSYOPS team arrived on the scene and began broadcasting appeals to surrender over loud speakers. Some of the NVA realized the futility of further resistance and gave up to the Americans. Among this group was an NVA sergeant who quickly agreed to go on the air and plead with the remaining NVA to give up. In a short while, more dazed and disoriented NVA soldiers began to stumble from the wreckage of Le Van Thuong and surrender to the Alpha Company troopers. By noon, Alpha Company advanced into the village without further resistance. Later in the day, Bravo Company from the 2/501st moved in to replace Alpha Company 1/502nd at its positions in the shortened lines of the cordon, while the exhausted Alpha Company troopers were returned to LZ Sally. For two more days, the Screaming Eagles held the cordon while NVA soldiers threw their lives away in futile attempts to break out and escape. Finally, during the morning of May 3rd, the enemy made its final attempt. Like the others before it, it too, ended in failure. The battle was over. The NVA lost 419 killed. But what was even more significant, the persistent 2nd Brigade paratroopers had captured 107 prisoners—the largest number of NVA captured in any single action up to that point in the war. The Americans had totally destroyed the 8th Battalion of the 90th NVA Regiment. In a period of five days, the enemy battalion had ceased to exist. Vast quantities of arms and equipment were seized by the 2nd Brigade paratroopers, and at the cost of only eight American and two South Vietnamese soldiers killed, and another fifty-six wounded. It was a great victory indeed!

Continual sweeps and cordon operations by the three battalions of the 2nd Brigade and mechanized elements of the 2/17th Cav kept NVA/VC forces off balance in the areas north and west of Hue and along the "Street without Joy."

WHILE CARENTAN II was in full-swing, 1st Brigade troopers were pulled away to take part in an even tougher mission, participating in Operation DELAWARE. On April 19th, elements of the 1st Brigade, along with the 1/502nd, moved down Highway 547 and 547A to interdict enemy supply routes and provide a blocking force for the 1st Air Cavalry's air assault into the heart of the A Shau Valley. The Brigade, supported by the 3rd ARVN Airborne Task Force, moved into the Rao Nho and Rao Nai valleys to establish Fire Support Base Veghel nine klicks east of the A Shau Valley.

While the 1/327th secured the area around FSB Veghel, meeting only scattered resistance, on April 25th, Company C, 2/327th engaged two NVA companies along Highway 547, fifteen miles southwest of Hue. While Charlie Company held contact, Alpha Company 2/327th moved into flank the dug-in NVA. Outflanked and outfought, the NVA pulled out leaving behind 32 dead and seven weapons. Charlie Company, 1/327th later found 6,300 rounds of anti-aircraft ammunition after a one day search, and then uncovered an even bigger cache two days later yielding 582 mortar rounds, 200 recoilless rifle rounds, and 50 grenades.

While the 1st and 2nd battalions of the 327th were dueling with the NVA forces near the A Shau Valley, their sister battalion was conducting sweep operations west of Phu Bai. In one of these operations, another Screaming Eagle was to pay the supreme sacrifice, and in so doing would be awarded the Congressional Medal of Honor. Private First Class Milton A. Lee, a radio operator with Company B 2/502nd, was on patrol with his company. His platoon was the lead element on the company sweep. Suddenly, the platoon found itself in the middle of a deadly kill zone, being ripped apart by NVA forces in well-concealed, reinforced bunkers. With half the platoon dead and wounded, the remainder of the surviving paratroopers sought cover to reorganize and treat their wounded. In the momentary confusion, Private First Class Lee moved through the heavy enemy fire rendering first aid to many of his wounded comrades. Shortly thereafter, the remnants of the platoon assaulted the enemy positions, while Private First Class Lee reported the situation to his company commander. While moving back to the forward elements of his platoon to relay orders to his platoon leader, Lee observed four NVA with automatic weapons and an RPG lying in wait to ambush the lead element of the platoon. Realizing the danger to his comrades, Lee removed his radio and passed it to another soldier, then stood and charged through murderous small arms fire to overrun the enemy position. After killing the NVA soldiers and capturing four automatic weapons and a rocket launcher, Lee again charged through a heavy barrage of deadly enemy fire toward a second enemy bunker he had spotted. Grievously wounded, he crawled to a spot where he could put accurate fire on the enemy position, and kept their heads down while his platoon maneuvered into position to destroy the bunker. As the victorious paratroopers overran the NVA bunker complex, Private First Class Lee quietly died from his wounds.

Operation DELAWARE came to a close on May 17th. The 1st Brigade companies had killed 318 NVA, captured three prisoners and 121 weapons during the month long operation. The Brigade also interdicted Route 547 and succeeded in cutting off its use as a resupply route for enemy forces fighting around Hue. However, the operation was a poor trade for the 139 American body bags that were filled and the loss of over 60 helicopters to the numerous enemy anti-aircraft positions that ringed the valley.

Operation CARENTAN II also ended on May 17, 1968. Paratroopers killed over 1,200 NVA, captured 151 prisoners and 581 individual and crew-served weapons during the 47-day operation in the countryside around the Imperial City of Hue. Twenty-eight 2nd Brigade and six South Vietnamese soldiers were killed in the cordon operations during the CARENTAN II. The paratroopers and soldiers of the 1st ARVN Division had succeeded in their mission of relieving pressure on Hue and its surrounding areas.

WHILE THE 101ST Airborne Division and its 1st and 2nd Brigades had moved north to deal the enemy a series of serious blows in I Corps Tactical Zone, 3rd Brigade paratroopers had remained behind in III Corps Tactical Zone to begin an eight month odyssey which would see them involved in combat in all four tactical zones. Paratroopers from the 2/506th earned their CIBs at the onset of the Tet offensive when they were loaded onto helicopters at their base in Phuoc Vinh and set down behind the 101st Division headquarters to begin 36 hours of heavy fighting around the Division base camp and the Bien Hoa air base, which left 150 enemy dead when the smoke had cleared. The 1/506th and the 2/17th Cav was "blooded" during Tet in the vicious, block-by-block street fighting that left the city of Song Be in ruins. Located sixty miles north of Bien Hoa, along the Cambodian border, Song Be had been the target of the 211th and 212th Viet Cong Infiltration Groups. Standing up and slugging it out with overwhelming enemy forces, the airborne battalion along with the cavalry men and the 31st ARVN Ranger Company recaptured the city and dealt the two main-force VC elements a severe blow.

The 3/187th Rakkasans "broke their cherries" by moving in and destroying a regimental base camp along the Dong Nai River south of Phuoc Vinh, killing more than 120 enemy soldiers. It was during this battle that the 101st Airborne Division would see its sixth Congressional Medal of Honor. On March 16, 1968, Captain Paul W. Bucha, commanding officer of Delta Company 3/187th, led his company in a combat assault into a suspected enemy stronghold to locate and destroy the enemy. Demonstrating both aggressiveness and courage, Captain Bucha and his men destroyed enemy fortifications and base areas and eliminated scattered resistance to their advance. Two days later, on March 18th, lead elements of Delta Company were engaged by an estimated enemy battalion, effectively pinning them down with heavy fire from numerous automatic weapons, heavy machine guns, RPGs, claymore mines and grenades. Captain Bucha moved forward to the threatened area and took control of the situation, ordering reinforcements to move up to aid the stranded soldiers. Spotting the heavy machine gun that had pinned down his lead element firing from a concealed bunker less than forty meters to the front of his position, Captain Bucha crawled forward through a hail of fire to single-handedly destroy the machine gun emplacement with grenades. During his advance, Delta Company's commanding officer was painfully wounded by shrapnel. As he was returning to his lead element, enemy soldiers attacked in human wave assaults. Realizing his men could not defend their present position against this type of determined attack, Captain Bucha ordered them to withdraw back to the company's positions where he could direct artillery upon the attacking enemy. When one of his fire teams was ambushed and cut off by the enemy while attempting to retrieve Delta Company wounded, Captain Bucha shouted for them to play dead while he directed friendly artillery fire around them. During the night Captain Bucha moved continually among his trapped company, redistributing ammunition and encouraging his troopers to hold on. Throughout the hours of darkness, he directed accurate supporting fire from artillery, helicopter gunships, and an Air Force "Spooky" gunship upon enemy strong points and assaulting elements, marking their positions with well-thrown smoke grenades. Using flashlights to mark his own position, Captain Bucha directed helicopter resupply of his company and three separate medivac extractions of seriously wounded Delta Company troopers, ignoring ongoing sniper fire from the surrounding enemy. At daybreak, Captain Bucha personally led a rescue party to retrieve the dead and wounded members of the ambushed fire team. When the battle finally ended later that morning, the enemy departed leaving 156 of their dead on the battlefield, now in control of a bloodied but victorious Delta Company.

THE 3RD BRIGADE was placed under the operational control of II Field Force after the Division left for I Corps shortly after the start of the Tet offensive. In this capacity, the Brigade became the "Fire Brigade" for II Field Force, much like its famous sister 1st Brigade had been for MACV during 1965-67. In this capacity, companies of the Brigade fought alongside the U.S. 9th Infantry Division south of Saigon in IV Corps Delta region.

ON MAY 6, 1968, another Screaming Eagle earned the Congressional Medal of Honor, during hostile action in Phuoc Long Province, north of Saigon near the Cambodian border. Sp4 Robert M. Patterson, a cavalryman with B Troop 2/17th Cav, was on patrol with his unit when B Troop's 3rd Platoon moved to attack enemy bunker positions to their front. Suddenly, interlocking machine gun fire from two positions pinned down the advancing squad. Unwilling to wait for someone else to get the job done, Specialist Robert Patterson decided to handle the matter himself. Yelling for two of his comrades to cover him with their M-16s, Patterson raced across the open terrain with his rifle and grenades and destroyed the two bunkers from where the VC machine gun fire was coming. Stopping momentarily to catch his breath, Patterson spotted another enemy bunker and went after it. He didn't stop until he had personally wiped out all enemy resistance.

When the battle was over, it was discovered that the young cavalryman had knocked out five enemy strong points and had personally killed eight enemy soldiers.

ON MAY 18TH, yet another Screaming Eagle would have his name enshrined in the rolls of America's Medal of Honor recipients. Sp4 Peter M. Guenette was serving as a machine gunner with Company D 2/506th on an operation near Quan Tan Uyen Province. His platoon was searching through a suspected enemy base camp when it came under light harassing fire from an entrenched squad of NVA soldiers. Believing they were faced by a small enemy delaying force at the entrance of the base camp, the Delta Company platoon moved to within ten meters of the enemy fortifications. Suddenly, the NVA opened up with a tremendous volume of small arms fire. Guenette and his assistant gunner immediately began to lay down a heavy base of suppressive fire. As Guenette momentarily ceased fire to allow his assistant gunner to toss a grenade into a nearby bunker, he saw a Chi Com grenade land a few feet to his right. Realizing the grenade's blast would hit him and at least three of his comrades, in addition to destroying his machine gun, Guenette shouted a warning, then dove on the enemy grenade absorbing the blast with his body. His personal sacrifice saved the lives of at least three of his comrades and enabled them to maintain their fire superiority.

THE 3RD BRIGADE soon became the star performer in a secret MACV operation designed to destroy North Vietnamese forces in the Central Highlands. The Brigade was notified to move to an undisclosed location in the highlands, a move so secret that 3rd Brigade paratroopers were ordered to remove all Division patches from their uniforms and to erase all unit markings from their helicopters. The operation was so secret its contingency plans were kept from all "foreigners." On May 25th, the Brigade moved to Dak To to join the 4th Infantry Division. In spite of all the secrecy and subterfuge, the Brigade failed to catch the NVA napping or even to impress him with its fancy footwork. Ten days later, the Brigade was back in Dak To loading aboard huge Air Force C-7As for a short flight to Dak Pek to relieve the surrounded Special Forces camp there. The airborne reinforcements, coupled with extensive B-52 arc-lights falling within 1500 meters of the camp's perimeter, soon convinced the NVA there were parts of the country they hadn't seen yet. The now well-seasoned wanderers of the 3rd Brigade returned to Dak To for the third time in two weeks, and mounted search and destroy operations in the steep, heavily jungled mountains in an effort to locate the enemy. With June came intelligence reports that indicated the enemy around Dak To had left the mountainous Central Highlands. Word came a day later for the 3rd Brigade to head back south to Phuoc Vinh in III Corps, wearing a little egg on its face. II Field Force's operations staff's well laid plans for the conquest of the Central Highlands had gone somewhat awry. Before the 3rd Brigade paratroopers could even unpack at Phuoc Vinh, word reached them to prepare to move to Cu Chi to join the 25th Infantry Division in operations against suspected enemy concentrations.

The Brigade kicked off Operation TOAN THANG—PHASE II by making immediate contact with a large force of NVA regulars. The Screaming Eagles, now bloodied in earlier battles, performed like seasoned veterans, undaunted by the new foe and the alien terrain composed of shallow rice paddies and thick hedgerows. It was a new kind of fighting for the 3rd Brigade troopers.

The Brigade then moved to another III Corps battleground, called Dau Tieng, where the Screaming Eagles went up against tough, determined NVA and VC elements dug-in among row after row of limbless rubber trees stretching in all directions across an old rubber plantation. Again, the combat at Dau Tieng was different from anything the 3rd Brigade troopers had yet experienced. Marked by sharp, vicious firefights that bloodied noses on both sides, but never really produced a total victor, Dau Tieng proved to be a lesson in futility. But the young Eagles proved up to the task.

Next stop on the Brigade's bandwagon was back to Cu Chi. The following three month sojourn was marked by numerous combat assaults and cordon operations designed to keep the local VC off balance. It was during one of these operations that Sp4 Frank A. Herda earned his Congressional Medal of Honor. Sp4 Herda was serving with Company A 1/506th on June 29, 1968, and was part of a battalion-sized night defense perimeter set up just outside Trang Bang, when a large enemy force attacked. While other enemy elements put down diversionary and indirect fire on the west side of the battalion perimeter, a group of about thirty sappers armed with hand grenades and small satchel charges attacked Company A's spot in the perimeter from the east. As the enemy sappers tried unsuccessfully to penetrate the battalion's lines, a last-ditch, desperate effort by five of VC commandos succeeded in breaching the wire. The five screaming enemy soldiers broke through and charged the position defended by Herda and two of his buddies, one of whom had been wounded in the earlier fighting and now lay helpless in the bottom of their foxhole. Herda brought the enemy soldiers under fire, shooting at them until they were within ten feet of his fighting position. One of them tossed a grenade into Herda's foxhole just as Herda fired the last round from his M-79, hitting one of the enemy soldiers in the head. Realizing he had a "live" grenade in his fighting position, Herda immediately dropped upon the grenade shielding its blast with his body. The resulting explosion wounded Herda grievously, but his actions prevented his comrades from being either severely wounded or killed, and enabled the last defender to destroy the remainder of the VC sappers.

After three months at Cu Chi, the Brigade received word to move again by way of Phuoc Vinh to rejoin the Division in I Corps, replacing the 82nd Airborne Division's 3rd Brigade which had been OPCON to the 101st Airborne Division since February 14, 1968. The 3rd Brigade's legacy as the "Wanderer's" of Vietnam was coming to an end. In the Brigade's first year in Vietnam, it killed 1,987 enemy soldiers, captured 62 prisoners, 375 detainees, 293 individual and 138 crew-served weapons, and 141 tons of rice. For the first time in the Vietnam War, the Screaming Eagles of the 101st Airborne Division would be together in one place. The Division would be responsible for a TAOR that had previously been the responsibility of a full Marine division and the larger, more mobile First Air Cavalry Division.

Operation NEVADA EAGLE was kicked off at a time when the NVA in central I Corps Tactical Zone were trying to pull their shattered forces together after their punishing defeat during Tet '68. Critical to their survival and to their ability to go back on the offensive in 1969, the NVA/VC units in Thua Thien Province had to rely on securing a share of the upcoming rice harvest. The mission of the paratroopers of the 1st and 2nd Brigades of the 101st Airborne Division was three-fold: to protect the villagers as they harvested their spring rice crop, to deny the enemy any part of that harvest, and to pacify that part of Thua Thien Province within its area of operations.

Working closely with the South Vietnamese district chiefs, the Screaming Eagles set about to accomplish their mission. Operation NEVADA EAGLE officially began on May 17, 1968, with the companies of both brigades moving into the countryside and coastal plains around Hue in search of the enemy.

The first significant combat of the operation occurred four days later on May 21st, when Camp Eagle was attacked by an NVA battalion supported by sapper teams carrying satchel charges. The assault began at 0030 hours and was preceded by a 400 round barrage consisting of 122mm rockets, 82mm mortars, and B-40 and 41 rocket-grenades directed against Division headquarters. The ground attack struck behind the covering barrage and was beaten back by headquarters troops, airborne infantrymen from the 2/502nd and supporting helicopters, but not before sapper teams had succeeded in penetrating deep into the heart of the sprawling 101st base camp. A sweep of the area the next morning, turned up 54 enemy dead and recovered 16 individual weapons, 40 unexploded satchel charges, 30 bangalore torpedoes, and over four dozen RPG rockets. The same night, 2/327th troopers were assaulted in their battalion night defensive perimeter by an unknown-sized enemy force. Responding with small arms and artillery fire, the 1st Brigade troopers succeeded in repulsing the attack.

The next morning, a sweep of the area outside the perimeter turned up 31 enemy bodies and a dozen weapons.

A few days later, 1st Brigade forces from the 1/327th discovered the first of a series of large NVA weapons and equipment caches they were to uncover while conducting screening operations in the dense triple canopy jungles west of Hue. Other elements of the same battalion found three light artillery pieces, a pair of 12.7mm anti-aircraft guns and a truck deep in the jungle below Fire Base Veghel. Three days later, paratroopers from the 2/327th turned up the largest single cache of Operation NEVADA EAGLE. Over 230 individual and crew-served weapons were unearthed from well-camouflaged storage bunkers, buried deep in the earth and hidden beneath several feet of overgrown brush. At the same time, paratroopers from the battalion's sister unit, the 1/327th were back to their old habit of depriving the enemy of his tools of the trade. In a jungle-covered motor pool less than five klicks from Fire Base Veghel, the 1st Brigade troopers discovered a fleet of 54 NVA trucks which they destroyed in place. For the hungry NVA in the area, it meant back to the bicycles.

While 1st Brigade forces were busy sweeping the jungles west of Hue for elusive NVA units, 2nd Brigade paratroopers, with the help of 2/17th cavalrymen, continued conducting their patented sweep and cordon operations throughout the rich rice paddies and among the numerous villages dotting the coastal plains. During the fourth week of NEVADA EAGLE, Delta Company 1/502nd troopers searched a village and uncovered 35 tons of rice earmarked for NVA forces back in the mountains. The same day, cavalrymen from the 2/17th Cav made a big discovery of their own, capturing six tons of harvested rice. Not to be outdone, the 2/501st unearthed 3,100 pounds while its sister battalion, the 1/501st, contributed another 2,400 pounds. But it wasn't to end there. The B Troop cavalrymen once again struck a blow against NVA overeating, by bringing in nearly nine tons, while Charlie Company 1/501st topped the Cav's find with another cache of nearly 10 tons. It continued like that for several weeks until after two months into Operation NEVADA EAGLE, the Division had confiscated nearly 325 tons of rice. That's 700,000 pounds of life sustaining groceries missing from the enemy's larders. There were to be some lean months ahead for the NVA/VC in central Thua Thien Province. The only saving grace was there would be over 1,100 fewer enemy soldiers in the food chain. And food wasn't to be the only shortage, as Screaming Eagles captured nearly 2,000 individual and crew-served weapons and large amounts of ammunition, grenades and rockets. On July 1, 1968 the Division was redesignated the 101st Air Cavalry Division—a title that lasted only seven weeks—and became an "airmobile" division, giving up its "airborne" status. Its inventory of 15,000 parachutes would be traded for more than 400 helicopters of various shapes, sizes and configurations, as the Division joined with the 1st Air Cavalry Division in pioneering the new airmobility concept that was to make the two organizations the most hard-hitting allied combat divisions in the Vietnam war. In mid-July, Major General Melvin Zais—"Lucky Eagle"— replaced Major General O.M. Barsanti—"Brave Eagle"— as the new Division commander. His promise to the Division would set the standard for his command, "My mission as your Division Commander is twofold: First, I came here to fight; second, I have a grave responsibility to take care of you."

ON APRIL 19TH, Major General Sidney Tolson, the commander of the 1st Cavalry Division, sent his 3rd Brigade, followed soon after by his 1st Brigade, air-assaulting into the northern end of the A Shau Valley. Plagued by bad weather, hostile terrain, an elusive enemy, and deadly accurate anti-aircraft fire, the cavalrymen spent nearly a month sweeping along the floor of the valley and up into the nearby foothills in a vain attempt to catch the NVA before they could escape across the border into Laos. But the NVA, still master players at the game of "keep-away", avoided the roving cavalrymen as they fled across the border into Laos, carrying with them as much of their weapons, equipment and supplies as they could remove. However, it hadn't kept them from ringing the surrounding ridgelines with heavy machine guns and anti-aircraft weapons designed to punish the 1st Air Cavalry Division and its supporting 3rd ARVN Regiment for trespassing into "their" domain. Resupply, medivac, and air support became a very risky proposition and quickly raised the stakes in an operation that failed to pay the dividends envisioned by its planners. Operation DELAWARE/LAM SON 216 uncovered a large number of enemy weapons and equipment, and briefly disrupted the enemy's undisputed enjoyment of the valley's amenities, but it failed miserably in its mission to destroy the NVA forces in the valley and deny them forever its use as a base area. For shortly after the Cav and their allies pulled out amid low hanging rain storms, not quite a full month after going into the valley, the NVA were moving back and hardly affected by the inconvenience of it all.

But MACV was obsessed with ending the enemy's domination of the A Shau. In August, it was the Screaming Eagles' turn to go into the "valley of death." Division planners took time from the long-running Operation NEVADA EAGLE, to lay out Operation SOMERSET PLAIN. SOMERSET PLAIN was designed to trap NVA forces in the A Shau Valley and cut off their supply routes from the west. On August 3, 1968, two 1st Brigade battalions, the 2/502nd and the 2/327th, air-assaulted into the valley, landing on the valley floor near the old A Luoi and Ta Bat Special Forces camps. Establishing forward support bases around the old airstrips, companies from the two battalions immediately began sweeping the surrounding jungles in an attempt to locate the enemy and uncover his hidden bases before he could evacuate them into Laos. As with the 1st Air Cav's A Shau invasion back in April, the 101st Air Cav would fare no better. On August 5th, two battalions of the 1st ARVN Division air-assaulted into the area secured by the 2/327th and immediately joined in the effort to locate the enemy. Then the paratroopers of the 1/327th joined its 1st Brigade brothers in the valley. Meeting only scattered resistance from NVA stay-behind forces, the Americans and South Vietnamese units soon learned the same frustration as their counterparts before them. American combat engineer and recon units took advantage of the situation to rappel onto a couple of nearby mountain tops east of the valley to clear away the thick vegetation, constructing bunkers, digging trenches and staking out concertina wire for the purpose of establishing a number of fire support bases. No one knew how to throw up fire bases in mountainous country like the 101st. It was a gift, an art-form, and the Screaming Eagles excelled at it.

As SOMERSET PLAIN began to wind down, other engineer units along with heavy teams from F Company, 58th Infantry (Long Range Patrol), commanded by Captain Kenneth Eklund, were infiltrated into the valley. Linking up with patrolling infantry units, the engineers began laying mine fields along the roads and trails that criss-crossed the floor of the valley. As the engineers plied their trade, guarded by the infantry, the Lurps slipped away unobtrusively to plant sensor devices and booby traps beside hidden trails, stream crossings, and road intersections along the base of the mountains. This time the enemy would find a few surprises waiting for him when he moved back into the valley.

On August 21st, fleets of Huey slicks and Chinooks from the 101st Aviation Battalion, escorted by gunships from the 2/17th Cav and 4/77th Aerial Artillery shuttled back and forth between Camp Eagle and the A Shau to remove the raiding units as quickly as possible. No one wanted to be the last to leave the deadly valley. However, stay behind teams from the Division long range patrol company lay hidden in the jungles along major NVA access routes to monitor the enemy's return into the valley.

From the NVA's point of view, Operation SOMERSET PLAIN left the A Shau Valley in a mess. The Americans and their South Vietnamese allies destroyed numerous enemy base camps, uncovered a multitude of weapons and supply caches, and rendered the road network running through the valley impassable and littered with minefields. The 17-day raid had only accounted for 170 NVA dead, four prisoners, and 58 weapons captured. But it was the second time in four months the enemy was to receive a very clear message, " There will be a stiff price to pay if you remain in the A Shau Valley." On August 29th, the Screaming Eagles shed the title of 101st Air Cavalry Division, and once again became known as the 101st Airborne

Division, but this time with the additional designation (Airmobile).

BACK TO NEVADA EAGLE

RETURNING TO OPERATION NEVADA EAGLE, the Screaming Eagles went back to the cordon tactics that had worked so well during CARENTAN II and the early phase of NEVADA EAGLE. But this time the cordon operations would be given a different twist. Previously, extensive artillery preparation, followed by airstrikes always preceded a cordon operation. While this procedure usually "softened up" the enemy trapped inside the cordon, it also caused a lot of collateral damage to the enclosed terrain and structures. In addition, it often warned the enemy they were in imminent danger of being surrounded, or at the very least attacked, giving them ample opportunity to "slip out the back way" before the cordon could be closed.

Under the new concept, a minimum of artillery and air power would be used prior to establishing the cordon. Instead, tight encirclements, night movements, deception and surprise tactics were employed to seal an area prior to the enemy being alerted. The "classic " cordon operation of the Vietnam war occurred as a direct result of this new philosophy—the Battle of Vinh Loc Island. On September 11, 1968, four companies from the 1/501st and the 54th ARVN Regiment air-assaulted onto the east coast of a 24-kilometer long island/peninsula that jutted out into the South China Sea. The VC had moved onto the island sanctuary after Tet and were still using it as an R&R center and a district supply base. Armored personnel carriers from the 3/7th ARVN Cav moved in from the north as U.S. Navy Swift Boats and armored barges from the Hue River Security Group cut off any escape to the sea. With the cordon in place, U.S. paratroopers and ARVN soldiers moved in to search the island. Caught totally by surprise, enemy soldiers tried desperately to go to ground. Those who couldn't attempted to mix with the local population. The U.S. and ARVN soldiers quickly set about to separate the wheat from the chaff. One terrified group of 213 detainees were set down at a secure collection point after having just experienced their first helicopter ride. A quick-thinking national policeman saw that the detainees were somewhat confused and euphoric after their airborne experience and decided to exploit the situation. He walked up, put his hands on his hips and shouted in Vietnamese, "All members of the K-4 Battalion over here, those with the C-118 over there!" Sixty-three VC soldiers dazedly followed his instructions.

When the operation finally ended ten days later, 153 enemy soldiers had been killed, 178 individual and crew-served weapons were captured, and 370 prisoners had been apprehended of which 126 were positively identified as part of the local Viet Cong infrastructure. As an added bonus, 56 more "Hoi Chanhs" seized their moment of opportunity to rally to the cause of the South Vietnamese government. Of this total 139 enemy soldiers decided to switch sides and volunteer for the ARVN forces. The Vinh Loc operation proved to be an ARVN recruiter's bonanza.

During several weeks of cordon operations—AN THAN, PHU VANG I-IV, TROUI BRIDGE CORDON—and with the assistance of a major typhoon, the new concept of encirclement without air and artillery prep had accounted for losses to the enemy of 1,178 men—against only 32 suffered by friendly forces.

By the end of November, the coastal plains had been cleared of sizable NVA elements and, for all intents and purposes, the Viet Cong infrastructure had ceased to exist as a threat to the South Vietnamese government. Operation NEVADA EAGLE shifted its focus westward to the steep, jungled mountains of the Chaine Annamitique. The monsoon season limited the scope of the war, forcing American units to go into the mountains in search of the enemy. It was a time of infantry sweeps in the high country, and small patrols and ambushes out in the coastal plains. Except for occasional forage missions into the populated coastal plains for food, the NVA was forced to hide back deep in their mountain sanctuaries to lick their wounds and replace their losses, if they were to go back on the offensive during the coming dry season.

Operation NAM HOA I ran from November 18th through December 7th. Conducted by the 2/501st and elements of the 3rd ARVN Regiment, the goal of the operation was to locate and destroy the 5th NVA Regiment, led by the notorious Colonel Mot. Staging out of fire support bases Panther II and Panther III, elements of the 2/501st swept the valleys southwest of Leech Island in search of the elusive 5th NVA Regiment. Continuous heliborne combat assaults, in conjunction with flanking maneuvers and massed fire power, were conducted to trap and destroy the enemy. When the operation drew to a close nearly three weeks later, 78 NVA had been killed, 65 individual and 13 crew-served weapons had been captured, and large quantities of ammunition and supplies, including 122 mm rockets had been destroyed. The price tag-six killed and 39 wounded. Operation RAWLINS VALLEY was conducted in Nam Hoa District in Thua Thien Province and was in response to reliable intelligence data that indicated the district was being used as a base area by the 6th NVA Regiment. The 1/506th, the 3/187th and elements of the 3rd ARVN Regiment conducted combat assaults and reconnaissance in force operations within the Nam Hoa District. NVA forces avoided contact, and the operation netted only eight enemy killed. But the operation, running from December 16-24, succeeded in forcing the 6th NVA Regiment to abandon its base areas and move deeper into the surrounding mountains, impeding their ability to launch operations in the near future from the Nam Hoa area.

Operation TODD FOREST began December 3, 1968, and involved the 1/506th and elements of the 1st ARVN Division. Similar in mission and scope to Operation RAWLINS VALLEY, TODD FOREST succeeded in destroying numerous bunker complexes and supply caches in Nam Hoa District. In addition, the operation netted 12 enemy killed, and 26 individual weapons captured. Large quantities of rice, mortar rounds, and Viet Cong currency were confiscated. Ending on January 13, 1969, TODD FOREST saw only two friendlies wounded during the operation. Operation PLATTE CANYON began January 6, 1969, and involved elements of the 2/502nd, the 1/327th, the 2/327th, the ARVN 7th Armored Cavalry Task Force, and the 54th ARVN Regiment. The operation was planned to go after NVA/VC supply and staging areas in the Ruong Ruong and Elephant valleys. Preceding the attack, fire bases Dagger and Cutlass were constructed to support the combined operation. Moving ahead of the maneuver elements, a reconnaissance platoon uncovered a large cache and staging area. Sweeping through the area, the maneuver elements secured the local population centers and several key installations located along QL1. The local Viet Cong infrastructure was substantially weakened when a number of its members were killed and captured during the operation. Overall losses for the NVA/VC in the area were 80 dead, 10 prisoners captured, with 72 individual and crew-served weapons collected by the allies. In addition, a large quantity of munitions, supplies and equipment was destroyed. Friendly forces lost 10 killed in action and 19 wounded. The operation officially ended February 5, 1969.

The next operation supporting NEVADA EAGLE was SHERMAN PEAK which began on January 24th. Delta Company 1/501st, the 1/502nd and the 3/3rd ARVN Regiment responded to increased enemy activity along Route 547 and on the Rao Nai River, indicating the NVA were moving reinforcements and supplies from rear staging areas in the A Shau Valley toward the coastal plains and specifically the vicinity around Fire Base Veghel. Featuring rapid, hard-hitting combat assaults and reconnaissance in force, the operation succeeded in slamming the lid on all enemy infiltration along Route 547. The operation concluded on February 9th with little actual contact and only a single NVA soldier killed in action. However, a large munitions cache was located and destroyed. Third Brigade elements from all three battalions and units from the 1st ARVN Division, struck deep into suspected base areas of the 6th NVA Regiment on January 24th in Operation OHIO RAPIDS. Encountering enemy trail watchers, snipers, and stay-behind squads, the allied commanders soon realized that the enemy was employing delaying tactics while their main forces withdrew north into Base Area 101. To counter this, the maneuver elements were ordered to pursue the enemy into the area around the Lgon O'Lau River just south of

Base Area 101. During this phase of the operation, the 6th NVA regimental command post was discovered and destroyed. Its destruction insured the 6th NVA Regiment would play no offensive role in the upcoming 1969 Tet season. The operation came to a close on February 28th accounting for 102 NVA/VC killed, five taken captive, and 73 individual and 15 crew-served weapons captured. Friendly casualties were only six U.S. and six ARVN killed.

The final collateral operation running in conjunction with Operation NEVADA EAGLE was Operation SPOKANE RAPIDS. Commencing on February 20th, SPOKANE RAPIDS saw elements from the 2/502nd, the 3/187th (OPCON to the 1st Brigade) drive deep into Nam Hoa District in response to intelligence reports indicating the 5th NVA Regiment was now using the area as a rear support base, and the Ta Trach and Pao Mai Rivers as direct lines of communication and resupply for their combat elements in forward operational areas. Once again believing the enemy would withdraw toward the Ruong-Ruong and A Shau valleys, 2/502nd companies jumped in to secure Fire Support Base Normandy and construct Fire Support Base Spear in the very heart of the operational area. Weather hampered the construction of FSB Spear, and by the time the maneuver elements were able to conduct operations the enemy had once again withdrawn from the area. The operation closed out on March 3rd with enemy losses of nine killed and two wounded. Friendly losses were three killed and 11 wounded.

A WANDERER RETURNS

October saw the departure of the 3rd Brigade of the 82nd Airborne Division—which had been OPCON to the 101st since February 14, 1968—for III Corps Tactical Zone, and the simultaneous return of the 101st's own 3rd Brigade—now commanded by Colonel Joseph B. Conmy, Jr.—to its operational control. The Brigade had moved seven times in combat operations, and upon arriving in I Corps Tactical Zone, established the unique record of being the only American Brigade-sized unit to have served in all four tactical zones.

A month after the 3rd Brigade arrived at Camp Eagle—in an overnight shift—the 1st Cavalry Division (Airmobile) departed I Corps for III Corps Tactical Zone to beef up the defense around Saigon, while the 3rd Brigade received orders to deploy to the now empty Camp Evans, some 20 miles north of Camp Eagle, and assume control of the Cav's old AO. Camp Evans became the 3rd Brigade's ninth home in eleven months. The 3rd Brigade quickly moved into the sprawling division-sized base camp, and within a week was conducting ground operations in its new area of responsibility.

The 3rd Brigade's new AO included the infamous "Street Without Joy," the deadly A Shau Valley, the Song Bo River, and the Son Trach River.

Every type of terrain feature common to Thua Thien Province could be found in the Brigade's new AO. Running back from the coast were white sand beaches interspersed with numerous tiny hamlets and fishing villages. Farther inland, beginning near Highway 1 and extending westward toward the mountains, were rice-rich coastal plains and gently rolling piedmont hills sparsely vegetated and dotted with ancient family gravesites. Then, rising sharply towards the sky was the legendary Chaine Annamitique—the ubiquitous mountain range with its impenetrable valleys and double and triple canopied jungles that harbored the deadly A Shau, Ruong-Ruong, and Elephant valleys.

WAR IN THE SOUTH

WITH THE WANDERING 3rd Brigade back with the Division, only the prodical 3rd Battalion of the 506th Infantry was still fighting its own war. The "bastard battalion," still based at Phan Thiet, spent the remainder of 1968 running operations DOUBLE EAGLE I-V. The short, back-to-back operations consisted of continuous patrolling interspersed with the heavy use of bushmaster or ambushing tactics. The Currahees succeeded in keeping the enemy in Binh Thuan Province from achieving his stated goals of disrupting the lives of the local citizenry and humiliating the South Vietnamese government. In addition to accomplishing their mission, the paratroopers of the 3/506th conducted joint operations with elements of the 44th ARVN Regiment, providing them with valuable training and motivation .

Final tallies for the battalion at the close of January 1969, for the preceding twelve month period running from Tet '68 to Tet '69 was 832 enemy killed in action, 24 prisoners of war, 396 detainees, 281 small arms and 86 crew-served weapons captured, 1,792 structures destroyed, 140 tons of rice, 1500 pounds of flour, 7000 pounds of wheat, over 42,000 rounds of small arms ammo, a multitude of equipment from sewing machines and radios to explosives and one truck. All in all 1968 had been a very productive year for the 3rd Battalion Currahees.

On February 1st, 1969, Task Force 3/506th initiated Operation SHERIDAN in the same AO, Binh Thuan Province and portions of Ninh Thuan and Binh Tuy provinces to the southwest. The operation involved continued heavy patrolling and bushmaster operations conducted by the Screaming Eagles for the purpose of protecting the city of Phan Thiet during the suspected enemy offensive of Tet '69. During operations HANCOCK EAGLE I and II, the Battalion was awarded the Valorous Unit Citation for its actions during the period of February 12-22. A total of 111 enemy soldiers were killed, and another five captured by the Currahees during this period. Nearly 50 small arms and 10 crew-served weapons, plus 40 tons of rice were taken from the enemy.

Operation HANCOCK EAGLE—PHASE III ran from February 23rd to April 3rd. During these battalion operations, HANCOCK QUEEN and HANCOCK FLAME, the 3/506th succeeded in killing another two dozen enemy soldiers and capturing additional weapons and equipment. It was becoming apparent the 3rd Battalion's operations had succeeded in curtailing enemy activities and bringing about pacification in Binh Thuan Province. Enemy contact during the remainder of 1969 remained light. During the fall of 1969, the Battalion's Delta Company made the Division's first amphibious assault. On November 3rd, the Battalion moved to Ban Me Thuot to provide road security operations on the vital supply route QL21 to the besieged camps, Bu Prang and Duc Lap, on the Cambodian border.

On December 20th, the Currahees moved to Qui Nhon for combined operations with the 173rd Airborne Brigade in the Crowsfoot Mountain Range, focusing on the destruction of enemy bunkers and fortified positions along its supply and infiltration routes. In a ferocious battle there, elements of the 3/506th killed over 90 NVA.

The battle for Hill 474 began when Bravo Company 3/506th uncovered a large weapons and ammunitions cache while searching a series of caves on Hill 474. The Currahees found five crew-served weapons, two 82mm mortars, two 57mm recoilless rifles, one 7.62mm Type 57 Soviet machine gun, and an NVA radio. After cataloging the captured equipment, the company established security and set down to eat chow. Suddenly, NVA snipers hidden in concealed caves around them opened up, wounding several Screaming Eagles. A short time later four medivac helicopters were shot trying to evacuate wounded paratroopers.

Incensed by the pounding taken by the dust-off helicopters, troopers from Bravo Company moved quickly into the caves and wiped out the enemy using nothing more than .45 caliber pistols and hand grenades. When it was all over, nearly a hundred dead NVA were found in the cave complex.

NEVADA EAGLE DRAWS TO A CLOSE

HARASSING ATTACKS BY rocket and mortar against U.S. base camps and fire support bases characterized the fighting in October and November. The Division responded by sending its long range patrols into the "rocket belt" to locate the NVA rocket teams. It was during one of these missions that a twelve-man "heavy" team from F Company 58th Infantry (Long Range Patrol) was surrounded by elements of the 5th NVA Regiment in the heart of the Ruong-Ruong valley southwest of Hue. The team had ambushed a ten-man NVA unit less than 400 meters from an enemy regimental base camp. Killing nine of the NVA in the ambush, including the regimental executive officer and a medical team, the Lurps recovered seven weapons, medical supplies and a large bag full of maps and documents. The team waited at the ambush site for either a reaction force or helicopters to extract them, but unfortunately, neither event was about to occur. Unknown to the team, its assigned helicopters from Bravo Company 101st Aviation Battalion—the Kingsmen—had been removed from their operational control and had been placed OPCON to one of the Division's brigades for a multi-battalion combat assault. As luck would have it, when the Lurps most needed their air support, it was busily engaged in another part of the country.

Ninety minutes later, trying to signal the Lurp company commander flying C&C overhead in a small LOH scout helicopter, the Lurp point man was gunned down by an enemy force that had moved up and surrounded the team. This initiated a five-hour firefight during which NVA forces tried on numerous occasions to overrun the team's position. The battle would see four Lurps killed, including the team leader, and the remaining seven wounded before a reaction force of 23 volunteers from F Company 58th Infantry (Long Range Patrol) combat assaulted into the jungle and fought its way through an encircling NVA reinforced battalion to reach the team's survivors. A back-up reaction force from D Troop 2/17th Cav landed behind the Long Range Patrol reaction force and secured the LZ while the dead and wounded Lurps were evacuated from the battleground by means of jungle penetrator and rope. Six members of the reaction force were subsequently wounded in the rescue attempt. Marking their positions with cigarette lighters, both reaction forces were extracted after dark by courageous Kingsmen pilots who hovered their Hueys over a heavily obstructed LZ while the Lurps and cavalrymen climbed ladders to get aboard. The lengthy combat action saw the subsequent awarding of one Distinguished Service Cross (with a recommendation for the Medal of Honor), six Silver Stars (with two recommendations for Distinguished Service Crosses), seven Bronze Stars with "V" devise, two Distinguished Flying Crosses and seventeen Purple Hearts. It was a sad day for the 101st Airborne Division. Although there was never a full and accurate accounting of enemy casualties, members of the reaction force claim to have charged through numerous enemy dead on their way to reach the trapped team at the top of the hill.

Action in December dropped off to virtually nothing as the enemy withdrew deeper into the mountains to his rear sanctuaries to rebuild and prepare for Tet '69 and the coming Spring offensive.

OPERATION NEVADA EAGLE officially ended on February 28, 1969. The 9-month long operation accounted for 3,299 enemy dead of which 1,384 were NVA and 1,915 were VC. There were 853 prisoners captured, of which 55 were NVA and 798 were VC. Hoi Chanhs numbered 714. The operation netted a total of 3,702 weapons and more than 667 tons of rice. American casualties were 205 killed in action and 1,822 wounded in action.

The operation succeeded in destroying the Viet Cong infrastructure in the coastal plains and driving the NVA deep into their mountain sanctuaries. Pacification was becoming a reality to the citizens of Thua Thien Province. The city of Hue enjoyed a peaceful Tet holiday season in 1969—the tab had been paid by the 101st Airborne Division.

VIETNAMIZATION, PACIFICATION AND BAD HAMBURGER?

THE FIRST MAJOR Division-wide operation of 1969 was KENTUCKY JUMPER. It saw Screaming Eagles returning to the A Shau Valley for the first time since their daring raid into the NVA stronghold in August 1968, during Operation SOMERSET. But KENTUCKY JUMPER was different. It was not a mere raid, designed to disrupt the resident NVA. No, KENTUCKY JUMPER was an invasion, with "conquest" as its goal. The 101st Airborne Division (Airmobile) had come to make the A Shau Screaming Eagle country. No one had been able to tame the valley before, and many had tried. In late '65 and early '66, U.S. Army Special Forces had invaded the A Shau with their CIDG strikers, building fortified camps at A Luoi, Ta Bat, and A Shau along the valley's floor. In March of 1966, the NVA sitting in the hills around the valley, decided they didn't want the camps interfering with their livelihood anymore, and went about closing them down one by one. For two years, the NVA enjoyed unchallenged ownership of the valley, until, in May of 1968, the 1st Cavalry Division, along with the 101st's 1st Brigade and the 3rd ARVN Airborne Task Force, struck deep into the valley, where they probed around through the thick vegetation for a couple of weeks before pulling out, patting themselves on the back for a job well done. Unfortunately, the skeletons of sixty Cav helicopters left behind as a parting shot at Operation DELAWARE attested to the firm resolve of the enemy soldiers in the valley.

The NVA soon moved back in again, totally undisturbed at the inconvenience of having to slip across the border into Laos while the American cavalrymen and paratroopers spent a couple of weeks storming around the valley uncovering a few caches and blowing up some bunkers. If the lines of communication had been open between the opposing forces, one could almost expect the NVA to query, " Was it as good for you as it was for us?"

In August, the Screaming Eagles decided that it was their turn to get star's billing, and "having a go at it," as the British would say. Operation SOMERSET PLAIN saw the valley full of Eagles for seventeen days while the landlords of the A Shau once again decided to take their ball and go home. The paratroopers managed to repeat the efforts of their cavalrymen brothers—without losing as many helicopters. Unfortunately, the results of SOMERSET PLAIN mirrored those of Operation DELAWARE. With untouchable sanctuaries just a hop, skip and a jump across the border into Laos, it was much easier and far less punishing for the NVA to back off while the Americans took their frustrations out on the jungle and a few diehard stay behinds. They had learned in the past that standing toe-to-toe with the Americans was not the way to win a decisive victory.

So KENTUCKY JUMPER was designed to end all that. The next 167 days would see three separate operations conducted under KENTUCKY JUMPER. The first of these would be Operation MASSACHUSETTS STRIKER kicking off on March 1, 1969. Hampered by inclement weather from the onset, the operation began with engineers from the 326th Engineer Battalion going in to erect a string of fire bases, among them FSBs Fury and Whip, along the eastern edge of the A Shau. Unable to deploy the 2nd Brigade maneuver battalions earmarked for the invasion because of poor weather conditions, Charlie Company 1/502nd air assaulted into the abandoned FSB Veghel as a diversion as the weather finally cleared. Landing in the middle of a company from the 816th NVA Battalion waiting in ambush, they were immediately embroiled in bitter fighting that would last through the night and into the next day. When the smoke and dust of the battle finally cleared, the O' Deuce troopers were left on the battlefield among the bodies of twelve dead NVA soldiers. The remainder of the battalion piled in on top of Veghel and quickly moved off in pursuit of the survivors of the enemy company. It wasn't long before the paratroopers discovered a mass grave with the bodies of eight more NVA soldiers killed in the fight with Charlie Company. For thirty-three days the enemy company ran, chased by the 1/502nd. On April 14th, the company linked up with the rest of the 816th NVA Battalion at the crest of Dong A Tay Ridge. All along the crest of Dong A Tay Ridge were deep, well built bunkers tied together by interconnecting tunnels and trenches. In those bunkers 300-500 men of the 816th NVA Battalion squatted patiently. They were no longer running.

Lieutenant Colonel Donald Davis, the commanding officer of the 1/502nd, suspected the battered enemy company he had been pursuing had holed up on Dong A Tay Ridge. However, he had no idea as to what waited for him and his troopers on the high ground above them. On April 17th, Colonel Davis sent Alpha Company up the side of Dong A Tay Ridge. Expecting sniper fire and trail watchers, the company was met head on by an intense barrage of small arms, machine gun, and RPG fire. In a matter of minutes Alpha Company's lead platoon had taken two dozen casualties of which half had been killed. Dragging its dead and wounded with them, the survivors retreated down the face of the mountain. Calling in artillery and air strikes to prep the ridgeline, Alpha Company was back on the attack with its platoons on line. They made it half way up the ridge before the NVA counterattacked, sending them reeling back down the mountain again.

Davis knew he was up against more than a single company. Sending his Charlie Company to set up a blocking force on the south side of the ridge, he ordered Bravo Company to maneuver around to the opposite side of the ridge and attack from there. It quickly met the same fate Alpha Company had suffered on the reverse slope earlier, taking ten casualties before withdrawing. Davis called in artillery and air strikes for two solid hours before sending Alpha and Bravo companies back against the ridge in a coordinated assault. Again the attackers were driven back. All three companies dug in around the base of the ridge as four separate artillery batteries pounded the ridge top the rest of the day and all through the night. The next morning, the enemy bunkers were still standing but their protective cover had been destroyed by the artillery pounding. Using 90mm recoilless rifles to knock out the exposed NVA bunkers, Alpha and Charlie companies attacked and reached the summit only to be thrown off again by another NVA counterattack.

For two more days, the fighting continued unabated until, finally, U.S. fighter-bombers succeeded in dropping two dozen 1,000 pound bombs with delayed fuses on top of the ridge. The "blockbusters" succeeded in collapsing the bunkers. Still a hundred diehard NVA were waiting when Alpha and Bravo companies got on line and finally took the ridge. It took several hours of tough fighting before it was finally secured. Dong A Tay was some of the toughest fighting the Screaming Eagles would face during the Vietnam war. They found 86 enemy bodies on the ridge, but later discovered an enemy hospital on the south side of the mountain where, according to a patient list, over half the 700 man NVA battalion had been killed. But the victory at "Bloody Ridge" as it soon became known had extracted a bloody price—thirty-five Americans had been killed and over a hundred wounded. It was only a prelude of the tough fighting to come in Operation APACHE SNOW.

In the early morning hours of March 29th, an NVA battalion reinforced by a Sapper company, launched a ground assault against FSB Jack, situated in the rolling hills southeast of Camp Evans. The infantry company and 155mm artillery battery on Jack, had been forewarned of the impending attack by three six-man Ranger reconnaissance teams from L Company 75th Infantry (Rangers), which had intercepted the NVA elements as they moved up to hit the fire base. Laying quietly in the eight foot high elephant grass as the enemy columns passed through their positions, the teams had radioed whispered warnings to their own radio relay team deployed on FSB Jack that they were about to be hit. At 0100, when the NVA opened with a withering barrage of RPGs and small arms fire, without the usual mortar prep, they were met by direct fire bee-hive rounds from the fully depressed 155's and an infantry company that had been standing by on a 100% alert.

In spite of the warning, enemy sappers still succeeded in breaching the perimeter and doing some minor damage before they were repelled.

As the NVA retreated back toward the mountains, they ran into the hidden Ranger teams. Cobra gunships and two "Puff the Magic Dragon" C-130 gunships were called in by the Rangers. The air power broke the back of the NVA for good. Dozens of NVA bodies were found outside the perimeter of Fire Base Jack the next morning. Three more dead NVA were found outside the Ranger positions, with dozens of blood trails running west through the elephant grass. U.S. casualties on Jack were light. The Rangers suffered two wounded.

Subsequent air assaults saw the remainder of the 1/502nd, along with the 2/501st, the 2/327th (OPCON to the 2nd Brigade on March 22nd and replaced by the 1/501st on April 15th), the 2/3rd and the 3/3rd ARVN Regiment, bring five maneuver battalions into the A Shau Valley. Combat assaults and fast moving reconnaissance in force quickly determined the NVA were once again avoiding contact and moving its main forces back across the border. But captured documents led to the discovery of one of the largest caches to date in the 101st's AO. When MASSACHUSETTS STRIKER came to a close on May 8th, 176 enemy soldiers had been killed by actual body count, two more had been captured, and 859 weapons had been taken out of circulation. Troopers from the 2/327th, operating in the southern A Shau, on March 22nd discovered several trucks and bulldozers along a heavy duty road being constructed by NVA engineers. In addition, on April 20th, Screaming Eagles of the 1/502, patrolling just south of Route 614—the "Yellow Brick Road"— in the northern end of the A Shau, uncovered a huge cache that included 14 trucks, over 600 brand new SKS rifles, ChiCom radios and field telephones, and large stocks of medical supplies.

WHILE MASSACHUSETTS STRIKER was going on, another battle took place in the A Shau Valley that bears telling here. On April 22nd, a FAC plane on a routine patrol over the northern end of the A Shau spotted some huts on a ridgeline below Dong Ngai mountain, in the sector known at Division as "the warehouse area"—a known NVA logistics center. The FAC pilot immediately called in an air strike on the huts. In a short period of time Air Force "fast movers" zeroed in on the FAC's marker rocket and began pounding the ridge with 250 and 500 lb. high explosive bombs. Suddenly, tremendous secondary explosions literally tore the top off the ridge. The bombs had found an NVA munitions storage area. The next day, B-52s pounded the area even harder with hundreds of tons of 1,000 pounders, causing even more secondary explosions. Division Intelligence decided to send in an aerial rifle platoon from the 2/17th Cav to do a BDA (bomb damage assessment) and to determine the size of the enemy storage area. The

CH-47 Chinook moved in to lower the platoon by ladder and was raked by a heavy burst of ground fire which sent it crashing into the jungle. Seven cavalrymen were killed in the crash and two others were seriously wounded. The dazed survivors crawled from the wreckage and set up a defensive perimeter around the crash site just in time to meet an attacking enemy platoon coming down off the mountain. The cavalrymen beat off the attack, inflicting heavy casualties on the enemy, but lost five more of their own in the process. Two more platoons from the Cav were rushed in to reinforce the crash site, and lost two more helicopters and ten men in the process. Hanging on through the night against repeated enemy attacks, and losing two light observation helicopters and a Cobra gunship in the process, the cavalrymen were in imminent danger of being wiped out. Their casualties had reached forty.

Staging out of Fire Support Base Blaze, a relief force consisting of Bravo Company 3/187th prepared to come in on the Cav's position, but aborted the combat assault at the last minute when the Cav took forty more casualties, beating back another daylight enemy attempt to overrun their perimeter. Instead, the relief force, now including Delta Company 3/187th, would attempt to combat assault into a prepared landing zone on top of Dong Ngai and then attack downhill toward the Cav perimeter, catching the NVA in a trap. After a pair of F-4s worked over the LZ with 500 lb. bombs, and Cobra gunships gave it a final prep, the first ship of the relief formation went into the single-ship LZ. It never made it out again. Intense enemy anti-aircraft fire turned the LZ into a deathtrap. Lieutenant Colonel Weldon Honeycutt, the 3/187th's commander, had a tough decision to make. He would have to reinforce the LZ or risk losing the paratroopers trapped on the LZ. He decided to reinforce. Three of the next five lift ships into the perimeter were shot down, the last one blocking the LZ. The surviving cavalrymen and aircrews, 58 in number, stripped the machine guns and ammunition from the four downed Hueys and set up a perimeter around the seven men injured in the crash. Two others had been killed. The survivors of Bravo Company held on for the rest of the night.

The next morning, the remainder of Bravo Company and half of Alpha Company combat assaulted into the lower LZ, securing it and helping the Cav evacuate its dead and wounded. Once completed, the paratroopers struck out for their trapped comrades above them.

At the higher LZ, the pilots of the downed Huey blocking the LZ managed to repair their ship and fly it out of the LZ. Delta Company immediately reinforced and managed to get five ships in and out of the LZ before the NVA woke up and shot the next two down.

Colonel Honeycutt landed on the lower LZ on the afternoon of April 25th and took charge of the operation. He set up a CP just before dark, then endured an hour long mortar attack followed by two company-sized infantry assaults which nearly overran the perimeter. Calling in napalm less than 50 meters from their positions, the paratroopers beat off the final attack and the enemy withdrew.

On the morning of April 27th, the Screaming Eagles went on the offensive. Alpha Company reinforced the upper LZ at first light, and succeeded in securing the high ground above it. With the upper LZ secured, Lieutenant Colonel Honeycutt ordered a massive air strike in the area between two LZs, then sent a platoon each from Bravo, Alpha and Delta companies attacking uphill. Each platoon began uncovering extensive arms and ammunition caches, protected by heavily reinforced enemy bunkers. Air strikes and recoilless rifle fire was utilized to deal with the bunkers. By the end of the day the three platoons had fought to within 200 meters of the upper LZ.

On the morning of the 28th, preceded by air strikes, the three platoons went back on the attack, while a platoon each from Alpha and Bravo companies began attacking downhill from the upper LZ. Thirty to forty NVA were caught between the two forces and killed. A linkup was effected in the afternoon, and a three hundred meter area surrounding the upper LZ was secured.

To exploit the situation, Lieutenant Colonel Honeycutt ordered in an engineer detachment to begin clearing the high ground above the upper LZ for a fire support base. By the evening of April 29th, three 105mm howitzer batteries were in place. Alpha Company set up shop to secure the new fire base, appropriately named "Airborne," while Bravo and Delta companies pushed off to root out the surviving NVA. Delta Company made contact and defeated an enemy platoon on the 30th, and in the process uncovered a large cache that contained twenty tons of rice and hundreds of RPG rounds and 122mm rockets.

During the next four days, Delta Company continued finding small caches and dealing with enemy snipers and trail watchers. On May 4th, it ran into an enemy company and after a vicious firefight overran their positions and drove them from Dong Ngai.

The 13-day battle for Dong Ngai had come to an end. The NVA had lost one of its largest logistical base areas in the A Shau. The 6th NVA Regiment had well over 100 of its soldiers killed and hundreds of tons of supplies and munitions destroyed. Surprisingly, for the ferocity of the fighting, the 3/187th had only five killed and fifty-four wounded. However, 2/17th Cavalry losses were significant with nine killed and 72 wounded.

ON MAY 8TH, the 3/187th was airlifted back to Camp Evans for a two-day rest before the "Big Show" started in the A Shau Valley around a mountain known as Dong Ap Bia. They were replaced on FSB Airborne by Alpha Company 2/501st from the 2nd Brigade. In the early evening hours on May 12th, while the battle for Hamburger Hill was just warming up, the 6th NVA Regiment crawled out of the caves it had been hiding in on Doi Thong Mountain, less than 2,500 meters from Dong Ngai, and began moving into position around FSB Airborne. Revenge was on their minds. They intended to pay the American paratroopers back for the loss of their logistics depot on Dong Ngai by destroying their new fire base and all of the men who guarded it.

The attack, early on the morning of May 13th, was preceded by a barrage of 82mm mortar fire, followed by a sapper attack by members of the K-12 Sapper Battalion. The assault lasted for three hours. When it ended at 0600, 40 NVA bodies were discovered in and around the perimeter. One other was captured. Drag marks and blood trails suggested that many more had been carried off. But the defenders also suffered heavy casualties. Twenty-six Screaming Eagles lay dead, and sixty-two more were wounded. The only victory at Airborne was that the fire base was held.

OPERATION BRISTOL BOOTS began on April 25th with the 2/327th, 3/5th Armored Cav Regiment (placed OPCON to the 101st Airborne Division on May 2nd), Charlie Company 2/34th Armor, and the 1/54th ARVN Regiment conducting airmobile operations south of Leech Island and armored cavalry assaults into the Ruong-Ruong Valley where intelligence had reported the massing of NVA heavy weapons, the stockpiling of war materials, and increased movement of enemy forces. The operation terminated on May 8th, with 22 NVA/VC killed, a single enemy captured, and 27 weapons liberated.

OPERATION APACHE SNOW, a XXIV Corps project, started on May 10th when the 3rd Brigade of the 101st Airborne Division (Airmobile), in conjunction with the 1st and 3rd ARVN Regiments, and in coordination with the 9th Marine Regiment 3rd Marine Division, air assaulted into the northern A Shau Valley. Under 3rd Brigade operational control were the 1/506th, the 2/501st, the 3/187th, Task Force 3/5th Armored Cav with Delta Company 2/506th OPCON to it. The 1st ARVN Regiment deployed its 2nd, 3rd and 4th Battalions, while the 3rd ARVN Regiment deployed its 1st Battalion. On D-Day the 1/506th, the 3/187th, the 2/501st, the 4/1st ARVN and a single company from the 2/1st ARVN conducted multiple battalion combat assaults along the Laotian border on the western side of the A Shau Valley.

The infantry assaults were well supported by ten full batteries of artillery sitting on multiple fire support bases on the eastern side of the valley. Arc-lights, tac air, aerial rocket artillery, tube artillery, and prepatory LZ reconnaissance by the 2/17th Air Cav Squadron prior to the combat assaults, saw to it all the maneuver battalions got on the ground without incident. Two battalions, the 3/187th and the 1/506th, had drawn initial objectives right up against the Laotian border, a side of the A Shau that had always been avoided in prior operations. The 1/506th had been tasked with interdicting Highway 923 from where it crossed the Laotian border to where it intersected Route 548 running up the middle of the A Shau Valley. The 3/187th had drawn the job of securing a huge mountain mass dominated by a peak known as Hill 937, or Dong Ap Bia. Division Intelligence believed it was being used as a way station for supplies being brought in from Laos. The 1/506th, patrolling out in two different directions from their landing zones, soon made contact with the enemy, but quickly eliminated its opposition, killing 12 NVA in the process. The 3/187th's Delta Company landed first along the spine of a secondary ridge just to the north of the imposing mountain mass known as Hill 937. Lieutenant Colonel Weldon Honeycutt, the battalion commander, was surprised that the landing had been unopposed and quickly ordered his Alpha and Charlie companies in on the same LZ. Keeping Charlie Company to secure the LZ along with the battalion headquarters, Colonel Honeycutt sent Delta Company to the south on a reconnaissance in force toward the top of 937, while dispatching Alpha to the north toward the Laotian border. Two hours after the initial combat assault, Lieutenant Colonel Honeycutt joined his battalion on the ground. Anxious to find the enemy before they could once again escape across the border, he released Charlie Company from its job of LZ security and sent them patrolling off in a different direction toward the border. Then, accompanied by his Headquarters Company and his heavy weapons platoon, Honeycutt moved off following in the tracks of Delta Company. Linking up with Delta about 1,000 meters below Dong Ap Bia at midday on the 10th, Honeycutt established a battalion CP and had his troops cut another LZ. He planned to establish a new CP on the top of Dong Ap Bia the next day. Little did he know that it would be ten more long and bloody days before his troopers would establish anything on the peak of Hill 937. By midafternoon, bunkers, fighting positions, and live NVA were sighted in the immediate vicinity of Dong Ap Bia. This served as a warning to Lieutenant Colonel Honeycutt that contact with the enemy was only a matter of time. But to take advantage of the lull, he decided to bring in Bravo Company, his battalion reserve, before the action started. With all four of his maneuver companies, plus his headquarters company on the ground by mid-afternoon, Honeycutt decided it was no longer time to cut bait. It was time to catch "fish." Anxious to secure the "high ground," he sent Bravo Company to accomplish just that. It was after 1600 hours when the company moved out. Three hundred meters away, the point platoon reached a deep saddle, and sent a squad to recon the opposite side. The NVA were waiting. Hit by

RPGs and small arms fire, the squad moved back across the saddle to where the rest of the platoon waited, and called in an airstrike. But by the time the skyraiders had done their thing, it was almost dark. Bravo Company decided to go into a night defensive perimeter and wait until the morning to continue the advance.

An hour and a half after daylight, Bravo Company was once more on the move, inching its way up the mountain, sensing that the enemy were waiting just ahead. Around 1500 hours the waiting came to an end. The point squad walked into an ambush and was decimated, suffering three killed and seven wounded. Contact grew more intense by the minute, and it soon became apparent the Rakassans had run into an NVA unit that had made the decision to stand and fight. The enemy (by now discovered to be the 7th and 8th Battalions of the 29th NVA Regiment—the Pride of Ho Chi Minh) were dug in deep along the face of Dong Ap Bia mountain, and were putting up a rather determined resistance to these initial probes by the 3/187th troopers. This action on the second day of the Operation APACHE SNOW would escalate into ten days of some of the most ferocious fighting of the Vietnam war. Over 16,000 artillery rounds and hundreds of helicopter gunship and tac air strikes would be used to "soften" the enemy positions. On May 18th, paratroopers actually approached within 25 meters of the crest of the mountain when the heavens opened and torrential rains turned the pulverized earth into cascading, slippery mud that offered zero purchase to the assaulting forces.

Before the battle for Dong Ap Bia finally came to an end on May 20, 1969, the 1/506th, the 2/501st and the 2/3rd ARVN, along with the 3/187th, were fed into the meat grinder. The final day of action—May 20th—saw all four battalions thrown into the attack simultaneously.

Hampered by the weather, well-placed enemy bunkers, trenches, and spider holes interconnected by a complex tunnel system, and by the sheer physical difficulty of attacking uphill, the American paratroopers and ARVN soldiers charged again and again into the face of incredible fire to finally eject the enemy from the mountain soon to earn the name "Hamburger Hill." The cost on both sides had been high. The official count listed the NVA suffering 691 killed in action, five captured, along with 241 individual and 40 crew-served weapons and vast amounts of equipment and supplies captured. A Special Forces reconnaissance patrol set up in position a cross the border in Laos where it could monitor the enemy withdrawal, counted approximately 1,100 dead and wounded NVA being carried off Dong Ap Bia. Allowing the continuous pounding from artillery and air strikes undoubtedly vaporized a large number of enemy soldiers along with their weapons and equipment, and it is very likely that the NVA suffered somewhere in excess of 1,800 dead and wounded during the joint allied assault on Hamburger Hill. American forces lost 55 killed in action and over 400 wounded in action. By all accounts, it was a great Allied victory, but the media soon turned it into a senseless and inane battle, without a strategic objective. Some rightly questioned why our troops were not pulled back while B-52s finished the job. That's a question for military historians, second guessers, and those who display incredible powers of hindsight. But Hamburger Hill was taken by ground-pounders, and to suggest alternative solutions after the fact is to discredit their courage and sacrifice. Although real estate was captured with the victory, it was abandoned again several days later. But then, this was the nature of the Vietnam war—a war of attrition, and body counts. At Dong Ap Bia, a reinforced, well-trained, and well-equipped NVA regiment was effectively destroyed before it could turn itself loose on the coastal plains around Hue. The price in American lives and dollars, though high, fell well within the "acceptable loss" ratios established by our military statisticians who decided such things. The most important result of the battle was perhaps the message it gave to the enemy—that there were no sanctuaries for them in South Vietnam. Operation APACHE SNOW officially ended on June 7, 1969. Shortly after the operation was over, General Melvin Zais, the Screaming Eagles' Division commander, was promoted to Lieutenant General and appointed XXIV Corps commander. Major General John M. Wright, Jr. took over command of the 101st Airborne Division (Airmobile).

THE FINAL MILITARY operation under KENTUCKY JUMPER, was MONT-GOMERY RENDEZVOUS. The operation began on June 8, 1969 when 3rd Brigade soldiers air assaulted into the ridges east of the A Shau in what was to be the final stage of the valley's conquest. Responding to intelligence reports which indicated that the 6th and 9th battalions of the 29th NVA Regiment, the 803rd NVA Regiment, and the 675th NVA Artillery Regiment were operating unimpeded in the northern end of the A Shau, the 1/506th and the 3/187th air assaulted into the area and began sweeping the surrounding foothills looking for the enemy. Simultaneously, in the floor of the valley, elements of the 326th Engineers, along with their equipment were being inserted by Chinooks and Flying Cranes. Their mission was to build a 1,500 foot airstrip near the old village of Ta Bat to accommodate C-7A Caribou aircraft. While this was going on in the center of the valley, engineers from the 27/18th Engineer Brigade were finishing up the final leg of Route 547, running from Camp Eagle to the A Shau. On June 20th, the first overland convoy reached the A Shau, as APCs from the 3/5th Armored Cav and 3/7th ARVN Armored Cav poured into the valley. The following week, tanks and self-propelled guns from the 3/5th and the 2/34th Armored reached the A Shau. Civilization had come to the valley.

Once again the enemy avoided contact with the massive American and ARVN forces patrolling the valley. The overpowering demonstration of massed armor was more than the NVA wanted to tackle.

However, on June 14th and 15th, NVA sapper teams and mortar units attacked FSB Berchtesgaden and FSB Currahee. The attack on Berchtesgaden was designed to knock out the 3rd Brigade Tactical Operations Center. It nearly succeeded. Colonel Joseph B. Conmy, Jr., the 3rd Brigade commanding officer was wounded in the attack as he fought off a sapper squad intent on destroying his command center. Colonel Conmy and the brigade sergeant major personally killed seven NVA sappers around the command bunker. The NVA lost 31 soldiers in the attack. FSB Currahee, hit the next day in a similar attack, cost the enemy another 55 killed.

MONTOGOMERY RENDEZVOUS PRODUCED two more Medals of Honor for Division soldiers. On July 11, 1969, Sp4 Gordon R. Roberts, was a rifleman with Company B 1/506th, during operations in the A Shau Valley. Roberts' platoon was moving along a ridgeline to relieve a friendly infantry company pinned down by heavily fortified enemy bunkers. As his platoon moved into position, they began receiving intense and accurate fire from hidden enemy bunkers located on higher ground on an adjoining hill. Realizing that his own platoon was now pinned down and unable to reach the trapped company, Specialist Roberts began crawling toward the enemy bunkers. When he got as close as the cover would allow, he jumped to his feet and charged the nearest bunker, firing as he ran. The two surprised enemy soldiers missed the attacking paratrooper, who quickly gunned them down. Roberts charged a second bunker, only to have his weapon shot out of his hands as he reached it. He grabbed up a rifle from a fallen comrade and silenced this bunker also. He quickly destroyed a third bunker with hand grenades. Now, deep inside the enemy positions and cut off from his platoon, Roberts did the only thing he could do, he continued his charge against a fourth enemy bunker, destroyed it, and fought his way into the perimeter of the trapped American company. Once he reached them, he helped them remove their wounded from exposed positions to evacuation points before returning to rejoin his unit.

During the period of July 15-19, 1969, Staff Sergeant John G. Gertsch, a platoon sergeant with Company E, 1/327th, earned his Medal of Honor posthumously for a series of valiant actions in the A Shau Valley. In an assault against a heavily fortified enemy position, Sergeant Gertsch took command of his platoon after braving enemy fire to rescue his badly wounded platoon leader. Under his leadership, the platoon beat back a determined enemy counterattack. A short time later, a small recon detachment from his platoon was attacked by an overwhelming enemy force. Sergeant Gertsch charged single-handedly at the enemy unit, fighting furiously and forcing them to withdraw, enabling two wounded comrades to be recovered. Wounded himself during a subsequent enemy attack, Sergeant Gertsch refused to be evacuated, continuing to lead his platoon. He spotted a medic from a nearby friendly unit treating a wounded officer. Seeing the two men were exposed to deadly and accurate enemy fire, Gertsch ran out into the open to draw the enemy fire until the wounded officer and the medic could reach safety. Before he could reach cover again, Sergeant Gertsch was killed.

When MONTGOMERY RENDEZVOUS ended on August 14th, with the airlift of the 3/187th back to Camp Evans, the operation had cost the enemy 451 killed, eight captured along with 270 individual and crew-served weapons liberated. The 9th Battalion of the 29th NVA Regiment had been run out of the country, and heavy casualties had been inflicted on the 803rd NVA Regiment. Operation KENTUCKY JUMPER had come to a close with the termination of MONTGOMERY RENDEZVOUS. The Screaming Eagle's 167 day sojourn in the A Shau had left its mark forever. Although the 101st Airborne Division had gone, the NVA's grip on the valley would never be the same. Most of its bases in the valley had been damaged or destroyed, its logistics system disrupted, its military forces decimated. Over 1,550 enemy soldiers were killed and 41 more were captured. The enemy lost 1,612 individual and 185 crew-served weapons. Hundreds of tons of supplies and equipment were destroyed. The Screaming Eagles had left behind an all-weather 1,500 foot airstrip, a completed highway running from Camp Eagle to the center of the valley, and numerous fire support bases dotting the high ground around the A Shau—mute testimony that if the enemy attempted to reestablish its presence in the A Shau Valley, the 101st Airborne Division would be back to kick them out again.

1ST BRIGADE LENDS A HAND

WHILE THE BATTLE of Hamburger Hill was being fought in the A Shau Valley, the NVA 2nd Division was threatening the Quang Tin Province Headquarters at Tam Ky under the protection of the American Division. Unable to pull its own elements out of the field, the American Division sent out a desperate call for help—a tactical emergency. Two NVA divisions were threatening to overrun the Marine airbase, and the nearby district capital of Tam Key. In addition, several U.S. fire bases, in particular LZ Professional, were under siege. With its maneuver battalions having full companies gobbled in and defeated in broad daylight, and its reserve companies busy defending beleaguered fire bases, the American Division had its back to the wall and was up to its collective ass in alligators. The 1st Brigade headquarters along with two 2nd Brigade battalions—the 1/501st and the 1/502nd—temporarily under the operational control of the 1st Brigade, prepared to answer the call. Beginning on May 15, 1969, the 1st Brigade, with its own supporting elements, deployed to Tam Ky and Chu Lai by air and sea lift. The full deployment took thirty-eight hours and required 66 C-130 aircraft sorties and a U.S. Navy LST. This was not the first time that the Brigade had joined the Americal Division in an operation. Twice before, the Brigade had fought with Task Force Oregon (later designated the Americal Division) during the battle for Duc Pho and again at Chu Lai.

The Americal Division's AO was one of the most diverse and extensive areas of operation in Vietnam. Unlike the 101st's AO just to the north, with its civilian population clustered along the coastal plains, the Americal's AO was characterized by villages and hamlets dispersed over the wide, gently rolling countryside that extended back a good distance from the coast. And although the division was numerically one of the largest U.S. divisions in South Vietnam, it lacked the helicopter assets possessed by the 101st Airborne Division. With more ground to cover and less mobility than its airmobile neighbor to the north, the Americal units were somewhat handicapped in their pursuit of the highly mobile enemy units, who after a couple of years of avoiding major contacts with the American soldiers, were suddenly standing toe to toe—and winning.

The 1st Brigade was to be a part of Operation LAMAR PLAIN and would serve the Americal Division well for the next 90 days. The first action the Brigade would see would be at Hill 270, where the Geronimos swept the battlefield and killed 25 NVA. Continual sweeps and reconnaissance in force uncovered numerous enemy base complexes, keeping the NVA reeling backward as they attempted to avoid contact with the hard-charging paratroopers from the 1st Brigade. In one cache alone, troopers discovered 29 SKS rifles, 72 AK-47s, a single M-1 rifle, three 60mm mortars, thirty-seven 122mm rockets, 13 cases of AK-47 ammunition, thirteen 75mm recoilless rifle rounds and numerous blasting caps and mortar fuses. Another nearby cache revealed two hundred 82mm mortar rounds and 78 RPG rounds.

LAMAR PLAIN saw another Screaming Eagle awarded the Congressional Medal of Honor, again posthumously. On June 2 1969, Sp4 Joseph G. LaPointe, Jr., a member of Headquarters and Headquarters Troop 2/17th Cavalry, was serving as a medic during a combat air assault outside of Tam Ky. His patrol was advancing from their LZ through an adjoining valley when it walked into a large enemy force, manning heavy automatic weapons, entrenched in well-fortified, mutually supporting bunker positions. Two of LaPointe's comrades at point position were seriously wounded in the opening burst of fire, while everyone else in the patrol moved to cover. Hearing the cries for help from the two wounded men, Specialist LaPointe left his position and ran forward under heavy machine gun fire to aid the wounded. To reach them he was forced to crawl through and area where he would be exposed to an enemy bunker. Calling for the rest of the patrol to cover him, LaPointe low-crawled across the kill zone and began to treat one of the wounded while shielding the other with his body. Suddenly, he was hit by a burst of fire from the nearby enemy bunker. Ignoring his own painful wounds, he continued administering aid to the two wounded men until he was hit a second time. Barely able to move, he crawled back to the wounded cavalrymen and once again tried to shield them with his body while he tried to dress their wounds. An enemy grenade fell among the three men mortally wounding all of them.

The arrival of the 1st Brigade to Tam Ky would provide the Americal Division with a capability it had been sorely lacking—air-mobility. The arrival of two NVA divisions in its AO had signaled a dramatic change in the type of war the Americal found itself embroiled in. Suddenly, full companies from the Americal Division were being engaged and soundly whipped in broad daylight by large NVA units, before help could arrive. Scout helicopters from the 2/17th Cav were the first elements of the 101st to deploy in the Americal AO. The "white" teams began operating alone, before the FACs and Cobras could come on line. They satisfied themselves with locating and marking enemy emplacements and with trying to locate the bodies of an Americal company that had gotten itself chewed up. It didn't take the Screaming Eagle scout pilots long to find the enemy—and the dead Americal soldiers. Calling in FAC directed F-4 Phantoms to suppress heavy NVA anti-aircraft fire, the scouts quickly discovered that they had stirred up a hornet's nest. They had located the 2nd NVA Regiment, and they weren't running.

Two infantry battalions were inserted to develop the situation, and immediately found themselves caught up in rotating blades of a meat grinder. Neither side was able to gain an advantage. For several days, each side would try to maneuver for a position of advantage, only to have its move countered by a similar move from the other side. At the end of the first week, only three helicopters were flyable from the combined assets of a air cav troop, an ARA battery, and a scout section. Americans killed in action was approaching one hundred. For the first time, 101st "pink" and "white" teams had run into an impenetrable wall of anti-aircraft fire that defied any and all attempts to reduce it. Not until the Screaming Eagles changed their tactics during the second week, did they gain a tactical advantage over the enemy. Only by increasing the numbers of choppers on their white and pink teams—going "heavy"—were they able to turn the tide of battle in their favor. By the end of the third week, the enemy was trying desperately to break contact. The American helicopters soon lost the main elements of the 2nd NVA Regiment, only able to account for a few stragglers. No one could figure out where the enemy had disappeared. But by the process of elimination, the Brigade determined the enemy had to be holed up in Death Valley in an area called Recon Zone Alpha. Aerial reconnaissance and infantry patrols turned up enemy emplacements but no enemy soldiers. The 2nd NVA Regiment had mysteriously disappeared. Then, running a final aerial recon, an aero-scout white team discovered a large enemy element in the open. Calling in ARA Cobras, the battle was joined once again. U.S. and South Vietnamese units were fed into the battle piecemeal, until the remnants of the 2nd NVA Regiment were finally forced to leave the battlefield—its commanding officer and most of his staff among the dead. Recon Zone Alpha would never go down in the history books as another Hamburger Hill or an Ia Drang Valley. But those who survived it—from both sides—would never forget its deadly ferocity. When Operation LAMAR PLAIN ended on August 14th, the 1st Brigade paratroopers had killed 519 enemy soldiers, and captured 257 individual and 18 crew-served weapons.

WHILE KENTUCKY JUMPER was in full swing, the 2nd Brigade, with the 1/327th and the 2/502nd under its operational control, was busy fighting its own war in the more hospitable, but equally deadly coastal plains and the foothills south of Camp Eagle in the Phu Loc District. Throughout the early summer months, the AO had seen an increasing amount of enemy initiated incidents. In June the Phu Loc area saw frequent attacks along QL1. These attacks culminated in an unsuccessful all-sapper attack on Fire Support Base Tomahawk. The old Hue-Da Nang railroad, recently reopened by the allies, was interdicted in several places, as was QL1. Intelligence reported enemy forces, both NVA and VC, were staging atop the "Bach Ma," a 4,500 foot ridge that housed the ruins of several palatial villas and old French resorts. In conjunction with the ARVN 54th Regiment, the two 2nd Brigade battalions air-assaulted directly onto the ridge line on July 13, 1969. They mounted a two-phased operation designed to defeat the NVA/VC forces around Phu Loc District and to drive them deeper into the mountains, out of reach of the civilian population centers and the lines of communication and transportation. The operation consisted of multiple air assaults into the area, followed by systematic search and destroy sweeps through suspected enemy base areas.

Once again, the enemy decided to run instead of meeting the paratroopers and their ARVN allies head-on. Phase I succeeded in its goal of pushing the Viet Cong Phu Loc Armed Battalion deep into the mountains, but failed in its bid to inflict heavy manpower and material losses on them. However, enemy initiated incidents decreased dramatically. Phase II saw a shift in operations to northern Quang Nam Province. Enemy contact remained light. The 2nd Brigade decided to facilitate future operations in this area by bringing in elements of the 326th Engineer Battalion to construct and leave behind a series of prepared landing zones and fire bases, including Fire Support Base Sledge, built among the ruins of the old French villas. More than 80 LZs were cleared in the area around Bach Ma and Phu Loc mountain areas. If the Eagles had to return to the district, they would be able to come in ready to fight. When the 2nd Brigade pulled out, they had killed 58 enemy soldiers and captured six others. In addition, a total of 57 individual and 10 crew-served weapons were taken from the enemy.

The next major operation after KENTUCKY JUMPER was RICHLAND SQUARE. It started just as the 1st Brigade returned to the Division after having been OPCON to the Americal Division for three months. This operation was to have significant impact on all future operations in the Division's Tactical Area of Responsibility. Vietnamization had become the "buzz-word" out of MACV. President Nixon had promised the American people that he was going to "bring our boys home," and "Vietnamization" was the program that was supposed to make it happen. After eight years of full American involvement, someone had finally determined that it was really South Vietnam's war. To American units in the field, this meant turning the war over to their ARVN contemporaries, whether they were ready or not. The 101st Airborne Division, blessed with a corresponding ARVN unit that was one of South Vietnam's finest divisions—the ARVN 1st Infantry Division—found the process of Vietnamization much easier to achieve than most other U.S. military units. Since its arrival in I Corps during Tet '68, the 101st had employed and enjoyed an outstanding working relationship with the ARVN 1st Infantry Division. So Vietnamization in the 101st TAOR was simply a matter of maintaining the usual way of conducting operations with ARVN participation—slowly but surely phasing out the degree of U.S. participation while assigning an increasingly bigger role to the South Vietnamese.

The basic concept of RICHLAND SQUARE was to provide the degree of security for the required accelerated pacification of the general population, while continuing the interdiction of enemy lines of communication and his base areas in the A Shau Valley.

Operation CUMBERLAND THUNDER, the 1st Brigade's role in RICHLAND SQUARE, saw the 1st Brigade team up with the 3rd ARVN Regiment, to go after the 5th NVA Regiment and local force units operating in the Phu Loc mountains. However, the NVA regiment played a well-executed game of "keep away" with the allied forces and managed to avoid any major contact. Occasional chance get-togethers with trail watchers, snipers, and food gathering parties provided some entertainment and kept the operation from being a total bore. Enemy losses were 83 killed in action, a single prisoner of war was captured along with 35 individual and three crew-served weapons.

OPERATION CLAIRBORNE CHUTE was conducted by the 2nd Brigade, in cooperation with the 1st ARVN Regiment, and was designed to protect the fall rice harvest in Thua Thien Province. Intelligence reports indicated the 7th Front and the 5th and 6th NVA Regiments would be moving into the lowlands to disrupt the harvest and to reap "their" share. On August 20th, friendly forces began conducting security patrols along QL1 and reconnaissance in force and screening operation in the rocket belt area. Elements from the 2/17th Cav carried out aerial reconnaissance keeping the sky full of "pink" teams—special hunter/killer teams composed of light aerial scout helicopters working with the deadly Cobra gunships—and "fireflys"—scout helicopters mounting high-intensity search lights and aerial flares. Saturation patrolling both above and on the ground interrupted the enemy efforts to infiltrate rice collecting parties into the populated areas. The rice harvest was completed without interruption. Enemy losses were put at 34 killed, two taken captive, and over 75 individual and crew-served weapons were captured. The operation ended on September 28th.

FINALLY, LOUISIANA LEE became the 3rd Brigade's contribution to RICH-LAND SQUARE. The 3rd Brigade, just back from operations with the Americal Division near Tam Ky-Chu Lai, in cooperation with the 3rd ARVN Regiment, maintained a strong allied presence in the A Shau Valley after the termination of Operation KENTUCKY JUMPER. Still suffering from heavy manpower and material losses during the A Shau battles, the enemy avoided face-to-face contact, and was satisfied to sit back and maintain a limited presence with indirect fire attacks against the firebases supporting LOUISIANA LEE. Allied forces practiced a form of economy of scale, deploying small reconnaissance teams in a saturation screen along the Laotian border. Enemy contact was answered by an infusion of air power. These tactics were very successful in keeping the pressure on the enemy and preventing him from gathering his forces for a major attack. Eventually, he would withdraw even further into Laos. The operation resulted in denying the enemy unperturbed use of the A Shau Valley. The Allies had placed a "use" tax on enemy operations in the A Shau. The cost of that tax was heavy. The NVA lost more large caches, suffered 67 killed, three prisoners captured and over 30 individual and crew-served weapons. The 101st Airborne Division and the 1st ARVN Division had made pacification in eastern Thua Thien Province a reality. For the first time in years, the Vietnamese in the area felt they were safe to conduct their lives without fear of intimidation, extortion, and death.

WHILE RICHLAND SQUARE was getting off the ground, Division staff planners were already conducting studies for a new operation called REPUBLIC SQUARE in the mountainous regions of the Division TAOR, especially the A Shau Valley. Consideration was given to the effect of the coming monsoon season upon the Division's ability to sustain operations once begun. The decision was made to sustain forces in the mountainous back country, especially the A Shau Valley. The rewards far outweighed the penalties. However, this decision was soon reversed when the Division was tasked with the mission of screening the redeployment of the 3rd Marine Division from Quang Tri Province.

An operational study indicated it would be impossible for the 101st Airborne Division and the 1st ARVN Division to maintain enough forces in both Quang Tri Province and the A Shau Valley to complete its mission, while at the same time maintaining the pacification efforts in the populated areas. The Screaming Eagles could only be stretched so far! While the 3rd Brigade prepared to move north to Quang Tri Province to cover for the departing 3rd Marine Division, the 1st and 2nd Brigades patrolled the lowlands and the piedmont areas to prevent the NVA/VC units, skulking back in the mountains, from refurbishing their food and manpower shortages at the expense of the Vietnamese population.

When Operation REPUBLIC SQUARE officially came to an end on December 6, 1969, all mission objectives had been achieved. The enemy had lost 254 killed and another 16 captured. Three others NVA/VC became Hoi Chanhs. Friendly forces had also captured 182 individual and crew-served weapons.

THE 3RD BRIGADE'S operation to screen the redeployment of the 3rd Marine Division was given the designation NORTON FALLS. Beginning on September 29th, the 1/506th and the 2/506th were airlifted by C-123s north to an old Marine airstrip and CIDG camp known as Mai Loc. It would serve as the 3rd Brigade command post during the entire 36-day screening operation.

On October 1st, eight Currahee companies combat assaulted into two separate landing zones south of the DMZ. Their mission was to deploy outward from their LZs and take up positions to protect the Marine withdrawal, utilizing small reconnaissance teams to monitor enemy movements into the area. The Screaming Eagles quickly established a pair of fire bases, Scotch and Schrapnel, located to provide mutual support for each other and the scattered infantry units. Enemy forces attempted to move in close to down the incoming helicopters, but Cobras from A Troop 2/17th Cav succeeded in suppressing their fire.

On October 5th, elements of the 1st Battalion swept out of Firebase Schrapnel and combat assaulted into an area just north of the fire base. Moving quickly and enjoying the element of surprise, the Currahees surged through an NVA cave complex, capturing a single enemy soldier, and uncovering a cache containing twenty-two 122mm rockets, over 100 mortar rounds, 20 grenades, 17 mines, 2 AK-47s, over 2,750 lbs. of fish, nearly two tons of rice and 405 tins of canned meat.

Utilizing their airmobility capability to the fullest, the Screaming Eagles maintained constant pressure on enemy forces in the vicinity. By the end of October, the 3rd Marine Division had successfully completed its redeployment and had departed Vietnam. The two Currahee battalions began their own redeployment back to Camp Evans as the 1st ARVN Division moved in to take over the AO. During NORTON FALLS, U.S. paratroopers killed 65 enemy and captured over 30 weapons, besides the contents of the large cache previously described.

BEGINNING ON OCTOBER 5th, Operation SATURATE saw the 1/327th, working with elements of the 54th ARVN Regiment and Thua Thien Sector forces, conduct combat operations in the Phu Thu District. The uniqueness of this operation is it was conceived, planned, executed and controlled entirely by the sector headquarters. It was not a joint US-ARVN operation. In the course of the two-month long operation, and in addition to its combat functions, the 1/327th conducted in-the-field training for the territorial forces. This assisted in the development of a Division training program aimed at upgrading the effectiveness of territorial forces in Thua Thien Province. This was an important contribution if Vietnamization was going to have a chance. Although U.S. forces killed only eight enemy soldiers during the two-month long operation, its overall result was the virtual elimination of the VC infrastructure from the Phu Thu District, with their strength at the beginning of the operation estimated at 50 to 70, reduced to 18 at the end. SATURATE was not a success statistically, and it would never rank among the list of famous American battles, but it was the first measurable success for the Vietnamization program and a positive sign of things to come.

1970 BRINGS CHANGES

OPERATION LOUISIANA LEE saw the withdrawal of American forces from the A Shau Valley. With the relocation of all the Division's maneuver battalions into the lowlands and the piedmont areas, the enemy quickly began a general eastward movement back toward the population centers. New lines had been drawn, the perimeter had been pulled in and strengthened. Both fighters were regrouping to catch their breath. No major offensive activity was forthcoming from the enemy units infiltrating back into the area where the piedmont met the mountains. The NVA appeared to be concentrating on the movement of supplies, establishing new forward base areas, and moving up its military units. But all the signs were there. The actions in the A Shau in '69 had forestalled the enemy's offensive plans, but they had not eliminated them. Under cover of the northeast monsoon, the NVA had set the stage for a new round of attacks.

Operation RANDOLPH GLEN was developed in coordination with the 1st ARVN Division and Thua Thien Province/Sector officials to provide a single philosophy regarding the fully integrated efforts to meet the goals of the Province Pacification and Development Plan. Vietnamizaton was to be the focus of American involvement in 1970, with emphasis on the training of local forces and combined operations with Regional Force and Popular Force units—something Special Forces had recognized years before. It was time to teach the Vietnamese how to fight their own war. The question was, had we waited too long? The general disposition of U.S. forces within the 101st Airborne Division's tactical area of operations would in the future serve to provide a screen of security around the populated areas of the coastal plains and the piedmont. The Division would maintain quick reaction forces to meet threats as they arose. Streamlined flexibility and hard-hitting, immediate response would be the Division's trademark. Extensive offensive operations with limited objectives would be conducted on the periphery of the populated areas, with periodic raids into the enemy's mountain staging areas. Occasional interdiction of the A Shau Valley would be conducted on a continuous basis, to prevent the enemy from reestablishing its supply bases with impunity.

In addition, dedicated 101st units would provide mobile training teams to train and upgrade territorial forces, especially in districts not under the continuous protection of the Division. Two entire battalions from the 101st, the 2/327th and the 3/187th, set up their tactical operations centers in their respective district headquarters. These "dedicated" battalions would function in close cooperation with their South Vietnamese counterparts. It was hoped by upgrading territorial forces to where they could take over the responsibilities for their own defense, it would have the effect of freeing Popular Forces to take over for Regional Forces, which would free Regional Forces to take over the responsibilities of ARVN units, which would free the ARVN for penetration operation s deep in the mountains—sort of an upgraded chain reaction.

Operation RANDOLPH GLEN, beginning on December 7, 1969, represented the game plan that would hopefully develop an autonomous Vietnamese capability for self-defense, and thereby self-determination. The U.S. forces were positioning themselves to "hand over the keys to the city." RANDOLPH GLEN proved to be a good start. When it ended on March 31, 1970, it had accounted for 670 enemy dead, 19 POWs, and 323 individual and 35 crew-served weapons captured. TEXAS STAR and JEFFERSON GLEN followed close on the heels of RANDOLPH GLEN. With MACV's new emphasis on pacification and Vietnamization, U.S. military units, including the 101st Airborne Division, entered into a phase of operation that saw a marked reduction in offensive capacity. During RANDOLPH GLEN, the enemy forces continued to position themselves closer to the population centers to where, by March 1970, they had become a significant threat to the success of the pacification effort in the lowlands. By April, the enemy forces in Thua Thien Province arrayed against the Division, had increased to levels greater than during the Tet Offensive of 1968. Although RANDOLPH GLEN had been effective in training and upgrading South Vietnamese military forces in the 101st's AO, it had inadvertently allowed the enemy the same opportunity to strengthen its own forces and upgrade its tactical and strategic capabilities. And it didn't take them long to infiltrate back into their old haunts abandoned during the mid to latter part of 1969. It was this aggressive infiltration TEXAS STAR would attempt to stop. On April 28, 1970, near the Song Bo river west of LZ Sally, Bravo Company 2/502nd killed 12 NVA during an attack on its night defensive perimeter. The next day they discovered 50 more enemy bodies in three bunker complexes destroyed by aerial rocket artillery from Alpha Company 4/77th ARA. On the night of April 29th, troopers from the 2/501st repulsed an attack on FSB Granite. The attack was repelled. The loss cost the NVA 22 dead and one captured.

On May 3rd, elements of the 2/502nd on a reconnaissance mission, with the help of ARA and air strikes, destroyed 27 NVA in a short battle near the Perfume River.

On May 9th, 2/502nd troopers on another reconnaissance mission ran into a reinforced NVA platoon fighting from bunkers. Again, in a short, vicious fight with the aid of ARA, airstrikes and artillery, the Strike Force soldiers killed 18 more NVA.

On May 17th, gunships from 4/77th ARA returned fire in the Vietnamese Salient area and killed another 35 NVA. On May 27th, recon elements from the 1/506th ambushed two NVA, only moments later to be "counter-ambushed" by an unknown-sized enemy force. Aerial rocket artillery was called in to support the beleaguered troopers. A total of 19 NVA were slain before the battle ended. Elements of the 2/327th were attacked on FSB Tomahawk, south of Camp Eagle, on the night of June 10th. Artillery from a neighboring fire base and Cobra gunships turned the tide. The NVA lost 21 more soldiers. On June 18th, the 2/17th Cavalry engaged several targets located within the 101st's tactical area of responsibility and killed 26 NVA. On June 25th, after a three-day operation in support of the 1st ARVN Division's Hac Bao Company, the 2/17th Cav chalked up 64 enemy killed. On the night of July 2nd, elements of the 2/506th killed 15 NVA when they were attacked in their night defensive position. On July 6th, a six-man long range reconnaissance team from L Company 75th Infantry (Rangers) made contact with an NVA company. Employing small arms fire and Cobra gunships, the Rangers killed 13 enemy. The bodies were discovered when a reaction force from D Troop 2/17th Cav came in to sweep the battleground. On July 8th, in the largest action of the year, ground elements of the 2/17th Cav spotted 150 to 200 NVA on the move near Khe Sanh. The Cav troopers with air support engaged the enemy, and in a battle lasting throughout the entire day, killed 139 and captured four.

This was the way it was during the summer and fall of 1970. Screaming Eagle units were finding the enemy everywhere, and taking the action to him. The enemy seemed to be avoiding major confrontations and the subsequent dramatic losses that accompany them. Instead, he demonstrated a willingness to sacrifice five men here, ten more there in brief, but sharp encounters with Division forces while he continued moving more men and materials into the mountains overlooking Hue—Camp Eagle—Camp Evans—LZ Sally. To once again infiltrate his forces to threaten the populated areas of Thua Thien Province, the enemy was forced to pay a dear price in this war of attrition. On May 25, 1970, Major General John M. Wright, Jr., passed the Division colors to Major General John J. Hennessey. General Hennessey was the fourth commanding general of the Division since it arrived in Vietnam in December 1967. A short while later, General Hennessey took a 3-week leave, his first in two years, and Assistant Division Commander, Brigadier General Sidney Berry, assumed temporary command of the Division.

TEXAS STAR, beginning on April 1 and running to September 5, was conceived as an operation designed to maintain the best of RANDOLPH GLEN, while restoring some form of offensive punch against the ever growing enemy threat. A thirteen day raid into the Khe Ta Laou River valley near FSB Maureen, an area overlooked for nearly three years as Screaming Eagles hunted the NVA in the mountains around the A Shau, produced some heavy fighting, and demonstrated the enemy was indeed "back." But he would indeed pay a steep price of admission. Operation TEXAS STAR would cost the enemy a total of 1,782 killed in action.

Unfortunately, the American military machine was by then caught up in the mad rush of a "reduction in force" in Vietnam. President Nixon had made a commitment to the American people to pull U.S. troops out of the war zone, and to turn the war effort over to the Vietnamese. Peace talks were already underway in Paris, with both sides arguing over protocol, power posturing, and personalities. As early as mid-1969, America's warriors were beginning to realize that they were risking their lives for a cause our government and our nation had already abandoned. It was only a matter of time before this would effect their resolve and their ability to conduct war. Discipline problems, racial tension, and drug abuse were spreading among U.S. units in Vietnam—primarily among rear echelon forces. But alarmingly, it was also beginning to show up among combat units. The problem was not one of major significance in the 101st Airborne Division. Although few in the division still wore the jump wings of U.S. Army paratroopers, the highly motivated, well-led sky-soldiers still possessed the spirit and dedication of the airborne. The importance of aerial reconnaissance and surveillance during this period of transition soon became apparent. The 2/17th Cavalry proved up to the task, but would pay a price in casualties and lost aircraft. Increased enemy activity in the South Vietnamese Salient in the vicinity of the abandoned U. S. Marine base at Khe Sanh, was on the rise. Ranger reconnaissance teams from Lima Company, 75th Infantry (Rangers), were making heavy contact during reconnaissance missions into western Quang Tri Province in the vicinity of Khe Sanh. An entire six-man recon team was wiped out on May 11th, 1970. Operating outside the artillery fan, plagued with foul weather and poor commo, other patrols also began to lose men resulting in a heavy toll from the Division's Ranger recon teams. With the Marines pulled out of western Quang Tri Province, the 101st Airborne Division (Airmobile) was forced to expand its AO to monitor enemy movement into South Vietnam through the Salient. It was during the early days of TEXAS STAR another Screaming Eagle became a recipient of the Medal of Honor. Since April, 1970, the NVA had been attacking U.S. fire support bases in an attempt to relieve the pressure on their movements in the A Shau Valley. On May 7th, it was Fire Base Maureen's turn. Private First Class Kenneth M. Kays had gone to Canada after his application for conscientious objector status was turned down and he received his induction notice. But he returned home 30 days later after having a change of heart. He contacted the Army and cut a deal—he would go into the Army if they would guarantee him service as a medic. Seven months later, he was in Vietnam, a medic with Delta Company 1/506th, on fire base security not far from the notorious A Shau Valley.

On the night of May 7, 1970, the 803rd NVA Regiment attacked Fire Base Maureen amid a hurricane of small arms fire, flashing RPG rounds and exploding satchel charges. A number of paratroopers were killed and wounded in the opening moments of the attack. Ignoring the intense fire, bank-shot tracers and ear-bursting explosions, Kays deserted the safety of his perimeter bunker and headed for a couple of his wounded buddies. As he was attempting to reach them, he heard something land next to him. In the flash of the next explosion he saw to his horror it was a satchel charge. Before he could react, it detonated. The blast severed the lower portion of his left leg. With the battle raging around him, Kays calmly applied a tourniquet around his ragged stump to stop the bleeding. With the tourniquet in place, Kays resumed crawling toward the wounded. He found the first soldier, dressed his wounds, then dragged him back to the company air station. Instead of having his own wound treated, Kays turned and crawled back into the carnage looking for more wounded paratroopers. Ignoring his own pain and fighting back shock, he crawled around the perimeter dressing the injuries of each wounded man he came to. In each case, Kays shielded the wounded with his body as he applied the dressings. At one point, he had to crawl outside the perimeter to reach one man, treat his wounds, then drag him to safety.

After five hours of fighting, the NVA attackers were driven away. Kays' company commander found him crawling toward another casualty. The young soldier refused treatment and medivac until all the other wounded had been evacuated. At this point he finally collapsed from loss of blood.

PROBABLY THE MOST impressive and compelling story of American courage, drive, and raw fighting ability occurred during the NVA siege of FSB Ripcord. When Operation RANDOLPH GLEN drew to a close in early 1970, it soon became apparent that the initiative established during the Division's A Shau Valley campaigns in 1969 had been lost trying to implement the pacification of the populated coastal plains and training the ARVN forces how to stand on their own two feet in fighting the enemy. Beginning in February, contact with enemy units infiltrating east from their Laotian base camps increased daily. When the operation finally ended on March 31st, units from the 101st Airborne Division's three brigades were already "standing in the door" and ready to go. It was once again time to take the war back to the enemy. Operation TEXAS STAR was designed to accomplish just that.

On March 4, 1970, the 2nd Battalion of the 506th Infantry Regiment, saw a new light colonel take over the reins of command from Lieutenant Colonel Howard G. Crowell, Jr. As in any situation where a popular commander is relieved of command for whatever reason, the new leader must often undergo a lengthy "now prove you're worthy to lead us" period before he is given the respect and admiration accorded his predecessor. At times this "cold shoulder" can prove a handicap and an embarrassment to the new commander, especially one who cannot fill the boots of his predecessor. In the case of Lieutenant Colonel Crowell, his boots would take a lot of filling. Lieutenant Colonel Andre C. Lucas, West Point Class of '54, saw this new assignment as both an honor and a challenge. It wasn't long before he had won the hearts and souls of the battle-hardened Currahees serving under him. Eight days after taking command, Colonel Lucas sent his Alpha Company on a company-sized exploratory reconnaissance into Fire Base Ripcord in a mountainous area overlooking the northeastern corner of the

A Shau Valley. The combat assault drew a heavy volume of RPG, mortar and small arms fire, indicating the presence of at least an enemy company. Alpha Company withdrew a short time later with moderate casualties, having accomplished its mission. There was no doubt about it, the enemy was in the area in strength. Charlie Company 2/506th was inserted on a nearby ridgeline to act as a blocking force behind the NVA company. During the next five days, its troopers participated in a number of running gun battles with "fleeing" NVA and killed five enemy soldiers—three of them members of the infamous K-12 Sapper Battalion. This proved to be a valuable bit of intelligence—sappers weren't used to entertain troops in the rear. It could only mean one thing—the enemy was planning to hit some of the towns and military bases beyond the mountains. They would have to be stopped before they could get there.

Operation TEXAS STAR began on April 1st, and saw the 2/506th's Delta Company OPCON to the 1/506th acting as a security force to protect the artillery battery on Fire Base Granite. At the same time Charlie Company conducted a combat assault into a mountainous area to clear the way for the construction of Fire Base Gladiator. The Screaming Eagles were moving back into the mountains.

The same day, Bravo Company assaulted onto Ripcord again and bumped into a bigger hornet's nest than Alpha Company had two weeks earlier. Recoilless rifle fire, in addition to RPGs, small arms and mortars combined to make the crest and slopes of Ripcord a dangerous place to live. While the battalion began to make the necessary moves to direct its attentions toward Ripcord, Bravo Company burrowed in deep and prepared to hold on.

While Charlie Company remained on Gladiator, Colonel Lucas ordered the battalion's Recon platoon to reinforce Bravo Company on Ripcord while Alpha Company CA'd onto a nearby ridgeline. Delta Company was sent on a long sweep toward Ripcord from the north with the mission of looking for the mortar and recoilless rifle positions threatening Bravo and Recon.

It soon became apparent the positions on and around Ripcord were tenuous at best, and the decision was once again made to extract the battalion's elements. On April 3rd, the last of the Screaming Eagles were lifted out, suffering six killed and 21 wounded. On April 4th, the Currahees were back in knocking on the door again. This time Charlie Company got the honors of assaulting into an LZ not far from Ripcord, secured by remnants of Alpha. With Alpha, Charlie, and Delta now on the ground, the operation began to pick up steam, and the enemy withdrew. On April 10th, Colonel Lucas decided once again to take Ripcord. Charlie Company got the honors and combat assaulted the abandoned fire base under the sound of friendly fire impacting in the surrounding mountains. There was no enemy resistance.

Charlie Company spent the next thirty days reinforcing Ripcord's fighting positions and strengthening the perimeter during the lull in action. Bravo Company outperformed Charlie during the following thirty day period. Except for the hard work and overabundance of sunshine, a thirty day stint at FB Ripcord was taking on the characteristics of a standdown. The NVA sneaked in once in a while to drop a few mortar rounds, just to let the Americans know they weren't forgotten. While Bravo and Charlie filled sandbags, Alpha and Delta roamed the hills and valleys around Ripcord looking for the enemy, with Delta seeing some success. Late in May, Recon also got in on the war and donated four dead NVA and a prisoner to the cause.

June saw little opposition from the enemy. On the 16th, Alpha Company took over base security on FB O'Reilly, and Delta moved onto Ripcord to spell Bravo for some patrolling. Charlie Company achieved a little success during the "dead" month.

In late June, radio intercepts, agent reports, and captured documents forewarned that an NVA attack on Ripcord was imminent. On July 1st, Alpha Company 2/506th was still securing Fire Base O'Reilly, Delta Company was protecting the Battalion TOC and the "redlegs" of Bravo Battery 2/319th Artillery on Fire Base Ripcord, Charlie Company was set up on nearby Hill 902, Bravo Company was sweeping the jungles southwest of Ripcord, and Recon platoon was screening across a wide band running from the northeast to the southeast corner of Ripcord. Echo Company, the battalions heavy weapons component, had recently moved six mortar tubes onto Ripcord and another three on O'Reilly.

Over the past three months, enemy sappers had attempted to penetrate the perimeter at Ripcord, but had always failed. On the morning of July 1, 1970, the siege of Fire Base Ripcord began with a barrage of recoilless rifle fire. Unbelievably, no one was injured in the initial onslaught. But by the end of the day, after eight successive barrages of recoilless rifle and mortar fire, six U. S. paratroopers were medivac'd from Ripcord. Two Chinook helicopters had also been shot down. During the day, Charlie Company, on nearby Hill 902, observed the enemy's heavy weapons being fired and adjusted deadly and accurate fire on the positions, causing serious losses. It would not be long before the enemy realized the source of its losses and decided to remove Charlie Company from its position on Hill 902. At 0345 hours on the morning of July 2nd, the NVA sent a company-size sapper attack against Charlie Company's defensive position. The enemy sappers were inside the perimeter before being detected. Their initial satchel charges confused the Screaming Eagles who did not understand if the explosions were mortars or satchel charges. When the enemy's small arms and RPGs joined it, the Currahees finally began to respond. The Americans fought like tigers. Their commander, Captain Thomas T. Hewitt, was killed early in the attack. Leaderless, the Currahees fought individually to throw the NVA sappers out of the perimeter. When the fight ended an hour later, Charlie Company counted eight dead among its ranks, with nearly fifty wounded. But the enemy had left 20 dead on the battlefield, with numerous blood trails and drag marks leading off the hilltop and into the jungle.

Captain Jeff Wilcox took over the reins of Charlie Company as it was extracted from Hill 902 and reinserted at another location. Ripcord continued to be the beneficiary of the NVA's main efforts, receiving continual mortar and recoilless rifle fire. Captain Rollison, Delta's commander, expected at any minute to get hit with a ground assault. Another Chinook was shot down, this time directly on the fire base.

Bravo Company, under the command of Captain Ben Peters, and Recon platoon, led by 1st Lieutenant Romig, continued to patrol through the jungles surrounding Ripcord, killing several NVA moving to support the enemy units assaulting the fire base.

On July 6th, Bravo and Delta companies flip-flopped positions, with Delta Company moving west toward Hill 1000 and the Recon platoon , which was probing toward expected enemy positions around the crest of the hill. The Recon platoon met heavy resistance and pulled back with its wounded. When Delta Company arrived on the scene, its commander sent a platoon forward to recover Recons abandoned equipment, and decided there was more on Hill 1000 than just a few NVA laying in ambush. He pulled back and plastered the crest with heavy artillery for a solid hour, then put his company on line and assaulted. In a very short period of time, Captain Rollison discovered he had stepped into a den of angry bears with only a stick for defense. Delta had little choice but to withdraw. However, low on ammunition and dragging along two dead and several wounded, Delta Company was having a difficult time breaking contact. Hovering at treetop height, Lieutenant Colonel Lucas arrived on the scene just in time, kicking out cases of smoke and fragmentation grenades. In spite of drawing heavy enemy fire the entire time they were over Delta's position, Colonel Lucas and his pilot escaped without being injured, even though the chopper took seven hits. The extra grenades and a few well-placed air strikes enabled Delta to break contact and withdraw. They had accounted for seven dead NVA by body count.

The next day, Delta Company, assisted by Charlie Company, attempted a second time to assault Hill 1000, but to no avail. The enemy was there and well-entrenched in heavily fortified bunkers. Delta Company was lifted out of the area on July 9th and combat assaulted to an LZ in the Fire Base O'Reilly area. Alone, Charlie Company moved back around to the east flank of Ripcord.

On July 10th, Alpha Company, under the command of Captain Charles Hawkins, combat assaulted to Charlie Company's LZ while Charlie Company moved in to secure Fire Base O'Reilly. Later that day, Alpha Company, along with Delta Company 2/501st (which had been placed OPCON to the 506th), commanded by Captain Straub, combat assaulted into an area just below Hill 805 located southeast of Fire Base Ripcord. On July 12th, the two companies had secured the hill amid light to moderate contact, destroying numerous bunkers and fighting positions in the process. It was then becoming obvious the enemy had dug in all around Ripcord. D/2/501st set up housekeeping on top of Hill 805, while Alpha Company moved to an LZ 200 meters away and dug in. That night Delta Company 2/501st got hit by a heavy barrage of mortar and RPG fire, and some well-directed small arms fire. From its position 200 meters away, Alpha Company was able to observe where the enemy fire pasting Delta was coming from. Captain Hawkins directed his troopers to place accurate fire on the enemy positions, forcing them to break contact after an hour. Alpha suffered no casualties, but Delta had 16 men wounded. Enemy dead littered the slopes of Hill 805.

On July 13th, Alpha Company moved off Hill 805 and went in search of the enemy within the confines of a rugged valley southwest of Ripcord. Delta would remain on Hill 805 until July 17th when it was evacuated. It had been bled white by heavy attacks during five straight nights it was on the hill.

For ten straight days, Bravo Company had been trapped in its bunkers on top of Ripcord. The constant shelling made life outside the bunkers almost impossible. Resupply was nearly impossible, and any attempt to land a helicopter was met by a renewed barrage of mortar fire. Throughout this constant deluge of falling rounds, Echo Company mortarmen and the artillerymen of Bravo Battery 2/319th performed brilliantly, putting out continual fire support for the infantry companies working the surrounding areas without missing a beat.

On July 18th, a fourth Chinook was shot down. Unfortunately, it crashed into the main artillery ammo dump on Ripcord and burst into flames. Over 400 rounds of 105mm ammo began to cook off and explode. The detonations lasted for 8 hours, destroying all six of Bravo Battery's howitzers, a pair of 106mm recoilless rifles, a counter-mortar radar set, a VHF radio, numerous bunkers, and operations centers on Ripcord's south side. The perimeter itself was intact, but the heart of Ripcord's defenses was a shambles.

On July 19th, Alpha Company killed two NVA and discovered a bonanza of valuable information on the bodies of the two dead NVA. The intell was quickly passed on to Colonel Lucas on Ripcord.

Delta Company 1/506th, commanded by Captain Don Workman, was placed OPCON to the 2/506th and inserted on a LZ a couple of kilometers east of Hill 805. Their insertion was "hot" as they encountered intense small arms, mortar, RPG and heavy machine gun fire going in. It appeared the NVA had strong defenses and adequate manpower covering every potential LZ within six klicks of Ripcord. Captain Workman succeeded in getting his company on the ground intact, and then moved them 600 meters away from the clearing and into a defensive perimeter. Secure for the moment, but burdened with several dead and nearly half the company wounded, Captain Workman radioed for help. Delta Company 2/506th would answer the call, combat assaulting into another LZ nearby. They, too, were met by a hail of small arms fire. Delta quickly established fire superiority, then assaulted the enemy's positions driving them off. The NVA left behind several of their dead along with a .51 cal. machine gun. Charlie Company, now under the command of Captain Kenneth Lamb, CA'd right behind Delta and secured the LZ for the extraction of D/1/506th. Captain Workman, D/1/506th's commanding officer, was killed during the final moments of the evacuation. But by nightfall, all three companies were out with their dead and wounded. In the meantime, Alpha Company had been pushing deeper and deeper into "Indian Country," and discovering more and more enemy fortifications. Feeling a lot of sympathy for George Armstrong Custer, Captain Hawkins knew that his position was precarious. But he had come to fight. By mid-morning on the 20th, he had his troops at the base of Hill 805. Hawkins sent half his company across the river which ran along the south base of the hill, and placed the remainder of his company in an ambush position on the bank above the water. His element across the river located a string of commo wire across the river and tapped into it. Setting up a hasty ambush around the wire tap, the Currahees stayed in position for five hours while the company interpreter and one of their Kit Carson scouts listened in. The Americans initiated contact twice during the time the wire tap was in service. Across the river, the other half of the company had busted two watering parties as they approached the stream.

The information gathered by the wire tappers proved invaluable. It stated that an entire NVA division, not just two regiments as previously thought, was waiting to hit Ripcord. It also revealed that the NVA division headquarters was at one end of the wire, while a regimental headquarters waited at the other end. Alpha Company pulled back and set up a defense perimeter for the night, calling in heavy artillery on the suspected enemy headquarters locations. During the 21st, Alpha Company elements killed several NVA, including a courier to the division headquarters carrying with him diagrams and a plan of attack for the NVA forces scheduled to hit Ripcord. After dark, Captain Hawkins moved his company a couple hundred meters away and set up in a defensive perimeter. He knew they had been in too long and had done too much damage to the enemy. The NVA would soon come in force to find them. When daylight arrived he planned to move west across the river and get away from the NVA hunting grounds they had stumbled into.

That same day, Brigadier General Sidney Berry, the acting Division Commander, made the decision to evacuate Fire Base Ripcord. It was obvious that the NVA had made the commitment to take Ripcord at all costs. Its position over their major northern infiltration route into the coastal areas was too much of a threat. For General Berry the cost of holding Ripcord was not worth the price in American lives. He gave Colonel Lucas orders to draw up plans and execute the evacuation on July 23rd. Charlie and Delta companies had already been returned to Camp Evans after the rescue of D/1/506th. Alpha Company and the Screaming Eagles manning the perimeter on Fire Base Ripcord were the only troopers left to bring in.

On the morning of the 22nd, Captain Hawkins received a coded message from Colonel Lucas to move his company to an LZ located just east of Ripcord. His point element moved no more than a 100 meters before surprising and killing three NVA. Moving up to exploit the situation, the point platoon ran broadside into an NVA battalion on the move. The enemy battalion immediately pivoted and assaulted Alpha Company with human wave attacks supported by mortar fire. Captain Hawkin's troopers were immediately embroiled in a fight for their lives, as they slowly constricted into a defensive perimeter. Outnumbered better than 6 to 1, the Screaming Eagles fought with the desperation of men marked to die. Airstrikes called by Captain Hawkins on his own positions and the timely arrival of helicopter gunship cover saved the day and the remainder of Alpha Company. Airpower broke the back of the NVA battalion. When it was over, Alpha Company suffered 90% casualties, and the NVA left over one hundred dead on the battlefield. Colonel Lucas, knowing that Alpha Company would not be able to evacuate with out help, ordered in Delta Company 2/506th to reinforce battered Alpha.

As darkness fell on the battleground, Delta was forced to abort its rescue attempt. The LZ was still aflame from the burning napalm. They would be back at first light to try again. In the meantime, Alpha Company had to hold out during the night.

Delta Company was on the ground at first light on the morning of the 23rd and force marched cross country to get to Alpha Company. Delta Company made the link-up, hacking and blowing a LZ in the middle of the jungle while Alpha provided security and treated its wounded. Twenty-one Huey helicopters later, Delta and Alpha companies had been plucked from the gates of hell and returned to Camp Evans to see to their wounded and bury their dead.

Up on Ripcord, the final evacuation was proceeding with dispatch. Pathfinders from the 101st were skillfully guiding the evacuation ships in, around and between incoming enemy mortars. Unbelievably, only one helicopter was lost to enemy fire. However, the enemy got in a heavy parting shot, as one of their mortar rounds found Colonel Lucas and his S-3, Major Tanner, as they stood discussing the final moments of the operation. Colonel Lucas had landed on Ripcord during the extraction to supervise and to set an example for his men. The battle for Fire Base Ripcord was over.

Ripcord was not a U.S. victory nor was it a defeat. However, it was the last major ground battle of the Vietnam War involving only American forces against the enemy.

Lieutenant Colonel Andre C. Lucas would posthumously receive the Congressional Medal of Honor for repeated displays of unparalleled bravery during the siege of Fire Base Ripcord. The citation reads: Lieutenant Colonel Lucas distinguished himself by extraordinary heroism while serving as the commanding officer of the 2nd Battalion. Although the fire base was constantly subjected to heavy attacks by a numerically superior enemy force throughout this period, Lieutenant Colonel Lucas, forsaking his own safety, performed numerous acts of extraordinary valor in directing the defense of the allied position. On one occasion, he flew in a helicopter at treetop level above an entrenched enemy directing the fire of one of his companies for over three hours. Even though his helicopter was heavily damaged by enemy fire, he remained in an exposed position until the company expended its supply of grenades. He then transferred to another helicopter, dropped critically needed grenades to the troops, and resumed his perilous mission of directing fire on the enemy. These courageous actions by Lieutenant Colonel Lucas prevented the company from being encircled and destroyed by a larger enemy force.

On another occasion, Lieutenant Colonel Lucas attempted to rescue a crewman trapped in a burning helicopter. As the flames in the aircraft spread, and enemy fire became intense, Lieutenant Colonel Lucas ordered all members of the rescue party to safety. Then, at great personal risk, he continued the rescue effort amid concentrated enemy mortar fire, intense heat, and exploding ammunition until the aircraft was completely engulfed in flames.

Lieutenant Colonel Lucas was mortally wounded while directing the successful withdrawal of his battalion from the fire base. His actions throughout this extended period inspired his men to heroic efforts, and were instrumental in saving the lives of many of his fellow soldiers while inflicting heavy casualties on the enemy.

ANOTHER SCREAMING EAGLE would also earn a posthumous Medal of Honor during Operation TEXAS STAR. Corporal Frank R. Fratellenico, a rifleman serving in Bravo Company 2/502nd, was on patrol with his company near FSB Barnett in south west Quang Tri Province on August 19th, when they ran into an estimated enemy company. Fratellenio's squad was pinned down by heavy fire from two enemy bunkers. Moving against the NVA positions, Fratellenio neutralized one bunker with well thrown hand grenades and was attacking the second when he was hit by enemy small arms fire, causing him to fall and drop a grenade he was preparing to throw. Realizing some of his comrades were in the impact zone of the fragmentary grenade, he grabbed it and fell on it, absorbing the explosion with his body. The battle resulted in the deaths of 25 enemy soldiers with another captured.

Heavy action beginning in late August and running through the end of September, centered around FSB O'Reilly north of the A Shau Valley, produced heavy enemy losses. Cobra helicopters from the 4/77th Aerial Rocket Artillery and the 2/17th Cavalry killed over 140 NVA in almost daily contacts with enemy forces dug in or maneuvering in the immediate vicinity of FSB O'Reilly.

OPERATION JEFFERSON GLENN, September 5, 1970–October 8, 1971, was the last installment of the 101st's commitment to leave Thua Thien Province pacified and in the hands of South Vietnamese forces capable of not only defending themselves, but of going on the offensive to drive the invading North Vietnamese from their country. Utilizing a network of fire support bases, aggressive patrolling and extensive aerial reconnaissance, the Screaming Eagles fought to prevent enemy thrusts into Thua Thien Province, while the South Vietnamese built their strength. The Division bought time for the government of South Vietnam to consolidate its positions, time paid for with the blood of young Eagles.

For its involvement in the many civil affairs programs during RANDOLPH GLEN, TEXAS STAR and JEFFERSON GLEN, the 101st Airborne Division (Airmobile) received the Vietnamese Civic Action Medal on May 23rd, 1970.

INTO CAMBODIA

FOR FOUR YEARS, eastern Cambodia had belonged to the NVA and main force VC units operating in South Vietnam's II, III and IV Corps tactical zones. The enemy had been there long enough to call it "home." These Cambodian sanctuaries had become "suburban havens" to the "suitcase-commuter" soldiers who crossed the border on a regular basis to wreak a little havoc then scamper back home for a little uninterrupted R&R. It was their job! American and ARVN units had been frustrated for years as they had repeatedly pursued NVA/VC elements right up to the border only to lose them as the invisible barrier slammed shut in their faces. Good old American politics once again proved to be the greatest slayer of American soldiers. You had to be there to appreciate the helplessness of the situation. There, just across an imaginary line, the B-3 Front had constructed a multitude of trails, roads, storage structures, hospitals, bunkers, motor pools, and every other significant military target one could imagine. The Cambodian sanctuaries had been a thorn in the side of the Allied war effort for a long time. Prince Sihanouk, Cambodia's leader, claimed neutrality but actually allowed Communist forces to operate freely along his country's border with South Vietnam. But all of that was about to change. While Sihanouk was on a trip to France during March, 1970, he was unseated in a coup by one of his generals, Lon Nol, who happened to be pro-Western. Lon Nol quickly demanded under the international rules of neutrality that the Communists take their business elsewhere. With its Khmer Rouge allies, the NVA responded by attacking Cambodian military outposts. Lon Nol appealed to the U.S. and South Vietnamese governments to expel the Communists. In 1969, elements of the B-3 Front crossed the border frontier and struck Ben Het during the summer and Bu Prang and Duc Lap in the fall. These attacks along with the normal east-west traffic across the border finally got the attention of the "people in high places " who establish the rules the rest of us live by. Now, with the leadership in Cambodia "begging for help" it was time to play a trump card. President Nixon was bold enough to make the decision. Cambodia was going to see an invasion—or at least a raid of some magnitude. The amazing thing was that it was supposed to be a surprise.

It was mid-April 1970, before the planners and the logistics people had completed their part of the equation. The primary goal of the Cambodian "incursion"—as a mollifying Richard Nixon would announce it to the American people—was to eradicate the enemy sanctuaries in Cambodia and destroy the NVA/VC forces defending them. On May 1st, with heavy artillery barrages preceding and the last of six arc-lights still pounding in the distance, the 1st Cavalry Division's Task Force Shoemaker pushed across the border into Cambodia. Operation TOAN THANG-43 was underway. Five days later, on May 6th, operations TOAN THANG-44 and BINH TAY-I, led by the U.S. 25th Division and 4th Divisions respectively, produced additional border crossings in an all out effort to invade enemy strongholds. Task Force 3/506th found itself part of Operation BINH TAY I, under operational control of the 4th Infantry Division. In spite of the six arc-lights preceding the invasion, several elements from the 3/506th were driven away from their intended primary landing zones by heavy enemy fire, and forced to land at alternative LZs.

Engineers from Headquarters and Headquarters Company 326th Engineer Battalion moved into Cambodia and hastily erected Fire Support Base Currahee to provide artillery support for Task Force 3/506th. A battery of 105mm howitzers from Delta Battery 2/320th Artillery Battalion arrived to provide that support. All the players were in place. During the next five days, elements of Task Force 3/506th uncovered numerous caches, destroyed dozens of enemy structures and discovered a large hospital complex. Contact was sporadic and in most instances limited to small, hit and run enemy units. However, as the operation continued, the task force began to run into progressively stiffer resistance as enemy units recovered from their surprise and began to respond to the invasion.

Then, encroaching monsoon weather moved in and threatened to shorten the length of the operation. On May 10th, Bravo Company, having just uncovered an enemy hospital complex and a sizable food cache, was engaged by an estimated NVA battalion, fighting from camouflaged, heavily fortified positions. The company soon discovered to its dismay that it was surrounded. Airstrikes, gunships and artillery from Fire Support Base Currahee were quickly employed to soften the enemy positions and keep the NVA at bay. During the night, the company ran dangerously low on ammunition. Its First Platoon, in a courageous assault, broke through the encircling NVA and brought reinforcements and a resupply to their trapped comrades, enabling them to hold out until daylight. The next day, Delta Company, commanded by Captain William C. Ohl II, linked up with Bravo and secured an LZ while the battered Bravo Company survivors were extracted to FSB Currahee. Bravo Company had suffered 8 killed and 28 wounded during the two-day battle against an entrenched NVA battalion. Delta Company later swept the contact area and turned up 47 dead NVA soldiers and located numerous blood trails exiting the area in several different directions.

On May 12th, Charlie Company, under the command of Captain Robert L. Acklen, Jr., discovered a large weapon's cache containing 760 small arms, 65 crew-served weapons, over one hundred 57mm recoilless rifle rounds, two hundred twenty-two B-40 rounds, twenty 75mm rounds, five hundred twenty-five 82mm mortar rounds, over 8,100 rounds of small arms ammunition, 155 pairs of NVA binoculars, and over one thousand hand grenades and assorted mines. The total amount of captured enemy weapons, munitions and equipment from the operation included vast amounts of food and medical supplies, 13 mortar tubes, two .51 cal. machine guns, 101 SKS rifles, 55 Chi Com submachine guns, 10 Soviet heavy machine guns, twelve Walther 9mm automatic pistols, 122 Soviet 7.62 automatic pistols, and over 800 other small arms and crew-served weapons. An entire field hospital was captured intact. Two U.S. radios and a starlight scope were also recovered.

In twelve short days, Task Force 3/506 had destroyed what it had taken the enemy four long years to build. The enemy lost 80 killed by actual body count with blood trails and body parts indicating much heavier casualties. Caught by surprise, the NVA had been unable to remove their large stores of food, weapons and munitions. It would teach them a valuable lesson— their cross border sanctuaries were no longer inviolate. Their fixed costs to conduct war had risen.

In the face of heavy tropical monsoon rains, Task Force 3/506th redeployed from Cambodia to FSB Wildcat inside South Vietnam, and immediately began Operation WAYNE JUMPER. Two days later, on May 18th, the 3/506th was airlifted to Plei Djereng. Over the next two months, the Battalion participated in a series of short operations which saw them moved around the II Corps and III Corps tactical zones like pawns on a chessboard. There was no significant action during any of these operations. After spending two fruitless days at Plei Djereng, on May 20th, the battalion moved by truck transport to Ban Me Thuot for Operation BYRON MOORE, a road clearing mission along QL21 that lasted 20 days. Local enemy forces avoided contact.

Released from BYRON MOORE on June 8th, Task Force 3/506th was airlifted to An Khe where it went into an 8-day refitting and retraining cycle prior to beginning Operation HANCOCK MACE. The battalion was airlifted to Song Mao and then combat assaulted into its AO on June 20th at the start of HANCOCK MACE. The operation lasted for two weeks and turned out to be another "dry hole." The next stop was to Phan Thiet, where the battalion immediately combat assaulted into Military Region 6 for Operation HANCOCK GOLD.

Starting on the 4th of July, HANCOCK GOLD would finally produce a little action, not much, but enough to keep the Currahees from rusting solid. On July 9th, the Recon 3/506th was hit by a command detonated claymore mine and small arms fire, suffering four killed and four wounded. They called in airstrikes on the enemy positions with unknown results. On July 10th, Delta Company troopers located and destroyed 45-50 abandoned enemy bunkers. On July 12th, a platoon from Bravo Company ran into a pair of VC and killed one of them before he could get away. Two days later, a platoon OP from Delta Company opened up on three enemy soldiers approaching their position and killed one. The enemy avoided any further contact with 3/506th troopers for the next seven days and the operation was terminated on July 21, 1970. The final operation for the 101st's "bastard battalion" was Operation JACK. The battalion was transported by convoy from An Khe to Tuy Phuoc District and inserted by truck into their new AO. The operation turned out to be just another "walk in the woods," and produced no combat activity. With things quiet for the 3/506th troopers in II Corps and III Corps tactical zones, the Currahee battalion was ordered to move north to rejoin its parent division. Things were once again beginning to heat up in the mountains around the A Shau Valley, and the return to the 101st Airborne Division of its missing battalion would go a long way toward strengthening the combat capability of the Division and stemming the tide of the NVA infiltration into the populated areas around Hue-Phu Bai. The 3/506th dejectedly began preparations for the move, beginning the actual deployment on August 20th. It would be a week later before the battalion with all of its support units would arrive at Phu Bai. On their arrival at hot and dusty Phu Bai, the 3/506th troopers immediately longed for their old stomping grounds to the south. They had developed a great sense of independence in their three years of operating on their own. But they soon accepted the fact that they would benefit from the added support that came with being part of a division-sized unit. The Battalion was informed that it was to become a part of the Division's 2nd Brigade, with its base camp located on the southeast border of the Phu Bai Combat Base—the old 2nd Brigade standdown area. On August 29th, Delta Company was air-lifted onto the previously abandoned FSB Brick. As soon as the Delta troopers consolidated, they walked off the fire base to begin patrolling in the immediate vicinity as Bravo Company landed behind them to provide security for the arriving engineers from the 326th Engineer Battalion. Fire Base Brick, overlooking the lower Son Ta Trach—Perfume River—and the infamous NVA stronghold—Leech Island, had been abandoned by the ARVNs three months earlier. It would now serve as a forward operational base for the Battalion. By mid-afternoon on the same day, Delta Battery 320th Artillery had arrived and set up its 105mm howitzers. Echo and Alpha companies had been air-lifted in and had moved off the hill, patrolling south and west, respectively. The next day Delta Company 3/506th, sweeping boldly through the heavily vegetated foothills of the Chaine Annamatique, foiled an NVA ambush, killing two enemy soldiers and capturing a pair of AK-47s.

On September 17th, Battalion elements air-assaulted into the mountains 10 klicks to the southeast and opened up FSB Pistol. Two days later, patrols from the 3/506th were probing deep into old enemy strongholds in the dangerous Elephant and the Ruong Ruong valleys . After conducting sweep operations around FSB Pistol for nearly three weeks, the Battalion returned to its rear area at Phu Bai for rest, refresher training and equipment overhaul. From October 13-31, the Battalion was OPCON to the 1st Brigade and began to conduct patrol operations into the mountainous area around Fire Base Birmingham. Deteriorating monsoon weather patterns soon terminated the operation and kept contact with the enemy at a minimum. From November 1-24, the battalion operated in the vicinity of FSB Arsenal, after once again returning to operational control of 2nd Brigade.

Continued bad weather resulted in light contact and made patrolling difficult if not altogether impossible. A quiet December closed out the year in the 101st Airborne Division's AO. The enemy was out there—waiting. He had been hurt time after time by the aggressive tactics of the Screaming Eagles, but if the NVA was anything, he was persistent. With the winding down of U.S. direct action involvement in Vietnam, the enemy seemed satisfied to sit back and bide his time. By the end of 1970, he knew for certain the Americans were on their way out. Time was on his side.

A CHANGING ROLE

THE BEGINNING OF 1971 saw the 101st Airborne Division once again on the move. The successful 1970 operations into Cambodia by joint U.S.-South Vietnamese forces had temporarily closed the sanctuaries and logistics centers available to the NVA/VC forces deployed against Saigon and its environs. It was a crippling blow to the enemy's war effort. The NVA had to depend entirely on its Laotian base camps and the Ho Chi Minh Trail if it were to continue its war effort at its previous level of intensity. North Vietnam began immediately to strengthen its hold on eastern Laos. The Ho Chi Minh Trail was improved and expanded. Anti-aircraft defenses were increased in an effort to protect the trail from allied air strikes. Steps were taken to counter MACV SOG operations in eastern Laos all the way down to the tri-border area. Security was strengthened at supply depots, rest areas, hospitals, truck parks and other facilities. Enemy armor and Soviet SAM batteries were brought in from North Vietnam to fortify the Trail. It was a reasonable assumption that the enemy's Laotian sanctuaries would be targeted for invasion by allied forces. After all, the Cambodian operations had handicapped enemy forces operating in III and IV Corps. The natural corollary was a similar thrust into Laos. Unfortunately, seven months would separate the two, allowing the NVA to prepare a suitable welcome. In addition, with the continuing withdrawal of U.S. forces during 1971, and the defensive posture assumed by all U.S. divisions and brigades remaining in country, the Laotian invasion would be a total South Vietnamese operation. Of course, American air power would still have to be a key factor, but for all intents and purposes, the South Vietnamese would have to go this one alone. The success of Vietnamization was about to face its first test.

The North Vietnamese, still reeling from the Cambodian invasion that had destroyed their timetable for an all-out invasion of South Vietnam, had rebounded by striking out against the four provinces comprising U.S. Military Region I (Quang Tri, Thua Thien, Quang Nam and Quang Ngai). The controlling American command in the area was XXIV Corps, and for the ARVN it was I Corps Headquarters. The U.S. XXIV Corps commander, Lieutenant General James W. Sutherland, had to counter this threat with only three major combat elements still under his control: The 1st Brigade 5th Infantry Division (Mechanized); the 23rd Infantry Division (Americal); and the 101st Airborne Division (Airmobile). The enemy's first move was to infiltrate a vast quantity of supplies and manpower into the A Shau Valley. With the pull out of occupying 101st Airborne units in late 1969, the old enemy stronghold was ripe for the retaking. In spite of continuous aerial patrolling by the 2/17th Cav, the NVA began to retake his old strongholds in the A Shau.

Intelligence gathered by aerial reconnaissance, long range patrols, agent reports, and sensors soon alerted XXIV Corps command to the danger. The 101st Airborne Division countered by occupying a series of forward fire support bases astride the enemy's routes of egress to the coastal plains and the populated areas around Hue-Phu Bai. Ripcord was the deepest fire base established by the 101st to thwart the NVA's plans, while Fire Base O'Reilly was manned by the ARVN 1st Infantry Division for the same purpose. Intense fighting around both fire bases during the summer of 1970 saw Ripcord evacuated in late July under heavy enemy attacks, while O'Reilly lasted until October when difficulty in resupply during monsoon weather forced its abandonment. The Ripcord/O'Reilly campaign failed to drive the NVA from rebasing in the A Shau, but it did succeed in blunting its planned offensive into the populated coastal plains. Temporarily, the opposing forces had reached a stalemate, but continued intelligence reports indicated the NVA were rebuilding across the border in Laos at a feverish pace.

On December 8, 1970, COMUS MACV—General Creighton Abrams— convened a special strategy meeting to discuss the NVA buildup in Laos. Intelligence pointed out a full-scale enemy logistical effort had begun along the Ho Chi Minh Trail in October, during the Laotian dry season. In spite of the daily dose of air strikes by at least thirty B-52 bombers and three hundred USAF, USN and USMC fighter/bombers, and continuous MACV-SOG raids and trail interdictions, the massive flow of food and medical supplies, war materials and manpower continued unabated. The experts pointed out huge stockpiles were being built up in the A Shau Valley, Base Area 611, and Base Area 604. In addition, 90% of the material coming down the Trail was being funneled through the Laotian town of Tchepone. Everything supported a MACV prediction of a four-part enemy offensive as soon as their material and manpower needs had been met. Their conclusion was:

1. A multi-division invasion of various targets in Quang Tri and Thua Thien provinces with Base Area 604 serving as the launch point into Quang Tri City, and Base Area 611 utilizing the adjacent A Shau Valley as a staging point for attacks against Hue-Phu Bai.

2. A renewed but limited attack in Cambodia, aimed primarily at the capitol of Phnom Penh to overthrow the pro-American Lon Nol govern-

ment.

3. A rebuilding operation along the Cambodian-South Vietnamese frontier to reclaim their vanquished sanctuaries.

4. A continued buildup in southern Laos throughout the dry season (October to April) with obvious consequences to Military Region I. The general conclusion among those present at the meeting was it would be foolish to wait for the enemy to take the initiative. It was an accepted fact he grew stronger with time, while U.S. forces grew weaker. Continuing troop withdrawals had not only reduced manpower, but it also had a debilitating effect on those still remaining. To attack the enemy in Laos would be dangerous and costly. He had been building up his fortifications in the area uncontested for over twenty years. A further handicap to the invasion had been imposed by the U.S. Congress in the form of the Cooper-Church amendment, passed in response to the public anti-war outcry over the Cambodian invasion. The amendment prevented U.S. ground forces, including those serving as advisors to the South Vietnamese military, from crossing any borders. This meant that an invasion or raid into Laos would have to be strictly an ARVN operation. U.S. ground forces would be able to support along the border as long as they refrained from crossing the line. However, U.S. aviation forces would have free-reign to carry the attack to the enemy. This last fact provided the only positive note to such a plan. Despite the danger of attacking into the heart of strong and well-equipped enemy forces, General Abrams made the decision to go ahead with the plan, subject to final approval from Washington. The offensive was not seen as an invasion of Laos, but, in effect, a spoiling raid toward the town of Tchepone designed to destroy enemy supplies and disrupt the NVA's planned offensive against I Corps military region. It was hoped by all concerned that the ARVN could wreak havoc across the border until the end of the dry season in April. If they could achieve this, it would forestall any large-scale NVA invasion that might pose a danger to the last U.S. units positioning to pull out of South Vietnam. Overall command of the ARVN ground forces would be in the hands of Lieutenant General Hoang Xuan Lam, the ARVN I Corps commander. U .S. forces would be used to open the invasion route to the Laotian border, and to conduct additional operations along the Laotian-South Vietnamese border from the A Shau Valley north to prevent enemy reinforcements in the south from reaching the invaders. The commanding general of XXIV Corps was assigned the following three duties:

1. To provide complete support for ARVN forces inside Laos. This was to include logistics, aviation, engineer, artillery and communications via Route 9 from the border back to the staging areas.

2. To reopen and support the Khe Sahn air field.

3. To provide and coordinate strategic and tactical air support for the

invasion through U.S. Air Force, Navy, and Marine Corps. These duties put into action meant elements from the 101st Airborne Division and the 1st Brigade of the 5th Mechanized Division would have to open, secure and patrol Route 9 from Dong Ha all the way through Khe Sanh and Lang Vei to the border. U.S. combat engineers would have to upgrade and maintain the dirt highway and reopen the Khe Sanh air strip. American artillery units would have to establish firebases along the border to support ARVN forces in Laos. Aviation units organic to or attached to the 101st Airborne Division would have to transport, supply, support, and medivac ARVN forces inside Laos. In addition, both U.S. commands would still have to conduct screening operations within their own TAORs. A tall order for American forces already tasked with providing security for operational areas too widespread for their capabilities. LAM SON 719/ DEWEY CANYON II, as the joint ARVN/American operation came to be known, was a tragedy in the making. General Sutherland was given approval on January 7, 1971, to go ahead with the final planning. The invasion was scheduled to begin in early February, immediately after the Tet holiday. For the first time during the preliminary planning stage, the ARVN command was brought in on the operation. The detailed plans attempted to make the best possible use of existing U.S. forces, although further analysis would show there was little allowance for unexpected contingencies. While the 1/5th Mechanized Brigade was tasked with the mission of opening Highway 9, establishing the supporting fire bases, and reopening the air strip at Khe Sanh, the 101st was given an even greater task:

1. To provide command and control for all U.S. Army Aviation units participating in the operation, including maintenance support (this was to include not only the helicopter, maintenance, and repair units organic to the Division, but also additional units attached from the Americal Division, 1st Aviation Brigade, and the 1st Marine Air Wing, which would more than double the number of helicopters normally available to the Division.)

2. To take over responsibility for the area of operations for the ARVN 1st Infantry Division when it moved into Laos. This included major parts of Quang Tri and Thua Thien provinces.

3. To attach required organic units to the 5th Mech ground task force.

4. To help secure the stretch of Route 9 from Dong Ha to LZ Vandegrift.

5. To provide helicopter support for all U.S. and ARVN units committed to the operation, on both sides of the border. Tremendous efforts were made to maintain security to prevent the NVA from getting wind of the coming invasion, even to the point of hampering preparations. But it was to no avail. It was impossible to mount an operation of this scale without

the enemy reading the signs. LAM SON 719 would fail to catch the NVA off-guard. For the purpose of deceiving the NVA of the true nature of the operation, elements of the 101st Airborne Division would drive into the A Shau Valley posing as a spearhead for further attacks against NVA base camps in the area. In addition, a 1,500-man Marine task force and the 7th Fleet would be standing by on station off the coast of North Vietnam while ARVN forces would assemble along the eastern DMZ poised to invade North Vietnam. Both of these feints would succeed in preventing NVA reinforcements from the A Shau Valley and along the DMZ from coming to the support of NVA units in Laos. Unfortunately, the NVA forces in Laos were of sufficient quantity and quality to handle the ARVN invasion force.

At Camp Eagle, things were moving along with the characteristic aplomb of a well-oiled machine. The planning group at the 101st Headquarters consisted of Brigadier General Sidney Berry (Assistant Division Commander for Operations), Brigadier General Olin Smith (Assistant Division Commander for Support), Colonel Don Siebert (Chief of Staff), Colonel Edward Davis (Commanding Officer, 101st Aviation Group), Lieutenant Colonel John Bard (G3), and Lieutenant Colonel Donald Rosenblum (Commanding Officer, Division Support Command). Major General John Hennessey, who had rotated back to the States on January 15th, was not present during this stage of the operation's planning. His replacement, Major General Thomas Tarpley, was not due until February 1st. For the second time in six months, the Division would be in the capable hands of Brigadier General Berry. Although these Screaming Eagle officers quickly got down to the impossible task at hand, many had reservations about the Division's ability to manage such an unprecedented operation of this magnitude. Just the list of aviation assets was staggering, besides the following aviation units organic to the Division: 101st Aviation Group, 101st Aviation Battalion, 158th Aviation Battalion, 159th Aviation Battalion, 2nd Squadron, 17th Air Cavalry 4th Battalion, 77th Aerial Field Artillery.

The following aviation units, mostly from the 1st Aviation Brigade, but also from the Americal Division, were also attached: 14th Aviation Battalion, 212th Combat Aviation Battalion, 223rd Combat Aviation Battalion, 71st Assault Helicopter Company, 116th Assault Helicopter Company (OPCON from the Americal Division), 174th Assault Helicopter Company (OPCON from the Americal Division), 132nd Assault Support Helicopter Company Troop B, 7th Squadron, 1st Air Cavalry Troop F, 8th Air Cavalry Troop C, 7th Squadron, 17th Air Cavalry HMH-463 (OPCON from the 1st Marine Air Wing), HMH-367 (OPCON from the 1st Marine Air Wing).

The 101st was also assigned the following aviation support units organic to DISCOM: 426th Supply & Service Battalion, 801st Maintenance Battalion, 326th Medical Battalion, 5th Transportation Battalion.

All in all, over 600 helicopters were to be operated, maintained and re-fueled by the 101st Aviation command. Its management would be overseen by Colonel Davis and General Berry—a staggering responsibility for both men. The 101st task force assigned to penetrate the A Shau Valley would be made up of four battalions and commanded by Lieutenant Colonel Paul F. Gorman, commanding officer of the Division's 1st Brigade. The 3/187th would be OPCON to the 1/5th Mech task force tasked with opening Highway 9. LAM SON 719 and its corresponding U.S. operation, DEWEY CANYON II, began on January 29, 1971. The ARVN forces would not invade Laos until February 8th. Meanwhile, hundreds of Huey slicks, Huey Charlie Model gunships, Loaches, Cobras and CH-47 Chinooks staged in various configurations all over the old Marine air strip at Khe Sanh. UH-1H model slicks from the Kingsmen, Commancheros, Phoenix, Dolphins, Ghostrid-ers, Lancers, and Black Widows sat in well-spaced clusters. AH-1G Cobras bearing the colorful names of Hawks, Toros, Redskins, and Blue Max waited like packs of hungry sharks ready for a kill. The first 101st Aviation casu-alties occurred on that same day as an A Company Huey "slick" from the 158th Aviation Battalion, piloted by WOs Paul Stewart and Tom Doody, was hit by 12.7mm anti-aircraft fire as it crossed the border with a load of ARVN Rangers. Trying to return to a friendly base, WO Stewart, the pilot, calmly announced over his radio, "Lead, Chalk Three is going inverted at this time." The helicopter was seen to go into the trees upside down and explode. There were no survivors.

Over Laos, small arms fire and deadly .51 caliber heavy machine gun fire was expected on each sortie and at every LZ. But RPGs were also used on final approaches with deadly effect. In addition, 23mm, 37mm, 57mm, 85mm and 100mm anti-aircraft artillery, some of it radar controlled was also encountered. The helicopter pilots had never before seen such an array of hostile weapons used against them prior to the Laotian incur-sion. Helicopters from the 158th Aviation Battalion transported ARVN paratroopers into Laos. Over the next few days they would leapfrog ARVN units over stalled mechanized and armored units all the way to Tchepone. The 101st pilots flew several sorties each day, day after day, defying all the rules for "safe" flying. Lieutenant Colonel Robert F. Molinelli's 2/17th Air Cav gunships were constantly running into NVA tanks, so many that they were running out of armor-piercing ammo before they ran out of targets. Targets of all types were plentiful, with gasoline pipelines, structures, sup-ply depots, bunkers, bridges, troop concentrations, anti-aircraft sites and just about every other target imaginable readily available. On February 18th, the 3/187th Infantry Battalion air-assaulted into the old U.S. Marine firebase known as "the Rockpile," just north of Vandergrift. An infantry battalion from the American Division, the 3/4th, had been trying to secure the mountain for several days and had been in almost constant contact with increasingly larger NVA forces. The mission of the 3rd Brigade battalion was to relieve the battered Americal battalion. The 3/187th, commanded by Lieutenant Colonel Bryan Sutton, had two killed and twelve wounded from its Echo Company within 30 minutes of landing. Among the wounded was his battalion operations officer, Major Ron Sharnberg. For several days, elements from the battalion made sporadic contact with small groups of NVA soldiers everywhere they turned. Fresh bunkers were found by nearly every patrol that ventured out. The amazing thing about the NVA was they seemed to be totally unconcerned an American Airborne battalion was operating within their midst. Elements of the 3/187th kept running into small groups of NVA who seemed unaware an enemy was anywhere around. On the night of February 21st, the NVA hit the perimeter of the Echo Recon platoon securing Fire Base Scotch and overran their positions. The paratroopers rallied and retook the hill suffering three wounded. The NVA left behind seven dead among Echo Recon's positions with several blood trails leading off into the surrounding cover. A diary found on one of the slain NVA soldiers indicated the enemy was scheduled to hit Bravo Company which was securing another hilltop nearby in the Rockpile. Before dark, the company's rifle platoons and a battalion sniper team were airlifted in to the hilltop. Everyone was quietly put on 100% alert. That night, the NVA struck. The snipers, spotting them through their starlight scopes, opened fire before the NVA assault forces reached the wire. Their single, well-aimed shots were deadly, and the enemy withdrew. Logistics was as mind-boggling a problem as the planners had first anticipated, but Colonel Donald E. Rosenblum, the commanding officer of the Division Support Command was up to the job. Working jointly with Brigadier General Olin Smith, the Assistant Division Commander for Support, Colonel Rosenblum coordinated the impossible task of keeping the wheels of transportation running smoothly. The 426th Supply and Service Battalion, under the command of Lieutenant Colonel Ken Jacobs, performed brilliantly, manning the refuel/rearm stations, scheduling transportation for DISCOM, and rigging the Division's helicopters with external loads. They kept supplies of food, ammunition, and replacements moving toward the front of the invasion forces, returning with the wounded and dead. Lieutenant Colonel William Beasley's 5th Transportation Battalion provided the maintenance, supply and repair for all the 101st's choppers. They quickly patched each helicopter brought in for repairs, performing miracles on some of the ships that should have been sent to the scrap yards. The 801st Maintenance, under command of Lieutenant Colonel Richard Nidever, was tasked with maintaining the Division's equipment—a seemingly impossible job in the midst of an all-out invasion. However, there were few complaints from the drivers and operators his battalion kept in business. With casualties heavier than expected, Lieutenant Colonel Robert Day's 326th Medical Battalion worked around the clock saving the lives of U.S. and ARVN soldiers who would not have had a chance without the unselfish efforts of the doctors, nurses, aids and technicians of the 326th Med. Rosenblum's four support battalions performed impossible tasks with little thanks or praise. Only those who realized where their next bullet, their food and water, the gas for their choppers, their mail from home came from could appreciate the efforts of those who served in the Division Support Command during LAM SON 719/ DEWEY CANYON II.

By the end of February it was obvious the ARVN operations inside Laos had ground to a halt. NVA forces had rebounded quickly, under the circumstances, and had counterattacked with a dreadful vengeance. And it wasn't reserved just for the ARVN forces across the border. Attacks were being pressed against nearly every U.S. installation from Lang Vei to Vandergrift to Khe Sanh. The NVA, supported by hundreds of large, radar controlled anti-aircraft guns, thousands of lighter 12.7mm and 37mm anti-aircraft guns, numerous tanks, and seemingly unlimited manpower, were striking boldly and in broad daylight to bring about as much damage as possible on the invaders and their support forces. As quickly as they were killed by allied forces, others seemed to take their place. Their backs were to the wall, and the enemy was pulling out all stops. By the middle of March, ARVN forces were desperately trying to get out of the hornets' nest they found themselves in. Some of the ARVN units managed to fight strong, well-organized withdrawals, punishing the NVA forces surging around them. But many ARVN soldiers had long ago given up any semblance of orderly withdrawal and had thrown away their weapons in a panic and were looking for any means possible to escape the carnage destroying them. Panic set in. Helicopter pilots reported a mad scramble for available space when they set down to drop off supplies or pick up wounded. Stories about dozens of ARVNs hanging from the skids of departing helicopters, and healthy soldiers tossing wounded comrades off medivacs to make places for themselves were all too common. On March 20th, a flight of ten 101st Aviation Battalion slicks, seven from Bravo Company (Kingsmen) and three from Charlie Company (Black Widows), were flying an emergency extraction mission for an ARVN battalion surrounded and in imminent danger of being overrun near FSB Brown. Six aircraft had already been shot down during two previous attempts to extract the ARVNs. When the ten helicopters arrived on the scene, their first approach was turned back by heavy anti-aircraft fire encircling the PZ. On the second approach, the lead aircraft sustained damages from the intense small arms fire, forcing the pilot to make another go-around. The second ship, flown by CWO Alan

Fischer and WO Ed Cash also took numerous hits, forcing them to break off and climb out. At 4,000 feet, the ship was hit again by what appeared to be a 37mm anti-aircraft gun and went into a steep dive. With the pilots knocked unconscious, the ship was doomed. But Fischer gained consciousness at the last minute and made a successful autorotation onto Delta One, which was at that time under siege. Chalks 3 and 4 were also hit on short final but continued into the PZ to pick up a load of troops. Severely damaged, both aircraft lifted off with a load of six ARVNs and made it out to complete their mission. Chalk 5, flown by CWO Bruce Sibley and Captain Steve Harris, was hit by an RPG and crashed into the trees nearby. Sibley was strapped in the left seat unconscious. Harris, in a daze from his wounds, ended up on the ground out in front of the wreckage. Sp4 Doug Purdy, the door gunner, was in intense pain, bleeding from a severe head wound. Sp5 Rich Ginosky, the crew chief, was shaken but uninjured in the crash. Seeing the futility of continuing their effort to extract the ARVNs, Chalks 7, 8, and 9 pulled out and aborted the mission. With the recent heavy losses among the U.S. aviation units, UH-1H's were becoming hard to replace. Chalk 10, piloted by Lieutenant Willis Wulf and WO Thom Beeson went to the aid of the crew of Chalk 5. As it approached the downed helicopter, they saw encircling NVA forces closing in around the wreckage of the Huey. Chalk 10 slipped into a hover over the crash site as all of the downed crew except Sibley climbed in. Offering an ideal target for the NVA gunners, the crew chief of the rescue ship was hit in the leg by enemy gunfire that ripped through the thin skin of Chalk 10. Sibley, hiding in a nearby bomb crater, waved frantically for Chalk 10 to get out of the area. Seeing Sibley was too injured to make it to the Huey on his own, Ginosky leaped from the cabin, ran back to Sibley's position and hauled him aboard. Meanwhile, Chalk 6, piloted by CWO Bill Singletary and WO Joe St. John slid into the PZ now under a heavy mortar barrage, and, without coming to a complete stop, picked up the crew of Chalk 2, escaping as enemy mortar rounds impacted on both sides of the aircraft.

Kingsmen commander Major Jack Barker, with a crew of Captain John Dugan, Sergeant Bill Dillender and Private First Class John Chubb led another sortie into the besieged PZ and took a direct hit from an RPG round and exploded in a ball of flame. The entire crew was lost. Further attempts at extracting the ARVNs were called off as suicidal. These were only a few examples of the professionalism and dedication of the American pilots who risked their lives repeatedly to save countless South Vietnamese soldiers and many of their own comrades from impending death. The magnitude of their sacrifices was unprecedented during the Vietnam war.

The main support base and the air field at Khe Sanh had been subjected to mortar and rocket shelling since the second week of the invasion. But by the middle of March, the shelling was almost continuous. The enemy had even moved up large 130mm guns and were pounding the old Marine base with regularity. The main area of bombardment was the part of the perimeter defended by Delta Troop 2/17th Air Cavalry. The Cav troopers had arrived early in the operation to provide security at the large base camp against the threat of NVA sappers who were expected to try to destroy the helicopters and the fuel points in an effort to nullify their support to the trapped ARVN units across the border. When the shelling increased in tempo—almost 20 rounds per hour—Colonel Sutton moved his 3/187th battalion from the Rockpile to Khe Sahn to provide added security to the Khe Sanh perimeter. Now, dug in between the positions manned by the 3/187th and the 4/77th Aerial Artillery, the Cav was still taking a beating.

During daylight hours, patrols from Delta troop and the 3/187th went out into the hills looking for the NVA. More often than not they found them. During the operation, the 3/187th killed 48 enemy soldiers, but at a heavy cost of nineteen of their own, including Colonel Sutton and Major Schranberg, who died in a helicopter crash. They were replaced by Lieutenant Colonel Robert Steverson, from the 5th Mech, and Major Chester Garret from the 3rd Brigade of the 101st.

On the night of March 23rd, the NVA came after the fuel blivets and helicopters at the Khe Sanh air strip. At 0315 hours, exploding satchel charges and ricocheting green tracers announced that the NVA sappers had already gotten through the wire. As a fuel blivet, a stockpile of 2.75 inch rockets, and a helicopter exploded, five enemy sappers slipped into the perimeter between the 2/17th Cav position and those of the 4/77th Aerial Artillery and jumped into a trench line. Screaming at the tops of their lungs, the NVA ran down the trench tossing satchel charges and hand grenades into the Cav's bunkers. Sp4 Michael Fitzmaurice and three other Delta Troop soldiers were in one of the bunkers taking three satchel charges. Seeing the danger, Fitzmaurice tossed out two of the satchel charges, then dove on the other smothering it under his outstretched flak jacket. The impact of the explosion tossed him back into the side wall of the bunker, bleeding profusely from the shrapnel that had riddled him. Blinded in one eye, blood streaming down his face, Fitzmaurice grabbed his weapon and charged out into the trench line and killed two of the sappers. Dropping his now empty rifle and grabbing up a machete, the young Screaming Eagle ran down the trench to the other three NVA sappers and chopped them to pieces in fierce hand to hand combat. It took several of his comrades to drag him back under cover. Specialist Michael J. Fitzmaurice became the seventeenth and final Screaming Eagle to be awarded the Congressional Medal of Honor during the Vietnam War.

The fighting at Khe Sanh air base lasted until daylight, after which three more sappers were trapped inside the perimeter and killed. The enemy had lost a total of fourteen sappers by actual body count, and another was captured. Numerous blood trails led off into the brush outside the wire. Three Americans were killed and fourteen more were wounded in the attack. But the assault had been defeated before extensive damage had been done to the helicopters on the flight line. LAM SON 719/ DEWEY CANYON II officially ended on April 6, 1971. The 101st Airborne Division lost 68 killed in action, 261 wounded in action, and 17 missing in action. Overall U.S. casualties were 238 killed in action, 1,149 wounded in action, and 42 missing in action. ARVN losses were 1,529 killed in action, 5,483 wounded in action, and 625 missing in action. U.S. helicopters lost in the operation totaled 107, with 618 damaged. Enemy losses were 13,914 killed in action, and 57 captured. The NVA also lost 5,170 individual weapons, 1,963 crew-served weapons, 2,001 vehicles, 11 combat vehicles, 106 tanks, 13 artillery pieces, 3 mortars, 98 radios, 1,250 tons of rice, and 170,346 tons of ammunition. It was obviously a great setback for the enemy. Official channels claimed the joint operation was another great victory, and the above statistics tend to support this claim. DEWEY CANYON II undoubtedly saw the ultimate success of its mission. But LAM SON 719, although it was effective early in its operation, rapidly degenerated into an ARVN rout. A few ARVN units performed admirably, but most turned and ran under the relentless NVA counterattacks. With their backs to the wall, the NVA proved superior to the ARVN when their backs were in the same position. From the viewpoint that Vietnamization was a success, LAM SON 719 was an unqualified defeat.

THE FINAL DAYS

When LAM SON 719 ended on April 6, 1971, the handwriting was on the wall. The war—at least the U.S. military's part in it—was over. The Fifth Special Forces Group and the 11th Armored Cavalry Regiment had pulled out of South Vietnam during the height of the Laotian campaign. The only major U.S. forces left in Vietnam by the middle of April 1971, were the 23rd Infantry Division (Americal), the 101st Airborne Division (Airmobile), the 3rd Brigade of the 1st Cavalry Division (Airmobile), the 1st Marine Regiment, the 5th Marine Regiment, the 1st Brigade of the 5th Infantry Division (Mechanized), the 173rd Airborne Brigade, and three separate battalions; the 1/1st Cavalry, the 1/10th Cavalry, and the 3/5th Cavalry.

Every U.S. unit, with the exception of the 101st Airborne Division and the 3rd Brigade of the 1st Cavalry Division, had already stood down from offensive action against the enemy. Assuming a defensive posture, these units went about the task of turning over their camps and equipment to the ARVN forces that would be relieving them.

The 101st Airborne Division (Airmobile), still in the middle of the long-running Operation JEFFERSON GLEN, began to gradually disengage from contact with the enemy. But the Screaming Eagles' "aggressive" disengagement succeeded in keeping the enemy at bay.

JEFFERSON GLEN, renamed OPORD 13-70 at the end of July, would continue to protect the coastal lowlands around Camp Evans-Hue-Camp Eagle, as the 101st began to wind down its operations and prepare to pass control to the ARVN 1st Infantry Division. When OPORD 13-70 officially came to an end on October 8, 1971, it was the last major ground combat operation of the Vietnam War. However, the Screaming Eagles would continue to take the war to the enemy with aggressive patrolling and ambushes and aerial interdiction right up until the end.

When LAM SON 719 ended, the ARVN 1st Infantry Division, still recovering from heavy losses sustained in the Laotian invasion, kicked off Operation LAM SON 720. This operation into the A Shau Valley to cut the enemy's supply routes was a four month operation that ended on August 13th and cost the NVA 3,800 killed and 900 weapons lost. Units from the 101st did not participate in a major role, but supported the operation by providing air transportation, artillery, gunships, and aerial and ground reconnaissance. Still 700 enemy dead and 75 crew-served weapons captured or destroyed were credited to U.S. forces. On April 23, 1971, a six-man Ranger team from L Company, 75th Infantry (Ranger), lead by Team Leader Sergeant Marvin Duren, was inserted on a ridgetop on the eastern side of the A Shau Valley. They were to serve as a radio relay team for a Ranger platoon laying anti-tank mines along Route 547A in the floor of the A Shau. Other Ranger reconnaissance teams and 2/17th Cav aerial scouts had for the past two weeks reported NVA tanks and tracked vehicles operating along the dirt highway. The insertion attempt at their primary LZ had been aborted due to enemy ground fire, so the team went in on its secondary LZ, in a saddle flanked by steep slopes. On the ground, Duren took point to lead the team off the LZ where it could "lay dog" long enough to determine if the NVA had monitored the insertion. They had. Fifteen yards out of the LZ, Duren was cut down by a burst from an enemy AK-47, that hit him twice in the right hip, chest and stomach. As NVA grenades exploded around him, and other automatic weapons joined in, Duren was hit again in the spleen, appendix, left lung, left arm and back. Firing from camouflaged bunkers, the NVA had the team pinned down in the saddle. At first, the rest of the team were unable to reach the badly wounded team leader. But a short time later, as Sergeant James Champion laid down suppressive fire with his M-203 grenade launcher, Sergeants Fred Karnes, the team RTO, and Steve McAlpine, an ex-Special Forces medic, crawled to where Duren lay. McAlpine quickly started a saline IV in his neck to prevent him from going into shock.

While preparations were being made to rescue the Ranger team, a Huey slick, flown by Captain Louis Spiedel from Bravo Troop 2/17th Cav, was inbound with Ranger Staff Sergeant William Vodden on board to take the place of the wounded Ranger team leader. As the aircraft passed over the battle torn LZ, Vodden leaped out and ran to join the rest of the Ranger team pinned down near the LZ. Enemy ground fire immediately hit the helicopter causing it to crash. Making sure that the assistant team leader had everything under control, Vodden looked up to see the door gunner from the downed Cav slick staggering across the LZ toward the Rangers' position. When the crewman fell behind a log, got up and fell again, Vodden left his position and ran out to retrieve the man. On the way back with the wounded door gunner, Vodden was hit in the leg, shattering his femur. As the NCO lay there treating his own wound, he observed a medivac helicopter from Eagle Dustoff, piloted by WO Fred Behrens and Captain Roger Madison, attempting to land amidst intense enemy small arms fire to extract Duren. McAlpine and assistant team leader, Sergeant John Sly, got up and dragged the badly wounded Ranger toward the waiting medivac. The Dustoff crew chief jumped from the medivac ship and ran to help, finally succeeding in getting the unconscious Duren on board. While Duren was being extracted, the crew chief from Speidel's downed Huey ran across the LZ and dropped at Vodden's feet. He told him that the two pilots were trapped upside down with their legs pinned in the wreckage, then tried to make it to the Rangers' perimeter. Heavy fire turned him back, so he returned to Vodden and told him he was returning to the downed helicopter, then disappeared over the crest of the hill. Meanwhile, the Eagle Dustoff medivac, piloted by Behrens, had returned to pick up Vodden. Coming in over the LZ, the ship landed on the LZ amidst the smoke of battle. Sp4 Isaako Malo, the Ranger team's junior scout, Karnes, McAlpine, Sly, Champion and the Cav door gunner climbed aboard. As the helicopter climbed out, it took several hits—two hitting WO Behrens in the foot and upper body, another killing the crew chief—and autorotated down on the LZ. The surviving crew and passengers spilled out opposite sides of the downed Huey, some heading for Vodden's position, Behrens dropping behind the closest cover he could find, the rest diving for a crater fifty feet away. A short while later, those at Vodden's location were joined by the crew chief from the downed Cav helicopter. During the entire operation, Cobra gunships from the 2/17th Cav had made pass after pass over the NVA positions preventing the enemy from overrunning the men trapped on the LZ. But as darkness fell, the gunships were forced to return to Camp Eagle. The heavy fire from the enemy positions ceased. The Cav crew chief reported he was going to go back to the crash site and attempt to extricate the two pilots. He took off with the surviving Dustoff crewman following behind. The two men returned a short time later, saying it would take special tools to get either of the pilots out of the wreckage.

Surprisingly, the enemy stayed put during the night. Karnes, Madison and Sly had spent a sleepless night together, not knowing if anyone else was alive or dead. In the morning, the three men crawled around the ridgetop looking for a radio. A sniper killed Sly. When Karnes showed up with a radio, Madison found out that an NVA battalion had been spotted moving up to reinforce whoever they were fighting. Madison spent the rest of the day directing air strikes and Cobra gunship runs on the enemy positions, often bringing it right up to their own perimeter. Later in the day, the two men learned one or more aero-rifle troops from the 2/17th Cav had landed to the north of them, while a couple of rifle companies from the 2/502nd had also combat assaulted down in the valley. The enemy had stopped them cold. Toward the end of the second day, Karnes and Madison decided to escape and evade. As they moved to the west off the side of the ridge, they ran into McAlpine who had just left a badly wounded Isaako Malo hidden in a hole on top of the ridge. Unable to carry the hip-shot Ranger, the three men decided to leave him where he was hidden and try to make it to the Cav troops. They moved down the mountain then turned north on a secondary ridge, then swung back east until they reached the Cav's perimeter. They were shocked to see dozens of dead and wounded in the Cav's positions. They had been mauled on insertion by the NVA, taking ten killed in as many minutes. A short time later, Madison was medivac'd out with the Cav's wounded. McAlpine and Karnes spent the second night with the survivors of the 2/17th Cavalry. Behrens spent the second day hiding alone among the NVA positions, wounded a third time by a sniper, hugging the Thompson submachine gun he had pulled from his wrecked helicopter. He had fired up half his magazine killing the sniper who had shot him, and had decided to save the rest for when the enemy tried to overrun his position. Friendly aircraft repeatedly strafed and rocketed the area around him. He screamed to alert any other survivors he was still alive, and breathed a sigh of relief when the Cobras adjusted their runs away from his location. He watched silently as khaki-clad NVA came out of their positions and dragged off their dead and wounded. The night was especially terrifying as enemy soldiers moved around in the surrounding darkness. Vodden, Champion, and the rest of the surviving helicopter crewmen tried to stay out of sight as each movement seemed to draw enemy fire.

The Cav crew chief continued checking up on the two pilots still trapped in the wreckage of the Huey, giving them moisture from some pulpy roots he had found. The men were in bad shape and getting worse by the hour. The three men decided Champion and the crew chief would try to escape and evade. The crew chief was armed only with a revolver. Champion, the stock of his M-16 shattered by an NVA bullet, had lost his webgear and rucksack, so Vodden divided his remaining magazines and frags, and gave the young Ranger his map and compass. At dusk on the second day, the two men moved out. A short time later, the crew chief returned to Vodden's position, telling him he had decided to stay and look after the injured pilots. Champion had gone on alone. An hour later, the two men heard firing down in the valley below them. Vodden believed he had just heard James Champion's "last stand."

During the night, enemy soldiers moved all around them. On two different occasions, Vodden had fired at the silhouette of a man standing over the edge of the crater that hid the two Screaming Eagles. Each time, for good measure, Vodden also tossed a grenade into the brush above them. On the third day, a scout helicopter appeared overhead followed by several Cobras making their deadly passes. Low flying fighter-bombers dropped their ordnance on the dug in enemy forces. The Cav crew chief slipped down the side of the ridge again to check on his pilots, and returned to report that the co-pilot had died sometime during the night. Off in the distance the two men saw a long string of helicopters approaching. They knew help was finally on the way. For the first time in three days they began to believe that they might get out of this alive.

In the afternoon, Vodden and the crew chief heard small arms fire and someone yelling. Then, miraculously, two L Company Rangers appeared ghostlike out of the brush. Sergeants Dave Rothwell and Don Sellner had reached two of the survivors. The Cav crew chief and Vodden were quickly medivac'd off the ridge. Karnes and McAlpine remained inside the Cav perimeter until the morning of the third day. The two men returned to the scene of the Ranger team's battle with a five-man reaction force composed of the Captain David Ohle, Sergeant Dave Quigley, Sergeant Herb Owens, and two other Rangers. General Tarpley, the Division Commander, had ordered an arc-light on the ridge for that afternoon, and the Rangers had volunteered to go in and try to recover anyone who had survived the three days on the ridge. Reaching the LZ, the seven Rangers came under intense fire from NVA hidden in bunkers. Everyone but Quigley was pinned down. Quigley rushed through the bunkers alone until he reached the LZ. He found Sly's body near the downed medivac aircraft. Crossing the LZ, he found many dead American soldiers from the 2/17th Cav and the 502nd who had tried to reach the trapped Rangers and helicopter crewmen. Bodies were everywhere. Then he found WO Fred Behrens, looking like a piece of Swiss cheese from all the holes in him. The NVA gunners had used him as a target for zeroing in their weapons. Unbelievably, Behrens was still alive and asked Quigley for something to eat. Quigley dropped him a can of apricots and a canteen and moved on. Captain Ohle had finally fought his way past the NVA bunkers and caught up to Quigley. The two Rangers found the Cav chopper three hundred yards down the side of the ridge, smashed flat as a pancake. Speidel was still alive, but would later loose both his legs at the hips. Owens and Quigley searched the ridge for Champion and Malo. They found Malo's weapon but no sign of either man. (Malo was released by the NVA in 1973—Champion was never seen again).

On August 3rd, the Rakkasans from the 3/187th were detached from the 101st Airborne Division and sent south to Cam Ranh Bay. The battalion would provide security for departing U.S. units by patrolling the surrounding mountains. On September 1st, LAM SON 810 began as 101st aviation units airlifted thousands of ARVN troops into western Quang Tri Province. During the months of April through October 1971, gunships from the 2/17th Cav, 4/77th Aerial Artillery, and the 101st Aviation Battalion roamed everywhere throughout the Division's AO, destroying enemy soldiers, supply points, and fortifications. The enemy was plentiful and paid a heavy price for their boldness to the 101st aerial hunters who were getting in their last "licks" before redeploying back to the States. This type of combat, small American elements running into major NVA units, and armed aerial interdiction, typified the contact that the Screaming Eagles would see during the rest of JEFFERSON GLEN/ OPORD 13-70. For its actions from March to October 1971, the 101st Airborne Division was awarded the Vietnamese Cross of Gallantry with Palm.

THE END OF THE VIETNAM RENDEZVOUS

The 101st Airborne Division (Airmobile) began its redeployment from Vietnam in November 1971. As the three brigades began to turn over their fire bases to ARVN units and withdraw to their base camps, the NVA avoided the last minute "going away" party they had given to other departing American units. The Division turned over Camp Evans, LZ Sally, and Camp Eagle, withdrawing to the air strip at Phu Bai, and finally to DaNang to close out of Vietnam. The Screaming Eagles were the last U.S. Army division to leave the combat zone in South Vietnam. Many of the soldiers from the 101st Airborne Division who still had six months or more remaining on their combat tours, were shipped south to strengthen the 3rd Brigade of the 1st Cavalry Division. Their presence would still be felt for another three months. Departing as it came in, the Division provided its own security to cover its own withdrawal. Finally, a single color-bearing battalion-sized element departed DaNang by plane for Ft. Campbell, Kentucky, in March, 1972. For the Screaming Eagles, its longest sustained combat mission was finally over. The Division had suffered over four thousand of its young Eagles killed in action. Over 50,000 others were wounded. But it had performed exceptionally well. The enemy would remember the Screaming Eagles long after they had gone. On April 6, 1972, the 101st Airborne Division (Airmobile) was officially welcomed home in a ceremony attended by Vice President Spiro T. Agnew and Army Chief of Staff General William C. Westmoreland. Major General Thomas M. Tarpley passed command of the Division to Major General John H. Cushman. Vice President Agnew summed up the past performance and the future mission of the 101st when he said at the end of his address: "...You can be proud of your service in Vietnam and you can look forward to a new challenge and new opportunity for the 101st Division in our armed force. Your job now will be to achieve a fully operational role as part of our strategic reserve. This will require continued personnel replacements and training to maintain the sharp dual edge—as both an airborne and an airmobile force—that you have had in Vietnam. While the new peacetime Army will be smaller, it must be strong and quick and versatile—serving as a deterrent to war and at the same time being ready for deployment in any emergency. It is a role to which the 101st, with its proud history and can-do spirit, will easily adjust. I am sure when duty calls, the Screaming Eagles will be ready.

Welcome home, and congratulations again on a mission well done."

The Eagle had returned.

CHAPTER FOUR

Air Assault

FROM SOUTHEAST TO SOUTHWEST ASIA

Thomas H. Taylor

1972-1991

T HE 101ST WAS the last U.S. Division brought back from Vietnam. One cannot speculate as to which troops were more elated, the NVA who had lost so many of their number to the 101st or the Screaming Eagles themselves, ending the last 13-month tours. Army Chief of Staff Westmoreland welcomed the final contingent on April 6, 1972, in a ceremony at Campbell Army Airfield. The next such return of the colors would be at the same site in the same month 19 years later.

Just home from Vietnam, the 101st was at approximately 20% strength. Preceding it had been the 173rd Airborne Brigade (Separate) which was then reconstituted as the 101st's 3rd Brigade, and remained parachutists. One by one, Major General John Cushman stood up battalions to flesh out the rest of the Division's skeleton. This was a process that would take 18 months, using the Army's new recruiting policy called "Unit of Choice." With the draft terminated and the all-volunteer Army (VOLAR) begun, Cushman relished the opportunity to obtain Screaming Eagles straight from civilian life.

To do so he dispatched Division "canvassers" with recruiters throughout the country. Under Unit of Choice they could sign up volunteers who would sew the Screaming Eagle on their first uniform, attend basic training together, then proceed to Ft. Campbell for advanced individual training (AIT) with the unit in which they were permanently assigned. Thus cohesion was very much enhanced, and the Division got about 10,000 of the kind of soldiers it wanted because it picked them even before their induction.

An additional attraction for prospective 101st volunteers was 'Eagle University,' a consortium of colleges and technical schools whom Cushman invited to create an on-post presence to offer educational opportunities, from high school equivalency to post-graduate credits, during duty hours. He was able to provide this time by introducing what was called the "XYZ" training cycle, whereby brigades conducted mission-oriented training at full strength for three days per week, performed post details and administrative functions for two others, and could devote the remaining two days for attendance at Eagle University or its high school counterpart called "Eagle Prep." Both institutions were open to dependents, and throughout America today many such alumni opened new phases of their lives because of the outside education made available to them at Ft. Campbell.

For his NCO corps, Cushman was fortunate to have many Vietnam veterans who requested assignment with the Division in order to remain at Ft. Campbell. But in 1971 it was not a sure thing that the Division would return to Ft. Campbell. Hunter Airfield (now part of Ft. Stewart, Georgia) had been turned over to the Army by the Air Force and seemed an excellent location for the 101st, especially since Ft. Campbell might be overcrowded if it continued as a training center as it had been during the Vietnam War. It would have been a difficult choice for the NCOs, whether to stay with the Division or stay at Ft. Campbell. Luckily, Cushman was able to keep both together.

By condoning violation of an Army regulation, he was also able to restore the original four-color Screaming Eagle patch to the Division's field uniform (called fatigues in Vietnam, battle dress uniform—BDUs—thereafter). "Subdued" (i.e., black and olive drab) patches had been dictated by regulation during the jungle war, though Vietnam Screaming Eagles largely exempted themselves and continued to wear the four-color patch as had their forbearers in World War II. But when Cushman took command of the Division, his only brigade wore subdued patches as prescribed by regulations. He set about to bring back the black-white-red and gold patches by appealing to the Division association. Bake sales and raffles by the association produced the money to buy the patches so that Cushman's conversion would be at no expense to the Army. He informed higher-ups at the Pentagon of what he was doing. They either winked or looked the other way; regulations were not so sacred as the spirit of a unit. There is something about wearing the full colored Screaming Eagle that affects spirit, in the past, the present, and in the future.

Cushman was succeeded in 1973 by Major General Sidney Berry, a former Screaming Eagle Brigade Commander in Vietnam, who presided over the final phase of the conversion of the Division from parachutes to helicopters when 3rd Brigade terminated jump status. Certainly it was wrenching to lose such a sentimental link (represented by the parachutist's badge and boots) to the original Screaming Eagles, but throughout its history "airborne" has meant not only "chutes" but gliders and powered aircraft of many sizes. It is a term that has evolved, just as "cavalry" at one time meant only horses, then transformed into armor.

Screaming Eagles never jumped tactically in Vietnam, but they considered themselves paratroopers nonetheless because "airborne" is a word that stirs the spirit more than it describes transportation. It does not so much distinguish how soldiers reach the ground but what they do once they arrive. That generic quality was verified by the passage from parachutes to helicopters in Vietnam, much the way gliders had passed in then out of the Division's inventory. The immediate post-Vietnam years produced a further transition, that from air mobile to air assault, and brought recognition in the form of the Air Assault School and the qualifications skill badge, first awarded to graduates in 1974.

In that same year the parenthetical designation "Air Assault" was added to the Division's official title. This updated combat personality was designed to present a new form of warfare to sophisticated enemies; i.e., the Soviet bloc. As an air cavalry then air mobile division (virtually synonymous), the 101st had used helicopters more for tactical mobility than as a weapon, the essential firepower of gun ships notwithstanding. Air Cavalry/Air Mobile somewhat assumed the enemy to be a light force. Air Assault took on all comers through the addition of three new - or greatly enhanced - capabilities: night vision, radar jamming, and anti-armor.

This comprehensive "new look" was yet to be fully endorsed in 1976 when Major General John Wickham took command. A major test occurred during the giant intercontinental exercise REFORGER 76, the Division's largest deployment since Vietnam. In the cramped and heavily built-up land corridors of Germany, the air assault division worked for the first time within a mechanized corps as it maneuvered, outnumbered against a simulated Soviet invasion.

The 101st had much to prove under difficult circumstances: a shallow defensive sector, urbanized or forested terrain, state of the art anti-aircraft defenses with only parity between opposing air forces. NATO Allies as well as EUCOM were watching closely to see whether costly, yet apparently fragile, heliborne forces could survive in even a mid-intensity environment. To show its worth, the 101st had not only to survive but do what no other division could: strike the second echelon of invasion and suppress wide areas in the enemy rear.

The air assault division's future was on the line. At the end of RE-FORGER 76, that future was assured. Way ahead and over the heads of mechanized forces, the 101st's lightning reactions in all situations opened a lot of eyes, many with envy. NATO had a new deep threat plus an incomparable covering force, and one that gave new meaning to mobile defense.

As a new and now favored weapons system, the 101st became the test bed for everything involving helicopters. It received new howitzers and the successor to the HUEY, the 12-passenger Black Hawk. The Cobra's anti-tank capabilities were gradually improved so that it was still highly effective in the Gulf War. By then the amazing Apache was the premier attack helicopter in the world, and the 101st was the first division to which it had become organic.

Also during Wickham's watch, the three-phase training cycle became a division institution: one brigade devoted to general support, one to local training, and one in major field exercises. Even with 100,000 acres, Ft. Campbell became too small for the far ranging operations toward which the Division was evolving, so lifts into Ft. Chaffee and Ft. Bragg became routine, and parts of the picturesque Land Between the Lakes in Kentucky was obtained for training.

Like the rest of the Army, Screaming Eagles immeasurably benefitted from much improved training facilities, especially as they related to realism. Acoustic sensors to provide fire effects proved to troops that they were hitting or being hit. Later, laser sensors would replace acoustics to produce the closest approximation to real fire fights, and very authentic battles would rage in the desert at Ft. Irwin.

The 101st, now once again an all-volunteer force, set itself strict as well as higher standards. The Army tradition of heavy drinking happy hours was abolished, and a driving while intoxicated ticket was enough to suspend a driver's license for months. In 1977, Ft. Campbell had the best safety record of all major posts.

VOLAR, of course, was a much smaller Army but also more inclusive. "One Army" was the concept, with the emphasis on one—not separate worlds for regulars and reservists. Consequently, the 101st had to take on a training mission in addition to its world wide strategic commitments. In the late 1970s, it led all FORSCOM active duty divisions in training assistance for National Guard and reserve units. A different sort of training went on within the Division's Officers Corps that came to be called "mentoring." Whatever "mentoring" involved, it worked; between 1976 and 78 alone, 24 generals rose from the ranks of lieutenant colonels and colonels serving with the 101st.

By 1980, the Division was included in XVIIIth Airborne Corps' role as the JCS Rapid Deployment Force focused on the Middle East where vast, open expanses provided ideal terrain for air assault tactics. Large scale joint and combined maneuvers began with JTX Bright Star in Egypt. In 1982, 1-502 was designated for a six-month tour with the Multinational Force and Observers (MFO), the peacekeepers in the Sinai. On a rotating basis, battalions of the 101st have been performing that mission ever since.

One such MFO mission ended in ghastly tragedy, the heaviest blow felt by the Ft. Campbell community since the height of the Vietnam War. Home bound for Christmas in a charter airliner, 248 Screaming Eagles, most from

3-502, crashed after takeoff from Gander, Newfoundland. Though shocked and shaken, the post mobilized all the comforts possible for the families of those who perished. There were many touching tributes and condolences, including a solemn visit by President Reagan, and Hopkinsville, Kentucky, dedicated a statue built and maintained by private donations. But the lasting memorial rose in a symbol of life, a grove of 248 Canadian Maple saplings planted between thoroughfares at Ft. Campbell. They grow to this day in memory of soldiers who had once trained nearby.

Gander, as the tragedy will always be remembered at Ft. Campbell, was the darkest cloud to envelop the community between the wars. But there was another kind of cloud, lesser but nagging, that wouldn't go away. With awesome firepower and unmatched tactical mobility, the 101st was relatively slow afoot when it came to strategic movement. This was because of bulk and weight. Department of the Army had made note of this handicap to more than one of the Division's commanding generals, but what was required to fight anywhere on the globe, at any level of intensity, seemed indispensable.

When Major General J.H. Binford Peay III took command in August 1989, the Army Chief of Staff flagged the Division's strategic mobility as an imperative improvement. The 101st would have to move out in fewer Air Force planes or its relevance in the Army's force structure could come into question. As international events would later unfold, Peay had less than a year to lighten the Division or it might be left behind as it had been for Grenada and Panama.

Though the 101st was in no way burdened with redundant or extraneous equipment, Peay subjected it to a zero based examination of what was needed when in a full deployment. It was all needed under one or another contingency in one of four theaters to which the Division could be committed, but by focusing on when it was needed, significant economies were possible particularly in air lift requirements. This economizing project was called Slim Eagle, In concept, it resembled a family's PCS move when the soldier has to get to a new station on short notice.

The soldier has to fly there with his orders in a brief case and uniform in a carry-on bag. Less essential baggage is checked in with the airline. Meanwhile, someone "self-deploys" the family car by driving it to the new station, and the household goods come later in a moving van. What Slim Eagle sorted out was what had to go with the soldier, what could self-deploy, and what could follow by surface transportation. It was laborious, exacting work to re-configure all the Division's personnel and equipment into these new categories, because Slim Eagle didn't mean simply that combat elements went first, then combat support, then combat service support. Effective, not just rapid, deployment required carefully considered slices of each.

Probably the most radical factor incorporated into Slim Eagle were plans to self-deploy many of the Division's helicopters. If permitted, they could have been flown to Panama faster than those air lifted from Ft. Bragg. A feasible route by way of Greenland was mapped out for self-deployment to Europe, and from there perhaps to the Middle East. Only southeast Asia was really out of range.

But southwest Asia was to be the Division's next rendezvous with destiny. It appeared on August 2, 1990, some three weeks after a retrospective celebration in Washington, DC—the 50th Anniversary of the U.S. Airborne. For that occasion the 101st was represented by a composite battalion and massed colors, festooned with battle streamers from World War II, Korea (187th), and Vietnam. The Division's veterans would be marching, too; before adjutants call, they mixed with the young soldiers and sensed how they longed for a trial by combat like that which they heard described by their Screaming Eagle forefathers.

Sooner than anyone ever imagined, the trial would begin, and 11 months later the Division would march again in Washington, carrying two new battle streamers labeled Desert Shield and Desert Storm.

THE GULF WAR

DEPLOYMENT

SUMMER 1990. NEVER officially begun, the Cold War was now unofficially over, and there was no doubt who had won. The free world's victory over communism in the 45-year struggle had been achieved without a shot being fired between the two super powers, though at a staggering cost measured in trillions of dollars. Deterrence had succeeded. The horrifying shadow of thermonuclear war was lifted from the face of the earth.

From editors, commentators, from statesmen in and out of government, came a ripple of praise for the essential role of the Armed Forces in the Cold War victory. They said now it was time to turn to the prospects of a world without war, time to consider worthy causes for the "peace dividend," sorely needed by the American economy battered by unprecedented national debt and budget deficits, tottering upon a decrepit infrastructure. To fund these and other pressing priorities, the military would have to shrink in size and expense. "Thanks for a job well done," was the message from the country to its Army—but clearly the job had been completed. Such was the mood of America in the summer of 1990. A new decade had begun, one which everyone expected to end with a much smaller Army serving a much more prosperous nation.

That time might be coming, but meanwhile the 101st would continue its mission of high readiness. In late July, key staff sections assembled at Ft. Bragg for a map exercise called Internal Look directed by 18th Airborne Corps (ABC). Though under contingency plans the 101st was tasked with a variety of global missions, the Division's principal role was as part of 18th ABC which itself was part of a joint aggregation designed to be the Pentagon's fire brigade for brush fires around the world. By 1990, it had become focused on the Middle East and converted into the land component of CENTCOM whose theater commander was General H. Norman Schwarzkopf. It was he who called for CPX Internal Look with an exercise scenario that assumed an invasion of Saudi Arabia by Iraq. The Cold War was over but that did not eliminate the possibility of hot war between other nations, conflicts that involved vital U.S. interests, and considered vital among them was access to Middle Eastern oil.

There were no U.S. bases within the geographic boundaries of CENTCOM, a fact that made it unique among the Pentagon's unified commands. Eighteenth Aiborn Brigade Corps was therefore configured to be strategically mobile—designed to move quickly from the United States to whatever hot spots appeared in the Middle East. The lightest of the corps' three divisions was the 82nd Airborne; the heaviest the 24th Mechanized. The 101st was assumed to be able to arrive between the two, its 400 helicopters heavier than the 82nd's parachutes but lighter than the 24th's tanks.

This sequence was the one played during Internal Look: the 82nd dashing to the Gulf by air, the 101st traveling in a mix of ships and planes, and the 24th bringing their armor entirely by sea. Results from the CPX indicated that the 18th ABC could become fully operational in Saudi Arabia some 60 days after being alerted. For the 101st, this wasn't fast enough. The lessons of Slim Eagle should speed things up. The Division was no longer something like a battleship with awesome fire power, but too slow getting from here to there in time for the decisive phase of battle, which was the opening phase. Slim Eagle had turned the 101st into a light missile cruiser.

Selecting out equipment and personnel that could follow on, Slim Eagle forged a spear point of combat power that moved far and fast. By 1990, Major General Peay believed he could get his forces into the Middle East as quickly as the 82nd and with more punch. CPX Internal Look showed this to be possible on paper, but there had been no validating test. As fate would have it, that test came within weeks after Internal Look.

On August 2, Peay was on leave in Virginia. At Ft. Campbell, G3 contemplated the Screaming Eagles' far flung peacetime operations. Units were all over the western hemisphere. An infantry battalion was training cadets at West Point, another battalion conducting jungle exercises in Panama, a third preparing for its peace-keeping role in the Sinai. Aviation assets were in Honduras, and key personnel, including a brigade commander, were evaluating reservists in several states. The brigades were neatly aligned with historical regiments. First Brigade (Colonel Tom Hill) was comprised of 1st, 2nd, and 3rd battalions of the 327th; 2nd Brigade (Colonel Gregg Gile, later replaced by Colonel Ted Purdom) had the same numbered battalions of the 502nd, and 3rd Brigade (Colonel James McDonald, later replaced by Colonel Bob Clark) the same numbers of the 187th. Cavalry, engineers, and artillery were represented as they had been since World War II, and Aviation Brigade (Colonel Tom Garrett) was practically identical with the Division's helicopter units that served in Vietnam.

The Gulf War arrived at Ft. Campbell on television. Almost as soon as it started, Saddam Hussein's invasion was over and accomplished. Kuwait had been swallowed in a matter of hours. The news came in late afternoon, after the duty day. Most Screaming Eagles were home, catching up with family activities. Perhaps television flickered in the background. Conversation stopped as regular programming was interrupted by news flashes. At the NCO and Officers Club, soldiers who had so recently participated in 18th ABC's CPX looked at each other wide-eyed. This was almost the Internal Look read-in scenario being repeated live on the networks!

Though Kuwait, rather than Saudi Arabia, was the victim nation, the kingdom looked to be next on Iraq's list of aggression, the second domino that would topple, and with it most of the world's oil reserves. Though America was not at war, Ft. Campbell instantly began to respond to imminent probabilities. In the Emergency Operations Center, long messages began to roll out of printers, mostly messages from corps. A soldier who was manning the EOC remembered them vividly:

"It was just like a big FTX except there weren't those words typed in capital letters at the top of the messages, 'THIS IS AN EXERCISE.' This was no exercise! It was real, though it seemed unreal."

Certain automatic actions were directed by FORSCOM, like cancellation of leaves and PCS as well as peak alert status. Plans were reviewed and briefing became almost continuous. The Division Chief of Staff, Colonel Joe Bolt, remarked that if Saddam Hussein had continued into Saudi Arabia on any morning in August, the Division wouldn't know about it until noon because everyone was in a briefing! The EOC became so crowded that most majors could attend briefings only by watching them on closed circuit television.

The 101st was well prepared by training and exercises to deploy, but in several ways Saddam's aggression presented novel challenges and revealed shortcomings in plans. Division-size deployment had never been accomplished since World War II (one brigade was already in the country when the rest of the 101st joined it in Vietnam). So within anyone's memory there was no precedent for the scale of deployment that began on August 7. The major problems were predominantly logistical.

Desert fatigues (DCUs) was one such problem. As a CENTCOM unit, the Screaming Eagles had them, but only one set per soldier. Now three sets were required, and the logistical system was pulsed to produce them. They were available, but in the wrong sizes. Since Vietnam, the basic physique of soldiers had changed: they were generally taller and slimmer now, a fact apparently unnoticed by the Quartermaster Corps. Thousands of DCUs arrived post haste at Ft. Campbell, but too many were too small. Cross leveling between units somewhat eased the shortfall, and contractors in Memphis and Philadelphia sewed around the clock to make up the difference. The right size DCUs arrived just in time so that every soldier deployed with at least two sets. Manufacture of desert boots, however, never caught up with demand. Most Screaming Eagles spent the entire war in the sand wearing jungle boots.

A higher technical problem emerged because data from the Time Phased Force Deployment List were in the process of being computerized and not yet complete. This "tip fiddle" could automatically designate the ship or aircraft for every soldier and piece of equipment, but the system was still being debugged when it was required to spell out the deployment of 18th ABC. Instead, tip fiddle had to be laboriously undertaken by hand, resulting in many hectic stops and starts, with troops waiting for aircraft and aircraft waiting for troops. That 500,000 service members and a million tons of equipment reached the Gulf in time was a major miracle made possible by sweat and sleeplessness of everyone in the joint logistical/transportation system.

For heavy equipment, pre-war plans called for rail movement. The deteriorated, weed choked rail spur into Ft. Campbell was found to be unsafe for trains to pick up loads that were to be delivered to the port of embarkation, Jacksonville, Florida. The only quick solution was to obtain commercial long haul trucking. The call went out on the truckers' CB radios. Soon 18-wheelers converged on Ft. Campbell from all over the southeast. Supplementing military convoys, hundreds of flat beds began a continuous 1,600-mile round trip—and a cavalcade of patriotism.

It started when a Chattanooga radio station was advised by highway patrols that unusually heavy truck traffic might clog the interstates. Instead of a warning, the citizens of Tennessee made it an opportunity to show support for the soldiers going to war. Day by day, crowds at highway overpasses grew into thousands. They came from as far away as Alabama and North Carolina to wave flags and shout encouragement to every troop convoy. They were answered by up-raised thumbs and "V's." Civilian flat beds, hauling everything from howitzers to dumpsters, responded with blasts on their air horns. Such scenes were picked up by network television and gave a boost of spirit to the entire country. Later, General Peay would describe such spiritual support as "combat power" during the ground war.

For Vietnam veterans bound for the Gulf, these eye-filling demonstrations were proof positive that their second war would be much different from their first. In the 17,000-man division, less than one hundred were Vietnam veterans; they included the three generals and all the colonels, most of the sergeant majors, and a few warrant officers. For almost all other Screaming Eagles, Iraqi guns would be the first they heard fired in anger.

At first it seemed that there might even be shooting at their arrival airfield in Dhahran, Saudi Arabia. No substantial forces stood between Dhahran and the Kuwaiti border when the air flow began. CENTCOM plans, as had been exercised in Internal Look, had to be modified in the light of potential Iraqi armor thrusts down the gulf coast. What General Schwarzkopf demanded immediately was tank killers.

This priority caused the Division to strip out attack and scout helicopters from planned Ready Brigade packages, form a hundred-helicopter aviation task force, and rush it to the Gulf. They arrived on August 19 and were screening the border region within 48 hours. On that same day, the first ship departed from Jacksonville carrying divisional heavy equipment. By coincidence this was the same ship that transported part of the 101st to Vietnam in 1967. Fittingly, it was named *American Eagle*. A thousand Screaming Eagles were in kingdom by August 25. In no small measure this vanguard slammed shut Saddam's most inviting window of opportunity.

With the Aviation TF came the Division Assault Command Post (ACP), under command of Brigadier General Hugh Shelton, the 101st's ADC for operations. Stepping onto the tarmac in Dhahran, he described his arrival as entering a blast furnace. Sun, heat (averaging 115°) and air clogged with talcum fine dust would be the most devastating enemies till autumn. Eight gallons of drinking water per day were required for every soldier just to survive, let alone train in the desert. From the start of Desert Shield, climate would dominate the Division's activities even more than it had in Belgium or the jungle.

G3 estimated that about 40% of 1990s Screaming Eagles had some desert training, but nothing on the scale required by the rigors of defending Saudi Arabia. As events turned out, there would be time enough to acclimate, to train "desert hard" before going into battle. Commanders soon realized that the Division's night fighting doctrine, enabled by devices like night vision goggles (NVG) and forward-looking infra red (FLIR), would be not only an advantage but a necessity so long as summer heat prevented much physical exertion. This daytime limitation would prevail until mid-October.

With advance parties from CENTCOM units landing every day, allocation of territory became a land grab. Saudi Arabia had not participated in Internal Look. They were not prepared for tens of thousands of "infidel" (non-Islamic) soldiers pouring into their xenophobic kingdom. By and large, Saudi authorities wished the Americans to be as isolated as possible with minimal contact between soldiers and civilians. This policy fit the Americans' desire for unrestricted training areas. With plenty of empty space (more than three times the size of Texas) and a sparse population (14 million), Saudi Arabia loaned the visitors pretty much all the vacant desert they wanted.

There would be frustrating negotiations about firing ranges, but never before had there been less friction between American forces in a war zone and their host nation. There would be no international fraternization, no war brides, no beer can strips. Indeed, there would be no beer—Saudi Arabia, the "Koran belt" of Islam, was as dry as its sand in August. This would be the Screaming Eagles most austere war.

Their roost would be a vast, partially constructed complex named King Fahd International Airport. Laid out in 1980 in an expanse of desert between Dhahran and the capital of Riyadh, King Fahd was about 70% completed by August 1990. It had the necessary acreage of tarmac to accommodate the 101st's helicopters. Shelton grabbed what he could of it—the rest had been appropriated by the Air Force—and recommended that the Division camp in the adjacent desert. Peay named the 101st's portion of King Fahd, plus the adjoining tent city, Camp Eagle II in recognition of the 101st's last overseas cantonment, Camp Eagle in Vietnam. The desert equivalent of the jungle base camp was usually abbreviated CE II, and nicknamed Ft. Camel.

The cotton tent city that arose next to King Fhad would be the largest for the Army since the Civil War. Canvas tentage was too heavy and bulky—remember Slim Eagle—to transport from the States. Thus, locally procured tents were the only alternative, and Arabs manufactured only cotton tents, primarily for pilgrims (hajis) trekking to Mecca. The tents were therefore light and mobile, not designed for permanency, and easily blown down. Nevertheless haj tents were the only ones available, so thousands of them each became "home" for eight or nine soldiers in a flapping shelter of about 300 square feet.

Second Brigade followed the Aviation TF in 56 C-141s and 49 C5A's, carrying 2,700 personnel, 487 vehicles and 123 equipment pallets. The heat, the jet lag from an 11-hour time change, forced a period of acclimatization that lasted about two weeks before new arrivals became truly effective. Fortunately Saddam did not exploit his early advantage that narrowed every week: five Screaming Eagles landed by August 18, a thousand by August 25; 2,000 by September 1; 5,000 by the 8th; 11,000 by the 15th;

14,000 by the 22nd, and the complete Division deployment (including an attached attack helicopter battalion) was accomplished by October 5. Slim Eagle had flown even better than Peay had hoped; the 101st was the first division in CENTCOM to report itself operationally ready.

Except for 2nd Brigade, most soldiers flew to the Gulf in airliners, part of the Civilian Reserve Air Fleet called into service for just such an emergency. Weight was critical for these flights, so every passenger was put on scales. Though combat loaded and carrying individual weapons, no one was allowed to exceed a total of 400 pounds for the person and his/her gear. About 700 Screaming Eagles at that time were women.

En route to the Gulf, members of the Division got a brief look at cities like Paris and Rome during refueling. At sea, a few Screaming Eagles served as equipment super cargoes, steaming across the Atlantic and Mediterranean, transiting the Suez Canal, down the Red Sea, through the Arabian Sea, then up the Gulf to the port of Dammam, a voyage that on average took 23 days. Sea movement had to be coordinated with air: to ease support requirements, Peay wanted no troops in the Gulf who could not marry up quickly with their heavy equipment.

Such coordination kept lights burning incessantly at Ft. Campbell as answers were sought for a myriad of logistical and personnel problems. Outside the offices was a teeming scene of packing, loading, moving. Vehicles, milvans and connex containers converged like filings to magnets. Hovering around this grim turbulence were the Division's families, convinced by what they saw that the entire Division would be gone before they could say goodbye.

The national media followed the same expectation. Nine television trucks parked just off post on rented farm land at the end of the departure airfield. The PAO found it impossible to convince them that the whole Division would not roll down the runway or out Gate 4 in the next hour. Such rumors had a way of feeding on themselves. Soldiers swamped the PX and commissary, buying items that would not be available in Saudi Arabia. That included almost everything. The auto shops bustled with departing men tuning cars they would leave with spouses. Loved ones from far away descended on Clarksville and Hopkinsville, filling the motels and restaurants—places of parting for a period no one could foresee. Both towns noted a rush for marriage licenses.

In the 101st's first order that began deployment was a vital section called the Family Care Plan. Probably no military base in the world supported its families better in more trying circumstances. An assistance hotline was immediately established, but this was just the beginning. Actually the beginning was back in recent history. first, there was the long record of brigade—size deployments that had generated component support groups down through the divisional pyramid, so that most problems caused by family separation had been dealt with before. Of course the crucial differences between the Gulf deployment and previous experience were in duration and size.

Heretofore, there had been a base—the Division—from which brigades departed and returned. Now the Division itself was pulling stakes with only post elements remaining as a support base, and these very much occupied with training replacements. In effect, the 101st was climbing aboard and pulling up the gangway behind it.

So the main, almost the sole, source of strength for the home front would have to come from the chain of concern; that is, rear detachments coordinating with numerous support groups. Many of them were specialty groups; e.g., for working mothers or those with problem children.

Every peacetime deployment in the past had had a known "end-x," a date certain when the soldiers would return. However, as the Gulf situation developed, the U.S. involvement became open ended. Into September the prevailing public opinion was that 18th ABC's deployment would be an effective show of force, and Saddam would back down. But as the media reported the Iraqi build up in Kuwait throughout the fall, anxiety increased. Clearly, the home front was in for a long war. With that understanding, most dependents felt they wanted to wait with the Ft. Campbell community, among people who were undergoing the same anxiety. Only five percent of dependents departed the post.

On television, week by week, Ft. Campbell watched reports of Saddam's consolidation of Kuwait. He commanded the fourth largest army in the world, the most modern outside Europe and the U.S., with the highest percentage of veterans anywhere. In the eight-year war with Iran (concluded in 1988), the Iraqi army had distinguished itself by a strategic offensive combined with tactical defense, the very combination that was to characterize Saddam's aggression against Kuwait. Operation Desert Shield was CENTCOM's plan to ensure that his strategic offensive was stopped at the Saudi border. Operation Desert Storm would challenge the strength of his tactical defense.

DESERT SHIELD

WHILE AWAITING TRANSPORTATION to the Gulf, the 101st's training program reflected what the Division expected to encounter. First priority was defense against NBC attack. Grisly pictures of gassed Kurds from northern Iraq were fresh in everyone's minds. For all outbound Army and Marine units, the fit and function of individual protective masks became the foremost concern for the first time since World War I.

Second, the soldiers had to bring themselves to peak physical condition to endure some of the most hellish heat in the world. To "practice misery," air conditioners for a time were turned off at Ft. Campbell—itself a pretty hot place in summer—in order to grow accustomed to constant discomfort. The G3 queried the advance party if any other methods might be helpful. Shelton replied, "Try sticking your head in a hair dryer all day"!

Third, soldiers were inculcated with precautions against terrorism. Widely unappreciated was Saddam's skill in psychological operations (PSYOP). His purpose was to erode public opinion supporting Desert Shield, and his method was to convince Americans that war against him would mean high casualties. He provided international media with film clips of his formidable arsenal, but perhaps his most potent threat was terrorism directed against CENTCOM forces. He called for religious war (jihad) against the infidels, and displayed the presence of infamous terrorists' organizations headquartered in Baghdad. At CE II, constant vigilance was the Division's main countermeasure expressed in many details.

An inviting target for hit and run mortar attacks, the perimeter of CE II was patrolled by aircraft and vehicles. Lines of soldiers at phone booths were broken up in order to foil drive-by shootings. Buildings at King Fahd were reinforced and partitioned to minimize damage from car bombs such as the one that killed hundreds of Marines in Beirut. SOPs were drilled so that if a soldier were captured by terrorists he knew how to react. Even packages from home were examined, and some blown up if not claimed immediately. The war against terrorists—who never appeared—began with the arrival of the first Screaming Eagle and didn't end until the last one departed. Like the Cold War, the counter-terrorist war was won by patient deterrence.

Fourth priority in the training program was a pre-deployment school to hone basic skills in field survival, featuring unsophisticated subjects like field sanitation, expedient care of individual weapons, and combat first aid. Such basic subjects correctly indicated that before the Division could win in the desert, it had to live in and with the desert. Peay took to studying the desert campaigns of World War II, recognizing the necessity for a "tether" between the field and the administrative hub. The hub would be CE II; the spokes (i.e., tethers) would be to the outlying Forward Operations Bases (FOBs), primitive places where the Division would both harden to the desert by training and at the same time perform its defensive mission.

That mission—to stop an Iraqi invasion of Saudi Arabia—was the same as had been rehearsed in Internal Look. The 101st knew it would be CENTCOM's covering force to identify, delay, disrupt and channelize an Iraqi attack anywhere along a front of several hundred miles, then participate in a corps counterattack to destroy the invaders. The Division would have plenty of space to exchange for the time needed to develop the counterattack; the depth of the 101st's sector was as large as Vermont and New Hampshire combined. With such an enormous area to cover, the 3rd Armored Cavalry and 12th Combat Aviation Brigade were attached, plus the 75th and 112th Field Artillery Brigades in direct support. Thus the 101st became a mini-corps with unprecedented firepower and mobility that included hundreds of tanks, Bradley fighting vehicles, self-propelled howitzers, and more attack helicopters than had ever been assembled under a major general's command.

In October, with cooler (90°) weather, the Division conducted an FTX to rehearse all the intricate coordination required by passages of lines and battle handoffs in a covering force mission. Typical of the complexities involved was the fire support plan, integrating computerized fire direction systems with less advanced methods. It all came together through the ingenuity of DIVARTY. For the Division's planners, it was almost a disappointment that the Iraqis never tried to penetrate the covering force. Evidence after the war indicated the Iraqis very much had that intention; Saddam even printed license plates for vehicles in the Eastern Province of Saudi Arabia, a region he planned to incorporate in a Greater Iraq.

Two key battle positions in the covering force plan were FOB's Bastogne and Oasis, both hundreds of miles north of CE II and a long way from anywhere except the border. The FOBs and CE II became the three rotation points for the Division's training cycle as they waited to see what Saddam would do. The rotation was by brigades, one refitting and standing down at CE II, another conducting company-size and counter-armor training at FOB Bastogne, and the third emphasizing house-to-house combat in a ghost town Screaming Eagles called FOB Oasis. This latter training indicated that Peay foresaw offensive possibilities if Saddam did not withdraw from Kuwait as the United Nations had demanded he do. Repeatedly, Saddam announced that he would never leave, and his hardening of defenses in Kuwait made the point. In the last quarter of 1990, Desert Shield took on the character of a sitzkrieg, both sides trying to stare the other down.

What would happen next awaited a presidential and congressional decision, whether to convince Saddam by besieging Iraq with economic embargo or dislodging him from Kuwait by force. The embargo option produced a plausible rumor that Divisions would be rotated in and out of Saudi Arabia, and the 101st would be one of the first to head home. "Home for Christmas" became the cry at both Ft. Campbell and Ft. Camel.

By a narrow margin, President Bush obtained congressional approval to eject Saddam from Kuwait by force. Rotation rumors were scotched by the movement of 7th Corps from Germany to the Gulf. As Garrett explained to his disappointed aviators, "7th Corps is coming to join us, not replace us." In November, Division planners began to develop offensive intentions.

As Churchill once noted about a successful desert campaign, "This is not the beginning of the end, but the end of the beginning." With this attitude, Screaming Eagles looked toward the end of Desert Shield and the beginning of Desert Storm. "The road home goes through Kuwait," replaced "Home for Christmas" as a slogan. Desert Shield had been an emotional roller coaster—an alternating sequence of rumors, positive and negative. As in no other war, there was extensive communication and feedback between the Gulf and home fronts.

Attitudinal communication came in a staggering volume of mail, much of it directed to "any soldier"; i.e., messages of support from America to be read by any soldier undergoing the privations of the desert. The other form of communication was by telephone, directed of course to specific soldiers. Instantaneous communication was a novel morale factor first encountered in Panama when soldiers could step into a phone booth and talk to home even as small arms crackled in the background.

Telephonic communication between soldiers and their families jumped official channels between the Division and its rear detachments, resulting in a credibility lag that spawned rumors. Frequently, after spouses talked on the phone, the stateside member passed around news about other soldiers in the unit. On the phone, a wife might learn that a buddy of her spouse was hospitalized with dysentery (a common disease before water sources were purified), and inform that man's wife. She knew nothing about her husband's illness because of the slow pace of outgoing mail that usually took two weeks from the Gulf to the States. The wife would demand information about her husband's condition from the rear detachment which then queried the Division. Before the official informational cycle was completed, the patient was probably back to duty. Thus, the chain of concern was constantly trying to catch up with information and rumors passed over myriad telephone connections. Despite budget-busting home phone bills and clogging of official lines at CE II with incoming calls, the chain of command recognized that the benefits of talking with loved ones outweighed the drawbacks in a way no staff study could verify. The phone was another tether, the one to home, the ultimate source of morale.

Morale, as with any Army, had negative and positive components that can work for or against the other. The input from the States was certainly positive, as much so as it had been negative during Vietnam. Desert soldiers could read—and sometimes see on CNN while they were at CE II—America's anxiety and affection, learn of it from the yellow ribbons sprouting like daffodils all over the country. Clearly, and almost unanimously, America stood behind what the Division was doing.

But what they were doing was largely unsatisfying. Yes, they were training to a sharper edge than ever before, and never before had the Division felt so ready. But getting ready can go only so far, and by Christmas that point had been reached so far as the defensive mission of Desert Shield was concerned. By then the negative component of impatience had set it. The diplomats were playing badminton with the prospects of war. Rumors set off emotional yo yos. War or a negotiated peace? It was difficult to mentally prepare for both. The 101st was like a prize fighter primed for a title match, but uncertain whether the opponent would enter the ring. Ultimately there was a target for this frustration, a dart board for the negative component of morale; Saddam Hussein and his brutal army, the causes of all the discomfort and dislocation. Even considering the likelihood of many casualties, the Division "wanted" the match, as prize fighters say. It would be a distinction that Screaming Eagles would get in the first punch.

In late September, Apaches of 1-101 Aviation Regiment received an order on a mission so secret that the aviators could not be told their targets. If peace talks failed, certain installations within Iraq were to be knocked out in the first minutes of the air war and in the dark of night. The raid would pave the way for an invasion of enemy skies, much the way the 101st had paved the way for Bradley's Army to hit the beachs of France. With the Division's history in mind, the raiders were named Task Force Normandy.

By Christmas the rest of the Division was well into its plans for Desert Storm. The troops were quick to notice that training became attack oriented; something at last was going to happen. As the desert cooled, the skies turned gray, and drizzle at the FOBs marked the beginning of the four-month rainy season. Despite visits by the President, senators, famous athletes and entertainers, the holiday season was lonely and depressing, but with the consolation that these would be the last holidays in the bleak sandscape. Home had never been so desirable, so appreciated, and "The road home leads through Kuwait!"

At Christmas, only the Division planners knew that the road instead would lead through Iraq. Desert Shield closed slowly like a curtain. Desert Storm, like its name, would be short and violent, the vent for six months of pent-up impatience.

As a retrospective on Desert Shield, a Screaming Eagle composed a parody of *The Twelve Days of Christmas,* with this last verse:

On the twelfth day in Saudi, my colonel gave to me twelve thousand sand bags, eleven plastic buckets, ten stinging scorpions, nine duck-board floors, eight faucets dry, seven hissing snakes, six running mice, five MREs, four cotton tents, three fold-up cots, two Evians—and a toilet without any seat.

The soldier was rhapsodizing about the amenities at CE II. At the FOBs, there were no creature comforts at all. Of the three sites in the training rotation triangle, CE II would be remembered for its tedium and its one compensation, the telephone tether with home. FOB Oasis was most memorable for its exotic character, an abandoned adobe town complete with minaret and the feel of a lost Foreign Legion outpost. FOB Bastogne was stunning for its isolation and the grandeur of the desert environment, stretching away to eternity. As an air oriented division, the Screaming Eagles probably saw, by flying over it, more desert than any other. A member of the 501st Signal described his first trip "up north," as the thousand of square miles around the FOBs were called:

"The FOBs were on a different planet. It was early in the morning when we flew out of King Fahd. Couldn't see much life after we crossed the highway. Civilization just stopped like there was a fence nobody could cross. It looked like pictures from space down there. Most of it was rocky plains at first with lots of gravel.

"Then there would be these beaches where the yellow sand begins. That's what it's like, a coastline with flat rock islands in huge bays of sand. Some of those bays were like the sea—you couldn't see the end of it, even from the air. That's what Arabia was famous for—those miles and miles of long dunes all the way to the horizon. I mean, we were flying at a thousand feet and the horizon was way out there.

"Nobody was talking, just looking out at all those mountain ranges of sand. They had designs like you see in fancy gardens—S's, X's, T's, and H's. Once and a while there were rock peaks sticking up like islands, but that just reminded you the rest was sand, sand, sand.

"Harrison said something before we landed, something like he thought he'd see the world when he joined the Army, but he never thought he'd see another world! That's the way it was up there, another planet, maybe Mars."

The vigil over the empty desert was almost over. As Arab nomads had for thousands of years, the 101st was headed toward a fertile valley, greened by a river they'd never seen but probably had read about in the Bible—the Euphrates. Armies had battled in the valley since biblical times, but soon soldiers would approach it as never before—from the air.

DESERT STORM

On January seventeen, Cody got the word;
Loaded up his Hellfires and revved his mighty bird.
He lifted off into the night and headed for Iraq.
They should've known the one-oh-one wouldn't cut 'em any slack!

THIS VERSE FROM *The Night the Eagle Screamed* was recorded in 1991 by Division Chaplain Herb Kitchens and heard on country-western radio stations throughout the southeast. His ballad memorialized the first strike of the air war, the initial thunder and lightning of Operation Desert Storm. The bolts were hurled by eight Apache attack helicopters from 1-101, commanded by Lieutenant Colonel Richard Cody. The octet, accompanied part way by four Air Force search and rescue ships plus a maintenance Black Hawk and a back-up Apache, comprised Task Force Normandy.

Their mission was to knock out two early warning radar sites, enabling hundreds of Allied fighter-bombers to enter Iraq undetected where they would destroy Saddam's principal command and control facilities in a devastating onslaught. The pair of sites, each more than 10 acres in size and protected by anti-aircraft weapons, were pickets in the Iraqi radar fence. Unless two holes were opened in the fence, the Air Force estimated 20% losses among their first sorties.

For surprise and secrecy, the Normandy raiders had to make their own way into Iraq, hit the targets and egress without outside support. The mission required men and machines to match its dangers. The 101st was tasked for both.

Cody's call for volunteers was answered by every aviator in 1-101, and probably his most difficult decision, among many in planning the raid, was selecting the TF Normandy crews. Because of utmost secrecy, neither location nor time of the raid could be revealed to them. Throughout the fall they had rehearsed night attacks on simulated targets and performed long distance navigation at sand dune altitude with FLIR and NVG. The sites, 40 miles apart, would have to be approached on the deck in order to get under the radar cones.

As rehearsals progressed, Cody grew confident about the attack phase of the raid; skillful flying and the immense firepower delivered by Apaches indicated the sites could be taken down in less than five minutes. But getting there was the major problem, requiring an auxiliary fuel tank that was not designed to be flown into combat. It would be anyway—that was the only way to execute the mission without refueling.

As described in Chaplain Kitchens' lyrics, the raiders took off from a secret airfield in northwestern Saudi Arabia during the first moonless hours of January 17, 1991. Through sporadic ground fire, the task force split into two four-ship flights for their respective targets. They had to reach them with stopwatch timing as cruise missiles fired by the Navy were to hit elsewhere on the fence at precisely 0238.

Each flight formed on a firing line within 45 seconds of that hour. Chief Warrant Officer Dave Jones perceived the historic importance of his first Hellfire, the opening observed shot of the war. "This one's for you, Saddam," he said on intercom as he sent the round down range; 20 seconds later a power generator exploded in a ball of flame.

The Iraqis truly did not know what hit them. Undetected by radar, standing off beyond range of anti-aircraft (which could not see them in the dark anyway), the Apaches mauled their targets so suddenly, thoroughly and permanently that Baghdad never learned what happened to the sites. Instead, waves of fighter-bombers delivered their pay loads in a pyrotechnic display watched by the world on television, narrated by astonished CNN reporters in a Baghdad hotel. Desert Storm began the way it would continue: with awesome speed and shock. The tenor and tempo had been set by TF Normandy who, in Schwarzkopf's words, "plucked the eyes" of Saddam's radar. Iraqi forces were virtually blind from then on.

For six weeks thereafter, Allied Air Forces pummeled the entrenched Iraqi army as Schwarzkopf rolled his ground formations up to the border. His strategy was to fool Saddam into thinking the counter-invasion would be along the Gulf coast, supported by amphibious landings. Actually, Schwarzkopf was massing on the western flank, positioning for a turning movement that would become known as "Hail Mary," an expression from football meaning a desperate, last second play. History should not be misled by this connotation because Hail Mary was really a meticulously planned, methodically executed logistical feat as much as a spectacular strategic success. Half a million personnel with millions of tons of material moved 500 miles over a single two-lane road day and night before the avalanche of combat power was in position to crush Saddam's vaunted army.

Chairman of the joint chiefs, General Colin Powell, described the effect Hail Mary intended on the Iraqi army: "to cut it off and then kill it." The 101st would have major roles in both the amputation and execution. Their first mission was to snip Saddam's main supply route (MSR) between Baghdad and Kuwait, then be prepared to support the "kill" phase of the campaign by turning east toward the key city of Basra. In the first phase, the 101st would leap ahead of Allied ground forces and operate somewhat independently within 18th ABCs AO. A French Light Armored Division, followed and supported by the 82nd Airborne, would attack north on the 101st's left flank. On their right, the 24th Mechanized Division and the 3rd ACR were to attack parallel with the Iraq-Kuwait border. To their right, 7th Corps—Schwarzkopf's Sunday punch—would strike at the Iraqis' center of gravity, their armored reserve of Republican Guard Divisions. Between 7th Corps and the U.S. Marines on the coast were the Pan-Arab forces to attack frontally across the Saudi-Kuwaiti border. No division in ARCENT had more important objectives than the 101st; the degree of Iraqi resistance would depend largely on whether they kept their supply lines open, and the magnitude of Saddam's defeat would depend on how much of his army could get away. The Screaming Eagles' landings were to stop both resupply and retreat.

Could the 101st do it? Before the Gulf War no one was sure, but everyone either hoped or believed, though both the dual mission and the force to accomplish it were unprecedented. As Powell noted, "The unique characteristics of the air assault division were finally going to be tested in combat. Fast moving, deep operations over a wide area were the purpose for which it was designed."

The design, begun in Vietnam when the 101st converted from a parachute to a helicopter division, had at last reached the final evolution of air assault. As previously noted, a lineage of forefathers could be traced to Lieutenant General H.W.O. Kinnard, the 101st's G3 in World War II, later commanding general of the 11th Air Assault Division, the prototype from which air cavalry developed.

The concept and doctrine had then devolved to General John Wickham who nurtured them as Army Chief of Staff. He is typical of many links of many ranks that connected the 101st's history to what it had become in January, 1991. The investment of thought and interest was as great as the enormous expense. The 101st readied to live up to its past, justify faith in its present prowess, and point to a future that would be novel in the history of warfare. Air assault, on the scale envisioned by the Hail Mary plan, was essentially a new means of warfare. Without link up with forces on the ground, never would so many and so much be inserted so far and so fast behind the defenses of a well-equipped, modern enemy.

For rough comparison, Operations Junction City and Delaware were corps-size airmobile campaigns in Vietnam; but neither sortied as many helicopters during a week as Peay would launch in three days. In Operation Overlord, the 101st and 82nd combined landed about as many troops as did the desert eagles on the D-day where the first objective was as far as England to Normandy; the second, the next day, as far as England to Holland. In both 1944 operations, quick link up with friendly armor was essential to withstand counterattack on the airheads. In 1991, the Division relied on its organic anti-armor capability. Incidentally, Peay's Black Hawks, the principal troop carriers, flew as fast as C-47s and his cargo ships, Chinooks, carried heavier loads.

But historical antecedents were for post-war contemplation. On January 17—as TF Normandy returned from an 18-hour flight to Camp Eagle II—the Division was beginning a 500-mile displacement to their future line of departure, the edge of a vast tract of desert on the Iraqi border called Tactical Assembly Area (TAA) Campbell. Here they would hone the plan that would add luster to their history, at the same time making history.

It was a plan to answer the ultimate question: How deep could the Division strike into Iraq, and how fast? The answer hinged on logistics; and logistics, more than any other factor, meant fuel—fuel for the HUMM-V's, the mules and anti-tank platforms for the infantry—but most important, aviation fuel for the fleet of more than 400 helicopters.

Fuel ruled—an ironic hegemony on the sands of the world's foremost petroleum producer. Indeed the fuel which powered the Allied Forces came from under those sands, first to be pumped, then refined, then transported to the front in titanic quantities.

In a decision of far reaching importance, Peay sided with his logisticians who recommended conversion of all ground vehicles to the same fuel used by helicopters, Jet A. This meant adjusting HUMM-V's carburation and injection, but the benefit of simplicity that a single fuel provided overrode all other considerations. Then came the most important question: How far could that fuel take 1st Brigade who would be making the initial landing in OPLAN Desert Rendezvous that called for a double leapfrog of brigades, ending with 3rd Brigade in the Euphrates Valley astride Highway 8, the Iraqi MSR. This was to be accomplished in 48 hours. The next phase of the plan would launch 2nd Brigade to another choke point on Highway 8 or east onto the fortified air base of Tallil; then, on order, the Division was to continue the attack toward Basra and possibly into the Tigris Valley, depending on other developments in the Hail Mary strategy.

The first phase of Desert Rendezvous alone involved an area the size of southern New England. The next two leapfrogs would vault distances as long as the mid-Atlantic seaboard. The 101st would push the capabilities of air assault to the limits, and these would be self-imposed except for political constraints. If Peay could convince CENTCOM, and the war continued long enough, he would have Screaming Eagles throughout the Tigris-Euphrates peninsula and in the environs of Baghdad. Meanwhile in TAA Campbell his planners grappled with the multi-faceted problems of getting from here to there with unprecedented speed.

On January 8, their planning was interrupted by a strong indication that Iraq sought to seize the initiative. Theater intelligence had produced reports that Saddam was contemplating a corps-size spoiling attack. Reliable sources marked the Wadi Al Batin as the axis of attack with King Khalid Military City (KKMC), the main Allied logistical base in the northern kingdom, as his objective. The Trans-Arabian Pipeline (Tapline) Road, MSR for 18th ABC, also would be severed by this thrust.

At the junction of the wadi, a 100-mile dry gulch, and Tapline Road was the oil pumping town of Hafer Al Batin. Seventh Corps was to have secured it, but their arrival from Germany had been delayed, leaving a wide gap in the Allied front. Second Brigade was rushed in to fill it. For the next three weeks they dug in—and bailed out their excavations as the rainy season flooded the wadi and the town with its critically important airfield. Supported lavishly by 7th Corps and 1st Cavalry Division Engineers, 2nd Brigade trenched a six-mile tank ditch in 48 hours as well as digging in battalion TOCs and supporting artillery. Outnumbered, but thoroughly ready, they watched over the parapets and into the mists for the Iraqi corps. It never materialized. For reasons that may never be known—the entire threat might have been the result of Iraqi dis-information—Saddam's spoiling attack was aimed along the coast where it briefly captured the Saudi town of Khafji. But another reason for his change of objectives may have been the reports from his spies in Hafer Al Batin that 2nd Brigade's positions were too hard to crack. On January 25, the Strike soldiers rejoined the 101st at TAA Campbell. Hafer Al Batin had been the last serious defensive operation for the Screaming Eagles. From then on, all thoughts were focused to attack.

Constant air strikes on the horizon were reminders that the Allies were now on the offensive. Flashes illuminated low rain clouds; unnatural thunder rolled south from around-the-clock bombardment, heard in the maze of tents, sand bag bunkers, camouflage nets and concertina that were now DMAIN. To bring the Division to TAA Campbell had required 358 C-130 sorties and 2,000 vehicles, many of them obtained through civilian contracts. The rocky plains rang with the strike of entrenching tools. This was a bleak, depressing and chilly wasteland, endured by Screaming Eagles because it was the last waiting place before the road home led through Iraq.

With this backdrop, Desert Rendezvous was honed to its final form, a two-inch thick document replete with annexes, tables and overlays. But it contained a major blank, a blank on the map. This was the LZs for 1st Brigade. The LZs were the locus of the perimeter required to protect the vital Forward Area Refuel Points (FARPs), which in turn depended on the round trip range of Black Hawks, the pace ships of Desert Rendezvous. That combat loaded range was no more than 80 nautical miles. For the leapfrog to succeed, a FARP had to be that close to both TAA Campbell and 3rd Brigade's objective on the Euphrates.

This double requirement restricted 1st Brigade's LZs to a goose egg only a few miles long in an AO bigger than Connecticut. Within that goose egg, LZs had to be found with surface conditions that would not cause "brownout," the only word that struck true fear in the air assault division.

Brownout can be lethal when loose sand coats the desert floor in such quantity that it roils up into blinding clouds of gritty dust swirled by rotor wash. This occurs on both take off and landing. The ingestion of sand into sensitive working parts is dangerous enough, and loose sand take offs were therefore avoided as much as possible during Desert Shield. But landing in brownout conditions is even more perilous because the pilot loses ground reference. With a large sling load, a Chinook can not even use its altimeter.

The Iraqi desert in the 101st's AO was a mystifying mosaic of surface conditions. There was no way to identify potential brownout conditions except to fly in and attempt landings. Even then, sand shifted by the wind or sodden by sudden rains could turn potential LZs into browned out maelstorms, or vice versa, in a few hours. Garrett would have taken his chances with such fickle conditions if his scouts could have undertaken preliminary reconnaissance, but this was not permitted by CENTCOM.

Though all his corps and division commanders begged to recon forward into Iraq, Schwarzkopf insisted otherwise. The air campaign prevented Iraqi counter-reconnaissance, but he would not tip off his massive left hook by reconning into Iraq. Not until G minus 7 days anyway. G (ground) Day had yet to be recommended by Schwarzkopf for approval by President Bush who was giving the diplomats every chance to talk Saddam out of Kuwait.

Thus Desert Rendezvous had to await confirmation of the most critical variable in the plan, the location of the first LZs. Yet planning had to go forward on the assumption that suitable LZs would be found inshallah— Arabic for "God willing"—a term much heard throughout G3 in January. For 1st Brigade, inshallah meant planning with a template, a goose egg on an overlay encircling a pivot where the hundreds of Black Hawks and Chinooks would, if they could, eventually land. The FARP with its defensive perimeter, wherever it would be, had to have a name, and the G3, Lieutenant Colonel Monty Hess, originally gave it an appropriate one, "7-Eleven," which was later changed to Cobra. Seven-Eleven was apt because that is what the site would be: a gas pump and convenience for people in a hurry. Those people were 3rd Brigade who would fly from TAA Campbell all the way to the Euphrates to cut Highway 8 in an area called AO Eagle. On the return trip, the Black Hawks that delivered them would have to refuel at the FARP protected by 1st Brigade.

Protection was defined to be prevention of direct and observed indirect fire on the extremely vulnerable POL facilities that comprised the FARP. And the FARP was not very compact. In an area the size of a county fair was the cargo helicopter refueling complex, while several miles away would be the attack helicopter FARP, somewhat smaller but closer to identified enemy defenses. Hill's template enclosed an area of about 200 square kilometers (nearly the size of Ft. Campbell), to be defended by only about 5,000 infantrymen, even after 1-502 from 2nd Brigade was added to his task force. If his four infantry battalions were strung along the planned perimeter, each soldier would be nearly a quarter mile apart. However, clear fields of fire and the scanty Iraqi forces suspected in the vast AO made such wide dispersal academic.

That was because Schwarzkopf had effectively fooled Saddam that the Allies' main attack would be on the coast; Iraqi defenses were loaded up there with the Republican Guard reserves close by. Slowly, as the air campaign progressed, the Iraqi general staff began to perceive the threat from the desert flank, but Peay's planners expected no more than 10,000 regular troops (most of them from the 45th Infantry Division) in positions to contest 1st and 3rd Brigade's landings. With a worse case scenario, Hill assumed his airhead could be attacked by as many as five battalions within three hours. They could be held off first by the air force hampering their movement, then attack helicopters delaying them as they drew nearer, then artillery to hit them, and finally strong points with TOWs to stop them. Tactical defense was not the principal problem: logistics were.

By innovative rigging, fast flying and superb coordination, Desert Rendezvous could provide for sufficient combat power on the ground after two lifts. From then on, priority would be for fuel delivery in two air transportable containers: gas bags (10,000 gallon capacity) and 500 gallon "blivets." For the first time, including peacetime, these unwieldy rubber bladders would be flown nearly full and sling loaded under Chinooks. They would have to be on time because 3rd Brigade's Black Hawks would return thirsty after the insertion into AO Eagle. If the pumps weren't ready to do the refueling, Cobra would be the world's largest and most vulnerable helicopter parking lot.

Even if Cobra went up as scheduled, the FARP would soon run dry if it was resupplied only by air, causing the schedule for subsequent operations to be delayed. Overland resupply by HEMITs (rough terrain gas tankers) from TAA Campbell was therefore essential. This meant field trains had to be organized into Task Force Citadel to cross some 80 miles of enemy held desert—if a land route to Cobra could be found.

The task force commander was Major John McGarrity, 1st Brigade's XO. His father had served in the Middle East where John became interested in the region's history. He learned of a famous 14th century Islamic explorer, Ibn Batuta, who once crossed the unexplored desert between Baghdad and Mecca, the city to which Muslims regularly travel for a religious pilgrimage called Haj. Batuta called the track he discovered, the Dub Al Haj, route of the pilgrim. Consulting both ancient and CENTCOM maps, McGarrity suspected that it was near TAA Campbell and went through Cobra. Because ground and aerial reconnaissance were denied until G minus 7, he had to confirm his hunch through interrogation of nomads who before the war regularly transited the region. Yes, they advised, there was a track in the direction of his interest. McGarrity thrilled when they told him it had a very old name, Dub Al Haj. Now the problem was to ensure that 20th century vehicles could follow a route that for 500 years had been traversed only by camels.

In mid-February the President and the Pentagon approved a G date of February 23. The long awaited reconnaissance could therefore begin on the 17th. Focus would be on Dub Al Haj (now designated MSR New Market) and siting the Cobra FARPs, the areas most sensitive for brownout. For this crucial investigation, Aviation Brigade worked like detectives.

The first clues to adequate surface conditions were from satellite and aerial photography. Areas showing gray often meant sabkhas, dry lake beds that became swales only during rainy seasons. Generally, such depressions had less loose sand than the surrounding desert, though drifting sand was another complication. The more rain, the more sabkhas filled; and because rainy seasons varied in amounts of precipitation, so too did the number of sabkhas that held water. No one, not even the reliable Air Force meteorologists, could predict how much rain was coming, so how many or which sabkhas would be wetted down enough to stop brownout remained open questions.

Nevertheless, sabkhas were the best prospects for LZs and FARPs. Within Saudi Arabia, Garrett sent out Black Hawks and Chinooks to try landings on promising sabkhas. Results were mixed; what looked good from photography often turned out bad and vice versa. Nature was not to be understood by map analysis alone. Now Peay, as Schwarzkopf had been, was pressed by his subordinates for permission to make crucial reconnaissance, and the most important ones were trial landings on sabkhas within Cobra. Peay directed that these be deferred to as late a date as possible and with an elaborate deception plan, so that even if recons compromised the landings sites the Iraqis would have the minimal time to react or reinforce.

Until then, attention turned to the proposed track for MSR New Market. Scouts and attack helicopters started forward in lengthening waves to determine what obstacles confronted TF Citadel. By day and night, Kiowas from 1-101 and 2-229 scouted for Apaches who brought back videos of key terrain. About 20 miles from TAA Campbell, the aviators discovered an escarpment where the trail wound uphill. Video study indicated that bunkers covered the pass. To learn more, Apaches conducted a reconnaissance by Hellfire. Iraqis poured out like flooded ants, threw down their arms, trying to surrender to orbiting helicopters! This was a situation not covered at Ft. Rucker. The aviators called back to DMAIN for instructions.

Despite permission for G minus 7 recons, CENTCOM had imposed the restriction of no infantry in Iraq. DMAIN split some hairs; pathfinders were part of Aviation Brigade so arguably they were not infantry. Therefore a platoon of pathfinders was loaded into Black Hawks to round up the prisoners (EPW). To preserve appearances, CENTCOM reported in a press conference that the EPWs had been "herded" over the border by Apaches.

The action on the escarpment presented a precedent but also a problem. If Iraqi troops were so willing to surrender (the initial group were border guards), what should be done about larger groups that might raise white flags if taken under fire from the air? Permission was obtained from corps to use small numbers of line infantry if required for capture. Almost immediately they were required. Farther up MSR New Market more Iraqis were blasted from bunkers. A reaction platoon from 2nd Brigade went out to bag them. This time the EPWs were regulars from the 45th Division. They revealed there were many more north on the trail, particularly at an escarpment which became known as "the toad in the road."

Toad became an objective on the morning of G minus 4, a sharp bend in the trail about half way up MSR New Market. Bedhouins had reported to McGarrity that a number of wells flowed from the escarpment here, the only year-round water source for many miles, and so a much used resting place for desert travelers. Toad could therefore support perhaps a battalion of Iraqi troops; moreover, the escarpment provided excellent observation to the south, the direction from where TF Citadel would be coming.

FLIR photography of Toad on the night of G minus 6 had revealed camouflaged structures and vehicles. Daylight aerial recon by 2-17 Cavalry brought evidence of an elaborate bunker complex for about a hundred troops. This intelligence correlated with some Air Force warnings of triple-A in the vicinity. As a major obstacle on MSR New Market, Toad would have to be cleared, but because of the rules of engagement in effect, this would have to be accomplished without a ground attack! The rules had been stretched to permit infantry to round up EPWs, but if there was serious resistance rather than prompt surrender at Toad, Peay might be in an embarrassing dilemma.

He directed Garrett to attack Toad from the air on G minus 3, a mission handed down to 3-101, the Cobra attack helicopter battalion. Some deception might result from using the older gunships rather than Apaches that would be strafing elsewhere, causing the Iraqis to believe that Apaches would be employed against priority targets. The Cobras then were a ruse within a bluff—make the Iraqis think Toad was unimportant and force it to surrender without commitment of sizable ground forces. In case the bluff didn't work, a battalion of Rakkasans stood ready at PZs to convince any diehards at Toad.

The Cobra's initial show of force was too convincing. During the air campaign, the Iraqis had developed a bunker mentality. Three-101s recon by fire and dune top buzzing of the escarpment drew no counter fire or even signs of life. Secondary explosions moved a lot of sand, uncovering mortar and triple-A positions, all unmanned. The aviators began to suspect—and DMAIN hoped—that perhaps the defenders had evacuated. However, Toad was too big a potential obstacle to wish away.

Calling in A-10s, Lieutenant Colonel Mark Curran commanding 3-101 began digging up Toad with 500 pound bombs, but still if there were Iraqis down there, they were bunker hunkers. The A-10s departed for other missions, and 3-101 was running out of ammunition. Early in the afternoon they had to break off the attack. As the Cobras went into a departing orbit, the Iraqis apparently felt they had held out and won. Foolishly they dribbled some fire into the sky, removing the possibility that Toad had been abandoned.

Two-229, Lieutenant Colonel Bill Bryan commanding, roared up from the south and relieved 3-101 like a tag team. The Apaches pounded the escarpment without signs of resistance, but with no signs of surrender either. Garrett flew up for a personal view of the situation. It had to change or the entire pre-G-day timetable would be thrown off. There were other targets for that night and many more crammed into the next three days. Toad would have to come down today, one way or another. Garrett recommended that 1-187 be committed while there was still daylight for them to take the objective. DMAIN disapproved—no troops could be lifted in until there were signs of surrender.

Except for resummoning A-10s, Aviation Brigade was out of ideas. But DMAIN had a last resort: 301st MI Battalion was printing up some surrender leaflets and a loudspeaker team was en route to Garrett's Tac CP. He was to escort them to the objective; if the Iraqis could not all be killed, perhaps they could be convinced.

The Apaches held their fire (and their breaths) as the PSYOP Black Hawk strewed leaflets over the objective, then landed amid the bunkers to broadcast a surrender appeal. A few Iraqis darted out like ground squirrels to listen and scoop up leaflets. This was enough of the sign DMAIN needed to launch an infantry company. Their arrival brought out the first white T-shirts and 50 EPWs. A Black Hawk landed to give them water and this compassionate gesture lured out more.

Isolated in bunkers, the Iraqis lacked unit cohesiveness and responsiveness to their chain of command (inter-bunker commo had largely been destroyed by the air attacks). Consequently, some bunkers were all too ready to surrender while others were bitter enders. To the 101st, this schizophrenia presented a paradox in the rules of war: what to do when half an enemy force is waving white flags while the other half is shooting at you? Toad was the first occasion the Screaming Eagles confronted this dilemma. For the 1-187—eventually the entire battalion, under Lieutenant Colonel Henry Kinnison, was committed at Toad—the solution was to keep firing as long as there was resistance. Enemy troops who tried to surrender just had to wait for their belligerent comrades to join them or die.

The Iraqi battalion at Toad had professionally improved the excellent natural defenses, and their fire (mostly high that failed to interlock) had 1-187 sucking sand until dark, when the enemy commander gave up with more than 400 troops and nine officers. The troops had been badly served by their officers, many of whom had abandoned Toad even before G minus 6 for the comforts of the Euphrates Valley. This battalion were regulars of the 45th Division, the most likely formation to be encountered during Desert Rendezvous. On the basis of this first significant clash, Peay determined that caution could be replaced by even more boldness once Cobra became operational on G-day.

That day was slipped to February 24 as Bush allowed a Soviet initiative to try talking Saddam out of Kuwait without a ground war. The delay proved to be a blessing for the 101st, allowing time for the all important search for Cobra's FARP sites. The entire Desert Rendezvous plan depended on finding some without brownout conditions, so Garrett felt he had to make the evaluation himself. Riding in an Apache, with four more from 2-229 escorting, he headed north as other flights into Iraq provided deception. In his daylight recon, he could not reveal too much interest in Cobra. If he did not find what he was looking for after a few touchdowns, the search would have to be undertaken at night.

What Garrett's flight found first was disturbing. A ridge, not shown on maps, over watching the planned LZs in the northern portion of Cobra appeared occupied. Two huge sabkhas seemed to be good FARP candidates, but as luck would have it one being used as an Iraqi latrine when the Apaches came over! The flight departed, then returned when no one was in sight. Garrett descended into brownout at widely scattered points—no joy, no place where Chinooks that would raise much more dust could land and refuel. The air assault division was prepared to conquer any enemy except the desert. The sifting sand would have to give them a break.

On the fourth touchdown it did. Garrett felt the Apache bump on a hard surface, while only a brief veil of dust obscured the horizon. The sabkha surface buckled under the ship's weight, radiating cracks in all directions, but this spot would be good enough unless more sand drifted into the sabkha. The 101st would have to take that chance. Garrett streaked back to TAA Campbell with the coordinates he came for: MU 705725 would be the location for Cobra's main FARP.

Hill pinned his defensive template at that spot, now the hub for final planning. Each battalion in 1st Brigade had been working with giant sand tables, some half the size of a football field, and now they walked through the phases of their air assault under the critical eye and questioning of Brigadier General Shelton. Commanders down to companies and separate platoons back briefed him on just what they would do in various situations. Because of the discovery of the unmapped ridge just north of the Cobra perimeter, 1-327s LZs were moved south. Planning adjustments continued right until the night of G minus 1.

Now that the FARP coordinates were in place, 426 Supply and Transportation (S&T) Battalion moved into the catbird seat. Commanded by Lieutenant Colonel John Broderick, their basic job was to fly some 200,000 gallons of fuel into Cobra, then pump it right out again, from 16 refuel points, into the gas tanks of hundreds of helicopters. Eight more points, for the attack ships, would be run by Aviation Brigade, but for G plus 1 operations and beyond, S&T would have to refill all 24 refuel points, assuming that TF Citadel reached Cobra in time (early morning of G plus 1).

This was a titanic task, and dangerous not just because of enemy action. The refuel points had to be up and pumping by H plus 2 hours, the first hour being consumed by flying up from TAA Campbell. To jump start such a huge flow rate meant refueling ships "hot": while their engines kept running, their blades spinning. Hot turbines next to gas fumes is the combination for explosion; one explosion could set off a chain reaction as pumps would be only 30 meters apart so as to stay tightly in a space where dust was least troublesome.

There was the additional hazard of crashes because of air traffic congestion and the ever present possibility of brownout. Garrett may have found just a tiny patch of clear surface. What conditions were on the remaining acres of the FARP was anyone's guess. Whatever they were, ships would be landing very near the pumps every 30 seconds, lining up nose to tail, taxiing up to a pump, topping off, then back into the sky. For G-day, Cobra would be the busiest airport in the world, directed by Corporal Alcus Davis, the air traffic controller with nothing but a back packed radio.

After the war, Broderick reflected on the unique tensions of the Cobra FARP:

"Everyone had to do exactly what the plan called for. No slack. No interpretations. Get in the pattern. Drop your load. Land in a near brownout, stand in line, refuel hot, and take off back into the pattern.

"You're putting yourself into other people's hands—strangers like the pump operator who signals you forward, jams a nozzle in your tank while he gets ready for the next ship. You life's in his hands for some long minutes. Then a voice you've never heard tells you to take off through a dust storm on a certain heading. He'd better be right because the air's full of ships listening to him—taking his orders.

"This isn't combat where you feel alone against the enemy. This is a test of trust in how well other guys can do their jobs. We had to develop that trust in rehearsals."

The rehearsals were just as important at the lift off area at TAA Campbell where there were other ominous hazards. The PZs were bunched together far more than the LZs would be. Power failure on take off would surely involve other ships filled with troops. And lift off would be simultaneous, causing the mother of all brownouts despite aluminum matting and oiling the sand to hold down dust.

Thus, as the days dwindled down to G minus 1, the Division became more acutely aware that the OPLAN would "push the envelope," stretch air assault's capabilities to untested boundaries. Garrett counseled his aviators to be prepared to do a lot of flying with the fuel light glowing. Normal maintenance schedules were suspended. Rotor blades, whose leading edges had been carefully preserved by painting and taping, would now be flown util they shook, then pulled off and replaced with new ones that had been stockpiled. In other words, when the ground war started, Aviation Brigade would fly like there was no tomorrow. Though few of his pilots had flown in Vietnam, Garrett reassured them that they were nonetheless veterans for having survived months of desert flying. The nape of the desert was still the principal and most dangerous enemy, the Iraqis would be a lesser threat.

By increasing scud attacks in all directions, the Iraqis seemed to sense that something big was about to happen to them. They were right; the final peace proposal (it was from Moscow) collapsed and Saddam had missed the last chance to save his army. G-day and H-hour were now firm. The 101st was ready to flip the switches and go. Over the TACSAT net came a short message from DMAIN, racing across computer screens, then spitting out hard copy, torn from the printer and rushed to the commanders:

SUBJECT: MESSAGE TO ALL SCREAMING EAGLES

1. DIVISION OPORD 91-1 IS EFFECTIVE FOR EXECUTION UPON RECEIPT OF THIS MESSAGE. G-DAY IS 240600C FEB 91.

2. THE DIVISION'S NEXT RENDEZVOUS WITH DESTINY IS NORTH TO THE EUPHRATES RIVER. GOD SPEED AND GOOD LUCK.

3. AIR ASSAULT. SIGNED MG PEAY

This meant 1st Brigade's Black Hawks were to lift off at 0600, but there was earlier work to be done. During the night of G minus 1, four Long Range Surveillance Detachments (LRSD) were inserted in and around Cobra to provide up-to-the-minute reports on enemy activity and weather. Then, starting at 0300, beacon teams would be dropped off as navigational aids for the Black Hawk flotillas lifting off at H-hour.

The LRSDs got on the ground undetected and transmitted encouraging reports: no Iraqis within the Cobra perimeter and those outside didn't seem especially alert. Moreover, clear skies prevailed over Cobra; visibility at 1st Brigade's LZs should be unlimited.

Those, unfortunately, were not the weather conditions at either TAA Campbell or AO Eagle where 3rd Brigade would be landing on G plus 1. Between the two locations the desert rose in a plateau with Cobra at about the center and the highest elevation. At the two ends, low ground often held fog. The beacon teams found that dense fog had oozed out during the night. In order to stay under Iraqi radar, they had to fly through the thick of it with Kiowa scouts groping ahead.

One of them struck a dune—miraculously neither aviator was killed—but the fiery accident boded ill for the entire Division's air assault, which was put on indefinite weather delay. Black Hawks could not fly over the fog lest they be detected by radar; they could not crawl through it because of fuel consumption. Once launched they had to maintain a constant 90 knots, producing the most economical mileage. Air speed higher or lower than 90 knots cut into the wafer-thin refueling margin.

Elsewhere along the 300-mile front, Schwarzkopf's juggernaut rolled into Kuwait and Iraq, leaving the 101st crouched in a sprinter's stance after the starting gun had gone off. Peay was not going to put at undue risk any of his 18,000 soldiers, but he was not going to let the Screaming Eagles be left behind either. The same fog that grounded the pathfinders was also blanketing TAA Campbell, but that had happened before. It usually lifted in a couple of hours. Peay ordered a new H-hour of 0700. At 0630 the scouts went up again but they could not dissipate the fog with their rotor blades. Slowly it receded north, not to be hurried by a thousand curses. Peay was forced to slip H-hour once more, but this time he insisted the 0800 was firm. That was it and that's that.

Salutes were exchanged right down the chain of command. We're going at 0800 come hell or heavy weather. Cameras came out to record the impending moment. Helicopters revved, their exhausts turning the dawn purple, drowning tense farewells and good wishes. Combat loaded, troops mounted into their aircraft, a scene reminiscent of a thousand combat assaults in Vietnam but in scale more like the departures from England for LZs in Normandy and Holland, spectacles when everyone is nearest to God and to each other.

Five hundred mem were in the first lift, rising from PZs churned by rotor wash into a giant dust cloud the size of a volcanic eruption. Ahead of them the fog bank loomed, the color of an old marshmallow. Soon they were in it, and a gray blanket seemed to have been thrown over the windshields. Blindly the Black Hawks followed the beacon signals. Thirty feet altitude and 90 knots, a test of faith. It lasted about 20 minutes, until they broke into clear sky a third of the way to Cobra. Ahead of them, 1-101 was already preparing the LZs.

With FLIR the Apaches had pierced the fog bank, the entire battalion out in front of the Black Hawks like destroyers searching for submarines ahead of a convoy. One-17 Cavalry was paving the way for another convoy, TF Citadel that bucked through the sand with 5,000 soldiers and hundreds of vehicles, a huge snaking column that took all of G-day to cross the border, with the leading HUMM-V scheduled to arrive at Cobra before the last left TAA Campbell, a span of over a hundred trail miles. Unless it was stalled by enemy action, TF Citadel would be like a military Baja race.

With the two-hour weather delay, time was even more important than before; Chinooks, as well as Black Hawks had to complete three round trips on G-day. The fog bank had compressed the air flow like an accordion, a warp of delay that could mean Cobra might not be ready to receive TF Citadel. If that happened the HEMITs could not deliver their 200,000 gallons of fuel to the FARPs. If that happened 3rd Brigade's Black Hawks could not be refueled. If that happened Desert Rendezvous would become a plan that fell apart early in its execution. There was only one way to bring the plan back on schedule: 1st Brigade would have to double time in securing Cobra.

A/1-327 was the first company to land on the sand, guided to their objective by attack helicopters working over the Iraqi defenders on the "surprise ridge" discovered by Garrett's recon. Lieutenant Colonel Frank Hancock rapidly deployed his battalion to take this high ground, the dominating feature outside Cobra. Opposing him was the reserve battalion of the 45th Division, commanded by an Egyptian-educated lieutenant colonel who had relatives in Detroit. His troops were well dug into a blocking position but expected to be attacked from the west by French armor. So effective had been the 101st's deception and counter-reconnaissance plan that the 45th Division believed that there were only Syrians screening the area where the Screaming Eagles had coiled in TAA Campbell.

Over the surprise ridge Apaches and Cobras kept the Iraqis' heads down, but with triple-A they were able to hold their own as equal volumes of red and green tracers crisscrossed between ground and sky. The balance of fire power tipped when Chinooks dropped off the first howitzer battery, and fire missions began to puff dust on the ridge. With very limited 105 ammunition to support their assault, 1-327 hurried forward in open formation. They were covered because coordination of close fire permitted the helicopters and howitzers to simultaneously beat up targets. Company objectives were pointed out on the march and marked by artillery. Rigorous physical conditioning from Desert Shield allowed 1-327 soldiers to lunge ahead rapidly over three miles of rocky, rising ground even while burdened with a hundred pounds of equipment. The plan had called for them to drop much of their loads before assaulting, but with the accelerated schedule everything had to get going at once.

Speed was also of the essence because sister battalions soon dispersed from their LZs in a wide arc that taxed the skimpy resources of DIVARTY on the ground, so 1-327 had to get on their objective before fire support picked up other priorities. D/1-327 had the battalion's TOWs that would have to take up the slack in supporting the assault. Mounted on HUMM-Vs, the TOWs got out in front, preceded by Recon Platoon's scouts on motorcycles.

As was greatly hoped for, 1-327s bold advance produced a psychological affect on the Iraqis. Closing on the ridge, the scouts saw some white T-shirts rising after Cobras pulled off. Quick thinking and good luck let D Company pick up a bull horn and an Arab linguist as they reached the base of the ridge. His message was part bluff, part threat: whatever it was, the little TOW/bike task force demanded surrender from the first line of terraced trenches on the ridge. A few Iraqis scampered out but behind them white flags were retracted as if the tiny show of force was not enough. Cobras moved in, chewing up the sand once more, showing that there was a lot more behind D Company. Over the bull horn, this message was emphasized.

It was not well received by many dug-in Iraqis, so small arms continued to zing until the ridge was rocketed once again. Ten or 15 more Iraqis gave up, indicating that there were wounded inside their bunkers. White flags now waved, but it was uncertain whether they indicated surrender or a request for truce to evacuate the wounded. Fortunately an Iraqi captain was among the first to come out with his hands up. He was convinced to recommend surrender to his company manning the second terrace of trenches, and he was handed the bullhorn for that purpose.

A psychological chain reaction set in: 339 EPWs, all veterans of the Iran war, stumbled down the ridge in various stages of shock. Well supplied and entrenched, they could have held out for days, but the avalanche that fell on them from the sky was too much and too quick for them to conduct a coordinated defense. For the 101st, the first ground action of Desert Rendezvous was an overwhelming success. Napoleon once told his marshalls, "Ask me for anything except time." Yet Peay had asked that of 1st Brigade—to make up on the ground, time lost by the weather delay— and they had done it.

Still, there was no time to waste. S&T elements were on the ground minutes after the first infantry, checking planned cargo LZs and pumping sites to see if they were in fact suitable. Some were, some weren't. Motorcycle couriers careened around Cobra, redesignating locations, waving off one flight, bringing in another, telling the fuel people to roll out hoses here instead of there. From a small hill at the south end of the main FARP, a giant gas station could be seen going up even as 1-327 was taking down the Iraqis on the escarpment. To the single air controller, Alcus Davis, it looked like chaos in a dust cloud, but his concerns were in the air.

His neck froze in permanent strain from observing flights as thick as gulls over a garbage dump, and his mouth grew dry from talking them all in and out. He controlled over 300 sorties before a ship arrived with his tower and relief. By then Cobra's perimeter had spread like an oil drop in all directions, a goose egg about 10 by eight miles. Within it a log base had sprouted like the sudden springtime bloom of desert foliage. Hasty depots, supply dumps, ammunition points, medical stations, equipment pools, computer stations, blivets, gas bags, Vulcans, HUMM-Vs, TOWs, trucks, radios and radars—all were amazingly up and running where a few hours before there had been only silent, empty desert.

Equally amazing is that there had been no casualties. Plenty of mishaps, malfunctions, damage, and close calls—but no American deaths. Seven ships, among the hundreds in the air, had crashed accidentally but none beyond repair. An Apache was struck over the ridge but wobbled into its FARP with a shredded tail rotor and severed hydraulic lines. This was the only damage inflicted by the stunned Iraqis, and not as serious as three loads that had to be cut by Chinooks, resulting in destruction of a commo van and 1st Brigade's computer equipment, Hill's vital hookup with the Division's sophisticated network of lap tops.

Hardly noticed amidst all the dust-raising activity in Cobra came a single Black Hawk. Landing near 1st Brigade's CP, it did not take off again like the other ships but instead connected to an auxiliary generator, and soon a small pop-up tent rose beside it. This was the ACP, a tiny brain cell from where the next phases of Desert Rendezvous would be directed. The most important phase was scheduled to thunder overhead the next evening—3rd Brigade winging toward Saddam's jugular.

Rains, much heavier than predicted, were sealing off the Euphrates Valley just as fog had obscured the PZs at TAA Campbell. It seemed that nature was Saddam's only defense. Even with acceptable weather, Highway 8 had always been "a road too far," because it could be reached by Black Hawks flying from TAA Campbell to maximum range but not by Chinooks.

Until TF Citadel's HEMITs topped off the FARP, 3rd Brigade's Chinooks could not refuel at Cobra en route to AO Eagle. That meant that before then Chinooks carrying artillery and mounted TOWs would have to be landed at a site, not yet confirmed, called LZ Sand about 40 miles short of the AO Eagle LZs, then motor march to link up with the infantry, an expedition called TF Rakkasan, commanded by 3-187's CO, Lieutenant Colonel Tom Greco. This split of 3rd Brigade had been the plan all along, but the closing weather around AO Eagle and LZ Sand now made success quite problematic.

If TF Rakkasan and 3rd Brigade could not link up in time, either could face annihilation by the two Iraqi Brigades at As Samiwah and An Nasiriyah which were mobile and within striking distance. An additional threat could appear from Iraqi forces pulling back from Schwarzkopf's ground attack. Peay remembered that the heaviest fighting at Bastogne, Belgium, had not been while the 101st was first encircled there, but when Von Rundstedt pulled out of the Bulge.

The first and most vital question for the ACP was to designate a site for LZ Sand. One-17 Cavalry, commanded by Lieutenant Colonel John Hamlin, set off to search for suitable ground. For the initial reconnaissance, Team Jerry, a detachment of pathfinders with 3-187's recon platoon led by Lieutenant Jerry Biller, flew along to touch down and test surface conditions. For deception, 2-229 roamed into the Euphrates Valley, shooting up military vehicles along Highway 8 and preventing counter-reconnaissance. The Apaches and 1-17 Cavalry were overflying terrain unlike any desert they had seen. Brush in the hills had suddenly grown green, carved by rushing wadis and dotted with sabkhas now bulging with water. Ironically, LZ Sand might have better been named LZ Mud. Fear of brownout changed to washout. Trial touchdowns sprayed water like lawn sprinklers. Pathfinders jumping down were stuck in muck knee deep. The aerial search headed into higher hills where, it was hoped, steeper terrain might mean faster water runoff. Skids disappeared into mud, but the pathfinders could at least walk around though their boots were almost sucked off. Biller wished he could have looked longer but it was past time for his team to get under way, even if he was leaving a marginal LZ for Greco, with more rain threatening. Team Jerry's motorcycles were underpowered for mud wrestling but they swerved off to the north to find a route into AO Eagle.

Labeled 41-A for the strip running by six gates at Ft. Campbell, this route had to carry Greco's howitzers towed by HUMM-Vs, scheduled to land the next day; but already Biller's bikes were slipping and sticking, a sure sign that going would be even worse for heavy laden HUMM-Vs. Scouting ahead of him, 1-17 Cavalry had more bad news: two immense irrigation ditches between him and AO Eagle were now overflowing with water.

This sudden inundation of the Euphrates Valley caused a momentous command decision back at TAA Campbell. Forecasts of even worse weather impelled Peay to consider an early insertion of 3rd Brigade, originally scheduled for dusk of G plus 1 in order to take advantage of the air assault division's night fighting advantage. But the oncoming rain front looked more dangerous than the Iraqis. Consulting with Colonel Bob Clark, Peay decided to move up the longest leap of his brigades by sending off the Rakkasans in early afternoon, rather than the evening of G plus 1.

By early morning of G plus 1, Biller was able to provide some essential information. Sometimes lost, often separated, Team Jerry had nevertheless slipped and slid in a meandering advance toward a bend in a pipeline which was to be 3rd Brigade's CP. The hills were like butter and the shallow valleys morasses. Though trafficability on 41-A would be treacherous for Greco, the accelerated schedule forced the risk. In the morning, Clark went up with Greco's first lift to see for himself what the risk would be.

En route he passed over Cobra, now swarming with vehicles after the arrival of TF Citadel. The reception committee had been organized by

CSM Bob Nichols who in the darkness had "herring boned" all the serials and guided them off into the perimeter in the dark of night. Lieutenant General Luck had warned before G-day that 45 HEMITs had to make it into Cobra or 3rd Brigade's ships would run out of gas. White with dust, 45 were parked and pumping when Clark flew by headed for LZ Sand. They had fueled Team Jerry's ships and now stood ready to refuel Clark's after 3rd Brigade's insertion. The linkup of TF Citadel with 1st Brigade had been the most important since Patton's armor broke through to Bastogne, Belgium. Now the Division bent all efforts to ensure a second linkup, that between TF Rakkasan winging toward LZ Sand, and 3rd Brigade saddling up at their PZs.

Their air assault would be another first—the side step of one Division (the 101st) over another (the 82nd). The All Americans had followed and supported the French armor who now screened Schwarzkopf's west flank. Passing through them, the 82nd veered northeast around Cobra on their MSR called Virginia. Clark's lifts would fly right over MSR Virginia, and 3rd Brigade had no land tail to cross the 82nd's convoys of 5-ton trucks; instead, Aviation Brigade would provide an aerial overpass.

At LZ Sand, TF Rakkasan's first lift hit the ground running—but then their boots had to be pulled out one at a time! Biller had not exaggerated the sticky going. Forty one-A was going to be 40 miles of no road. Clark saw Greco off, then flew ahead to see how Team Jerry was doing. They had struggled and fish-tailed along all night, the only Allied ground force for a hundred miles, but daylight found them bogged down in front of an irrigation ditch after taking small arms from buildings that dotted the plains. Turning back for TAA Campbell, Clark overflew LZ Sand where he told Greco to put small dozers in front of his task force to push causeways over the ditches. Greco set out at once, even before his entire command had flown in. He would have to risk dispersing his forces in order to make up time.

Third Brigade's first lift was 65 Black Hawks, V's in trail. Like a slow moving barrage of arrows, they flew over the southeast corner of Cobra, an unforgettable sight for those aloft and below. The dusty, tired troops of 1st Brigade gave thumbs up to the Rakkasans who signalled back with V's for victory. The ball had been handed off from Hill to Clark who was now going for a score.

But with landings set for daylight in AO Eagle, the gamble was now greater than had been anticipated by OPLAN Desert Rendezvous. The Iraqis would see the obvious threat to the MSR of their army that was decisively engaged in Kuwait. The Iraqi brigades at As Samawah and An Nasiriyah could be expected to react with violent desperation. Before Clark could take them on, he'd need the anti-tank and artillery support of TF Rakkasan. Until then he'd have to rely on attack helicopters.

The Iraqi reaction was surprising in that it came from the diplomatic level. Foreign minister Tariq Aziz protested to the United Nations that the air assault into the Euphrates Valley was outside the Security Council mandate. No fair hitting us in Iraq—the war's supposed to be in Kuwait! Aziz went on radio to describe the outrage to his nations: "The forces of aggression have barbarically deployed in these areas (AO Eagle) with a show of muscle by dropping troops from helicopters."

These troops that so alarmed Baghdad had a new concern of their own: where the desert had been unpopulated, the fertile bottom land of AO Eagle was heavily cultivated with numerous farmers and herders living in huts. Third Brigade's three LZs had been selected to minimize civilian contact and none of them was prepped. This bold and humanitarian consideration was validated when the landings received no ground fire.

Overriding all other considerations was the importance of setting up before dark. There were only three hours of overcast daylight remaining when the first lift went in, increasingly less for following lifts that continued until rain joined with darkness to abort further landings in AO Eagle and diverting about half of 3rd Brigade into Cobra where they would spend the night. The Rakkasans who had made it to AO Eagle moved immediately to their objectives.

The first was on the south bank of Euphrates, outside the town of Al Khidir (population about 15,000) where Highway 8 and a double-tracked railroad doglegged in a loop of the river. Here a company of 3-187 (the rest were with TF Rakkasan) set up a blocking position. Three miles east, 2-187, Lieutenant Colonel Andrew Berdy, understrength because of the diversions to Cobra, emplaced a flanking position on the road. One-187 was brigade reserve along the pipeline after seizing an air strip and pumping station five miles east of Clark's CP, called Waco, the destination for TF Rakkasan.

Third Brigade was thus deployed in the shape of a two-prong fork, 3 and 2-187 deployed on the tips, connected with 1-187 at Waco, with 41-A forming the handle leading down to LZ Sand. With only about a thousand troops in AO Eagle, they had nevertheless snipped Saddam's MSR. A sleepless night began as they awaited the Iraqis' tactical reaction.

It came in a dribble, in "onesies and twosies" as Clark was to recall, a piecemeal series of probes that did not amount to a counterattack. It seemed the Iraqi army did not comprehend what all those Black Hawks had carried in. Peay's bold decision to risk a skeleton force on the Euphrates early appeared to have worked. All would be well if Clark made it through the night and weather cleared sufficiently for him to assemble his entire brigade the next day. Weather, once again, would be the major determinant.

On the river the weather became a mixture of rain and airborne sand, driven by high winds that taught the Americans another Arabic, word,

Schmall, which means "from the north." In New England it would be called a nor'easter, the most ferocious of storms in the region. During the night the Schmall blinded the Rakkasan's NVG, costing them the advantages of night ambush. Fortunately only civilian vehicles approached the roadblocks in the first hours after they were emplaced.

At Cobra, the wind carried only stinging sand but the higher elevation meant higher velocities. The night would be remembered for its name, "The Schmall from Hell." It was a war stopper. Aircraft were grounded, even the attack ships which provided the anti-armor protection for Clark. Convoys plowing north on MSR New Market had to pull over. Even radio signals went into a communications black hole. Troops pulled their tents or ponchos around themselves and just hunkered down. Some donned their gas masks to filter the air. At DMAIN wooden latrines and fuel drums bounded across the rocky sand like tumbleweed. Paint from vehicles was sandblasted down to gleaming steel. Any loose cloth or canvas flapped with the sound of a machine gun.

With even commo cut off, 3rd Brigade in AO Eagle knew they were on their own until the winds eased. The road blocks continued their missions, knowing that they could not be reinforced. Around midnight, 2-187 stopped its first military vehicle, shredding it in the opening fire fight on the Euphrates. The situation was complicated by Iraqi soldiers in civilian trucks and civilians driving abandoned military trucks. In every ambush, the Rakkasans went beyond the call of duty to prevent loss of civilian lives, and even risked their own lives to save those of EPWs. Despite 3rd Brigade's restraint, the Iraqis could not break through a single roadblock.

The most ticklish action of the night was at the pump house and Darraji air strip where Iraqis seemed to be regrouping. Unless expelled by 1-187, they would be in position to prevent link up with TF Rakkasan. C Company got the pump house mission, requiring them to cross a mile of open flatland with only support from organic weapons. Stealth, silence and guts took them to the pump house complex enclosed by a barb wire fence. The lead squad snipped open a breach and rushed the concrete cluster of buildings, flushing an Iraqi platoon toward the air strip across a hundred meters of soggy ground. A Company passed through C to seize the strip from a company of Iraqis alerted by the capture of the pump house.

Without cover and concealed only by darkness, A Company fanned out for a devilish night attack. A third of the way to their objectives, the Iraqis opened up in quantity, but wildly. With C Company's supporting fire, A Company closed on the air strip and took it with no loss of life. The Iraqis seemed to have washed away with the rains and disintegrated from the shock of 1-187s attack. They abandoned 60mm mortars, heavy machine guns, RPGs, plus triple A that could have mowed down A Company like a scythe. The Iraqis seemed as stunned by the air assault as the Screaming Eagles had been stalled by the Schmall.

Like arctic explorers immobilized by a blizzard, the Cobra airhead could only wait it out. Before the Schmall from Hell arrived, 2nd Brigade (less 2-502 which was corps reserve) had made it into Cobra where they planned for on order mission. The most likely one was Tallil, an air base about 90 miles east of Cobra, but more like a fortress, a concrete maze of hangars and bunkers, the size of Dulles International Airport, all within a formidable fence and protective berm. First rate Iraqi units manned Tallil, their major air force and air defense base in southern Iraq, and they had been reinforced by armor. If the 101st got the mission it would be the "hardest" objective ever given to an air assault force since German glider commandos took down the Belgium fortress of Eban Emael.

Slowed, but not stopped by the Schmall, the 24th Mech had progressed so rapidly that they seemed to be in better position to take Tallil, but by the evening of G plus 1 corps had not irrevocably decided which division would draw the mission. So Purdom kept Tallil centered on his plate, conducting and table walk-throughs of a scheme of maneuvers that would begin with a prep by two full attack helicopter battalions and a unique fire support plan that called for artillery to be landed outside the berm ahead of the infantry and fire into the air base as the Black Hawks landed on the runways. Purdom would have a four-battalion brigade for Tallil if the Schmall abated enough for 2-502 to be lifted into Cobra. Meanwhile, he kept an eye on another on order mission, Objective Gold, a choke point on Highway 8 some 80 miles east of AO Eagle.

For eventualities like Tallil and Gold, Aviation Brigade had to reposition scores of aircraft, Schmall or no Schmall. When winds ebbed to 40 knots, Black Hawks tried to struggle up MSR New Market while Chinooks went the other way. With wind assistance, the latter set speed records; heading north, however, ships had to set down when gusts almost forced them back into Saudi Arabia.

The Division's major elements were separated, scattered over a hundred miles, and isolated by the Schmall. Only short wave radio was reliable, and on BBC they learned more about the war than heard on their tactical nets. At 0400 London reported that Saddam had ordered his army out of Kuwait. This drew a laugh because Schwarzkopf had more control over their movement than Saddam. Then came sobering news that a scud had killed a dozen U.S. soldiers in Dhahran. The war was far from over.

But the Schmall finally was. Early on the morning of G plus 2, forward security from Clark's CP saw 2-17 Cavalry's scouts over the southern horizon. In clearing skies, radio contact was made. The scouts were over watching TF Rakkasan, and soon its vehicles could be seen lurching down the last low hills. It would be hours before the tail of the columns closed at Waco, but the final big linkup had been accomplished. As the porous ground began to dry—the single benefit from the high winds—Greco rushed his TOWs and supporting artillery to rejoin his battalion and fill out their positions outside Al Khidir. The 800 Rakkasans who had RONed at Cobra lifted into firm LZs. Saddam's last chance to reopen his MSR had blown away like a leaf in the Schmall.

Clearing weather also brought Peay a new mission. Forget Tallil, corps ordered: the 24th Mech would divert a brigade to take it down. They were streaming eastward to close the noose at Basra. The 101st was to turn east as well, first to establish an FOB on an Iraqi bombing range now in the hands of the 3rd ACR, then prepare to cut off Iraqi withdrawal north of Basra.

The new FOB was called viper, a hundred miles from Cobra. Second Brigade would establish it as a launching pad to an engagement area (Thomas), the last choke point in Schwarzkopf's plan to annihilate Saddam's army in Kuwait. Corps' FRAGO determined the 101st's new plan, called The Audible, a brief oral order from the ACP that would shift 5,000 soldiers, hundreds of helicopters and vehicles, even quicker than Patton changed directions in the Battle of the Bulge.

Viper was designed to function like an aircraft carrier in a sea of sand, a launching pad for attack helicopters to cut Saddam's last escape route to the north, a causeway across marshland. Minutes were precious to perform the cut because Saddam was pulling out as much as fast as he could. Even before 2nd Brigade piled into Viper and secured its perimeter, 1-101 and 2-229 were off interdicting the retreat. As they did, 3-327 saddled up for insertion into an engagement area near Ash Shanin, near the Iranian border, to be named for the battalion's commander, Lieutenant Colonel Thomas. He and his soldiers were spoiling for a fight, as his only action at Cobra had been in scaring off some errant French tanks.

What the Apache crews saw, what they found, what they destroyed on the causeway, they reported to the Viper TOC—and it all indicated that the last day of fighting was fast approaching. The two-battalion task force for EA Thomas would go in the next morning if the war was still going on. Contradicting air assault doctrine, all landings to date and those projected were daylight operations, but doctrine is theoretical and war is reality. Boldness prevails in a pursuit, and by G plus 3, the ground campaign throughout the theater was surely in the pursuit phase.

The tempo of pursuit was most affecting Aviation Brigade where aviators and aircraft were approaching or past the red line. Garrett's pre-war warning that they must be prepared to fly 'till they die seemed close to fulfillment. Red lights on the fuel gauge were reflected in the pilots' red eyes. No one had more than a few hours sleep in the last 48. But they had to press on, so the Iraqis would break before they did.

Things were equally exhausting for support elements. On the evening of G plus 2 for example, 1-101's land tail arrived at Cobra after 20 hours with the Schmall in their faces on MSR New Market. Don't unload, Cody told Sergeant Major Erhke—keep moving the FARP 90 miles east to Viper tomorrow at 0300.

Once more there was a great stirring of dust, this time for the launching rather than landing of an air assault brigade. First and 3rd had lifted off from the oiled-down pads of TAA Campbell, but 2nd's PZs were on raw sand at Cobra. For an hour it seemed the Schmall had returned as billowing dust clouds choked the ground. By the time the air cleared, 2nd Brigade's first lift was touching down far away at Viper.

Though not vulnerable to Iraqi fire, Viper was nonetheless a dangerous airhead. Formerly a bombing range, the area within 2nd Brigade's perimeter was strewn with unexploded munitions, mostly cluster bomblets that could be set off by the weight of a foot. Drifting sand concealed the lethal duds so that much of Viper amounted to a mine field. Engineers ran out of tape to mark huge areas. Extreme personal caution was really the only protection. It did not have to be urged by the chain of command. Everyone near a short wave radio could hear BBC reporting more and more indications of Iraqi disintegration. The end of the war was forecast, and no one sought the distinction of being the last casualty.

The approaching end could be seen as well as heard; Saddam had torched Kuwait's oil fields, the smoke rising tens of thousands of feet, blackening the eastern horizon with the cremation of the tyrant's plunder. He did so from megalomaniac spite, but also to obscure targets from air strikes, and in this he succeeded.

Rolling smoke streamed over the causeway, turning day into night; not a night that could be penetrated by FLIR or NVG, but the darkness of smut on windscreens and instruments. Moreover, heavy carbon content in the air threw off laser ranging so that Hellfiring became erratic and inaccurate. Fire support coordination was very uncertain with ground forces moving so rapidly and tac air roaming far and wide. In effect, the entire north Kuwait-Basra region had become a free for all in a free fire zone.

The lifts for EA Thomas were planned to cut across a corner of this cauldron, a 120-mile passage more dangerous than any Iraqi resistance on the ground. Like a piston, VII Corps' advance had forced a mixed mass of broken units and refugees up the Basra corridor. LZs planned for Thomas were already filling with the human backwash of war. The more the ACP (now displaced to viper) studied the chaotic situation, the higher the hopes that it would be obviated by complete Iraqi surrender.

Only their ground to air fire remained potent. Forced low by oil field smoke, tac air could be heard by triple-A gunners before the fighters could see them. Forced by these circumstances up into SAM range, a USAF F-16 was hit and its pilot ejected, breaking his leg. As he descended in his chute he screamed a Mayday, picked up by B/1-101 over the causeway and by an AWAC who called for emergency assistance—the Iraqis were shooting at the pilot as he floated down. Aviation Brigade's TOC at Viper responded. Two-229 would attempt a rescue with two Apaches and a Black Hawk.

The F-16 pilot was disoriented, and the coordinates of his landing passed on by the AWAC were way off. The SAR flight entered a hornet's nest of green tracers. An Apache was badly shot up and the Black Hawk shot down. In the waning hours of the war, Peay's forces were reminded that even victory has a price that is never a bargain. In the rescue attempt for which they volunteered, five soldiers of 2-229 were killed and three captured (later to be repatriated)—the Division's most serious battle casualties.

There would be no more, because around 0200 corps notified Division that indeed a cease fire would begin later in the morning. The hour was slipped to 0500 then 0800, news that most Screaming Eagles first heard on short wave radio from an announcement by President Bush. The 101st had completed its 100-hour war. On the morning of January 27, 1991, they felt as though they had competed in a 100-meter dash. The racers to the Euphrates were leaning on their knees, catching their breath.

Now with the race won, they knew they had done well, but not better than their expectations—those would have only been exceeded by the capture of Saddam in his headquarters. The desert eagles were not overly impressed that in three days they had slashed across several hundred miles of enemy terrain and grabbed a huge army by the throat. That was the objective of OPLAN Desert Rendezvous and it had been achieved. So when the cease fire silenced the desert, the prevailing feeling of those who had accomplished unmatched feats of arms was "No big deal."

It would be for military historians to disagree—it was in fact quite a big deal—and drew apt comparisons with Germany's blitzkrieg of Poland; that is, something new and transforming in warfare. In the years between the Vietnam and Gulf War, the 101st had examined and tested what an air assault division could do—then did it in the desert. The world had not been paying much attention to what was going on at Ft. Campbell, so it was the world, not the Division, which was startled by the unique air assault campaign into Iraq. What the Screaming Eagles thought about themselves could be expressed in the Olympic motto: "stronger, faster, higher." Constantly improving capabilities, in other words, bettering what was already the best. Contemptuous of complacency, impatient for improvement, the Division had never stopped getting better.

But what specifically were the elements of the Gold Medal performance? First, some constants, and the first of those is the Screaming Eagle mystique. From the start (1942), the Division was all-volunteer. There were periods in its history when it was not, but except for the brief non-airborne interval in the 1950s, the "I want to be with the best" espirit carried over from volunteers to those involuntarily assigned. That's a mystique; it can't be analyzed or quantified, but it's either there or it's not, and everyone knows it.

The mystique was self-perpetuating because so many people, having at some point in their Army careers experienced the mystique, wanted to again come under its influence. This resulted in NCOs and officers regularly serving with each other—"growing up" with each other—in the Division as they advanced through the ranks. This long term familiarity, like the slow aging of wine, produced enormous benefits. In extremely fast-paced, quick-changing action such as occurred during The Audible, the mutual understanding between principal players amounted to a sort of telepathy. There's no way to teach telepathy, but there is no way to lose it when soldiers know each other from "way back."

Another constant is how quality attracts quality. Whatever causes the mystique, the result is that it attracts the best, just as it brings out the best. In this way, the Division did not remain homogeneous despite its core of "repeaters." New blood was infused because the attraction of the mystique was not allowed to produce a closed club. In 1992, Colonel Hill was the Division Chief of Staff during the 50th anniversary for the 101st's activation. In this capacity he met the former Division commanders who visited Ft. Campbell for the occasion. He was more impressed by the diversity of their personalities rather than their similarities. The 101st has always been like that - very different people with the same purpose and allegiance to the same traditions.

The 101st's traditions have less to do with "dining ins" and similar rituals than with standards. Other elite units have more emphasized the ceremonial trappings by reason of history of propinquity to Washington. The 101st's history is relatively brief as compared to several other distinguished divisions, and relatively isolated at Ft. Campbell the 101st has never performed much as show troops. "Keep your eye on the job to be done" is a line from the Division's march, and the job has always been to fight and win. Distractions have rarely been allowed to intrude.

The mystique and repeated gravitation of those who felt it, the Division's traditions as expressed in uncompromising standards and single-minded purpose were the most important constants in the 101st's development between its second and third wars. To account for its stunning success in the Gulf, two other factors are foremost: technology and public support.

Even though air superiority had swung to the Allies before Normandy, the 101st went into combat with an overall technological disadvantage in organic and supporting arms vis a vis their enemy: e.g., initially the U.S. was better only in field artillery, and the German 88 remained the best direct fire piece throughout the war. Public support remained high all throughout the time the Division was overseas.

In Vietnam, the Division came ashore with a distinct edge in fire power and mobility. Gradually over seven years, both advantages diminished as Soviet technology produced counter measures for the benefit of the NVA. Public support for American troops was high initially but subsequently eroded.

In the Gulf—the 101st's technological advantage was exponentially higher than the Iraqis—night vision, mobility, accuracy of fire and location finding are prime examples—and remained so during the campaign which, coincidentally, was eight months, the same period the Division had fought in Europe. Public support was also high from beginning to end of the Gulf War and, because of television was even more visible than it had been during World War II.

Another decisive factor must be mentioned in comparing the three wars, that of mission. In World War II and the Gulf, the mission was distinct and well understood at all ranks; whereas in Vietnam, it was as equivocal as the motto foisted upon 1st Brigade, "Diplomats and Warriors." Such a dual mission required two contradictory mentalities to fit under two hats.

Other interesting comparisons can be made, such as the influence of terrain and the effect of population in operational areas. Generally, like the bird of prey for which they are named, Screaming Eagles prefer an open range without many people around their targets.

At the end of their third war, with so much accomplished so quickly, a mood of after action anti-climax quite naturally set in at the 101st's far flung air heads. A hundred hours earlier, the most heard question was, "When do we go to war?" Now it was "When do we go home?" President Bush had promised quick return, and the haste of redeployment vitiated an orderly regress to Saudi Arabia. Second Brigade had been the first brigade to deploy and so were scheduled to return first. A thousand Strike soldiers were lifted out of Viper but became snarled in southbound air traffic from Rafha. Eventually reaching King Fahd, they encountered a force that stopped Schwarzkopf's Army as Saddam never could. This was the U.S. Department of Agriculture, who demanded such fine tooth comb cleansing of equipment—to prevent Middle Eastern microbes from being introduced into the U.S.—that soldiers spent more time scrubbing away dust and sand, then they had fighting the Iraqis.

The cease fire had hardly been signed when the Iraqis began ignoring its terms. This was an effort to test the coalition's cohesiveness and exploit the

American public's enthusiasm to "bring the boys home." The boys were just as anxious, but Iraqi cheating required 3rd Brigade to return to AO Eagle a few days after withdrawing to Cobra. It was nearly a month before the entire Division was relieved by a cavalry regiment and an aviation brigade, the last DISCOM convoy crossing back into Saudi Arabia on March 25. TAA Campbell was broken down and the bulk of the Division reassembled at CE II, then flew out on civilian aircraft between April 3 and 15, the colors returning with Peay on the 12th. Heavy equipment again went by sea, so that the last Screaming Eagle departed Saudi Arabia on May 1.

The Ft. Campbell community sprang a surprise party for the home bound victors. Post and unit support groups had held the fort, held together, and upheld morale for eight months under extremely trying circumstances. Though Peay requested a low-key welcome, the support groups and rear detachments had too much to celebrate, so they ambushed each plane with overwhelming pride, gratitude and joy.

Nothing like this outpouring of emotion had been seen before, except from the cheering throngs that saw off the Division's convoys en route to Jacksonville. Then the atmosphere had been electric with support and patriotism, along with prayers. Those sentiments were very much present for the returning flights, but even more so was the sense of sheer relief.

The Division's rear detachment commander throughout the war was Lieutenant Colonel Dan Lynn. Originally slotted to command a battalion in 1st Brigade, he was instead designated assistant chief of staff when the war broke out. Missing the war had been a grievous professional disappointment, but the importance of supporting the home front was a challenge as vital as it was unique. Deployment had been a mad house, Desert Shield a house haunted with rumors and alarms, Desert Storm a three-day television marathon, and now homecoming was as hectic as deployment had been. In March, communications hummed between King Fahd and Kentucky more than at any time during the war. Manifests had to be accurate because families were traveling from all over the nation to meet particular planes. Lynn's phone never stopped ringing with arrival inquiries.

CE II confirmed manifests only after a plane took off. That provided some 15 hours for families to assemble. ETAs went out through the chain of concern. Meanwhile it worked out an SOP that applied to every incoming flight.

The plane would roll up to a huge hangar dedicated for receptions and no other purpose. Civilian pilots opened a hatch over the cockpit where a returning soldier raised the colors of the units aboard. The plane slowly taxied toward the hangar where greeters—many of whom were there simply for the emotional experience—waved and cheered. This was a tip off for what was coming, but then the greeters disappeared into the hangar like guests for a surprise party.

Groggy from jet lag, the returnees did not yet realize what was about to happen. First weapons had to stacked, later to be racked before a two-week leave commenced. Then, disarmed and unsuspecting, the 400 passengers entered the huge vault of the hangar and rubbed their eyes. It was festooned with signs, banners and flags. A National Guard band struck up, and the civilians rushed for their soldiers. Somehow partners found each other without guidance, and the hangar became the scene of a thousand private moments in an unimaginable public swirl. Even reporters, television and airline crews broke into tears from emotional overload.

There were no speeches in the hangar—the band just played on above the shouts and crying, over the pop of flash bulbs that sounded like a fire fight. They caught pictures of feet swept off the floor, toddlers lifted high on shoulders, lips and bodies locked for however long. Thus, in a colorful mixture of camouflage and civilian clothes, each plane load dissolved into a tearful whirlpool.

The band played unnoticed for about 20 minutes, then the crowd hushed for the *Star Spangled Banner*. The final notes were greeted with a thunderous cheer louder than anyone had ever heard in a stadium. The desert war was over, and lives began anew.

There would be parades and accolades, a clamor for public appearances, speeches and welcomes aplenty for several months, as reality merged reluctantly into history. There was rarely a tribute that did not include the invocation, "God bless America." To look around the hangar, to listen how it echoed with joy, was to realize that God had blessed America—most of all with mercy, as no one could more appreciate than the Screaming Eagles, all home and reunited with their loved ones.

The nation savored an afterglow that even extended back in time to enclose the returnees from Vietnam decades before. All across America, speakers addressing the victory celebrations asked that outpourings of gratitude include the neglected service and dedication of Vietnam veterans. This was surely the nation's wish; President Bush said as much, but nowhere was it better expressed than in a poem on a sign at the Bangor, Maine, airport, the first arrival point for hundreds of home bound flights.

Freddy McHugh was airborne, proud of the 101st.
But in '68 in Vietnam, the VC did their worst.
Freddy came home under a flag, to stay in Maine's cold ground.
Others came back, time after time—but no one was around.
Thank you, troops of Desert Storm, for bringing us back home.
Home at last, from a war long past—home from Vietnam.

There was not a single Screaming Eagle who was present for the return of the Division colors on both occasions—the first on April 6, 1972, the second April 12, 1991—but the locale was a uniting symbol, Campbell Army Airfield. In Vietnam, no division had been more associated with helicopters than the 101st, but during the inter-war years the helicopter became the Screaming Eagles' almost exclusive hallmark. The progression through the sky had been simple: from airborne to air mobile to air assault, but the arduous development and training for this transformation was the work of decades and tens of thousands of dedicated soldiers. Yet as much as had changed, the overall mission remained the same. This was expressed prophetically by Brigadier General Bill Lee the day after the Division was activated, and quoted by Major General Peay at the first 101st Division Association Reunion after the Gulf War:

"Due to the nature of our armament and the tactics in which we shall perfect ourselves, we shall be called upon to carry out operations of far-reaching importance, and we shall habitually go into action when the need is immediate and extreme."

In the Gulf War, the 101st went immediately—it was the first division in theater to be declared operationally ready—and when the ground war began, no division carried out operations of more far-reaching importance. Tradition, training and technology are what did it—plus that undefinable mystique.

———◆·×·◆·×·◆———

CHAPTER FIVE

Medal of Honor Recipients

SERGEANT FIRST CLASS WEBSTER ANDERSON, UNITED STATES ARMY

THE PRESIDENT OF the United States of America, authorized by Act of Congress, 3 Mar 1863, has awarded in the name of The Congress the Medal of Honor to Sergeant First Class Webster Anderson, United States Army, for conspicuous gallantry and intrepidity in action at the risk of his life above and beyond the call of duty:

Sergeant First Class (then Staff Sergeant) Webster Anderson, who distinguished himself by conspicuous gallantry and intrepidity in action while serving as Chief of Section in Battery A, 2nd Battalion, 320th Artillery, 101st Airborne Infantry Division (Airmobile) against a hostile force near Tam Ky, Republic of Vietnam. During the early morning hours on 15 Oct 1967, Battery A's defensive position was attacked by a determined North Vietnamese army infantry supported by heavy mortar, recoilless rifle, rocket-propelled grenade and automatic weapons fire. The initial enemy onslaught breached the battery defensive perimeter. Sergeant Anderson, with complete disregard for his personal safety, mounted the exposed parapet of his howitzer position and became the mainstay of the defense of the battery position. Sergeant Anderson directed devastating direct howitzer fire on the assaulting enemy while providing rifle and grenade defensive fire against enemy soldiers attempting to overrun his gun section position. While protecting his crew and directing their fire against the enemy from his exposed position, two enemy grenades exploded at his feet knocking him down and severely wounding him in the legs. Despite the excruciating pain and though not able to stand, Sergeant Anderson valorously propped himself on the parapet and continued to direct howitzer fire upon the closing enemy and to encourage his men to fight on. Seeing an enemy grenade land within the gunpit near a wounded member of his guncrew, Sergeant Anderson, heedless of his own safety, seized the grenade and attempted to throw it over the parapet to save his men. As the grenade was thrown from the position it exploded and Sergeant

Anderson was again grievously wounded. Although only partially conscious and severely wounded, Sergeant Anderson refused medical evacuation and continued to encourage his men in the defense of the position. Sergeant Anderson, by his inspirational leadership, professionalism, devotion to duty and complete disregard for his own welfare was able to maintain the defense of his section position and to defeat a determined enemy attack. Sergeant Anderson's conspicuous gallantry and extraordinary heroism at the risk of his own life above and beyond the call of duty are in the highest traditions of the military service and reflect great credit upon himself, his unit and the United States Army. (This award supersedes the Distinguished Service Cross awarded to Sergeant Anderson for extraordinary heroism displayed on 15 Oct 1967 as announced in General Orders Number 343, Headquarters, United States Army Vietnam, dated 30 Jan 1969.)

CAPTAIN PAUL W. BUCHA
UNITED STATES ARMY

BY DIRECTION OF the President, under the Joint Resolution of Congress approved 12 Jul 1862 (amended by act of 3 Mar 1863, act of 9 Jul 1918 and act of 25 Jul 1963), the Medal of Honor for conspicuous gallantry and intrepidity at the risk of life above and beyond the call of duty is awarded by the Department of the Army in the name of Congress to:

Captain Paul W. Bucha, 306-44-7783, Infantry, United States Army, who distinguished himself during the period 16 to 19 Mar 1968 while serving as commanding officer, Company D, 3rd Battalion (Airborne), 187th Infantry, 3rd Brigade, 101st Airborne Division on a reconnaissance-in-force mission against enemy forces near Phuoc Vinh, in Binh Duong Province, Republic of Vietnam. The company was inserted by helicopter into the suspected enemy stronghold to locate and destroy the enemy. During this period Captain Bucha aggressively and courageously led his men in the destruction of enemy fortifications and base areas and eliminated scattered resistance impeding the advance of the company. On 18 March, while advancing to contact, the lead elements of the company became engaged by the heavy automatic weapon, heavy machine gun, rocket-propelled grenade, Claymore mine and small arms fire of an estimated battalion-size force. Captain Bucha, with complete disregard for his own safety, moved to the threatened area to direct the defense and ordered reinforcements to the aid of the lead element. Seeing that his men were pinned down by heavy machine gun fire from a concealed bunker located some 40 meters to the front of the positions, Captain Bucha crawled through the hail of fire to single-handedly destroy the bunker with grenades. During this heroic action Captain Bucha received a painful shrapnel wound. Returning to the perimeter, he observed that his unit could not hold its positions and repel the human wave assaults launched by the determined enemy. Captain Bucha ordered the withdrawal of the unit elements and covered the withdrawal to positions of a company perimeter from which he could direct fires upon the charging enemy. When one friendly element retrieving casualties was ambushed and cut off from the perimeter, Captain Bucha ordered them to feign death and he directed artillery fires around them. During the night Captain Bucha moved throughout the position, distributing ammunition, providing encouragement and insuring the integrity of the defense. He directed artillery, helicopter gunship and Air Force gunship fires on the enemy strong points and attacking forces, marking the positions with smoke grenades. Using flashlights in complete view of enemy snipers, he directed the medical evacuation of three ambulance loads of seriously wounded personnel and the helicopter supply of his company. At daybreak Captain Bucha led a rescue party to recover the dead and wounded members of the ambushed element. During the period of intensive combat, Captain Bucha, by his extraordinary heroism, inspirational example, outstanding leadership and professional competence, led his company in the decimation of a superior enemy force which left 156 dead on the battlefield. By his conspicuous gallantry at the risk of his own life in the highest traditions of the military service, Captain Bucha has reflected great credit on himself, his unit, and the United States Army. (This award supersedes the Distinguished Service Cross awarded to Captain Bucha for extraordinary heroism during the period of 16 Mar to 19 Mar 1968, as announced in United States Army, Vietnam, General Orders Number 822, 1969.)

LIEUTENANT COLONEL ROBERT G. COLE
UNITED STATES ARMY

THE PRESIDENT OF the United States of America, authorized by Act of Congress, 3 Mar 1863, has awarded in the name of The Congress the Medal of Honor posthumously to:

Lieutenant Colonel Robert G. Cole, United States Army, for conspicuous gallantry and intrepidity in action at the risk of his life above and beyond the call of duty.

Lieutenant Colonel Cole distinguished himself with 3rd Battalion, 502nd Parachute Infantry Regiment, 101st Airborne Division, during combat operations on 11 Jun 1944, in France. Colonel Cole was personally leading his battalion in forcing the last of four bridges on the road to Carentan when his entire unit was suddenly pinned to the ground by intense and withering enemy rifle, machine gun, mortar, and artillery fire placed upon them from well prepared and heavily fortified positions within 150 yards of the foremost elements. After the devastating and unceasing enemy fire had for over one hour prevented any move and inflicted numerous casualties, Colonel Cole, observing this almost hopeless situation, courageously issued orders to assault the enemy positions with fixed bayonets. With utter disregard for his own safety and completely ignoring the enemy fire, he arose to his feet in front of his battalion and with drawn pistol shouted to his men to follow him in the assault. Catching up a fallen man's rifle and bayonet, he charged on and led the remnants of his battalion across the bullet-swept open ground and into the enemy position. His heroic and valiant action in so inspiring his men resulted in the complete establishment of our bridgehead across the Douve River. The cool fearlessness, personal bravery, and outstanding leadership displayed by Colonel Cole reflect great credit upon himself and are worthy of the highest praise in the military service.

SPECIALIST FOUR MICHAEL J. FITZMAURICE
UNITED STATES ARMY

THE PRESIDENT OF the United States of America, authorized by Act of Congress, 3 Mar 1863, has awarded in the name of The Congress the Medal of Honor to:

Specialist Four Michael J. Fitzmaurice, United States Army, for conspicuous gallantry and intrepidity in action at the risk of his life above and beyond the call of duty:

Specialist Four Michael J. Fitzmaurice, Troop D, 2nd Squadron, 17th Cavalry, 101st Airborne Division, distinguished himself on 23 Mar 1971 at Khe Sanh, Republic of Vietnam. Specialist Fitzmaurice and three fellow soldiers were occupying a bunker when a company of North Vietnamese sappers infiltrated the area. At the onset of the attack Specialist Fitzmaurice observed three explosive charges which had been thrown into the bunker by the enemy. Realizing the imminent danger to his comrades, and with complete disregard for his personal safety, he hurled two of the charges out of the bunker. He then threw his flak vest and himself over the remaining charge. By this courageous act he absorbed the blast and shielded his fellow soldiers. Although suffering from serious multiple wounds and partial loss of sight, he charged out of the bunker and engaged the enemy until his rifle was damaged by the blast of an enemy hand grenade. While in search of another weapon, Specialist Fitzmaurice encountered and overcame an enemy sapper in hand-to-hand combat. Having obtained another weapon, he returned to his original fighting position and inflicted additional casualties on the attacking enemy. Although seriously wounded, Specialist Fitzmaurice refused to be medically evacuated, preferring to remain at his post. Specialist Fitzmaurice's conspicuous gallantry, extraordinary heroism, and intrepidity in action at the risk of his life contributed significantly to the successful defense of the position and resulted in saving the lives of a number of his fellow soldiers. These acts of heroism go above and beyond the call of duty, are in keeping with the highest traditions of the military service, and reflect great credit on Specialist Four Fitzmaurice and the United States Army.

CORPORAL FRANK R. FRATELLENICO
UNITED STATES ARMY

By DIRECTION OF the President, under the Joint Resolution of Congress approved 12 Jul 1862 (amended by act of 3 Mar 1863, act of 9 Jul 1918 and act of 25 Jul 1963), the Medal of Honor (Posthumous) for conspicuous gallantry and intrepidity at the risk of life above and beyond the call of duty is awarded by the Department of the Army in the name of Congress to:

Corporal Frank R. Fratellenico, 069-44-0577, United States Army, who distinguished himself on 19 Aug 1970 while serving as a rifleman with Company B, 2nd Battalion, 502nd Infantry, 1st Brigade, 101st Airborne Division. During an assault that day against a North Vietnamese army company near Fire Base, Barnett, Quang Tri Province, Corporal Fratellenico's squad was pinned down by intensive fire from two well-fortified enemy bunkers. At great personal risk, Corporal Fratellenico maneuvered forward and, using hand grenades, neutralized the first bunker which was occupied by a number of enemy soldiers. While attacking the second bunker, enemy fire struck Corporal Fratellenico, causing him to fall to the ground and drop a grenade which he was preparing to throw. Alert to the imminent danger to his comrades, Corporal Fratellenico retrieved the grenade and fell upon it an instant before it exploded. His heroic actions prevented death or serious injury to four of his comrades nearby and inspired his unit which subsequently overran the enemy position. Corporal Fratellenico's conspicuous gallantry, extraordinary heroism, and intrepidity at the cost of his life, above and beyond the call of duty, are in keeping with the highest traditions of the military service and reflect great credit on him, his unit, and the United States Army.

FIRST LIEUTENANT JAMES A. GARDNER
UNITED STATES ARMY

By DIRECTION OF the President, under the Joint Resolution of Congress approved 12 Jul 1862 (amended by act of 3 Mar 1863, act of 9 Jul 1918 and act of 25 Jul 1963), the Medal of Honor for conspicuous gallantry and intrepidity at the risk of life above and beyond the call of duty is awarded posthumously by the Department of the Army in the name of Congress to:

First Lieutenant James A. Gardner, 05321930, United States Army. On 7 Feb 1966 Lieutenant Gardner's platoon was advancing to relieve a company of the 1st Battalion (Airborne), 327th Infantry, that had been pinned down for several hours by a numerically superior enemy force in the village of My Canh, Vietnam. The enemy occupied a series of strongly fortified bunker positions which were mutually supporting and expertly concealed. Approaches to the position were well covered by an integrated pattern of fires including automatic weapons, machine guns, and mortars. Air strikes and artillery placed on the fortifications had little effect. Lieutenant Gardner's platoon was to relieve the friendly company by encircling and destroying the enemy force. Even as it moved to begin the attack, the platoon was under heavy enemy fire. During the attack, the enemy fire intensified. Leading the assault and disregarding his own safety, Lieutenant Gardner charged through a withering hail of fire across an open rice paddy. On reaching the first bunker he destroyed it with a grenade and without hesitation dashed to the second bunker and eliminated it by tossing a grenade inside. Then, crawling swiftly along the dike of a rice paddy, he reached the third bunker. Before he could arm a grenade, the enemy gunner leaped forth, firing at him. Lieutenant Gardner instantly returned the fire and killed the enemy gunner at a distance of six feet. Following the seizure of the main enemy position, he reorganized the platoon to continue the attack. Advancing to the new assault position, the platoon was pinned down by an enemy machine gun emplaced in a fortified bunker. Lieutenant Gardner immediately collected several grenades and charged the enemy position, firing his rifle as he advanced to neutralize the defenders. He dropped a grenade into a bunker and vaulted beyond. As the bunker blew up, he came under fire again. Rolling into a ditch to gain cover, he moved toward the new source of fire. Nearing the position, he leaped from the ditch and advanced with a grenade in one hand and firing his rifle with the other. He was gravely wounded just before he reached the bunker, but with a last valiant effort he staggered forward and destroyed the bunker and its defenders with a grenade. Although he fell dead on the rim of the bunker, his extraordinary actions so inspired the men of his platoon that they resumed the attack and completely routed the enemy. Lieutenant Gardner's conspicuous gallantry and intrepidity, above and beyond the call of duty, were in the highest traditions of the United States Army.

STAFF SERGEANT JOHN G. GERTSCH
UNITED STATES ARMY

By DIRECTION OF the President, under the Joint Resolution of Congress approved 12 Jul 1862 (amended by act of 3 Mar 1863, act of 9 Jul 1918 and act of 25 Jul 1963), the Medal of Honor (Posthumous) for conspicuous gallantry and intrepidity at the risk of life above and beyond the call of duty is awarded by the Department of the Army in the name of Congress to:

Staff Sergeant John G. Gertsch, 189-36-5254, United States Army, Company E, lst Battalion, 327th Infantry, 101st Airborne Division, who distinguished himself during the period 15 to 19 Jul 1969 while serving as a platoon sergeant and platoon leader during combat operations in the A Shau Valley, Republic of Vietnam. During the initial phase of an operation to seize a strongly defended enemy position, Sergeant Gertsch's platoon leader was seriously wounded and lay exposed to intense enemy fire. Forsaking his own safety, without hesitation, Sergeant Gertsch rushed to aid his fallen leader and dragged him to a sheltered position. He then assumed command of the heavily engaged platoon and led his men in a fierce counterattack that forced the enemy to withdraw. Later, a small element of Sergeant Gertsch's unit was reconnoitering when attacked again by the enemy. Sergeant Gertsch moved forward to his besieged element and immediately charged, firing as he advanced. His determined assault forced the enemy troops to withdraw in confusion and made possible the recovery of two wounded men who had been exposed to heavy enemy fire. Sometime later his platoon came under attack by an enemy force employing automatic weapons, grenade and rocket fire. Sergeant Gertsch was severely wounded during the onslaught but continued to command his platoon despite his painful wound. While moving under fire and encouraging his men he sighted an aidman treating a wounded officer from an adjacent unit. Realizing that both men were in imminent danger of being killed, he rushed forward and positioned himself between them and the enemy nearby. While the wounded officer was being moved to safety Sergeant Gertsch was mortally wounded by enemy fire. Without Sergeant Gertsch's courage, ability to inspire others, and profound concern for the welfare of his men, the loss of life among his fellow soldiers would have been significantly greater. His conspicuous gallantry, extraordinary heroism, and intrepidity at the cost of his life, above and beyond the call of duty, are in the highest tradition of the United States Army and reflect great credit on him and the Armed Forces of his country.

SPECIALIST FOUR PETER M. GUENETTE
UNITED STATES ARMY

BY DIRECTION OF the President, under the Joint Resolution of Congress approved 12 Jul 1862 (amended by act of 3 Mar 1863, act of 9 Jul 1918 and act of 25 Jul 1963), the Medal of Honor for conspicuous gallantry and intrepidity at the risk of life above and beyond the call of duty is awarded posthumously by the Department of the Army in the name of Congress to:

Specialist Four Peter M. Guenette, 122-38-7322, United States Army, who distinguished himself while serving as a machine gunner with Company D, 2nd Battalion (Airborne), 506th Infantry, 101st Airborne Division (Airmobile) during combat operations in Quan Tan Uyen Province, Republic of Vietnam, on 18 May 1968. While Specialist Guenette's platoon was sweeping a suspected enemy base camp, it came under light harassing fire from a well-equipped and firmly entrenched squad of North Vietnamese army regulars which was serving as a delaying force at the entrance to their base camp. As the platoon moved within 10 meters of the fortified positions, the enemy fire became intense. Specialist Guenette and his assistant gunner immediately began to provide a base of suppressive fire, ceasing momentarily to allow the assistant gunner time to throw a grenade into a bunker. Seconds later, an enemy grenade was thrown to Specialist Guenette's right flank. Realizing that the grenade would kill or wound at least four men and destroy the machine gun, he shouted a warning and smothered the grenade with his body, absorbing its blast. Through his actions, he prevented loss of life or injury to at least three men and enabled his comrades to maintain their fire superiority. By his conspicuous gallantry at the cost of his own life in keeping with the highest traditions of the military service, Specialist Guenette has reflected great credit on himself, his unit and the United States Army.

SPECIALIST FOUR FRANK A. HERDA
UNITED STATED ARMY

THE PRESIDENT OF the United States of America, authorized by Act of Congress, 3 Mar 1863, has awarded in the name of The Congress the Medal of Honor to:

Specialist Four Frank A. Herda, United States Army, for conspicuous gallantry and intrepidity in action at the risk of his life above and beyond the call of duty.

Specialist Four Herda (then Private First Class), who distinguished himself on 29 Jun 1968 while serving as a grenadier with Company A, 1st Battalion (Airborne), 506th Infantry, 101st Airborne Division (Airmobile) near Trang Bang, Republic of Vietnam, Company A, was part of a battalion-size night defensive perimeter when a large enemy force initiated an attack on the friendly units. While other enemy elements provided diversionary fire and indirect weapons fire to the west, a sapper force of approximately 30 men armed with hand grenades and small charges attacked Company A's perimeter from the east. As the sappers were making a last, violent assault, five of them charged the position defended by Specialist Herda and two comrades, one of whom was wounded and lay helpless in the bottom of the foxhole. Specialist Herda fired at the aggressors until they were within 10 feet of his position and one of their grenades landed in the foxhole. He fired one last round from his grenade launcher, hitting one of the enemy soldiers in the head, and then, with no concern for his own safety, Specialist Herda immediately covered the blast of the grenade with his body. The explosion wounded him grievously, but his selfless action prevented his two comrades from being seriously injured or killed and enabled the remaining defender to kill the other sappers. By his conspicuous gallantry at the risk of his own life in the highest traditions of the military service, Specialist Herda has reflected great credit on himself, his unit and the United States Army. (This award supersedes the Distinguished Service Cross awarded to Specialist Herda for extraordinary heroism on 29 Jun 1968, as announced in United States Army, Vietnam, General Orders Number 1589, 1969.)

STAFF SERGEANT JOE R. HOOPER
UNITED STATES ARMY

BY DIRECTION OF the President, under the Joint Resolution of Congress approved 12 Jul 1862 (amended by act of 3 Mar 1863, act of 9 Jul 1918 and act of 25 Jul 1963), the Medal of Honor for conspicuous gallantry and intrepidity at the risk of life above and beyond the call of duty is awarded by the Department of the Army in the name of the Congress to:

Staff Sergeant Joe R. Hooper, RA 19670872 (then Sergeant), United States Army, who distinguished himself by conspicuous gallantry and intrepidity on 21 Feb 1968, while serving as squad leader with Company D, 2nd Battalion (Airborne), 501st Infantry, 101st Airborne Division, near Hue, Republic of Vietnam. Company D was assaulting a heavily defended enemy position along a river bank when it encountered a withering hail of fire from rockets, machine guns and automatic weapons. Staff Sergeant Hooper rallied several men and stormed across the river, overrunning several bunkers on the opposite shore. Thus inspired, the rest of the company moved to the attack. With utter disregard for his own safety, he moved out under the intense fire again and pulled back the wounded, moving them to safety. During this act, Staff Sergeant Hooper was seriously wounded, but he refused medical aid and returned to his men. With the relentless enemy fire disrupting the attack, he single-handedly stormed three enemy bunkers, destroying them with hand grenades and rifle fire, and shot two enemy soldiers who had attacked and wounded the chaplain. Leading his men forward in a sweep of the area, Staff Sergeant Hooper destroyed three buildings housing enemy riflemen. At this point he was attacked by a North Vietnamese officer whom he fatally wounded with his bayonet. Finding his men under heavy fire from a house to the front, he proceeded alone to the building, killing its occupants with rifle fire and grenades. By now his initial body wound had been compounded by grenade fragments. Yet, despite the multiple wounds and loss of blood, he continued to lead his men against the intense enemy fire. As his squad reached the final line of enemy resistance, it received devastating fire from four bunkers in line on its left flank. Staff Sergeant Hooper gathered several hand grenades and raced down a small trench which ran the length of the bunker line, tossing grenades into each bunker as he passed by, killing all but two of the occupants. With these positions destroyed, he concentrated on the last bunkers facing his men, destroying the first with an incendiary grenade and neutralizing two more by rifle fire. He then raced across an open field, still under enemy fire, to rescue a wounded man who was trapped in a trench. Upon reaching the man, he was faced by an armed enemy soldier whom he killed with a pistol. Moving his comrade to safety and returning to his men, he neutralized the final pocket of enemy resistance by fatally wounding three North Vietnamese officers with rifle fire. Staff Sergeant Hooper then established a final line and reorganized his men, not accepting treatment until this was accomplished and not consenting to evacuation until the following morning. His supreme valor, inspiring leadership and heroic self-sacrifice were directly responsible for the company's success and provided a lasting example in personal courage for every man on the field. Staff Sergeant Hooper's actions were in keeping with the highest traditions of the military service and reflect great credit upon himself and the United States Army. (This award supersedes the Distinguished Service Cross awarded to Staff Sergeant Joe R. Hooper for extraordinary heroism on 21 Feb 1968 as announced in General Orders Number 2749, Headquarters, United States Army, Vietnam, dated 7 Jun 1968.)

PRIVATE FIRST CLASS KENNETH M. KAYS
UNITED STATES ARMY

THE PRESIDENT OF the United States of America, authorized by Act of Congress, 3 Mar 1863, has awarded in the name of The Congress the Medal of Honor to:

Private First Class Kenneth M. Kays, United States Army, for conspicuous gallantry and intrepidity in action at the risk of his life above and beyond the call of duty:

Private First Class (then Private) Kenneth M. Kays, United States Army, distinguished himself on 7 May 1970 while serving as a medical aidman with Company D, 1st Battalion, 506th Infantry, 101st Airborne Division near Fire Support Base Maureen, Thua Thien Province, Republic of Vietnam. On that date a heavily armed force of enemy sappers and infantrymen assaulted Company D's night defensive position, wounding and killing a number of its members. Disregarding the intense enemy fire and ground assault, Private Kays began moving toward the perimeter to assist his fallen comrades. In doing so he became the target of concentrated enemy fire and explosive charges, one of which severed the lower portion of his left leg. After applying a tourniquet to his own leg, Private Kays moved to the fire-swept perimeter, administered medical aid to one of the wounded and helped him to an area of relative safety. Despite his own severe wound and excruciating pain, Private Kays returned to the perimeter in search of other wounded men. He treated another wounded comrade, and using his own body as a shield against enemy bullets and fragments, moved him to safety. Although weakened from a great loss of blood, Private Kays resumed his heroic lifesaving efforts by moving beyond the company's perimeter into enemy-held territory to treat a wounded American lying there. Only after his fellow wounded soldiers had been treated and evacuated did Private Kays allow his own wounds to be treated. These courageous acts by Private Kays resulted in the saving of numerous lives and inspired others in his company to repel the enemy. Private Kays' conspicuous gallantry and heroism at the risk of his life are in keeping with the highest traditions of the service and reflect great credit on him, his unit, and the United States Army.

SPECIALIST FOUR JOSEPH G. LA POINTE JR.
UNITED STATES ARMY

THE PRESIDENT OF the United States of America, authorized by Act of Congress, 3 Mar 1863, has awarded in the name of The Congress the Medal of Honor posthumously to:

Specialist Four Joseph G. La Pointe, Jr., United States Army, for conspicuous gallantry and intrepidity in action at the risk of his life above and beyond the call of duty:

Specialist Four La Pointe, Headquarters and Headquarters Troop, 2nd Squadron, 17th Cavalry, 101st Airborne Division, who distinguished himself on 2 Jun 1969, while serving as a medical aidman during the combat helicopter assault mission in Quang Tin Province, Republic of Vietnam. Specialist La Pointe's patrol was advancing from the landing zone through an adjoining valley when it suddenly encountered heavy automatic weapons fire from a large enemy force entrenched in well-fortified bunker positions. In the initial hail of fire, two soldiers in the formation vanguard were seriously wounded. Hearing a call for aid from one of the wounded, Specialist La Pointe ran forward through heavy fire to assist his fallen comrades. To reach the wounded men, he was forced to crawl directly in view of an enemy bunker. As members of his unit attempted to provide covering fire, he administered first aid to one man, shielding the other with his body. He was hit by a burst of fire from the bunker while attending the wounded soldier. In spite of his own painful wounds, Specialist La Pointe continued his lifesaving duties until he was again wounded and knocked to the ground. Making strenuous efforts, he moved back again into a shielding position to continue administering first aid. An exploding grenade mortally wounded all three men. Specialist La Pointe's courageous actions at the cost of his own life were an inspiration to his comrades. His conspicuous gallantry, intrepidity and selflessness are in the highest traditions of the military service and reflect credit on him, his unit, and the United States Army.

PRIVATE FIRST CLASS MILTON A. LEE
UNITED STATES ARMY

BY DIRECTION OF the President, under the Joint Resolution of Congress approved 12 Jul 1862 (amended by act of 3 Mar 1863, act of 9 Jul 1918 and act of 25 Jul 1963), the Medal of Honor for conspicuous gallantry and intrepidity at the risk of life above and beyond the call of duty is awarded posthumously by the Department of the Army in the name of Congress to:

Private First Class Milton A. Lee, 452-8A-2563, United States Army, who distinguished himself by conspicuous gallantry and intrepidity in action above and beyond the call of duty on 26 Apr 1968, near the city of Phu Bai in the Province of Thua Thien, Republic of Vietnam. Private Lee was serving as the radio telephone operator with the 3rd Platoon, Company B, 2nd Battalion, 502nd Infantry, 1st Brigade, 101st Airborne Division (Airmobile). As lead element for the company, the 3rd Platoon received intense surprise hostile fire from a force of North Vietnamese army regulars in well-concealed bunkers. With 50 percent casualties, the platoon maneuvered to a position of cover to treat their wounded and reorganize, while Private Lee moved through the heavy enemy fire giving lifesaving first aid to his wounded comrades. During the subsequent assault on the enemy defensive positions, Private Lee continuously kept close radio contact with the company commander, relaying precise and understandable orders to his platoon leader. While advancing with the front rank toward the objective, Private Lee observed four North Vietnamese soldiers with automatic weapons and a rocket launcher lying in wait for the lead element of the platoon, As the element moved forward, unaware of the concealed danger, Private Lee immediately, and with utter disregard for his own personal safety, passed his radio to another soldier and charged through the murderous fire. Without hesitation he continued his assault, overrunning the enemy position, killing all occupants and capturing four automatic weapons and a rocket launcher. Private Lee continued his one-man assault on the second position through a heavy barrage of enemy automatic weapons fire. Grievously wounded, he continued to press the attack, crawling forward into a firing position and delivering accurate covering fire to enable his platoon to maneuver and destroy the position. Not until the position was overrun did Private Lee falter in his steady volume of fire and succumb to his wounds. Private Lee's heroic actions saved the lives of the lead element and were instrumental in the destruction of the key position of the enemy defense. Private Lee's conspicuous gallantry and intrepidity at the risk of life above and beyond the call of duty are in keeping with the highest traditions of the military service and reflect great credit in himself, the 502nd Infantry, and the United States Army.

LIEUTENANT COLONEL ANDRE C. LUCAS
UNITED STATES ARMY

By DIRECTION OF the President, under the Joint Resolution of Congress approved 12 Jul 1862 (amended by act of 3 Mar 1863, act of 9 Jul 1918 and act of 25 Jul 1963), the Medal of Honor (Posthumous) for conspicuous gallantry and intrepidity at the risk of life above and beyond the call of duty is awarded by the Department of the Army in the name of Congress to:

Lieutenant Colonel Andre C. Lucas, 552-36-9069, Infantry, United States Army, who distinguished himself by extraordinary heroism during the period 1 to 23 Jul 1970, while serving as the commanding officer, 2nd Battalion, 506th Infantry, 101st Airborne Division at Fire Support Base Ripcord in the Republic of Vietnam. Although the fire base was constantly subjected to heavy attacks by a numerically superior enemy force throughout this period, Lieutenant Colonel Lucas, forsaking his own safety, performed numerous acts of extraordinary valor in directing the defense of the allied position. On one occasion, he flew in a helicopter at treetop level above an entrenched enemy directing the fire of one of his companies for over three hours. Even though his helicopter was heavily damaged by enemy fire, he remained in an exposed position until the company expended its supply of grenades. He then transferred to another helicopter, dropped critically needed grenades to the troops and resumed his perilous mission of directing fire on the enemy. These courageous actions by Lieutenant Colonel Lucas prevented the company from being encircled and destroyed by a larger enemy force. On another occasion, Lieutenant Colonel Lucas attempted to rescue a crewman trapped in a burning helicopter. As the flames in the aircraft spread, and enemy fire became intense, Lieutenant Colonel Lucas ordered all members of the rescue party to safety. Then, at great personal risk, he continued the rescue effort amid concentrated enemy mortar fire, intense heat, and exploding ammunition until the aircraft was completely engulfed in flames. Lieutenant Colonel Lucas was mortally wounded while directing the successful withdrawal of his battalion from the fire base. His actions throughout this extended period inspired his men to heroic efforts, and were instrumental in saving the lives of many of his fellow soldiers while inflicting heavy casualties on the enemy. Lieutenant Colonel Lucas' conspicuous gallantry and intrepidity in action, at the cost of his own life, were in keeping with the highest traditions of the military service and reflect great credit on him, his unit and the United States Army. (So much of General Orders Number 9993, Headquarters, 101st Airborne Division (Airmobile), APO San Francisco 96383, dated 26 Aug 1970, as pertains to the award of the Silver Star (Posthumous) to Lieutenant Colonel Andre C. Lucas, 552-36-9096, Infantry, United States Army, for gallantry in action on 7 Jul, 1970, is revoked.)

PRIVATE FIRST CLASS JOE E. MANN
UNITED STATES ARMY

THE PRESIDENT OF the United States of America, authorized by Act of Congress, 3 Mar 1863, has awarded in the name of The Congress the Medal of Honor posthumously to:

Private First Class Joe E. Mann, United States Army, for conspicuous gallantry and intrepidity in action at the risk of his life above and beyond the call of duty:

Private Mann, Company H, 502nd Parachute Infantry Regiment, Army of the United States, distinguished himself on 18 Sep 1944 in the vicinity of Best, Holland, when his platoon, attempting to seize the bridge across the Wilhelmina Canal, was surrounded and isolated by an enemy force greatly superior in personnel and fire power. Acting as lead scout, Private Mann boldly crept to within rocket launcher range of an enemy artillery position and, in the face of heavy enemy fire, destroyed an 88mm gun and an ammunition dump. Completely disregarding the great danger involved, he remained in his exposed position and with his M1 rifle killed the enemy one by one until he was wounded four times. Taken to a covered position, he insisted on returning to a forward position to stand guard during the night. On the following morning the enemy launched a concerted attack and advanced to within a few yards of the position, throwing hand grenades as they approached. One of these landed within a few feet of Private Mann. Unable to raise his arms, which were bandaged to his body, he called, "Grenade," threw his body over the grenade and, as it exploded, died. His outstanding gallantry and his magnificent conduct were an everlasting inspiration to his comrades for whom he gave his life.

SERGEANT ROBERT M. PATTERSON
UNITED STATES ARMY

BY DIRECTION OF the President, under the Joint Resolution of Congress approved 12 Jul 1862 (amended by act of 3 Mar 1863, act of 9 Jul 1918 and act of 25 Jul 1963), the Medal of Honor for conspicuous gallantry and intrepidity at the risk of life above and beyond the call of duty is awarded by the Department of the Army in the name of Congress to:

Sergeant Robert M. Patterson, 244-78-4310 (then Specialist Four), United States Army, who distinguished himself on 6 May 1968 while serving as a fire team leader of the 3rd Platoon, B Troop, 2nd Squadron, 17th Cavalry during an assault against a North Vietnamese army battalion which was entrenched in a heavily-fortified position near La Chu, Republic of Vietnam. When the leading squad of the 3rd Platoon was pinned down by heavy interlocking automatic weapon and rocket propelled grenade fire from two enemy bunkers, Sergeant Patterson and the two other members of his assault team moved forward under a hail of enemy fire to destroy the bunkers with grenade and machine gun fire. Observing that his comrades were being fired on from a third enemy bunker covered by enemy gunners in one-man spider holes, Sergeant Patterson, with complete disregard for his own safety and ignoring the warning of his comrades that he was moving into a bunker complex, assaulted and destroyed the position. Although exposed to intensive small arm and grenade fire from the bunkers and their mutually supporting emplacements, Sergeant Patterson continued his assault upon the bunkers which were impeding the advance of his unit. Sergeant Patterson single-handedly destroyed, by rifle and grenade fire, five enemy bunkers, killed eight enemy soldiers and captured seven weapons. His dauntless courage and heroism inspired his platoon to resume the attack and to penetrate the enemy defensive position. Sergeant Patterson, by his conspicuous gallantry and intrepidity in action, at the risk of his own life, has reflected great credit upon himself, his unit and the United States Army.

STAFF SERGEANT CLIFFORD C. SIMS
UNITED STATES ARMY

BY DIRECTION OF the President, under the Joint Resolution of Congress approved 12 Jul 1862 (amended by act of 3 Mar 1863, act of 9 Jul 1918 and act of 25 Jul 1963), the Medal of Honor for conspicuous gallantry and intrepidity at the risk of life above and beyond the call of duty is awarded posthumously by the Department of the Army in the name of Congress to:

Staff Sergeant Clifford C. Sims, 240-72-8383, United States Army, who distinguished himself on 21 Feb 1968, while serving as a squad leader with Company D, 2nd Battalion (Airborne), 501st Infantry, 101st Airborne Division, near Hue, in the Republic of Vietnam. Company D was assaulting a heavily fortified enemy position concealed within a dense wooded area when it encountered strong enemy defensive fire. Once within the woodline, Sergeant Sims led his squad in a furious attack against an enemy force which had pinned down the 1st Platoon and threatened to overrun it. His skillful leadership provided the platoon with freedom of movement and enabled it to regain the initiative. Sergeant Sims was then ordered to move his squad to a position where he could provide covering fire for the company command group and to link up with the 3rd Platoon, which was under heavy enemy pressure. After moving no more than 30 meters, Sergeant Sims noticed that a brick structure in which ammunition was stocked was on fire. Realizing the danger, Sergeant Sims took immediate action to move his squad from this position. Though in the process of leaving the area two members of his squad were injured by the subsequent explosion of the ammunition, Sergeant Sims' prompt actions undoubtedly prevented more serious casualties from occurring. While continuing through the dense woods amidst heavy enemy fire, Sergeant Sims and his squad were approaching a bunker when they heard the unmistakable noise of a concealed boobytrap being triggered immediately to their front. Sergeant Sims warned his comrades of the danger and unhesitatingly hurled himself upon the device as it exploded, taking the full impact of the blast. In so protecting his fellow soldiers, he willingly sacrificed his own life. Staff Sergeant Sims' conspicuous gallantry, extraordinary heroism and intrepidity at the cost of his own life, above and beyond the call of duty, are in keeping with the highest traditions of the military service and reflect great credit upon himself and the United States Army.

SERGEANT GORDON R. ROBERTS
UNITED STATES ARMY

BY DIRECTION OF the President, under the Joint Resolution of Congress approved 12 Jul 1862 (amended by act   of 3 Mar 1863, act of 9 Jul 1918, and act of 25 Jul 1963), the Medal of Honor for conspicuous gallantry and intrepidity at the risk of life above and beyond the call of duty is awarded by the Department of the Army in the name of Congress to:

Sergeant (then Specialist Four) Gordon R. Roberts, 271-48-4872, who distinguished himself on 11 Jul 1969, while serving as a rifleman in Company B, 1st Battalion, 506th Infantry, 101st Airborne Division, during combat operations in Thua Then Province, Republic of Vietnam. Sergeant Roberts' platoon was maneuvering along a ridge to attack heavily fortified enemy bunker positions which had pinned down an adjoining friendly company. As the platoon approached the enemy positions, it was suddenly pinned down by heavy automatic weapons and grenade fire from camouflaged enemy fortifications atop the overlooking hill. Seeing his platoon immobilized and in danger of failing in its mission, Sergeant Roberts crawled rapidly toward the closest enemy bunker. With complete disregard for his own safety, he leaped to his feet and charged the bunker, firing as he ran. Despite the intense enemy fire directed at him, Sergeant Roberts silenced the two-man bunker. Without hesitation, Sergeant Roberts continued his one-man assault on a second bunker. As he neared the second bunker, a burst of enemy fire knocked his rifle from his hands. Sergeant Roberts picked up a rifle dropped by a comrade and continued his assault, silencing the bunker. He continued his charge against a third bunker and destroyed it with well thrown hand grenades. Although Sergeant Roberts was now cut off from his platoon, he continued his assault against a fourth enemy emplacement. He fought through a heavy hail of fire to join elements of the adjoining company which had been pinned down by the enemy fire. Although continually exposed to hostile fire, he assisted in moving wounded personnel from exposed positions on the hilltop to an evacuation area before returning to his unit. By his gallant and selfless actions, Sergeant Roberts contributed directly to saving the lives of his comrades and served as an inspiration to his fellow soldiers in the defeat of the enemy force. Sergeant Roberts' extraordinary heroism and intrepidity in action at the risk of his life were in keeping with the highest traditions of the military service and reflect great credit upon him, his unit and the United States Army.

SPECIALIST FOUR DALE E. WAYRYNEN
UNITED STATES ARMY

By DIRECTION OF the President, under the Joint Resolution of Congress approved 12 Jul 1862 (amended by act of 3 Mar 1863, act of 9 Jul 1918 and act of 25 Jul 1963), the Medal of Honor for conspicuous gallantry and intrepidity at the risk of life above and beyond the call of duty is awarded posthumously by the Department of the Army in the name of Congress to:

Specialist Four Dale E. Wayrynen, 472-54-2836 (RA17721421), United States Army, who distinguished himself with Company B, 2nd Battalion, 502nd Infantry, 1st Brigade, 101st Airborne Division, during combat operations on 18 May 1967 near Duc Pho, Quang Ngai Province, Republic of Vietnam. His platoon was assisting in the night evacuation of the wounded from an earlier enemy contact when the lead man of the unit met face to face with a Viet Cong soldier. The American's shouted warning also alerted the enemy who immediately swept the area with automatic weapons fire from a strongly built bunker close to the trail and threw hand grenades from another nearby fortified position. Almost immediately, the lead man was wounded and knocked from his feet. Specialist Wayrynen, the second man in the formation, leaped beyond his fallen comrade to kill another enemy soldier who appeared on the trail, and he dragged his injured companion back to where the point squad had taken cover. Suddenly, a live enemy grenade landed in the center of the tightly grouped men. Specialist Wayrynen, quickly assessing the danger to the entire squad as well as to his platoon leader who was nearby, shouted a warning, pushed one soldier out of the way, and threw himself on the grenade at the moment it exploded. He was mortally wounded. His deep and abiding concern for his fellow soldiers was significantly reflected in his supreme and courageous act that preserved the lives of his comrades. Specialist Wayrynen's heroic actions are in keeping with the highest traditions of the service, and they reflect great credit upon himself and the United States Army.

ACKNOWLEDGMENTS

The year "1994" was memorable for many of us. Fifty years earlier, this country was at war, a war in which our forces were engaged in mortal combat around the world. In 1944 Allied Forces set foot upon European soil as part of the greatest invasion in the history of warfare.

The 101st Airborne Division was born during that war and was one of the great participants that spearheaded the entry into enemy territory, an enemy that threatened the very survival of civilization in the Western world.

This division was less than two years old when it began its first combat as part of the new concept of vertical envelopment behind enemy lines. In 1994 it participated in the commemoration of that event, along with many of the veterans who were involved in the original invasion, when the 50th Anniversary was celebrated on 6 June 1994 in France.

This book attempts to commemorate the exciting record of 52 years of 101st Division history, from 1942 to 1994, from the many veterans of World War II, Korea, Vietnam, Southwest Asia, the Middle East, and all the intervening years, to the present day soldiers, who stand ready to respond to worldwide commitments.

This history is a product of many hands and minds, research, writing, follow-up, pleading, encouraging, brow-beating, discussion, cajoling, threats, frustrations, coordination and fatigue. It represents the efforts of a very large group of dedicated individuals.

First of all, we are indebted to the primary authors of the narrative section. They are:

John Hanlon - WWII and after years, 1942-1956.

John L. Burford - Fort Campbell and training years, 1956-1967.

Gary Linderer - Vietnam, 1965-1972.

Thomas H. Taylor - Fort Campbell training, Desert Shield/Desert Storm, 1972-1992.

Special recognition goes to the active division, which accepted the monumental task of submitting the details of all the individual units, while still accomplishing the many tasks on its busy schedule.

Appreciation is extended to the Curator of the Don F. Pratt Museum, Rex Boggs, and the Division Historian, First Lieutenant Edward Kroszkewicz, who provided many services, and acted as the conduit for the material submitted by the active division.

Also to Ivan G. Worrell, the executive secretary of the 101st Airborne Division Association, and the Association which took the responsibility for contracting to publish this history.

Finally, my gratitude to all veterans of the 101st Airborne Division *Screaming Eagles*—this is YOUR HISTORY!

—Robert E. Jones, History Coordinator

Index

Printed in the USA
CPSIA information can be obtained
at www.ICGtesting.com
JSHW082151140824
68134JS00014B/171